Foundations of Economic
Value Added

Second Edition

THE FRANK J. FABOZZI SERIES

Foundations of Economic
Value Added

Second Edition

JAMES L. GRANT

WILEY

John Wiley & Sons, Inc.

To Barbara and Our Family

Published by John Wiley & Sons, Inc., Hoboken, New Jersey
Published simultaneously in Canada

For general information on our other products and services, or technical support, please contact our Customer Care Department within the United States at 800-762-2974, outside the United States at 317-572-3993 or fax 317-572-4002.

Wiley also publishes its books in a variety of electronic formats. Some content that appears in print may not be available in electronic books.

For more information about Wiley, visit our web site at www.wiley.com.

ISBN: 0-471-23483-4

Printed in the United States of America

10 9 8 7 6 5 4 3 2 1

Contents

The pendulum swing of investors and corporate decision makers' focus over the past few years has probably not been this extreme for at least a generation. Growth for the sake of growth has been replaced with intense scrutiny of capital usage and payback. Risk has changed from loss of opportunity to loss of capital. Most importantly, valuation and all of its individual components has highlighted the need to reconcile what market expectations already reflect at today's stock price in terms of actual company fundamentals and outlook.

The concept of economic profit now more popularly known as economic value added has been constant during this dramatic change in market and economic environment. In a perverse way, though, it has taken a bear market, recession, corporate scandals and change in the systemic risk environment to bring increased attention to advanced financial statement analysis.

In 1997, I was working at Credit Suisse Asset Management, responsible for the firm's active large-capitalization portfolio management, Select Equity. The product was unique in that it was managed using economic profit-based analyses as its foundation. Although some product literature describing the process existed, there was market demand for a more comprehensive white paper to establish the validity of economic profit ingrained into this so-called new style of investing. Despite a successful history of implementing this concept on real world assets under management, a suspicion arose because the economic profit "style" emphasized cash flow returns on capital rather than earnings-per-share. It also emphasized substituting the company's cash flow volatility to measure risk rather than beta, a unique approach at the time.

Several books had been written principally for the corporate user dealing with economic profit and other value-based metrics but none were available dealing substantially with the linkage to stock price and investment performance. The broad acceptance into the commonplace of Wall Street was still in the future. This to me represented an irony in that corporations seemed to be more fluent in the knowledge and understanding of the principles behind economic profit than Wall Street analysts, the primary user of financial statements and influential in interpreting and valuing businesses. In searching for an academic to assist me in crafting a white paper, I came across the first edition of *Foundations of Economic Value Added* authored by Dr. James Grant. The book was groundbreaking because it was the first to create a bridge between these constituents. Dr. Grant and I have collaborated on many projects over the years since then including coauthoring a book, *Focus on Value*, further explaining economic profit as a practical tool for corporate and investor decision making.

In between the time of the first and second editions of *Foundations of Economic Value Added*, much progress has been made in advancing many of the tenets that were part of the original edition. However, like most business endeavors and even portfolio management, gains tend to be uneven and compressed. It is perhaps unfortunate that the increased acceptance and rapid adoption of economic profit based analyses in research has occurred after investors have lost confidence in management, financial statements, and Wall Street research. Though the concepts are intact, it is refreshing to see continued refinement in the application and implementation of economic profit principles.

The second edition of *Foundations of Economic Value Added* is a book to be read, underlined, written in, and reread. It offers readers the opportunity to not only learn the basic elements of value-based financial statement analysis but also illustrates the linkage between corporate decision making regarding capital allocation and stock price in a powerful and common sense way.

James A. Abate, CPA, CFA
Investment Director
Global Asset Management (USA), Inc.

Foundations of Economic Value Added, Second Edition is a greatly expanded version of the first edition. In this context, the second edition provides a much broader and sharper focus on the role of economic profit in the theory of finance, the empirical relevance of EVA as a measure of corporate financial success, and how to apply EVA principles when evaluating companies, industries, and even market economies. In this expanded work, there are several new chapters on economic profit including how to estimate EVA with standard accounting adjustments, enterprise and stock price valuation using free cash flow and economic profit models, the EVA role of positive and negative economic depreciation, and the development of an EVA-based factor model approach to estimating the cost of capital.

Having said that, it is important to emphasize that *Foundations of Economic Value Added, Second Edition* holds to the founding tenets of the first edition. To repeat, graduates of corporate finance (some of whom are perhaps now CFOs) will recall that in a well functioning capital market, the firm's operating and investment decisions can be made independently of shareholder "tastes" (or utilities) for present and expected future consumption. In this rational setting, the favorable NPV—equivalently, the discounted positive average EVA—announcements by corporate managers are wealth enhancing for all of the firm's existing shareholders, while the investor-perceived negative NPV announcements unfortunately destroy shareholder value. Whether corporate managers realize it or not, this efficient market condition is why they can make investment decisions according to the classic net present value rule.

Likewise, the modern principles of corporate finance reveal that if the capital market is indeed efficient, then these discounted positive average-EVA growth decisions can largely be made without regard to the particular method (debt versus equity) of corporate financing. In effect, the EVA-enhancing decisions by managers in a levered firm (a company with long-term debt) have the same wealth impact as if the firm were totally unlevered (that is, debt free). However, with market imperfections, corporate managers need to consider the discounted EVA impact of the firm's effective debt-tax subsidy and/or potential agency benefits arising from debt financing due to the presumably lower weighted average cost of capital.

As with corporate finance, EVA has many investment applications. For instance, if the firm's market capitalization (debt plus equity value) falls short of the EVA-based intrinsic value, then its outstanding bonds and stocks would be undervalued in the marketplace. By purchasing the mispriced securities of firms having, for example, relatively low NPV-to-EVA multiples, the active investor may reap windfall capital gains on the firm's outstanding debt and equity securities. Stock price rises in this active investing scenario because the discounted positive EVA announcements increase the true earnings pie for investors, while bond investors may reap windfall capital gains due to credit upgrades on the firm's risky debt. Hence, securities analysts and investment managers can also see that EVA has joint pricing implications for the valuation of the firm's outstanding debt and equity securities.

In the development of the first and now second edition of *Foundations of Economic Value Added*, I have benefited from many insights from professional associates. John Stahr, Wayne Archambo, and Paul Price were duly acknowledged in the first edition, and I am still grateful for their early comments in shaping my understanding of the practical significance of economic profit principles when evaluating companies, industries, and market economies. In this second edition, I am most grateful for comments and insights received from my professional colleague, James Abate of Global Asset Management in New York, who contacted me shortly after the publication of the first edition of this book. It has been a great pleasure to develop and see EVA principles in action from the dual perspectives of stock selection and portfolio risk control. Jim and I also coauthored *Focus on Value: A Corporate and Investor Guide to Wealth Creation* (John Wiley & Sons, 2001) from which advanced EVA insights in that book—such as the EVA-based factor model approach to estimating the cost of capital—are also included herewith.

On the research side, I am most grateful to Al Ehrbar and Bennett Stewart of Stern Stewart & Co. for their "no questions" asked policy in supplying MVA and EVA data on the Performance 1000 Universe. For the record, my enthusiasm about EVA (and its discounted MVA equivalent) as an innovative tool in measuring true corporate profit has in *no* way been influenced by anyone at Stern-Stewart. I would also like to thank Meredith Grant Anderson (Ph.D. candidate in physics at Carnegie Mellon University), and Ganesh Jois (MBA candidate in the Honors Program at Baruch College) for their quantitative research assistance in constructing the numerous exhibits in this book. Last, but hardly least, an enduring word of thanks goes to Frank J. Fabozzi of the Yale School of Management. His encouragement and flexibility over the years has made it a real pleasure to write both editions of *Foundations of Economic Value Added*. As mentioned before, it was Frank, not I, who had the initial insight to expand upon my EVA study in the Fall 1996 issue of the *Journal of Portfolio Management*.

James L. Grant

James L. Grant is President of JLG Research, a company specializing in economic profit research, and a member of the finance faculty at Baruch College of the City University of New York. Dr. Grant serves as a Special Adviser to Global Asset Management in New York. He holds a Ph.D. in Business from the University of Chicago's Graduate School of Business and has been a featured speaker at industry conferences on value-based metrics. Dr. Grant serves on the Editorial Advisory Board of the *Journal of Portfolio Management*. He has published several articles in investment journals, including *JPM* and the *Journal of Investing*. Dr. Grant is the coauthor of *Focus on Value: A Corporate and Investor Guide to Wealth Creation* (with James A. Abate) and coauthor and coeditor (with Frank J. Fabozzi) respectively of *Equity Portfolio Management* and *Value-Based Metrics: Foundations and Practice*.

CHAPTER 1

The EVA Revolution

In a market-driven economy many companies will create wealth. Other firms however will undoubtedly destroy it. Discovering those economic factors that lead to wealth creation and destruction among companies is important to many constituencies, not the least of which is corporate officials and investment managers. For corporate managers, wealth creation is fundamental to the economic survival of the firm. Managers that fail (or refuse) to see the importance of this imperative in an open economy do so at the peril of the organization and their own careers.[1]

Finding the "best" companies and industries in the marketplace is of primary importance to investment managers. With the proper financial tools, portfolio managers may be able to enhance their active performance over-and-above the returns available on similar risk indexed-passive strategies. A new analytical tool called EVA is now assisting this wealth-discovery and company-selection process. The innovative changes that this financial metric have spawned in the twin areas of corporate finance and investment management is the driving force behind what can be formerly called the "EVA revolution."

EVA IN PRACTICE

The analytical tool called EVA, for Economic Value Added, was commercially developed in 1982[2] by the corporate advisory team of Joel Stern

---

[1] It goes without saying that, in principle, a nonmarket economic system will create *less* wealth than a market-oriented system.

[2] It should be noted that the commercial development of EVA did *not* just happen overnight. It was the outgrowth of early economic profit innovators like Joel Stern who recognized the practical limitation of accounting earnings. For example, see Joel M. Stern, "Earnings Per Share Don't Count," *Financial Analyst Journal* (July/August 1974).

and G. Bennett Stewart III.[3] This financial metric gained early acceptance from the corporate community because of its innovative way of
looking at the firm's real profitability. Unlike traditional measures of
profit—such as EBIT, EBITDA, and net operating income—EVA looks
at the firm's "residual profitability," net of both the direct cost of debt
capital and the *indirect* cost of equity capital.[4] In this way, EVA serves
as a modern-day measure of corporate success because it is closely
aligned with the shareholder wealth-maximization requirement.

Large firms like Coca Cola, Diageo, Lilly (Eli), Guidant, and SPX have
used EVA as a guide to creating economic value for their shareholders.
Bonuses and incentive pay schemes at these firms have been built around
the manager's ability (or lack thereof) to generate positive EVA within the
firm's operating divisions. Positive payments accrue to managers having
divisional operating profits that on balance exceed the relevant "cost of
capital," while negative incentive payments may occur if the longer-term
divisional profits fall short of the overall capital costs. Thus, by accounting
for both the cost of debt *and* equity capital, EVA gives managers the incentive to act like shareholders when making corporate investment decisions.

EVA is also gaining popularity in the investment community. The
June 1996 Conference on "Economic Value Added" at CS First Boston
and the "roll out" of Goldman Sachs' EVA research platform in May
1997 is testimony to this exciting development. Indeed, "buy side" investment firms like Global Asset Management and Oppenheimer Capital use
EVA in their stock selection, portfolio construction, and risk control pro-
cesses.[5] Other large investment firms are taking a serious look, and EVA is

---

[3] EVA® is a registered trademark of Stern Stewart & Co. For insightful discussions
of the EVA® metric, along with many applications of how this economic profit measure can be used in a corporate finance setting, see (1) G. Bennett Stewart III, *The
Quest for Value* (New York: HarperCollins, 1991), and (2) Al Ehrbar, *EVA: The
Real Key to Creating Wealth* (New York: John Wiley & Sons, Inc., 1998).

[4] In this book, the acronym/words, EVA, economic profit, and residual profitability
(income) are used interchangeably. Strictly speaking, one can distinguish between
EVA to the firm (as emphasized in this book), and economic profit/residual profitability to the stockholders. This combined (albeit less stringent) view of EVA-based
metrics points to the potential benefits of economic profit improvement on both the
firm's risky stocks and bonds (via credit upgrades). For a finer distinction of EVA-
based concepts, see Pablo Fernández, *Valuation Methods and Shareholder Value
Creation* (London, UK: Academic Press, 2002).

[5] For EVA in action, see James A. Abate, *American Focus Equity Investment Strategy
Profile*, Global Asset Management (USA) (January 2001). For an explanation of the
EVA approach to stock selection, see (1) the chapters in this book on company and industry analysis, and (2) James L. Grant and James A. Abate, *Focus on Value: A Corporate and Investor Guide to Wealth Creation* (New York: John Wiley & Sons, Inc., 2001).

also making meaningful inroads in the world of global performance ana-
lytics. Moreover, recent empirical studies in the *Journal of Portfolio Management* (among other finance and investment journals) shows that EVA
is being advanced in both the academic and financial communities.[6]

EVOLUTION OF EVA

The evolution of economic profit—economic value added (EVA)—is a
fascinating study with historical roots that can be traced back to the
classical economists' notion of "residual income." For instance, consider the definition of economic profit made in 1890 by famous British
economist, Alfred Marshall, regarding the real meaning of a business
owner's "profit:"[7]

> What remains of his profits after deducting interest on his capital
> at the current rate may be called his earnings of undertaking or
> management.

Based on Marshall's statement, it is evident that the economists' definition of profit—namely, a residual view of income or economic profit—is
radically different from the accounting measures of profit in use today,
such as EBIT, EBITDA, or net operating income. That is, a key distinction
between economic profit and accounting profit lies in the classical economists' notion that a company is not truly profitable unless its revenues
have (1) covered the usual production and operating expenses of running
a business, and (2) provided a normal return on the owners' invested capital. In a more fundamental sense, this residual view of income is really
what today's economic profit movement is really all about.

While EVA is rooted in classical economic theory, three pioneering
20th century American economists—Irving Fisher during the 1930s,[8] and
Nobel Laureates Franco Modigliani and Merton Miller in the late 1950s
to early 1960s[9] —expanded upon the fuller meaning of economic profit in

---

[6] For examples, see (1) James L. Grant, "Foundations of EVA for Investment Managers," *Journal of Portfolio Management* (Fall 1996), and (2) Kenneth C. Yook and
George M. McCabe, "An Examination of MVA in the Cross-Section of Expected
Stock Returns, *Journal of Portfolio Management* (Spring 2001).
[7] Alfred Marshall, *Principles of Economics*, Vol. 1 (New York: MacMillan & Co.,
1890), p. 142.
[8] Irving Fisher's pioneering work on the NPV theory of the firm is described in *The
Theory of Investment* (New York: Augustus M. Kelley Publishers, 1965, reprinted
from the original 1930 edition).

a corporate valuation context. Irving Fisher established a fundamental link between a company's net present value (NPV) and its discounted stream of expected cash flows. In turn, Modigliani and Miller showed that corporate investment decisions—as manifest in *positive* NPV decisions— are the primary driver of a firm's enterprise value and stock price—as opposed to the firm's capital structure mix of debt and equity securities.

Basically, the theory of economic value added rests on two principle assertions: (1) a company is not truly profitable unless it earns a return on invested capital that exceeds the opportunity cost of capital, and (2) that wealth is created when a firm's managers make positive NPV investment decisions for the shareholders. We'll expand on these EVA tenets of wealth creation as we move forward in this book. For now, let's look at some operational definitions of EVA that have shaped the current economic profit movement as well as introduce the link between a company's economic profit and its market value added.

OPERATIONAL DEFINITIONS OF EVA

There are two popular, or operational, ways of defining EVA—namely, an "accounting" way and a "finance" way.[10] From an accounting perspective, EVA is defined as the difference between the firm's net operating profit after tax (NOPAT) and its weighted-average *dollar* cost of capital. As a result, EVA differs from traditional accounting measures of corporate profit including, EBIT (earnings before interest and taxes), EBITDA (EBIT plus depreciation and amortization), net income, and even NOPAT because it fully accounts for the firm's overall capital costs. This analytical difference is important to the firm's owners because the EVA metric is net of both the direct cost of debt capital and the *indirect cost* of equity capital—as reflected in the shareholders' required return on common stock. In this context, EVA can be expressed in more general terms as:

---

[9] See Franco Modigliani and Merton H. Miller, "The Cost of Capital, Corporation Finance, and the Theory of Investment," *American Economic Review* (June 1958), and "Dividend Policy, Growth and the Valuation of Shares," *Journal of Business* (October 1961).

[10] The author views an "accounting" approach to estimating EVA as one that rests on conventional accounting income and balance sheets, footnotes to financial statements, plus necessary external information such as "beta" used in CAPM. In turn, a "finance" approach to estimating EVA is viewed as one that rests primarily on a discounting or present value process with the goal of determining market value added, enterprise value, and stock price.

$$EVA = NOPAT - \$ \text{ Cost of Capital}$$

In this expression, the firm's *dollar* cost of capital is calculated by multiplying the *percentage* cost of capital by the amount of invested capital according to:

$$\$ \text{ Cost of capital} = [\% \text{ Cost of capital}/100] \times \text{Capital}$$

In turn, the percentage cost of capital is obtained by taking a "weighted average" of the firm's after-tax cost of debt and equity capital as shown by:

$$\% \text{ Cost of capital} = [\text{Debt weight} \times \% \text{ After-tax debt cost} \\ + \text{Equity weight} \times \% \text{ Cost of equity}]$$

EVA: The Finance Interpretation

From a finance perspective, EVA is defined in terms of how it relates to the firm's "market value added." In this context, MVA (or NPV) is equal to the present value of the firm's expected future EVA. Additionally, since MVA is equal to the market value of the firm less the "book capital" employed in the business, it can easily be shown that EVA is related to the *intrinsic value* of the firm and its outstanding debt and equity securities. Stating these concepts in more formal terms yields the familiar value-based relationship between the firm's "market value added (MVA)" and its "economic value added (EVA)" according to:

$$MVA = \text{Firm value} - \text{Total capital}$$

$$MVA = [\text{Debt } plus \text{ Equity value}] - \text{Total capital}$$

$$MVA = PV \text{ of expected future EVA}$$

These general financial definitions have important implications for the firm's owners. Companies having positive EVA momentum should on balance see their stock (and perhaps, bond) prices go up over time as the increasing profits net of the overall capital costs leads to a rise in the firm's "market value added." In contrast, firms with returns on invested capital that fall short of the weighted-average cost of capital should see share price declines as the adverse EVA outlook lowers the intrinsic (present) value of the firm.

Hence, by incorporating EVA into the company evaluation process, securities analysts and/or portfolio managers may enhance the overall pricing accuracy of their research recommendations. Also, with EVA corporate managers have an innovative financial tool for assessing whether their *planned* investment in real assets will lead to wealth creation (positive NPV) for the shareholders.

MVA AND EVA: A SIMPLE EXAMPLE

As a simple illustration of the present value relationship between the firm's MVA and EVA, consider a two-period world where NSF's (for, "New Start-up Firm") investment and financing opportunities are like those listed in Exhibit 1.1. The exhibit indicates that if NSF invests $100 million today in real assets, then it can expect to create $15 million of positive EVA in the future period.[11]

With a "discount rate" or cost of capital of 10%, the "net present value" of NSF's investment opportunity is $13.64 million:

$$
\begin{aligned}
NPV &= MVA \\
&= \$EVA(1)/(1 + COC) \\
&= \$15/(1.1) = \$13.64 \text{ million}
\end{aligned}
$$

The $13.64 million in "market value added (MVA)" shows that NSF is a wealth creator. By adding this positive NPV figure to NSF's initial capital investment of $100 million, one obtains the market value of the firm, at $113.64 million:

$$
\begin{aligned}
V &= Capital + MVA \\
&= \$100 + 13.64 = \$113.64 \text{ million}
\end{aligned}
$$

EXHIBIT 1.1 NSF Corporation

Time Period	Investment ($ millions)	EVA ($ millions)
0 (today)	100.0	0.0
1	0.0	15.0

Weighted Average Cost of Capital (COC) = 10%

---

[11] Note that if NSF's future EVA is $15 million, then its cash resources at period 2 (before capital costs) must be $125 million. This is because in a two-period "world," interest and return of loan principal—at $10 million and $100 million respectively—will be due in period 2. We'll look at the specifics of an EVA-based wealth model in the next chapter.

Moreover, if one makes the convenient assumption that NSF's capital investment is financed with 100% debt, then the aggregate equity capitalization of the firm is the $13.64 million in market value-added (MVA). With 1 million shares of common stock outstanding, each share is then worth $13.64 ($13.64 million/1 million shares) in market value terms. Thus, in this simplifying "two-period" example, the firm's aggregate MVA (or NPV) is equal to the present value of its expected future "economic value added (EVA)."

MVA and EVA: Growth Considerations

The basic EVA and MVA linkage outlined above can also be extended to a multiperiod framework. Without getting into complicated pricing details here, one can use a "constant growth" EVA model to show the pricing importance of both the firm's near-term EVA outlook and its long-term EVA growth rate in determining overall corporate (or enterprise) valuation. In this "Gordon-like" model,[12] the relationship between the firm's MVA and its EVA outlook for the future is expressed as:

$$MVA = EVA(1)/(COC - g_{EVA})$$

In this expression, EVA(1) is the firm's current EVA outlook (one-year ahead forecast), g_{EVA} is the firm's assessed long-term EVA growth rate, and COC is the familiar weighted-average cost of debt *and* equity capital.

The constant-growth EVA model shows that the firm's market value added (MVA) is positively related to its near-term EVA outlook, as measured by EVA(1), as well as the firm's assessed long-term EVA growth rate, g_{EVA}. As shown, the firm's MVA is also negatively related to any unanticipated changes in the weighted-average cost of (debt and equity) capital, COC. However, in view of modern day capital structure principles (*à la* Miller-Modigliani), this "cost of capital" interpretation does not imply that the firm's corporate debt policy has any meaningful

---

[12] The constant growth valuation model is generally attributed to Myron Gordon. See, Myron J. Gordon, *The Investment, Financing, and Valuation of the Corporation* (Homewood IL: Irwin, 1962).

Gordon popularized a dividend growth model in terms of a dividend stream that is growing at a constant rate over time—hence, the "constant-growth DDM." The text discussion suggests that the same discounting procedure can be applied to estimate MVA (or NPV) when it is reasonable to assume that EVA is growing at a constant rate.

impact on the valuation of the firm and its outstanding debt and equity shares.[13]

PREVIEW OF WEALTH CREATORS

Let's now take a preliminary look at the MVA and EVA relationship for major U.S. wealth creators and destroyers.[14] The MVA and EVA characteristics for five large U.S. wealth creators—including General Electric, Cisco Systems, Microsoft Corporation, Wal-Mart Stores, and Merck— for the 11-year period covering 1990 to 2000 are shown in Exhibits 1.2 and 1.3. These large capitalization companies were listed by Stern Stewart & Co. as the top-five U.S. wealth creators (based on MVA ranking) in their 2001 Performance Universe.

Exhibit 1.2 shows that wealth creators like General Electric (#1), Cisco Systems (#2), and Merck (#5) have substantially positive MVA that grows rapidly over time. At year-end 2000, General Electric's net present value was $426,616 million, while Cisco Systems and Merck were reporting MVA values of $272,131 and $203,689 million, respectively. During the 11-year period spanning 1990 to 2000, General Electric's net present value was growing at a compound yearly rate of nearly 34%. Moreover, over the 11-year reporting period, Cisco's MVA was actually growing at an annualized rate of 86% (!), while Merck was reporting a respectable average MVA growth rate of about 21%.

Exhibit 1.2 also reveals that the MVA values for the top-five U.S. wealth creators declined mostly[15] from year-end 1999 to 2000. For example, General Electric's MVA declined by about $45,000 million (or $45 billion) while Cisco Systems and Wal-Mart each experienced MVA declines of around $76,000 million. Indeed, Microsoft's MVA declined by a *staggering* $412,000 million—from $629,470 to $217,235 million—between 1999 and 2000. As with Cisco et al., the MVA decline for Microsoft was due in part to the general slowdown in economic

---

[13] Peter Bernstein eloquently captures the essence of the original "M&M (Miller-Modigliani)" capital structure principles when he states that—"the cost of capital depends far more on the quality of corporate earning power than on the structure of paper [debt and equity] claims." For Bernstein's insightful comment on corporate debt policy, see Peter L. Bernstein, "Pride and Modesty," *Journal of Portfolio Management* (Winter 1991).

[14] We'll look at the MVA-EVA relationship for some U.S. wealth destroyers in the next section. The financial characteristics of wealth creators and destroyers will be examined in much greater detail in upcoming chapters.

[15] Merck's MVA actually rose from 1999 to 2000, from $143,001 to $203,689 million.

activity—especially in the technology and telecommunication industries—and thus the precipitous decline in the U.S stock market commencing in the first half of 2000. Additionally, Microsoft's sharp decline
in MVA was due to serious legal challenges from competitors arising
from its alleged "bundling" of software with the Windows operating
system.

Exhibit 1.3 shows the source of the positive net present value being
generated by the five U.S. wealth creators shown in Exhibit 1.2. Specifically, this exhibit reveals that wealth creators like General Electric,
Microsoft, and Merck have substantially positive MVA because their
EVA is both positive and growing at a substantial rate over time. At
$5,943 million, General Electric's 2000 EVA is not only positive, but it
also grew by 25% over the 1990–2000 period. With MVA and EVA
growth rates in the 20–30% range during this decade, the two exhibits
suggest that General Electric's net present value largely "tracked" the
diversified conglomerate's ever-rising "economic value added." Likewise, Microsoft's ten-year EVA growth rate, at 39%, seems to have provided the necessary fuel for its abnormal MVA growth rate, at 40%.

EXHIBIT 1.2   Market Value Added: Top-Five Wealth Creators in Performance
Universe: 1990–2000

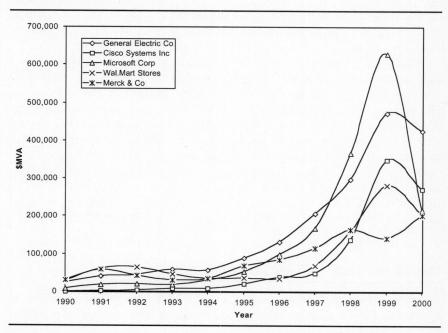

EXHIBIT 1.3   Economic Value Added: Top-Five Wealth Creators in Performance Universe: 1990–2000

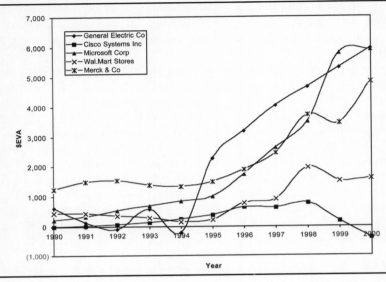

Exhibit 1.3 also shows that Cisco Systems had tremendous growth in its EVA up to 1998. During this period, the networking firm's EVA grew from just $9 million in 1990 to $775 million in 1998. This represents an astonishing EVA growth rate of 90% that, in turn, is joined with Cisco's MVA growth rate of 100%. On the other hand, Cisco's EVA peaked at $775 million in 1998, then declined to $182 million in 1999, and actually turned negative in 2000, at –$365 million. Interestingly, Cisco was apparently overvalued in 1999 as its MVA peaked at $348,442 during that year in the presence of its falling EVA. Cisco continued its MVA decline in 2000 with the major sell off in technology stocks to end the year at $272,131 million. Thus, taken together, the MVA and EVA relationships shown in Exhibits 1.2 and 1.3 are not only beneficial in describing the financial characteristics of wealth creators, but exhibits like these can be used to assist in the discovery of mispriced securities.[16]

PREVIEW OF WEALTH DESTROYERS

Exhibits 1.4 and 1.5 show the MVA and EVA relationships for five U.S. firms that—ironically enough—became large wealth destroyers in recent

---

[16] Later chapters will focus on the EVA approach to equity securities analysis.

times. Specifically, the two exhibits report the MVA and EVA experiences of First Union Corporation (#996), Lucent Technologies (#997),
General Motors (#998), WorldCom (#999), and AT&T (#1000) for the
11-year period covering 1990 to 2000. These companies were listed as
the bottom five firms—based on MVA rankings—in the 2001 performance survey by Stern Stewart & Co.

Exhibit 1.4 shows that the net present value estimates for the five U.S.
wealth destroyers are strikingly different from the reported MVA values
for the "New (and Old) Guard" of modern capitalism—including, wealth
creators like General Electric, Cisco Systems, Microsoft, Wal-Mart Stores,
and Merck. Indeed, as of year 2000, this exhibit shows that AT&T alone
wasted some $87,000 million (or $87 billion) in net present value. Also,
Lucent Technologies' MVA dropped from about $200,000 million to nearly
−19,000 million between 1999 and 2000. In turn, WorldCom's MVA dropped
from about $96,000 million in 1999 down to about −$32,000 million as of
year 2000.[17] Unfortunately, the MVA evidence reported in Exhibit 1.4
shows that during the 1990s these telecom giants were largely investing in
projects that had a *negative* net present value.

EXHIBIT 1.4   Market Value-Added: Bottom-Five Companies in Performance
Universe: 1990-2000

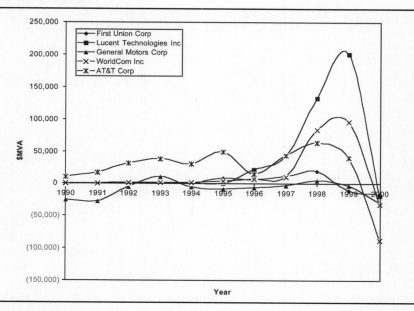

EXHIBIT 1.5   Economic Value Added: Bottom-Five Companies in Performance
Universe: 1990–2000

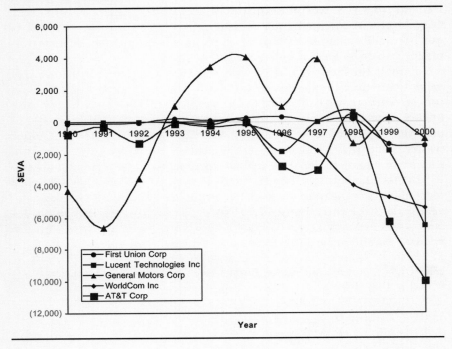

Exhibit 1.4 shows that General Motors' MVA experience during the 1990s was rather dismal, too. This large wealth destroyer had nine out of 11 years of negative net present value (including 1990). Indeed, General Motors' MVA for year 2000, at –$29,171 million, was actually *lower* than its MVA for 1990, at –$24,708 million. In effect, the market value of the automaker was consistently below the "book capital" (or invested capital) employed in the business. This means that General Motors' "price-to-book value" ratio was generally below unity during the 1990s. Amazingly, General Motors' shareholders seem plagued by an entrenched management that largely invests in capital-intensive projects having a negative net present value. Indeed, the intransigent automaker was third from the bottom in the MVA rankings for year 2000, and it was "dead last" in the Stern Stewart Performance Universe for 1995.

Exhibit 1.5 shows the EVA experiences for the five U.S. wealth wasters. As expected, the source of the negative net present value (Exhibit 1.4) for these companies is due to their (mostly) negative and volatile

EVA experiences over the 11-year reporting period.[18] For instance, AT&T was posting a negative EVA of –$745 million at year-end 1990. By 2000, this U.S. wealth destroyer's EVA had declined to –$9,972 million. Meanwhile, AT&T's net present value (MVA, in Exhibit 1.4) was quite volatile during the 1990s, with positive net present value that ultimately turned grossly negative in 2000. During 2000, investors *finally* woke up to the fact that persistently negative EVA destroys shareholder value. Moreover, it appears that the "bubble" in telecom stocks that occurred during the late 1990s (see Exhibit 1.4 for 1998 and 1999) burst in 2000 when investors realized that companies like AT&T, Lucent Technologies, and WorldCom were plagued by a systematic pattern of negative EVA. Negative EVA is clearly evident in Exhibit 1.5 for the three telecom companies over the 11-year period spanning 1990 to 2000.

Exhibit 1.5 also shows that General Motors had considerable volatility in its EVA during the 1990s. At 1990, the automaker's profitability *net* of the overall capital costs was –$4,271 million. Coinciding with this adverse EVA figure is General Motors' negative MVA of –$24,708 million. Although General Motors' EVA improved considerably up to 1995, the automaker experienced a volatile decline in its EVA through year 2000. Associated with this, the mostly negative MVA values (Exhibit 1.4) during this decade suggests that investors—whether correctly, or incorrectly so—still lacked confidence in General Motors' fundamental ability to generate economic value added. Thus, we again see that the joining of MVA and EVA (Exhibits 1.4 and 1.5) can be used to distinguish between wealth creators and wealth destroyers. The joining of MVA and EVA can also be used to identify overvalued and undervalued securities in the capital market.

---

[18] It is interesting to note that the *contemporaneous* relationship between MVA and EVA is generally more robust for wealth creators than wealth destroyers. For example, the average correlation of MVA with EVA during the 1990–2000 period for the five wealth creators shown in Exhibits 1.2 and 1.3 is 0.68. The MVA-EVA correlation for these wealth creators ranges from –0.21 for Cisco Systems up to 0.8 to 0.9 for the *other* four wealth creators.

In contrast, the average correlation for the wealth destroyers shown in Exhibits 1.4 and 1.5 is 0.43. The MVA-EVA correlation ranges from –0.46 for World-Com, up to about 0.5 for Lucent and General Motors, and 0.7 to 0.8 for AT&T and First Union Corporation, respectively. The financial implications of these correlation differences among wealth creators and wealth destroyers will be explained in a later chapter.

ACCOUNTING IRREGULARITIES AND INFORMATION INTEGRITY

At the time of this writing, the "buzz" on Wall Street was about dubious (at best) accounting practices employed by prominent U.S. companies to prop up earnings and stock price. For example, the U.S. Securities and Exchange Commission accused WorldCom—among other U.S. companies such as Enron and Global Crossings[19]—of defrauding investors by transferring some $4 billion in line operating expenses from the income statement to its capital accounts. These unannounced accounting transfers were presumably made by WorldCom's management (or its auditors) to show higher operating margins and operating earnings during 2001 and the first quarter of 2002.

While a detailed investigation of accounting irregularities at companies like WorldCom is beyond the scope of this book, it is worth making a few comments on the EVA consequences of the accounting improprieties. First, if it is publicly known—as it eventually would be with an "on balance" sheet transfer—that a company were going to capitalize an expense rather than write it off, then operating earnings in the current year would obviously go up. From an accounting perspective, such a transfer would make a company look more profitable, and thus presumably worth more money to investors. However, from an EVA perspective, the mere shifting of an expense to a capital account would lead to an annual capital charge that, in principle, should be "fully reflected" in economic profit. Specifically, while the current year's operating earnings might look higher, other things the same, all future profitability would be lower by an equivalent present value amount.[20]

From an EVA perspective, the firm's enterprise value and stock price could in principle remain invariant to the "on balance" sheet capitalization of the expense. Even if the transfer from the income statement to the balance sheet were not formally announced by management, EVA accounting would normally pick this transfer up, as the revised capital account (on the EVA balance sheet) would generate a capital charge equal to the amount of transferred expense *times* the opportunity cost of invested capital. In a nutshell, EVA accounting—as opposed to GAAP

---

[19] Enron and Global Crossings were among a growing list of large capitalization companies that defrauded investors with either "off balance" sheet or "on balance" accounting irregularities. We'll focus on WorldCom, as the long distance carrier was among the largest wealth destroyers in 2000 that we previewed in Exhibits 1.4 and 1.5.

[20] Consider the simple case of a capital item that forever remains on the balance sheet. According to EVA accounting, the present value of the annual interest charge would equal the amount of capital placed on the balance sheet: where "interest" each year is calculated by multiplying the capital amount by the opportunity cost of invested capital.

accounting—automatically picks up the capitalization of expensed items through the dollar capital charge. Obviously, *serious* EVA troubles arise for investors when "on balance" sheet items like revenue are artificially inflated, or when "off balance" sheet accounting gimmickry is used by management (or its auditors) as with the notorious case of Enron that was discovered in late 2001.[21]

Although sophisticated investors might recognize the EVA consequences of dubious accounting changes, the lack of accounting transparency for the average investor leads to a *precipitous* decline in investor confidence. Worse yet, the lack of information integrity in accounting numbers leads to outright investor capitulation—as apparently happened during the summer of 2002. Also, other things the same, the increased risk of investing in the stock market leads to a rise in the cost of capital. While a rise in the cost of equity capital in particular leaves GAAP accounting earnings unchanged, a rise in the weighted average cost of capital causes a decline in EVA and a concomitant decline in enterprise value and stock price.

Returning to WorldCom, it is interesting to note that a close inspection of Exhibits 1.4 and 1.5 shows that the telecom giant's accounting gimmickry in 2001 was just the "nail on the coffin" for this large U.S. wealth destroyer. In particular, Exhibit 1.5 shows that WorldCom's EVA was close to zero from 1990 to 1992. After that, the telecom giant's EVA was consistently negative in the eight years spanning 1993 to 2000. Moreover, by year-end 2000, WorldCom's EVA was grossly negative, at –$5,387 million. Coincidently, Exhibit 1.4 reveals that during 2000 the telecom firm's heretofore positive MVA was completely wiped out! Indeed, World-Com's MVA was a staggering –$31,808 million at year 2000.

As with AT&T and Lucent, it is clear from Exhibit 1.4 that the sharp rise in MVA that occurred during 1998 and 1999 was clearly not sustainable. That is, the MVA bubble in the telecommunication industry stocks finally burst in 2000 in the presence of persistently negative EVA for these wealth-destroying companies. By joining MVA with EVA, a casual market observer (or possibly, and informed SEC official or federal regulator) is left wondering why and how the stocks of telecom giants—such as AT&T, Lucent Technologies, and WorldCom—were so "hyped" during the late 1990s. Unfortunately, shareholders in companies like WorldCom were harmed by a lack of accounting transparency—or dearth of information integrity in the accounting numbers— while shareholders of companies in the telecom industry more generally were harmed by a fundamental *inability* of the underlying companies to generate sustainable economic value added.

---

[21] Moreover, accounting improprieties are downright illegal!

EVA HORIZONS

Before delving too deeply into the conceptual and empirical side of EVA, it is important to spell out to the reader what this book *is* and is *not* designed to do. First, this book *is* designed to explain the conceptual, empirical, and practical role of EVA in determining the enterprise value of the firm and its outstanding stock. In this context, the book focuses on the theory of economic value added as well as the application of EVA principles in practice. Additionally, the book sheds light on the empirical role of EVA in the cross section of U.S. companies and industries, along with the economy-wide influence of this economic profit metric.

Foundations of Economic Value Added shows how to apply economic profit principles in valuing companies and industries. In this context, the book shows how to (1) estimate EVA with basic and advanced accounting adjustments, (2) how to capitalize economic profit to determine a company's net present value (NPV), and (3) how to use published financial reports—such as company reports from Value Line—to estimate a company's future EVA, and in turn, its current market value added. Corporate managers and investors to assess whether the firm's outstanding securities are valued correctly in the marketplace can use these EVA valuation procedures.

Foundations of Economic Value Added also develops quantitative techniques that can be used by investors to find the most attractive companies and industries in the capital market. Linear and nonlinear regression techniques—including the Nobel prize-winning Markowitz portfolio model—are applied in an EVA context to find attractive investment opportunities. Also, the book develops a macro EVA model—based on the positioning of the economy-wide return on invested capital (ROC) and the cost of capital (COC)—to explore some exciting financial happenings at the macro-economic level. The EVA applications at the industry and economy level are updated versions of the original ones, and as such they still warrant exploration by the reader.

On the other hand, this book does *not* argue that EVA is the only measure of corporate profitability and success that should be used by managers or investors in determining the warranted value of the firm and its outstanding shares. Given the continued empirical "infancy" in EVA research, the author does not find it instructive to engage in the popular "Metric Wars" (ROE versus EVA, for example) that seem to detract from recognizing the strategic importance of this financial measure.[22] Suffice it to say at this point that EVA is a "top-down" approach

---

[22] For a practical discussion of competing profit measures and players, see Randy Myers, CEO, "Metric Wars" (October 1996).

to looking at the firm's real profitability. Moreover, it does so in a way that is intrinsically related to the firm's net present value. At the very least, the reader should find that the EVA research described here offers new insights that are consistent with the general principles of wealth maximization.

Finally, it should be mentioned that Stern Stewart & Co. should be credited (applause!) for their efforts in commercializing an innovative measure of corporate profit—that, in practice, can serve as the manager or investor's tool for estimating a company's "economic value-added." Having said that, it is also important to recognize that they are not the only individuals in finance or accounting to develop a practitioner approach to estimating the firm's profits net of overall capital costs. In this context, Robert Anthony of Harvard University is known in the field of managerial accounting for his early efforts at adjusting corporate profits for the associated capital costs. Additionally, published research during the 1970s by Alfred Rappaport, among others, is consistent with estimating the firm's weighted average cost of capital in a (CAPM) way that is consistent with the commercial EVA product.[23] Moreover, in the theory of finance, EVA is one of many *equivalent* ways of estimating the market value of the firm and its outstanding shares.

SUMMARY

The financial motivation for taking notice of the "EVA revolution" should be crystal clear. In a prospective sense, economic profit analysis suggests that companies that are experiencing positive EVA momentum should see their stock prices go up over time, as the increasing profitability *net* of the capital costs leads to a rise in the market value of the firm. In contrast, companies having negative EVA reports should see a noticeable decline in their equity values as the adverse real profits lead to a fall in the firm's net present value. In practice, EVA changes are also likely to impact, either positively or negatively, the firm's credit rating, and therefore the valuation of its risky bonds. Discovering these financial happenings before they occur is at the heart of the EVA revolution.

In the next two chapters we'll explore the role of EVA in the theory of finance. In Chapter 2, it will be shown that EVA is positive when the firm's after-tax return on invested capital is greater than the cost of capital. In this context, the firm creates market value added (MVA) by investing in projects having a positive "net present value." When EVA is

---

[23] See, Alfred Rappaport, "Strategic Analysis for More Profitable Acquisitions," *Harvard Business Review* (July/August 1979).

on average negative, however, the firm's managers destroy wealth by investing in capital projects having after tax returns that fall short of the weighted average cost of debt and equity capital. In Chapter 3, we'll examine the link (or lack thereof) between corporate financing decisions and economic profit. Here, we'll see that the EVA impact of the capital structure decision depends on whether the capital market is largely perfect, or imperfect. The theory of finance then serves as a backdrop for the EVA developments and applications that follow.

CHAPTER 2

EVA in the Theory of Finance I: Investment Decisions

Anyone who has had a course in finance knows that managers should invest in wealth-creating projects that have a positive net present value. But what does it mean for managers to invest in positive NPV projects when most of the available financial data has little if any resemblance to the kind of cash flow information that is required to make informed capital budgeting decisions? This is *precisely* where EVA as the practitioner's guide to measuring the period (annual or otherwise) contribution to shareholder value goes to the head of the corporate finance class—or more aptly, to the head of the corporate board!

Unlike accounting profit, the link between economic profit and shareholder value is transparent.[1] In principle, the net present value of any company is equal to the discounted stream of expected EVA generated by its current and future assets not currently in place.[2] This chapter

---

[1] While EBITDA and net income contains several important accounts—such as selling, general, and administrative expenses and cost of goods sold—that show up in the EVA calculation, accounting profit *per se* does not fully "account" for the owner's required return on invested capital. As we will shortly see, EVA is the annualized equivalent of a company's net present value. Unlike EVA, the discounted value of a company's accounting profit does *not* produce the enterprise value of the firm nor the NPV addition to invested capital.

[2] Fama and Miller provide a lucid discussion of the division of a company's enterprise value into contributions from existing assets and future growth opportunities. See Eugene F. Fama and Merton H. Miller, *The Theory of Finance* (Holt, Rinehart, and Winston, Inc., 1972).

For recent applications of the classic "Investment Opportunities Approach to Valuation (IOAV)," see (1) Chapter 7 of this book, (2) Aswath Damodaran, "Value Creation and Enhancement: Back to the Future," *Contemporary Finance Digest*, Winter 1998, and (3) Stanley Kogelman and Martin L. Leibowitz, "The Franchise Factor Valuation Approach: Capturing the Firm's Investment Opportunities," *Corporate Financial Decision Making and Equity Analysis*, ICFA (Charlottesville, VA: Association for Investment Management and Research, 1995).

builds on a wealth-discovery theme by examining the role of economic profit in the theory of finance. We'll begin with the neoclassical Fisherian Wealth Model[3] to show the fundamental link between NPV and the *annualized* EVA equivalent. We'll then see how other prominent economic profit measures such as cash flow return on investment (CFROI) evolve out of the same market value rule that guides managers to act in the best interest of the firm's shareholders.

Following that, we'll focus on the real meaning of a company's enterprise value-to-capital ratio. This development is especially important for investors who look at price relatives—such as the price-to-earnings and price-to-book value ratios—when evaluating companies and their outstanding shares. In the next chapter, we'll explore the formal link (or possibly, the lack thereof) between EVA and capital structure decisions in the theory of finance.

TWO-PERIOD NPV MODEL

Consider a two-period world where an investment today of, say, C = $100 million (or 100% of any initial capital amount) leads to an *unlevered* after-tax cash flow of $125 million in the future period.[4] For convenience, we'll denote this one-time expected cash flow as "NOPAT."[5] Further suppose that the firm's cost of capital, COC, is 10%. Based on these assumptions, the gross present value, GPV, of the firm's investment decision is simply the present value of the expected future cash flow:

---

[3] Irving Fisher's pioneering research on the NPV theory of the firm is described in Irving Fisher, *The Theory of Investment* (New York: Augustus M. Kelley, Publishers, 1965, reprinted from the original 1930 edition).

[4] There are two noteworthy items here: First, the numbers used in this example are the same as those introduced in Chapter 1 for NSF (for New Start-up Firm). Second, and more importantly, the after-tax cash flow of $125 million is *before* financing charges—hence, the operative phrase *unlevered* after-tax cash flow. This is central to the EVA calculation because the opportunity cost of debt *and* equity capital shows up in the dollar cost of capital.

[5] In practice, NOPAT refers to a firm's net operating profit after tax. Because we are using a two-period model to show the link between NPV and EVA, the NOPAT figure (at $125 million) shown in the text includes the initial investment (at $100 million) and the dollar return-on-invested capital (at $25 million). In equation form, this can be expressed as $C \times (1 + ROC)$, where C is the capital investment and ROC is the after-tax operating return-on-invested capital. This two-period interpretation of NOPAT is different from the conventional view of NOPAT as after-tax operating profit or the dollar return earned on an "on-going" firm's existing assets, namely $C \times ROC$.

$$\text{GPV} = \text{Present value of expected cash flow}$$
$$= \text{NOPAT}/(1 + \text{COC})$$
$$= \$125/(1 + 0.1) = \$113.64 \text{ million}$$

In turn, the net present value, NPV (or MVA in financial jargon[6]), of the firm's investment decision is given by:

$$\text{NPV} = \text{MVA}$$
$$= \text{GPV} - C$$
$$= \text{NOPAT}/(1 + \text{COC}) - C$$
$$= \$113.64 - \$100 = \$13.64 \text{ million}$$

Due to the wealth-creating investment, the firm's managers have added $13.64 million (or 13.64%) to the initial capital employed. The corporate or "enterprise" value of the firm is therefore:

$$\text{Enterprise value} = \text{Market value of debt} + \text{Market value of equity}$$
$$= C + \text{NPV}$$
$$= \$100 + \$13.64 = \$113.64 \text{ million}$$

Exhibit 2.1 provides a visual representation of the two-period Fisherian Wealth Model. Assume that the firm's ability to transform current resources into future resources can be represented by a Production Possibilities Curve (PPC). Further assume that the firm has *no* internal start up funds such that the invested capital, C = $100 million, is raised entirely from external capital market sources. The length "C = $100" in Exhibit 2.1 represents the amount borrowed to finance the capital investment. As before, assume that the initial investment generates an *unlevered* after-tax cash flow, NOPAT, of $125 million in the future period—which, in a multiperiod context can be viewed as the after-tax cash flow generated next period *plus* the net present value of all future after-tax operating cash flows thereafter.

With NOPAT of $125 million, the after-tax cash flow from the firm's production decision is represented by the vertical distance in Exhibit 2.1 from length "C" up to the PPC. At $113.64 million, the present value of the anticipated NOPAT is the firm's gross present value. The horizontal length noted as GPV in the exhibit represents this distance. Moreover, the firm's net present value, at $13.64 million, is measured along the horizontal axis by the difference between the gross present value, GPV at $113.64 million, and the initial capital of $100 million.

---

[6] In practice, Stern Stewart (among others) use MVA to denote NPV.

EXHIBIT 2.1   Wealth Creation with Positive NPV

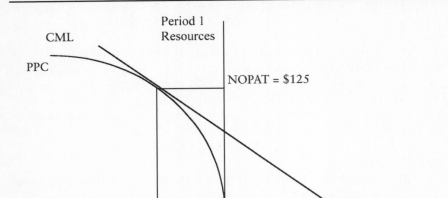

WEALTH CREATION WITH POSITIVE EVA

Up to this point *nothing* has been said about EVA as a financial tool for measuring the NPV of the firm's investment decision. This means that, in principle, we can speak of wealth creation without formally introducing a periodic measure of economic profit. Having said that, it is important to emphasize that one of the major goals of the EVA revolution is to promote a cash-operating measure of profit—albeit economic profit as opposed to accounting profit—that at the very least is consistent with the measurement and creation of shareholder value.

Based on the figures supplied in the two-period NPV illustration, it is a straightforward matter to show that the firm's expected future EVA is $15 million (or 15% of the initial capital). This economic profit figure results from subtracting the expected financing payments—including "interest" (at $10 million) and the return of "loan principal" (at $100 million) to external suppliers of capital—from the expected future cash flow, denoted previously as NOPAT:[7]

---

[7] Note again that for an *ongoing* concern, EVA is the difference between the unlevered net operating profit after tax, NOPAT, and a dollar charge for capital employed in the business—measured by the amount of capital *times* the weighted-average cost of capital, $C \times COC$.

$$
\begin{aligned}
\text{EVA} &= \text{NOPAT} - \$ \text{ Capital charge} \\
&= \$125 - \$100 \times (1 + 0.1) \\
&= \$125 - \$110 \\
&= \$15 \text{ million}
\end{aligned}
$$

With positive EVA at $15 million, the firm's cash operating profit after tax, NOPAT, is more than sufficient to cover the anticipated expenses—including a "rental charge" and the return of borrowed principal (in the two-period model), $C \times (1 + \text{COC}) = \$110$ million, on the capital employed in the business.

The EVA Spread

We can now use the two-period NPV model to explain the residual return on capital (RROC), or the "EVA spread." Specifically, the EVA spread refers to the difference between the return on invested capital, ROC, and the cost of capital, COC. To show this, we'll begin by unfolding NOPAT (*again*, in terms of a two-period model) into the firm's initial capital and the rate of return on that capital according to:

$$
\text{NOPAT} = C \times (1 + \text{ROC})
$$

In this expression, ROC is the firm's "operating cash flow return on investment" and "C" is the initial capital investment. With this development, we can express the firm's NPV directly in terms of both EVA and the residual capital return (ROC *less* COC) according to:

$$
\begin{aligned}
\text{NPV} &= \text{NOPAT}/(1 + \text{COC}) - C \\
&= C \times (1 + \text{ROC})/(1 + \text{COC}) - C \\
&= C \times (\text{ROC} - \text{COC})/(1 + \text{COC}) \\
&= \text{EVA}/(1 + \text{COC})
\end{aligned}
$$

In this combined expression, we see that the firm's NPV derives its sign from the difference between the operating cash flow return on investment, ROC, and the weighted average cost of capital, COC. The spread between ROC and COC is often referred to in the economic profit literature as (1) the "residual return on capital," (2) the "surplus return on capital," (3) the "excess operating return on invested capital," and, of course, (4) the "EVA spread." Furthermore, the above development shows that the net present value of the firm is equal to the present value of the anticipated economic profit stream—whereby economic profit is defined by the formula, EVA = NOPAT − $COC. Moreover, upon substituting the numerical values into the "two-period" NPV formulation, we obtain:

$$
\begin{aligned}
\text{NPV} &= \text{MVA} \\
&= \$125/(1.1) - \$100 \\
&= \$100 \times (1 + 0.25)/1.1 - \$100 \\
&= \$100 \times (0.25 - 0.10)/1.1 \\
&= \$15/1.1 = \$13.64 \text{ million}
\end{aligned}
$$

In this example, the firm's anticipated ROC is 25%, the assessed residual return on capital is 15% (RROC, or the EVA spread), and the firm's assessed economic profit is equal to $15 million.

Exhibit 2.2 shows how the firm derives its net present value in an economic profit context.[8] Recall that EVA is simply the difference between the firm's estimated NOPAT and the dollar capital charge (also *recall* that in the two-period NPV illustration one must include the return of loan principal, $100 million). At $15 million, this economic profit amount is labeled "EVA" in Exhibit 2.2. Upon discounting the firm's economic profit back to the current period by the cost of capital, at 10%, we obtain the firm's net present value, at $13.64 million. Hence, the firm's net present value is in fact equal to the present value of the anticipated future EVA. Likewise, the multiperiod relationship between NPV and the future stream of economic profit follows from this result.

EXHIBIT 2.2   Wealth Creation with Positive EVA

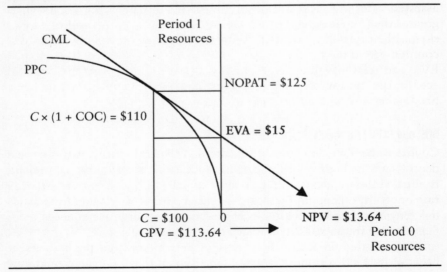

---

[8] Note that Exhibit 2.2 (and Exhibit 2.4 for that matter) are drawn out of proportion. However, the *key* NPV–EVA results remain.

EXHIBIT 2.3   Microsoft Corporation: Return on Capital, Cost of Capital, and Residual Return on Capital: 1990–2000

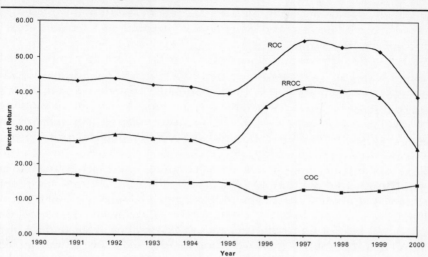

In sum, the two-period wealth model is robust. It shows that the firm makes a positive NPV addition to invested capital if and only if the assessed after-tax cash operating return on invested capital, ROC, is greater than the weighted average cost of capital, COC. Another way of saying the same thing is that the firm's NPV is positive because its discounted economic profit, EVA/(1 + COC), is also positive. In principle, EVA and related value-based metrics[9] are consistent with the classical economists' notion of "profit" because they *directly* measure whether a firm makes a wealth addition to invested capital.

ROC and COC: Microsoft Corporation

Consider the EVA experience of Microsoft Corporation over the past decade, which highlights the financial importance of having a positive residual return on capital. In this context, Exhibit 2.3 shows the after-tax rate of return on capital (ROC), the cost of capital (COC), and the residual return on capital (RROC) for the computer software services company during the 1990–2000 period.

As revealed in Chapter 1, Microsoft had a large positive MVA because its EVA was both positive and growing at an exceptional rate

---

[9] We'll look at another well-known economic profit metric, namely CFROI (Cash Flow Return on Investment) in a later section.

for most of the 1990s. In Exhibit 2.3, we see that the firm's large positive EVA (and therefore, MVA) was due to its strongly positive residual
return on capital—whereby, the after-tax rate of return on invested capital is greater than the cost of capital (*equity* capital, in Microsoft's case)
by a substantial margin.

Exhibit 2.3 shows that Microsoft's after-tax return on capital varied
from 44.16% in 1990, to a high of 54.75% in 1997, and then settled
(can you imagine!) at 39.06% by year-end 2000. For the 11-year reporting period, the computer software services company had an outstanding
average return on capital of 45.54%. Meanwhile, Microsoft's cost of
capital ranged from a high of 16.90% in 1991 (up slightly from 1990),
to a low of 10.74% in 1996, and then settled at 14.29% by year-end
2000. The firm's average cost of (equity) capital was 14.20% for the 11-
year reporting period shown in the exhibit.

Taken together, the capital return and capital cost findings for
Microsoft indicate that the "residual return on capital" was substantially positive for the reporting period. In this context, Exhibit 2.3
shows that the residual return on capital (RROC) ranged from 27.32%
in 1990, up to a high of 41.82% in 1997, and then settled at 24.77% by
year-end 2000. The exhibit also reveals that volatility in this technology
firm's residual capital return (and therefore, its EVA) is due primarily to
variations in the after-tax return on capital (ROC). In contrast, the cost
of capital (COC) for Microsoft was relatively stable during the 11-year
reporting period. Overall, the EVA findings for Microsoft are quite
remarkable: The company not only generated considerable residual
returns on invested capital—due to its highly desirable computer software products—but it also exhibited substantial "staying power" in the
presence of serious legal challenges from competitors and the U.S. Jus-
tice Department in the late 1990s.

The empirical findings for Microsoft also illustrate the role of the
"residual return on capital" in the wealth creation process. The company
graphs presented in Chapter 1 and in this chapter suggest that firms having positive EVA do so because the after-tax return on invested capital
exceeds the weighted average cost of capital. In turn, the positive EVA
announcement is clearly "good news" to the shareholders as it leads to a
sizable increase in the firm's market value added. This favorable NPV
(MVA, in financial jargon) result is one of the major predictions that
evolve from the neoclassical wealth model. It also emphasizes the role of
"positivism" in the application of modern financial principles.[10]

---

[10] This positivistic view of EVA and wealth creation is a breath of "fresh air" in a
market plagued by accounting scandals during 2002.

CASE B: WEALTH DESTRUCTION WITH NEGATIVE EVA

The two-period wealth model can also be used to gain some insight on the financial characteristics of wealth destroyers. To see this, suppose that the firm's managers anticipate that a $100 million outlay will generate an after-tax cash flow of, say, $107.50 million in the future period. The NPV consequence of the firm's 7.5% ($107.50/$100) investment opportunity is shown in Exhibit 2.4.

Exhibit 2.4 shows that the firm's initial capital is $100 million. The exhibit also shows that the firm's expected cash operating profit—namely, NOPAT—is $107.50 million. Upon subtracting the company's expected capital costs, at $110 million, from the anticipated cash operating profit, at $107.25 million, the manager (or investor) sees that the firm is left with negative residual income, at –$2.5 million. This dollar residual is the firm's expected EVA in the reduced operating (that is, ROC now at 7.5%) environment.

Note that if a company is a wealth destroyer in the future (due to the negative anticipated EVA), then it must also be a wealth waster in the present. By discounting the negative EVA by the 10% cost of capital, COC, one obtains the adverse net present value result:[11]

EXHIBIT 2.4   Wealth Destruction with Negative EVA

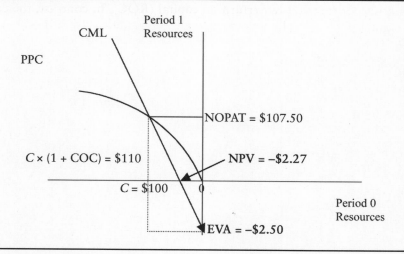

[11] In practice, a firm may have "real options" (EVA or otherwise) that offset an initial negative net present value assessment. For a discussion of real options—including options to abandon or to expand—see Stephen A. Ross, Randolph W. Westerfield, and Bradford D. Jordan, *Fundamentals of Corporate Finance* (New York: Mc Graw-Hill Irwin, 2003).

$$
\begin{aligned}
\text{NPV} &= \text{MVA} \\
&= \text{EVA}/(1 + \text{COC}) \\
&= -\$2.50/1.1 \\
&= -\$2.27 \text{ million}
\end{aligned}
$$

As a wealth destroyer, it should be apparent that the firm's NPV is negative because the after-tax return on invested capital, ROC at 7.5%, falls short of the cost of capital, at 10%. In this context, the net present value of –$2.27 million can also be obtained by multiplying the firm's residual return on capital, at –2.5%, by the initial capital, at $100 million, and then discounting this EVA result:

$$
\begin{aligned}
\text{NPV} &= \text{MVA} \\
&= C \times (\text{ROC} - \text{COC})/(1 + \text{COC}) \\
&= \$100 \times (0.075 - 0.1)/(1.1) \\
&= -\$2.27 \text{ million}
\end{aligned}
$$

Hence, in this two-period illustration, the company's negative NPV is due to the poor EVA outlook. The adverse EVA outlook is in turn caused by the negative residual return on capital (ROC – COC), at –2.5%. In a well-functioning capital market, the firm's managers would *not* be able to attract the necessary debt or equity capital to fund the proposed investment.[12]

ROC and COC: WorldCom Inc.

A fascinating, yet unfortunate, case of a recent wealth destroyer is WorldCom. In July 2002, the telecommunications giant filed for Chapter 11 bankruptcy protection. At that time, this was the largest corporate bankruptcy in U.S. history. As explained in Chapter 1, WorldCom's problems were much larger than those caused by the alleged accounting gimmickry that occurred during 2001 and the first quarter of 2002. Specifically, the telecom giant had consistently negative EVA in the eight-year reporting period spanning 1993–2000. Exhibit 2.5 provides a closer look at the EVA happenings for WorldCom by showing the firm's after-tax return on capital (ROC) versus the cost of capital (COC), and the residual capital return (RROC) for the 1990–2000 period. Notably, the exhibit shows that WorldCom's post-tax return on invested capital was consistently below the cost of capital after 1992.

---

[12] This is true even if the after-tax return on invested capital, ROC of 7.5%, were higher than the firm's after-tax cost of debt.

EXHIBIT 2.5   WorldCom: Return on Capital, Cost of Capital, and Residual Return on Capital: 1990–2000

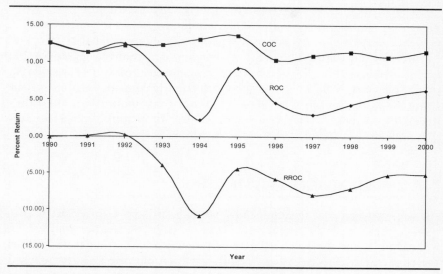

Specifically, Exhibit 2.5 shows that from 1990–1992, WorldCom's after-tax return on capital was about the same as its cost of capital, around 12%. In 1993, a notable EVA event occurred when the telecommunication giant's capital return fell *below* 10%. At that time, WorldCom's return on capital was 8.51%, while its cost of capital was 12.37%. The exhibit also shows that from 1993–2000, the telecom giant's return on invested capital ranged from lows of 2.23% and 2.95% in 1994 and 1997, respectively, to a high of *only* 9.21% in 1995. Meanwhile, WorldCom's cost of capital was consistently above the 10% watershed mark during the 11 year reporting period.

Moreover, the average return on capital for WorldCom during the 1990–2000 period was 7.26% while the firm's average capital cost was 11.82%. Taken together, the capital return and capital cost experience for the telecommunications giant produced a sharply negative "residual return on capital" during the eight years spanning 1993–2000. Not surprisingly, the average residual return on capital for WorldCom was negative, at –4.56%, over the reporting decade. These negative EVA findings for WorldCom can be see in Exhibit 2.5 by focusing on either (1) the mostly negative gap between the ROC and COC series, or (2) the mostly negative residual return on capital series during 1990–2000.

The empirical findings for WorldCom are indicative of the financial dangers that result when a company's after-tax capital returns fall short of the capital costs. With a positive after-tax return on capital for each year during 1990–2000, it would seem that the telecommunications giant was making money—albeit, a generally smaller amount when measured relative to capital as the years progressed. However, the EVA evidence reveals that WorldCom was in fact a *major* wealth destroyer for most of the 1990s. The firm's persistently negative EVA spread—that began in the post-1992 years—was the economic source of the collapse in the telecom giant's market value added (MVA) that occurred at the century's turn. Indeed, WorldCom's filing for Chapter 11 bankruptcy protection in July 2002 was just the "nail in the coffin" for a company that was already busted from an EVA perspective.[13]

CASE C: WEALTH NEUTRALITY WITH ZERO EVA

As with positive or negative EVA, we can use the two-period wealth model to examine the financial consequences of *zero*-expected EVA. If, for example, the firm's assessed return on invested capital is 10%, then the expected EVA is zero. This results because the expected cash operating profit—namely, NOPAT—from the firm's investment opportunity is the same as the anticipated capital costs, at $110 million. In this instance, the company's aggregate net present value must be zero:

$$
\begin{aligned}
NPV &= MVA \\
&= C \times (ROC - COC)/(1 + COC) \\
&= \$100 \times (0.1 - 0.1)/(1.1) \\
&= 0.0
\end{aligned}
$$

Note that if a company has *zero*-expected EVA in the future—therefore, *zero*-expected NPV in the present—then its enterprise value must be the same as the initial capital. In our two-period illustration, the firm's enterprise value must be $100 million. Also, with the 10% investment opportunity, the firm's residual return on capital is zero, and the enterprise value-to-capital ratio is unity.[14]

---

[13] It is interesting to note that General Motors—an "Old Economy" company—has been one of the largest U.S. wealth destroyers in recent times. For example, the automaker's MVA ranking in the Stern Stewart Performance Universe was 1,000 (dead last!) in 1995, 990 in 1999, and 998 in 2000, respectively. Yet, unlike the "MVA bubble" that occurred for "New Economy" companies like WorldCom, there was *no* MVA aberration for General Motors during the 1990–2000 period. Apparently, investors did not get caught up with "Old Economy" companies in the stock market hype that impacted technology and telecom firms during the late 1990s.

Practically speaking, if a company has unused capital resources, then the current shareholders would be just as well off if managers were to pay out the unused funds as a dividend payment on the firm's stock. In the event of capital market imperfections—due perhaps to differential tax treatment of dividends and capital gains—the shareholders might be better off if the firm's managers were to repurchase the firm's outstanding common stock. In principle though, the stock repurchase program is a wealth-neutral (or zero NPV) investment activity.

Moreover, managers should take corporate actions that result in wealth-neutrality seriously when they do not have discounted positive EVA opportunities for the future. Although stock repurchase programs do not create any new wealth for the shareholders, they do not destroy it either. In contrast, managerial actions (or inactions) that result in wealth losses to the shareholders like those experienced by AT&T, General Motors, and WorldCom in recent years were financially unconscionable, especially when the albeit unexciting, yet wealth-preserving financial alternatives were available for the shareholders.

REAL MEANING OF THE VALUE/CAPITAL RATIO

Wall Street analysts commonly speak in terms of the "price-to-earnings" and "price-to-book value" ratios. Along this line, one of the key benefits of the economic profit approach to measuring financial success is that we can see *why* a company has a price-to-book ratio, for example, above or below unity. We can show this NPV and EVA connection by simply dividing the firm's enterprise value, V, by invested capital, C, according to:

$$V/C = C/C + NPV/C$$
$$= 1 + NPV/C$$

From this, we see that a firm's enterprise value-to-capital ratio, V/C, exceeds *one* if and only if—in a well functioning capital market—the firm has positive net present value. In contrast, the V/C ratio falls below unity when the firm invests in wealth destroying or negative NPV projects—such that the NPV-to-Capital ratio turns negative. Moreover, upon substituting the EVA findings that we obtained before into the enterprise value-to-capital ratio produces:

---

[14] The enterprise value-to-capital ratio will be unfolded into NPV and EVA components in the next section.

$$
\begin{aligned}
V/C &= 1 + [EVA/(1 + COC)]/C \\
&= 1 + [C \times (ROC - COC)/(1 + COC)]/C \\
&= 1 + (ROC - COC)/(1 + COC)
\end{aligned}
$$

From this, we see that wealth-creating firms have an enterprise value-to-capital ratio that exceeds *unity* because they have positive net present value. The source of the positive NPV is due to the positive discounted economic profit. In turn, EVA is positive because the firm's after tax cash return on investment, ROC, exceeds the weighted average cost of capital, COC. These relationships point to the central role of EVA and related economic profit metrics in the theory of finance.

Upon substituting the values from the two-period NPV model[15] into the enterprise value-to-capital ratio yields:

$$
\begin{aligned}
V/C &= 1 + [\$15/(1.1)]/\$100 \\
&= 1 + [\$13.64]/\$100 \\
&= 1 + [0.25 - 0.10]/(1.1) = 1.1364
\end{aligned}
$$

Hence, with economic profit measures there is little uncertainty as to (1) why a wealth-creating firm has a value-to-capital ratio (or "price-to-book" ratio in popular jargon) that exceeds *one*, and (2) why a wealth destroyer has a value-to-capital ratio that lies below unity. Unlike accounting profit measures, economic profit metrics give managers and investors alike the necessary financial tools to see the *direct* relationship between corporate investment decisions—made both now and in the foreseeable future—and their expected impact on shareholder value.[16]

RELATEDNESS OF ECONOMIC PROFIT METRICS

While EVA is perhaps the best-known economic profit measure, it is *not* the only value-based metric used in practice by managers and investors. CFROI, for cash flow return on investment, is another prominent economic profit measure that is consistent with the principles of wealth

---

[15] We'll use the values from the initial *positive* NPV opportunity.

[16] That economic profit metrics can be used in business valuation, however, is based on the assumption that the capital market is reasonably efficient. If the capital market were price inefficient, then EVA estimates would not be "fully reflected" in stock prices. In turn, market inefficiency creates active investment opportunities for informed investors that seek to trade the equity *and* debt securities of mispriced companies.

maximization.[17] Although accounting differences exist, cash flow return on investment is analogous to the internal rate of return (IRR) concept that is widely used in capital budgeting analysis.

Specifically, CFROI is the after-tax rate of return (IRR) on a company's *existing* assets. In principle, CFROI is that rate that sets the present value of the after-tax operating cash flows equal to their investment cost. Like any IRR, CFROI is that rate which sets a company's net present value equal to zero. Consequently, the firm's NPV is positive if CFROI exceeds the "hurdle rate" or cost of capital, while the firm's net present value is negative when the anticipated cash flow return on investment falls short of the required return on invested capital.

Since CFROI is based on both current *and* distant cash flows—while EVA seems a snapshot of the firm's current economic profit—it is tempting to argue that the former economic profit measure is more closely aligned with promoting shareholder value over the long term. Such a comparative interpretation is incorrect however when one realizes that economic profit (EVA) is the *annualized* equivalent of the firm's net present value (as we have seen in the two-period NPV model). Also, if for some reason the firm's managers compare CFROI to a hurdle rate that is inconsistent with the weighted average cost of capital, COC, a wealth-destroying *agency* problem exists between the firm's managers and owners.

Wealth Equivalency of EVA and CFROI

While competing economic profit proponents like to promote their metrics as "best practice," it is important to emphasize that value-based measures such as EVA and CFROI are theoretically equivalent ways of looking at the firm's net present value (or shareholder value added). This wealth *equivalency* between the two economic profit methodologies is based on the following consideration: On the EVA side of the wealth creator ledger, the firm's NPV can always be viewed as the present value of the anticipated economic profit. In this context, EVA is the *yearly* (or periodic) equivalent of the firm's net present value.

On the CFROI side of the wealth creator ledger, the firm's NPV is positive when CFROI on the average exceeds the corporate-wide hurdle rate. But EVA, and therefore NPV, is positive if and only if the firm's residual return on capital (IRR[18] *minus* COC) is greater than zero. We'll now see that cash flow return on investment (CFROI) is the same internal

---

[17] CFROI® is a registered trademark of Holt Value Associates, LP. For a complete discussion of the innovative CFROI approach to measuring economic profit, see Bartley J. Madden, *CFROI Valuation: A Total Systems Approach to Valuing the Firm* (Woburn, MA: Butterworth-Heinemann, 1999).

[18] We'll shortly see that ROC is equal to IRR in the two-period NPV model.

rate of return that drives the *sign* of economic profit when measured relative to the cost of invested capital.

As mentioned before, cash flow return on investment (CFROI) is that rate which sets a company's net present value equal to zero. In the two-period illustration, the firm's CFROI is that rate which sets the discounted value of the expected cash operating profit less the investment cost, C, equal to zero:[19]

$$0 = NOPAT/(1 + CFROI) - C$$

From this, we see that the firm's expected cash operating profit, NOPAT, can be expressed in terms of the initial capital, C, and the cash operating return on invested capital, ROC, and CFROI measures according to:

$$NOPAT = C \times (1 + ROC)$$
$$= C \times (1 + CFROI)$$

Upon substituting this expression into the two-period NPV formula, we obtain the formal relationship between the firm's net present value and its cash flow return on investment (CFROI) according to:

$$NPV = C \times (1 + CFROI)/(1 + COC) - C$$
$$= C \times (CFROI - COC)/(1 + COC)$$
$$= EVA/(1 + COC)$$

As expected, the firm's net present value is positive *if and only if* CFROI (or the expected IRR) is greater than the cost of capital, COC. Otherwise, wealth is destroyed when CFROI falls short of the weighted average cost of debt *and* equity capital. But these capital return *versus* capital cost conditions are the same wealth creating (or destroying) conditions that drive (1) the assessed residual return on capital, RROC, and (2) the sign and dollar amount (when linked to the initial capital investment) of the firm's economic profit, EVA.

Based on the two-period illustration, the firm's expected operating cash return on investment, ROC = CFROI, is 25% ($25/$100). With a cost of capital of 10% ($10/$100), the firm's residual return on capital, RROC, is 15%. In addition, since CFROI exceeds the cost of capital,

---

[19] In practice, CFROI is estimated using a measure of gross operating profit as opposed to net operating profit after tax (NOPAT). But this is really an accounting detail since gross cash flow and gross investment measures can be used interchangeably with net cash flow and net investment information to obtain the same economic profit results.

the firm's assessed economic profit is positive, EVA at $15 million. As before, the net present value is positive at $13.64 million:

$$NPV = C \times (CFROI - COC)/(1 + COC)$$
$$= \$100 \times (0.25 - 0.10)/(1.1) = \$13.64 \text{ million}$$

Hence, the firm is a wealth "creator" due to its *jointly* attractive CFROI (measured relative to COC) and EVA condition. At 1.1364 ($113.64/$100), the firm's enterprise value-to-capital ratio is greater than unity because of the *positive* net present value opportunity.

CFROI: Real World Considerations

Before moving on, it should be noted that the CFROI measure is informative, yet more complex than a typical IRR calculation. For example, Peterson and Peterson[20] provide a helpful guide on how to estimate CFROI (and EVA), along with a discussion of the conceptual issues that arise in the estimation process. After intensive examination of the 1993 Annual Report of Hershey Foods Corporation (including the income statement, balance sheet, and footnotes), they estimate the *gross* operating cash flow and investment items that are pertinent to the CFROI calculation.[21] Their *nominal* CFROI findings for Hershey Foods Corporation for 1993 are shown in Exhibit 2.6.

EXHIBIT 2.6   Nominal CFROI Inputs for Hershey Foods Corporation for 1993

Gross Cash Investment	=	$2,925.86 million
Gross Cash Flow	=	$427.16 million
Nondepreciating Assets	=	$522.97 million

Existing asset life = 18 years
IRR = 13.31%

Source: Pamela P. Peterson and David R. Peterson, *Company Performance and Measures of Value Added*, ICFA (Charlottesville, VA: Association for Investment Management and Research, 1996).

---

[20] See, Pamela Peterson and David Peterson, *Company Performance and Measures of Value Added*, ICFA (Charlottesville, VA: Association for Investment Management and Research, 1996).
[21] While in theory EVA and CFROI are equivalent measures of wealth creation, there are several value-based accounting issues that separate the two measures in practice. As noted before, CFROI uses a measure of gross operating profit while EVA uses net operating profit (NOPAT). Also, EVA is measured in nominal dollar terms while CFROI is a percentage real rate of return, among other differences.

Based on Hershey's 1993 Annual Report, Peterson and Peterson find that the internal rate of return on the firm's *existing* assets is 13.31%. Although many accounting adjustments[22] were made to arrive at this point, the estimated IRR is *not* the firm's actual CFROI. As the authors note, there are two practical differences between CFROI and the standard IRR calculation. First, the inputs to the CFROI model are stated in current monetary equivalents. That is, past investments are "grossed up" to the current period by a historical inflation factor while gross operating cash flows are inflation-adjusted back to the present time period.

In light of current dollar adjustments (at that time), the CFROI for Hershey Foods Corporation drops from 13.31% to 10.25%. This percentage difference is important. If the firm's "hurdle rate" were somewhere between the two figures, the unsuspecting (or less informed) manager or investor—with an *unadjusted* CFROI estimate of 13.31%—might incorrectly gauge the firm to be a "wealth creator" having positive NPV. Second, in practice, the firm's cash flow return on investment is stated in *real* terms as opposed to nominal terms. Hence, the real CFROI measure is impacted by the inflation assumption used by the manager or investor in the after-tax operating cash flow and gross investment estimation process.

Peterson and Peterson also point out that CFROI measurement concerns arise because the estimated real return on the firm's invested capital is *not* compared to an inflation-adjusted cost of capital measure using the standard COC formulation. If correct, then the CFROI approach to shareholder value may give rise to an *agency* conflict between managers and owners. This could happen unless the estimated "hurdle rate"—due to many real world challenges to estimating COC in practice—is somehow a more descriptive measure of the *equilibrium* required rate of return on the firm's invested capital. In Chapter 9, we'll look at the standard accounting adjustments that are necessary to estimate CFROI (and EVA) in practice. At that time, we'll revisit economic profit measurement issues in greater detail.

MVA AND EVA: SOME LARGE-SCALE EMPIRICAL EVIDENCE

The empirical relationship between MVA and EVA can be examined in a more general context by analyzing the financial data collected by Stern Stewart & Co. In particular, they report EVA-related data for the 1,000 largest capitalization U.S. firms, ranked by market value added. Some of the more pertinent financial information listed in the Performance Universe include:

---

[22] Unfortunately, there exists an "army" of accounting adjustments that are necessary to estimate economic profit measures such as EVA and CFROI in practice. We'll cover economic profit measurement challenges in Chapter 9.

EXHIBIT 2.7 MVA-to-Capital versus EVA-to-Capital Ratio: All Companies in Performance Universe at Year-End 2000

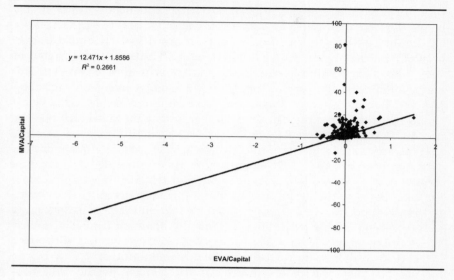

- ■ Market Value Added (MVA)
- ■ Economic Value Added (EVA)
- ■ Operating Capital
- ■ Return on Capital (%ROC)
- ■ Cost of Capital (%COC)

As before, EVA is equal to the firm's net operating profit after tax (NOPAT) less the dollar cost of capital. MVA is defined as the market value of the firm (debt and equity capitalization) less the operating capital employed in a business. As demonstrated in this chapter, the firm's market value added is also equal to the present value of its expected future EVA.

Exhibit 2.7 shows the statistical relationship between the MVA-to-Capital (dependent variable) and the EVA-to-Capital (explanatory variable) ratios for the companies listed in the Performance Universe at year-end 2000. The exhibit reveals that a statistically meaningful relationship exists between the two measures of corporate financial success. With a slope coefficient (or "EVA beta") of 12.47 and a t-statistic of 19, the size-adjusted EVA factor is a significant financial variable. In this regard, it is helpful to note that an explanatory variable—like the EVA-to-Capital ratio—is generally considered to be statistically significant when the t-value exceeds (the absolute value of the number) two. Moreover, the regression statistics reported in Exhibit 2.7 reveal that 27% (adjusted R^2) of the cross-sectional variation in the MVA-to-Capital ratio for large U.S. companies at year 2000 is explained by contemporaneous movements in the EVA-to-Capital factor.[23]

Exhibit 2.8 reveals the underlying source of the positive relationship between the MVA and EVA variables in the Performance Universe at year 2000. The exhibit looks at the statistical role of cross sectional variation in both the cost of capital and the residual return on capital on MVA-to-Capital ratios of large U.S. companies. Notably, the exhibit shows that the size of the difference between the after-tax return on capital, ROC, and the cost of capital, COC, has a significant impact on the average firm's ability to generate "economic value added" for the future. That is, with a slope of 11.6 and a t-statistic of 19.11, the residual return on capital has a significant impact on the MVA-to-Capital ratio for firms listed in the Performance Universe. Taken together, the empirical results reported in Exhibits 2.7 and 2.8 suggest that "good firms" do in fact have favorable stock (and presumably bond) prices because their after-tax return on capital exceeds the weighted average cost of capital.

It is also interesting to see that the cost of capital factor shown in Exhibit 2.8 has a significant positive impact on the average MVA-to-Capital ratio for companies listed in the Performance Universe at year-end 2000. With a slope of 66.64 and a t-statistic of 10.91, the cost of capital factor is helpful in understanding the cross-sectional variation in the MVA-to-Capital ratios for large capitalization U.S. firms. This finding may be due in part to an underlying positive association between the firm's after tax return on capital and the cost of capital, whereby high returning, yet inherently more volatile companies and industries (like technology, for example) have a relatively high required rate of return.

EXHIBIT 2.8 Multiple Regression Statistics for Performance Universe at Year-End 2000

$$\text{MVA/Capital} = -4.63 + 66.64\text{COC} + 11.60[\text{ROC} - \text{COC}]$$
$$(t\text{-value}) \quad (-7.57) \quad (10.91) \quad (19.11)$$

$$\text{Adjusted } R^2 = 31\%$$

[23] For year 2000, the regression of MVA on EVA (unadjusted for firm size) also yields an adjusted R^2 of 27% (rounded). As with the t-statistic on the capital-adjusted EVA factor, the t-value on the unadjusted EVA factor is highly significant.

EXHIBIT 2.9   MVA-to-Capital versus EVA-to-Capital Ratio: Performance Universe at Year-End 2000 (Net of Outlier)

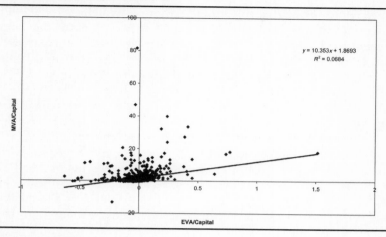

Regression Caveats

Before moving on, it should be noted that the statistical association between MVA and EVA (whether it is size adjusted or not) is especially variable and highly sensitive to presumed data "outliers" in the Performance Universe.[24] With respect to the first caveat, it is important to note that the adjusted R^2 over the 1996–2000 period for the size-adjusted EVA (on MVA-to-Capital) regressions fluctuates from 64% in 1997 up to 94% in 1998, then down to just 2% in 1999. The average R^2 for the capital-adjusted regressions is 45%. Also, during the 1996–2000 period, the percentage of variation explained in the unadjusted EVA-on-MVA regressions fluctuates from 47% in 1996 and 39% in 1997, then down to 23% in 1999. The average R^2 value obtained in the unadjusted EVA regressions over the five-year reporting interval is 34%.

With respect to the second (regression) caveat, consider what happens to the statistical results for large capitalization firms listed in the Performance Universe when the capital-adjusted MVA-EVA data point for Wellpoint Health Network—with negative operating capital at year-end 2000—is eliminated from the scatter plot shown in Exhibit 2.7.[25] With elimination of WLP, Exhibit 2.9 shows that the adjusted R^2 for year 2000 drops from 27% down to 7%. In statistical terms, this means

---

[24] The choice of keeping or eliminating a data outlier in a scatter plot is always a "Catch 22" situation: You are damned if you do, and damned if you don't!

[25] Indeed, Wellpoint Health Network was hardly a "well" company. The firm's negative operating capital and negative residual return on capital led to "spurious" MVA-to-Capital and EVA-to-Capital ratios of –73.82 and –5.26 (in decimal!).

that careful attention must be paid to the underlying scatter of MVA and EVA data points. In economic terms, this means that the relatively low percentage of MVA (-to-Capital) variation explained for the representative firm in the Performance Universe may now mask the contemporaneous MVA and EVA differences between wealth creators and wealth destroyers. In Chapter 5, we'll unmask the differential financial characteristics of U.S. wealth creators and wealth destroyers.

SUMMARY

This chapter examines the role of EVA in the theory of finance with an emphasis on investment decisions. In this context, we found that EVA is the *annualized* (or annuity) equivalent of the firm's net present value. From a capital budgeting perspective, we found that managers should accept investment opportunities having discounted positive economic profit. In turn, they should reject investment opportunities with discounted negative EVA. Whether or not investors should buy or sell the stocks of companies with favorable or unfavorable EVA opportunities depends on whether these opportunities are already "fully reflected" in stock prices. We'll look at the security selection and portfolio management implications associated with positive or negative EVA opportunities in Chapter 13.

We also found that EVA is *not* the only metric that is consistent with the principles of wealth maximization. Specifically, we examined the theoretical equivalency of EVA and CFROI in the context of the difference between a company's return on capital, ROC, and the cost of capital, COC. If CFROI exceeds the "hurdle rate," then in principle a company has a positive EVA spread and therefore positive economic profit. If CFROI falls short of COC, then economic profit is negative and the firm points in a direction of wealth destruction. However, if for some reason the "hurdle rate" used in CFROI analysis is not the same as the cost of capital (COC, including the weighted average cost of debt *and* equity capital), an agency problem may exist between the firm's owners and managers.

In the next chapter, we'll explore the role of EVA in the theory of finance with an emphasis on financing decisions. This EVA discussion encompasses the internal versus external sources of funding decision— which is commonly referred to in the corporate finance literature as the "debt versus equity" decision. The goal here is to examine the market conditions under which investment decisions alone impact shareholder value, or the market conditions (albeit, market imperfections) under which investment and financing decisions jointly determine economic profit and shareholder value. At the heart of this debate is the "MM (Modigliani-Miller)" versus traditionalist positions on capital structure.

CHAPTER 3

EVA in the Theory of Finance II: Financing Decisions

The "just right" way of financing a company's investment opportunities is a highly controversial issue in the study of corporate finance. In a perfect capital market, the method of financing a company's growth opportunities has *no* meaningful impact on the EVA and net present value created by the firm's investment decision. In this "MM (Modigliani-Miller)" context, the enterprise value of a firm is invariant to the capital structure—or debt versus equity—decision. In contrast, in an imperfect capital market, both the investment opportunity *and* the financing decision may impact a company's economic profit and NPV in a meaningful way.[1]

In this chapter, we'll examine the economic profit consequences of the capital structure decision. We'll begin with a two-period wealth model to show the EVA and NPV impact of the decision to finance a company's investment opportunities with external sources (typically viewed as debt financing) *versus* internal sources (equity financing in the capital structure controversy) of funds.[2] In doing so, we'll highlight the irrelevance of capital structure decisions on economic profit and NPV in a perfect capital market. Following that, we'll use the "MM Proposi-

---

[1] See Franco Modigliani and Merton H. Miller, "The Cost of Capital, Corporation Finance, and the Theory of Investment," *American Economic Review* (June 1958), and "Dividend Policy, Growth and the Valuation of Shares," *Journal of Business* (October 1961).

[2] Fama and Miller employ a "two-period" wealth model to show the irrelevance of internal *versus* external financing decisions in a perfect capital market—see Eugene F. Fama and Merton H. Miller, *The Theory of Finance* (Holt, Rinehart, and Winston, Inc., 1972). In this chapter, we'll examine the irrelevance of corporate debt policy in an EVA-NPV context.

tions" to develop a set of EVA-based propositions concerning the wealth impact (or lack thereof) of corporate financing decisions.

We'll then relax the perfect capital market assumption to see how imperfections—such as the tax deductibility of interest expense and agency costs—within the capital market leads to the relevance of both investment and financing decisions on EVA and shareholder value. Given the practical imprecision of the pricing impact of capital structure, we'll conclude the chapter by recognizing that managers (and investors) should largely focus on that something which we can all agree has a meaningful impact on shareholder wealth—namely, strategic investment decisions (via internal growth opportunities or external growth opportunities through corporate acquisitions) that have a discounted *positive* economic profit.

EXTERNAL VERSUS INTERNAL FINANCING

In Chapter 2, we looked at the economic profit and wealth consequences of a simple, yet meaningful investment opportunity. We used a two-period wealth model to show that if a company could invest $100 million in the present and expect to receive $125 million in the future that the expected EVA on the investment opportunity was $15 million. Additionally, the NPV of the investment decision was $13.64 million (or 13.64% of the initial capital investment).

With 100% external financing, we found that the expected economic profit was $15 million because the dollar cost of capital—at $110 million, including $10 million of "interest" and the $100 million return of loan principle—needed to be subtracted from the net operating profit after taxes, NOPAT at $125 million, to arrive at the company's expected EVA. Moreover, at $13.64 million, we found that the net present value (NPV) was in fact the present value of the anticipated economic profit. Exhibit 3.1 provides another look at the investment opportunity with a focus on the financing decision.

EVA Impact of Internal Financing Decision

Suppose that instead of using external funding sources, the firm's current owners provide the initial capital of $100 million. With this assumption, Exhibit 3.2 shows that the Production Possibility Curve shifts to the right by this dollar amount and now begins at "plus 100" rather than at zero. Given a perfect capital market, we see that nothing of any real value has changed. That is, with 100% internal financing, the PPC *merely* shifts to the right (by $100 million) without any impact on shareholder wealth—measured by NPV along the horizontal axis. As

Exhibit 3.2 shows, the NPV addition to the firm's invested capital is still equal to $13.64 million. As before, there are several ways of interpreting this result. We'll look at the net present value added to the owner's initial capital from an economic profit perspective.

EXHIBIT 3.1   Wealth Creation with Positive EVA (100% External Financing)

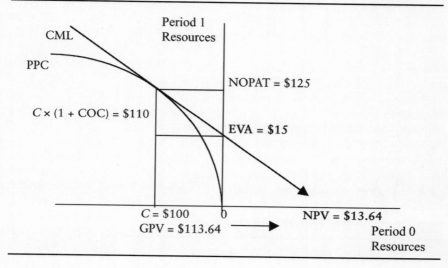

EXHIBIT 3.2   Wealth Creation with Positive EVA (100% Internal Financing)

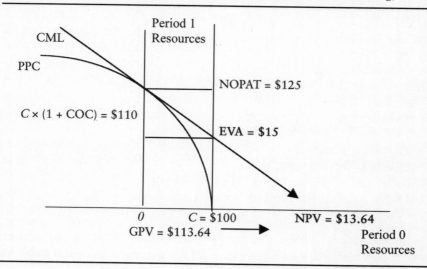

By looking up in Exhibit 3.2 from the initial capital of $100 million—along the positive side of the horizontal axis—we again see the anticipated net operating profit after taxes, NOPAT, of $125 million. Upon subtracting a capital charge of $110 million from NOPAT we obtain the estimated EVA of $15 million. This results because the expected capital charge (at $110 million in the two-period model, including a $10 million "opportunity cost" and the return of owner's capital of $100 million) still applies even though the firm is financed *entirely* with internal equity financing.

Indeed, the capital charge must still be "paid" regardless of whether the initial capital is supplied by external investors—the first financing assumption repeated in Exhibit 3.1—or by the firm's current owners— the second financing assumption shown in Exhibit 3.2. Moreover, upon discounting the anticipated EVA, at $15 million, back to the present time period yields the same NPV figure, at 13.64 million, that we obtained before with 100% external financing. This EVA and NPV result is the essence of the original Modigliani and Miller position on capital structure that we'll now unfold in greater detail.

CAPITAL STRUCTURE THEORY: A CLOSER LOOK

In 1958, Franco Modigliani and Merton Miller forcefully argued that capital structure decisions that merely vary the mix of debt and equity securities on a company's balance sheet have no impact on enterprise value (MM Proposition I) and the cost of invested capital (MM Proposition III).[3] Given the firm's investment decision, their capital structure propositions imply that economic profit and net present value (NPV) are invariant to the corporate leverage decision. In other words, wealth is created in the MM world by investing in positive NPV—equivalently, discounted *positive* economic profit—opportunities. As a practical consequence, the substitution of debt for equity shares or the substitution of equity shares for debt by managers is a *dubious* way to create economic profit and shareholder value.

Pivotal Role of the Cost of Equity

Without getting into all the Modigliani-Miller details,[4] we can use "MM Proposition II" to shed light on the seemingly paradoxical idea that the cost of capital—that is, COC—is invariant to changes in the

---

[3] See Modigliani and Miller, "The Cost of Capital, Corporation Finance, and the Theory of Investment."

[4] Fama and Miller lucidly explain the "MM Propositions" in the *Theory of Finance*.

mix of debt and equity securities on a company's balance sheet. Specifically, MM Proposition II states that the expected return on a "levered" firm's—typically viewed as a company with long-term debt outstanding—stock is a linear function of the debt-to-equity ratio, D/E. We can express this required return relationship as:

$$r_e = COC_u + (COC_u - r_d)D/E$$

In this expression, r_e is the required return on the levered firm's stock, COC_u is the expected return or cost of capital for an equivalent business risk "unlevered" firm, r_d is the cost of debt capital, and D/E is the ratio of debt to equity.[5] A graphical depiction of this expected return-leverage relationship is shown in Exhibit 3.3. With this formula, Modigliani and Miller argue that the expected return on levered stock is *linearly* related to the debt-to-equity ratio—one of several measures that can be used to capture financial risk. Indeed, MM Proposition II is a pivotal reason why the firm's enterprise value (MM Proposition I) and the cost of invested capital (MM Proposition III) are invariant to the corporate debt decision. We'll examine this key MM development in the context of the cost of capital.

EXHIBIT 3.3 Modigliani-Miller Required Return on Levered Firm

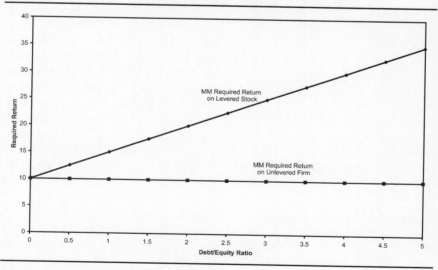

[5] We use lower case notation to denote the required return components of the levered COC—namely, r_e and r_d respectively.

In more formal terms, we know that the cost of capital for the levered firm is a weighted average cost of debt and levered equity. We'll denote this as COC_l. Upon substituting MM Proposition II into the general cost of capital formulation, we obtain:

$$\begin{aligned} COC_l &= w_d \times r_d + w_e \times r_e \\ &= w_d \times r_d + w_e \times [COC_u + (COC_u - r_d)D/E] \\ &= COC_u \end{aligned}$$

In this expression, the cost of capital for the levered firm, COC_l, is equal to the cost of invested capital for the equivalent business risk unlevered firm—namely, COC_u.[6] This in turn implies that changes in the mix of debt and equity shares—as well as any internally induced debt and equity yield changes caused by variations in the debt-to equity ratio—will have *no* meaningful impact on the weighted average cost of capital. Hence, corporate managers and investors alike must pay particular attention to real as opposed to illusory forces that impact the cost of invested capital.

Invariance of Financing Decision on Wealth Creation

We can now further explain the irrelevance of capital structure on economic profit and NPV in the context of the two period wealth model.[7] Specifically, in a *two*-period framework, we found that the firm's NPV can be expressed as the present value of its anticipated economic profit according to:

$$\begin{aligned} NPV &= EVA/(1 + COC) \\ &= [NOPAT - C \times (1 + COC)]/(1 + COC) \\ &= C \times [ROC - COC]/(1 + COC) \end{aligned}$$

In the first expression, EVA is the firm's estimated economic profit and in the second expression NOPAT is the unlevered net operating profit after taxes. In turn, ROC is the after-tax return on invested capital and COC

---

[6] Strictly speaking, the invariance of cost of capital to changes in corporate debt policy applies in a world of (1) no taxes, and (2) a world with corporate taxes, but *no* deductibility of debt interest expense. We'll examine the cost of capital issues that apply in a world with taxes and deductibility of debt interest expense at a later point.
[7] This EVA-NPV explanation is also covered in Fabozzi and Grant. See "Value-Based Metrics in Financial Theory," Chapter 2 in Frank J. Fabozzi and James L. Grant (eds.), *Value-Based Metrics: Foundations and Practice* (New Hope PA: Frank J. Fabozzi Associates, 2000).

is the weighted average cost of debt and equity capital. The letter C in the two-period model denotes the firm's initial capital investment.

Since NOPAT is the firm's net operating profit after taxes, but *before* financing costs—equivalently, NOPAT is the after-tax operating earnings of an "unlevered" company—and because C is the firm's fixed capital investment, we see that the wealth impact of the financing decision boils down to the impact of corporate debt policy on the weighted-average cost of capital. However, for Modigliani-Miller reasons that were explained before, the firm's cost of capital is *independent* of changes in the mix of debt and equity shares on the balance sheet.[8] Consequently, we now see why $COC_l = COC_u = COC$ in the two-period NPV model.

TOWARD A SET OF EVA PROPOSITIONS

The MM Propositions of corporate finance have a profound message for managers and investors. Specifically, if COC is unaffected by internal changes in the mix of debt and equity on a company's balance sheet, then the firm's assessed economic profit, NPV, and enterprise value must all be independent of the corporate financing decision. In the MM framework, the source of the firm's NPV—and therefore its *annualized* EVA equivalent—is derived from wealth-enhancing investment decisions that have an after-tax return on invested capital (ROC) that on average exceeds the cost of capital, COC. Moreover, in the MM world, the invariance of the economic profit spread (ROC – COC) to capital structure change is due to the invariance of ROC and COC in the two-period NPV formulation.

We can now use the MM capital structure foundation to enumerate a set of EVA-based propositions:

EVA Proposition I:
Given the investment decision, the firm's economic profit is invariant to the capital structure decision. This occurs because (1) ROC is the after-tax return on an unlevered company, and (2) in a perfect capital market, COC is independent of the financing decision.

EVA Proposition II:
The net present value of a company is independent of the corporate financing decision. This is the present value equivalent of EVA Proposition I since EVA is the *annualized* (or annuity) equivalent of a firm's NPV.

---

[8] See Modigliani and Miller, "The Cost of Capital, Corporation Finance, and the Theory of Investment." Again, to the extent that taxes apply, we'll assume (at this point) a world with corporate taxes, but *no* deductibility of debt interest expense.

EVA Proposition III:
In a perfect capital market, the firm's enterprise value is independent of the capital structure decision. This follows from EVA Propositions I and II and because the value of the firm can always be expressed as invested capital *plus* the NPV addition to invested capital.

Thus, we see that the MM propositions play a pivotal role in directing how managers and investors should proceed when assessing the economic profit and wealth consequences (NPV) of capital structure decisions. In a nutshell, their arguments suggest that investing in positive net present value (therefore, discounted positive EVA) opportunities is the "real key" to creating wealth. Moreover, in a well-functioning capital market, the decision to finance a company's growth opportunities with debt versus equity (or a combination of the two funding methods) is secondary to the set of EVA and NPV investment opportunities.

TRADITIONAL VIEW OF CAPITAL STRUCTURE

Up to this point, we have emphasized the economic profit and wealth implications of the Modigliani-Miller position on capital structure. This MM focus reinforces our earlier conclusions using the two-period Fisherian wealth model concerning (1) the positive role of investment decisions and, (2) the irrelevance of the capital structure decision in a well-functioning capital market.

Given that imperfections exist within the capital market, we would be remiss for not shedding light on the economic profit and NPV consequences of the traditional approach. Whether rightly or wrongly so, the traditional approach to capital structure holds that debt matters in the valuation of a company and its outstanding shares of common stock. Arguably, it is the approach to corporate debt policy that is used most often in practice by corporate managers and investors. By covering these divergent viewpoints, we'll have a better understanding of the conditions under which the capital structure decision has a meaningful impact on the creation of economic profit and shareholder value.[9]

As with MM, the traditional approach can be examined in a world with no taxes and a world with taxes and deductibility of debt interest expense at the corporate level. We'll begin the traditional capital struc-

---

[9] This section introduces the extreme complexity of the capital structure decision in a world with imperfect markets. It is not meant to be a complete examination of the voluminous work on capital structure that either competes with or challenges the Modigliani-Miller theory.

ture discussion in a no tax world—or better yet, a world with taxes, but *no* deductibility of debt interest expense. In this setting, we'll see that "debt matters" not just because of the tax issue, but also because of an *inefficient* pricing response by investors to changes in the level of equity risk as debt is varied on the balance sheet. In the traditional view, the inefficient pricing response to leverage leads to an increase in EVA and NPV because the cost of capital goes down in the presence of a higher debt-to-capital ratio.

Inefficient Risk Pricing in the Traditional View

In the traditional view of capital structure, it is argued that investors do not always have the information and/or the time needed to closely monitor changes in the level of debt relative to equity. Consequently, there is a period of time where the expected return or required return on the levered firm's stock does not fully account—in the MM sense—for the added financial risk that is associated with higher levels of debt.[10]

In more formal terms, the incomplete response by shareholders to changing debt levels means that the required return on levered stock is (for a time) less than the perfect market response as reflected in MM Proposition II. We can capture this risk pricing *inequality* for the levered firm's stock in terms of:

$$r_{e,T} < r_{e,\text{MM}}$$
$$r_{e,T} < [\text{COC}_u + (\text{COC}_u - r_d)\text{D/E}]$$

In this expression, $r_{e,T}$ is the expected return on the levered firm's stock in the traditional view, while $r_{e,\text{MM}}$ is the Modigliani-Miller required return on levered stock that we looked at before.

The cost of capital implication of this risk pricing inequality is transparent. That is, if the required return on levered stock is not fully responsive to changes in the debt-to-equity ratio (or any other leverage ratio) then corporate managers can utilize debt financing to lower COC. Unlike MM, this means that investment *and* financing decisions are no longer separable.

Hence, corporate managers have *two* ways to increase economic profit and shareholder value in the traditional view. They should look for investment opportunities that enhance shareholder wealth, and they should finance those positive investment opportunities up to the "target level" with a judicious mix of debt and equity. Moreover, if the traditional

---

[10] The traditional view of capital structure is a general one that predates the 1958 paper by Modigliani and Miller.

view is applicable in real world capital markets, then economic profit and shareholder value may rise in a *doubly* beneficial way to the announcement of investment opportunities that are financed with a sizable amount of debt.

Leverage Effects on ROE

We focused on the mispricing of equity risk as the fundamental reason why corporate debt policy in the traditional model can be used to enhance shareholder value. From the traditional perspective, we could just as easily show that a larger proportion of debt in the firm's capital structure leads to *higher* accounting profitability ratios—such as earning per share and return on equity.

Let's use the traditionally based "Dupont formula" to show the impact of leverage on the accounting return on equity.[11] In this context, the return on equity (ROE) can be expressed in terms of the return on assets (ROA) and the inverse of one *minus* the corporate debt ratio according to:

$$ROE = ROA/(1 - D/A)$$

In this expression, ROA is the accounting rate of return on assets, and D/A is the debt-to-asset measure of corporate leverage.

With a proportionately higher level of fixed obligations in the firm's capital structure, the Dupont formula shows that ROE goes up—since the denominator in the formula goes down as D/A rises.[12] Conversely, as the debt/asset ratio declines relative to the firm's return on assets, its rate of return on equity (ROE) goes down—as the denominator in the Dupont formula now goes up. In effect, when the debt-to-asset ratio rises relative to ROA, a *smaller* amount of equity capital is generating the same amount of accounting profit—hence the shareholder return on equity rises. On the other hand, a decline in ROE happens when a *larger* equity base is being used to earn the same amount of after-tax accounting profit.

Accounting Leverage: A Numerical Illustration

As a simple example of the link between the accounting ROE and leverage, assume that the firm's profit after tax were $10 (perhaps in millions), and its assets were $100 (million). Also assume that the firm is *initially* equity financed such that debt-to-asset ratio is equal to zero.

---

[11] The breakdown of ROE into several underlying ratios using the Dupont formula is explained in Chapter 8.

[12] This of course assumes that ROA is fixed by a *given* investment decision.

With 100% equity financing, the firm's accounting return on equity (ROE) is the same as its ROA, at 10%:

$$ROE = 0.1/(1.0 - 0.0)$$
$$= 0.1 \text{ or } 10\%$$

Now assume that the firm's corporate treasurer decides to engage in a financing strategy that effectively swaps the equity shares for more debt, such that D/A rises to, for example, 40%. With this *pure* change in capital structure, the firm's return on equity rises from 10% to 16.7%:

$$ROE = 0.1/(1.0 - 0.4)$$
$$= 0.167 \text{ or } 16.7\%$$

As the firm moves to what it perceives to be a "target" capital structure, we see that the ratio of accounting profit-to-stockholder's equity goes up. With a leverage change, it can also be shown that a firm's earnings per share would rise as well. Consequently, in the traditional view, it is argued that investors should be willing to pay *more* for the firm's enhanced profitability (as reflected in accounting profit measures such as EPS and ROE) and now seemingly dearer shares.

ROE Volatility

Before proceeding, it may seem odd that investors should somehow feel better off just because the firm has a higher debt level. This of course is the general thrust of what Modigliani and Miller were trying to say. Indeed, the flipside of the traditional Dupont formula is that it can be used to illustrate the underlying volatility in the accounting return on equity at varying debt levels.

Exhibit 3.4 shows what happens to ROE when the return on assets varies from 10% to –10% in the presence of corporate debt levels ranging from 0% to 70%, respectively. Notice that as a business expands or contracts—that is, ROA goes from 10% to –10%—with a debt load of 10%, we see that ROE fluctuates from 11.1% on the high side down to –11.1% on the low side.

In turn, Exhibit 3.4 shows that with a debt load of 40%, the ROE numbers swing from 16.7% down to –16.7%. As the business expands or contracts with a 50% debt load, the shareholder's return on equity is even more volatile, with ROE figures ranging from 20% on the positive side and –20% on the negative side. On balance, the exhibit reveals that increasing leverage in "good times" conveys volatile benefits to the shareholders, while rising corporate debt loads in "bad times" is a source of heightened financial concern.

EXHIBIT 3.4   ROE Impact of Corporate Debt Policy

	Corporate Debt Ratio							
	0.0%	10%	20%	30%	40%	50%	60%	70%
	ROE %							
Expansion: ROA = 10%	10	11.1	12.5	14.3	16.7	20	25	33.3
Contraction: ROA = -10%	-10	-11.1	-12.5	-14.3	-16.7	-20	-25	-33.3

According to MM Proposition II, the leverage-induced volatility in the accounting return on equity, ROE, should already be reflected in the required return on levered stock, $r_{e,MM}$. Clearly, what is key here from the Modigliani-Miller perspective is not the debt per se, but rather the business-risk changes that impact the expected return on unlevered stock—in other words, COC_u, the cost of capital for the unlevered firm. Along this line, managers and investors must be particularly cognizant of business-risk changes that result in heightened volatility in invested capital returns (ROC) and sudden changes in the (unlevered) cost of capital.

A GRAPHICAL LOOK AT MM AND TRADITIONAL VIEWS

Based on the preceding foundation, let's now take a graphical look at the MM and traditional positions on capital structure. Exhibit 3.5 shows how corporate debt policy impacts the levered firm's cost of capital in MM and traditional viewpoints, while Exhibit 3.6 shows the resulting impact of competing capital structure positions on enterprise value and shareholder value.[13]

Exhibit 3.5 shows that in the traditional view the cost of capital falls as the firm adds debt to its capital structure. This happens because investors do not see the rising level of debt relative to capital and therefore do not require a higher level of expected return to compensate for the added financial risk.[14] As the presumably lower cost debt is substituted for higher cost equity, the exhibit shows that the levered firm's

---

[13] Note that the EVA impact of capital structure decisions is implied from the impact of corporate debt policy on NPV. This follows from the fact that EVA is the annualized equivalent of a company's net present value.

[14] Of course, taxes *with* deductibility of debt interest expense provide further ammunition to the traditional argument that "debt matters."

cost of capital, COC_1, declines as the company moves toward its "target" debt-to-capital ratio of, say, 40%.[15]

EXHIBIT 3.5   Impact of Capital Structure Change on Cost of Capital

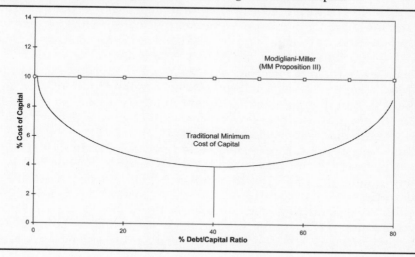

EXHIBIT 3.6   Impact of Capital Structure Change on Enterprise Value

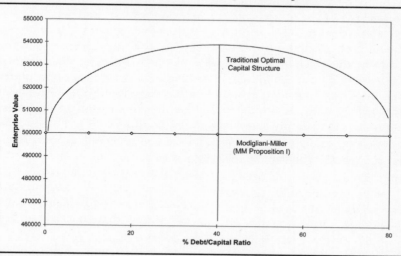

---

[15] The traditional view largely looks at bank rate financing when estimating the cost of debt. It does not fully consider the *indirect* equity cost arising from a higher debt burden and heightened financial risk for the shareholders.

Beyond the target debt-to-capital ratio, Exhibit 3.5 points to a sharp rise in the levered cost of capital. This happens in the traditional view because investors finally "wake up" to the increased risk of bankruptcy. They then respond to heightened financial risk with a dramatic rise in the required return on levered stock (not shown in the exhibit). This causes the levered firm's cost of capital to rise sharply with concomitant negative effects on economic profit, NPV, and of course enterprise value. (We'll see the latter of these variables in Exhibit 3.6.) Thus, in the traditional view, corporate managers have an incentive to finance their capital budgeting projects on the average with a "target" mix of debt and equity. Moreover, in this view, debt policy impacts the cost of capital in a significant way—and, if correct, one that corporate managers and investors need to be apprised of.

In sharp contrast, Modigliani and Miller argue that the cost of capital is invariant to the corporate debt decision. This position is represented graphically by the horizon line in Exhibit 3.5 that starts at the unlevered firm's cost of capital and then remains flat over varying degrees of financial leverage. As noted before, the invariance of the levered firm's COC to changes in the debt-to-capital (or debt-to-equity) ratio is a reflection of the perfect capital market response by ever observant investors to changing levels of corporate debt.

Also, as reflected in MM Proposition II, the expected return on levered stock (recall Exhibit 3.3) is linearly related to the debt-to-equity ratio. Because of the efficient pricing of financial risk, the cost of capital remains invariant to the corporate debt decision. This leads to the rather profound cost of capital invariance result in the Modigliani-Miller position on capital structure. Specifically, in the MM view, managers and investors would be much better off looking for investment opportunities having discounted positive economic profit (equivalently, positive NPV) rather than spending valuable shareholder time looking for inefficient capital structures that simply give shareholders an illusion of wealth creation.

Impact of Competing Positions on Enterprise Value

Exhibit 3.6 shows the capital structure implications of traditional and MM positions on enterprise value. In the exhibit, V_u represents the enterprise value of the *unlevered* firm—a firm having no long-term debt outstanding—while V_l denotes the *levered* firm's enterprise value. In the traditional view, we see that when the debt-to-capital ratio rises from 0% to the *target* level of, say, 40%, the enterprise value of the firm and its stock price go up. Over this debt range, the firm's enterprise value goes up presumably because of the "good news" resulting from the falling cost of levered capital shown in Exhibit 3.5. In other words, the leveraged induced decline in COC and the concomitant rise in economic profit (due to lower capital costs for a given NOPAT) cause investors to pay more for the levered firm's outstanding shares.[16]

On the other hand, if the debt-to-capital ratio exceeds the 40% target level (again, see Exhibit 3.5), then economic profit, NPV, and enterprise value will decline as the heightened financial risk leads to an ever-rising cost of capital. At that point, the cost of levered capital rises due to sharp increases in the required return on equity capital. With a 50% debt load, corporate managers have pushed debt *beyond* the target level, and therefore should engage in substantial "delevering" activities that effectively swap bonds for more equity shares. Moreover, if the 40% debt level is in fact an optimal one, then economic profit, NPV, and enterprise value decline with any sizable movement to the left *or* right of the target capital structure position. These traditionally based EVA and valuation effects are a reflection of the possibility (see Exhibit 3.5) that the cost of capital is higher for any debt-to-capital ratio that is different from the presumed optimal level.

Again, MM argue that the firm's enterprise value is invariant to the corporate leverage decision in a well-functioning capital market. This is shown graphically in Exhibit 3.6 by the horizontal line emanating from the unlevered firm's enterprise value and continuing at that level over varying levels of the debt-to-capital ratio. Of course, the invariance of enterprise value to corporate debt policy is a reflection of the invariance of the levered cost of capital to the debt changes shown in Exhibit 3.5. Finally, the invariance of both enterprise value (MM Proposition I) and the cost of capital (MM Proposition III) are a reflection of the continuously responsive expected return on levered stock (MM Proposition II) to changes in the firm's corporate debt decision. Moreover, given the firm's investment decision, the invariance of economic profit (NOPAT *less* $COC), NPV, and enterprise value to changes in corporate leverage all follow from the infamous MM propositions.

TAXES WITH DEDUCTIBILITY OF DEBT INTEREST

As mentioned before, the capital structure irrelevance argument of Modigliani and Miller rests on the assumption of a well-functioning or

---

[16] In the original Modigliani-Miller model, the higher EPS generated by corporate leverage is offset by a rise in the investor's required return on equity (in CAPM, for example, beta is linearly related to leverage). Consequently, in a perfect capital market, the company's stock price remains unchanged in the presence of a debt-induced rise in EPS and accounting ROE.

perfect capital market. In the real world, we know that market imperfections exist such that the capital structure mix of debt and equity financing may impact both the economic profit and the net present value of the firm. In this context, the capital structure controversy boils down to those factors that lead to capital market inefficiencies and the significance of their impact on the weighted average cost of capital, COC.

One of the more significant market imperfections is the question of corporate taxes *with* deductibility of a company's debt interest expense.[17] This tax imperfection can impact economic profit because a company receives a yearly debt tax subsidy that shows up in the cost of capital. Specifically, it can be shown that in a world with taxes *and* deductibility of debt interest expense, the firm's weighted average cost of capital boils down to:

$$COC_l = COC_u \times [1 - t_e \times D/C]$$

In this expression t_e is the firm's "effective" debt tax subsidy expressed as a rate, and D/C is the "target" debt-to-capital ratio. As before, COC_l is the cost of capital for a levered company, while COC_u denotes the cost of invested capital for an equivalent business risk unlevered firm.

Notice that if a company's debt tax subsidy rate is positive—as emphasized in the traditional view of capital structure—then the levered firm's cost of capital is *lower* than the cost of capital for the unlevered firm. In this case, the anticipated economic profit and the currently measured NPV of the levered firm would be *higher* than that available to unlevered shareholders. On the other hand, if a company's debt tax subsidy rate were zero—as argued in the original MM paper—then the levered firm's cost of capital would equal the cost of capital for the unlevered firm. When this happens, a company's economic profit, NPV, and enterprise value are invariant to the packaging of debt and equity securities on the balance sheet.

Consider how the levered COC might vary over a range of tax subsidy rates. With an unlevered COC of 10%, and a debt tax subsidy rate of 35% (approximately the corporate tax rate), we see that the cost of capital for the levered firm is only 6.5% (in the extreme case of 100% debt). If the effective tax subsidy rate were 20%, then the levered COC would be 8%. Notice too that for any tax subsidy rate greater than zero, the levered COC is lower than the unlevered COC. In these situations, the economic profit, NPV and the enterprise value of the levered firm would be noticeably higher than the corresponding values for the unlevered firm. Moreover, with a lower cost of capital, the levered firm

---

[17] We'll look at the capital structure impact of agency costs in the next section.

would have a larger capital base than the unlevered firm because if would presumably accept more projects at the lower cost of capital—for example, a "hurdle rate" of 6.5% versus a 10% rate would make it easier for managers to accept more projects.

Based on the levered COC formula (and the numerical application), we see that the capital structure issue boils down to the magnitude of the debt tax subsidy rate on the cost of capital. Given that companies are allowed to deduct the interest expense on their outstanding debt obligations, it would seem obvious that the levered firm's shareholders would reap the pricing benefits of a debt-induced tax subsidy. In the real world, it would seem that the capital structure decision would be of strategic relevance to the firm's shareholders.

Having said that, it is important to note that Miller argues that even in a world with corporate taxes, deductibility of interest expense, and a system of progressive income taxation that the firm's effective debt tax subsidy rate, t_e in the levered COC formula, is *close* to zero.[18] If Miller's debt-tax argument is applicable in real-world capital markets, then the levered firm's cost of capital is again equal to the cost of capital for an equivalent business risk unlevered company. Not surprisingly, the firm's assessed economic profit (EVA) and its NPV would be independent of the particular method of financing—including the supposed "just right" mix of debt and equity financing.

As a practical matter, we should not really question the existence of a debt tax subsidy on economic profit, NPV, and enterprise value. But we should also recognize that the benefit of a debt tax subsidy to the levered firm's shareholders may be overestimated, especially, as Miller argues when one considers the offsetting tax effects of leveraged capital structures. On balance, it seems fair to say that shareholders are better served when managers focus their efforts on investment decisions that lead to economic profit enhancement, rather than spending an inordinate amount of time on tax-related financing strategies that merely serve to repackage the mix of debt and equity securities on the balance sheet. In this context, managers should emphasize wealth creation via discounted positive economic profit as opposed to capital structure changes that in the end give shareholders an illusion of wealth creation.

AGENCY COSTS

Before moving on, it is important to shed light on another capital market imperfection that may tip the balance toward debt financing. Specifi-

---

[18] See Merton H. Miller, "Debt and Taxes," *Journal of Finance*, May 1977.

cally, Jensen argues that in a world with transaction costs, it is physically and financially difficult for dispersed shareholders in large on-going companies to discipline managers in a way that would maximize the discounted stream of economic profit.[19] After all, large companies have many shareholders who each hold a relatively small percentage of the outstanding stock. Moreover, investors with small stock holdings are geographically dispersed and—unless pushed too far—are not likely to attend annual shareholder meetings or join activist shareholder groups.

Given the practical limitations of monitoring manager actions with equity financing, Jensen argues that debt goes to the head of the financing table. In this regard, debt securities have restrictive covenants that "kick in" should a firm have difficulty meeting its promised interest and/or principal payments. Just as importantly, restrictive covenants become effective should the enterprise value of the firm fall too far and too fast relative to the outstanding value of the debt. Accordingly, debt is visible, debt is ever present, and debt is vigilant in the sense that bond covenants can be used to limit or restrict the investment decisions of managers should their decisions have a destructive impact on the firm's enterprise value—and by inference, a destructive influence on its economic profit and NPV.

Exhibit 3.7 shows why debt financing—via leveraged buyouts according to Jensen—may be preferable to equity financing in a world where transaction costs are significant. With debt financing, the enterprise value of the firm need only decline by a small amount before bondholders would use legal covenants to limit or restrict the inappropriate investment decisions by the firm's managers. With equity financing, however, the presence of transactions costs delays or prevents the ability of small investor groups from getting together to monitor the inept decisions of managers before it is too late.[20]

At the extreme—meaning a world where stockholders have virtually no ability to monitor managers because of prohibitive transactions costs—Exhibit 3.7 suggests that companies should be financed with 100% debt. According to Jensen, the presence of significant transactions costs provides an organizational incentive where companies are financed with debt. The tool *de jour* for implementing the "eclipse" of the large public corporation is through leveraged buyout (LBO) partnerships that effectively eliminate public equity. The danger though is that these highly leveraged deals may

[19] This section provides an overview of the economic profit role that levered capital structures may have in disciplining corporate managers (agents) to act in the best interests of shareholders (principals) in a world with agency costs. For an in-depth discussion of the transactions cost role of corporate debt policy in creating ownership value, see Michael C. Jensen, "Eclipse of the Modern Corporation," *Harvard Business Review* (September-October 1989).
[20] The debt and equity support levels—at 80% and 20%, respectively—shown in Exhibit 3.7 are presented for illustrative purposes only.

EXHIBIT 3.7   Enterprise Value Support Levels (Gray Scale) with Agency Costs

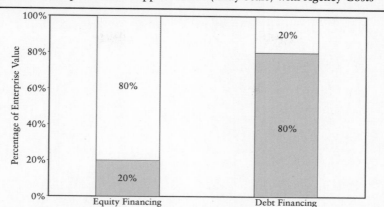

recreate the bureaucracy of public corporations if LBO partners earn their keep by taking large front-end fees for implementing the deal and/or management compensation that is loosely tied to economic profit improvement.

While the capital structure reasoning is different, this is the same financing conclusion—namely, that debt financing is preferable to equity financing—that we saw before when the effective debt tax subsidy rate is sufficiently positive in the levered COC formulation. Indeed, we could model the effective tax subsidy rate in the levered COC to capture the potential economic profit benefits of (1) the debt-interest tax subsidy that we examined before, and (2) the benefit of using debt financing as a monitoring tool to reduce or eliminate the agency conflict between managers (agents) and owners (principals). Although the math might be elegant, the results would only serve as reminder of the extreme complexity of the capital structure decision on economic profit, NPV, and enterprise value.

SUMMARY

In this chapter, we examined the role of capital structure and its variation impact on economic profit, NPV, and enterprise value. In a perfect capital market, we found that the mix of debt and equity securities on a company's balance sheet has no impact whatsoever on the firm's economic profit or its net present value. This is the essence of the original Modigliani-Miller position on capital structure when viewed from an economic profit lens. In contrast, we found that in an imperfect capital market, the mix of debt and equity securities on the balance sheet is of strategic financial relevance to the firm's shareholders.

With capital market imperfections, the levered firm's economic profit is higher than the economic profit of an equivalent business-risk unlevered company. This happens because the levered cost of capital is lower (for a time) than the cost of capital for the debt free or unlevered company. This is the essence of the traditionalist position on capital structure when viewed from an economic profit perspective. Moreover, it was argued that agency cost or transaction cost impediments to monitoring managers can tip the balance sheet toward debt financing levels that go *beyond* the traditional notion of a target mix of debt and equity financing.

By setting a capital structure foundation in this chapter, we can proceed to a more informed discussion of the cost of capital and its variation impact on the discounted stream of economic profit. Later on, we'll visit the business risk factors that affect economic profit via changes in the cost of capital for the unlevered firm—namely, COC_u. This added foundation is important because the cost of capital for the unlevered company is the primary component in the levered COC formulation. Moreover, once a company reaches its target capital structure, subsequent variations in the cost of capital for the levered firm would be largely attributable to EVA risk factors that drive the unlevered cost of capital.

CHAPTER 4

Basic Economic Profit

While the EVA theory chapters have shown that the concept of economic profit is robust—because true profit *must* be measured net of the opportunity cost of invested capital—it turns out that the actual measurement of economic profit is quite complex. Indeed, Stern Stewart, CS First Boston, Goldman Sachs, and other influential EVA players have found that there are over 150 accounting adjustments that could be made to estimate economic profit in practice.

In this chapter, we'll abstract from all the EVA accounting details and instead look at *basic* economic profit. The EVA goal here is twofold: (1) to illustrate the essential ingredients of economic profit measurement without getting tangled up in a plethora of EVA accounting adjustments and, (2) to illustrate the EVA advantage over traditional accounting profit measures such as EBIT, EBITDA, and net operating income. Some of the more important refinements to estimating economic profit in practice—such as the EVA treatment of research and development expenditures, restructuring costs, lease expense, and change in LIFO/FIFO and deferred income tax reserves (in priority order, more or less)—are explained in detail in Chapter 9.

LEVERED AND UNLEVERED FIRMS

Central to the economic profit calculation is the distinction between levered and unlevered firms.[1] A *levered* firm, like most real-world firms, is one that is financed with both debt and equity sources of financial

---

[1] The concept of levered and unlevered firms plays a central role in the development of the Modigliani-Miller (MM) principles of corporate finance. Eugene F. Fama and Merton H. Miller employ these company classifications in their pioneering book, *The Theory of Finance* (New York: Holt, Rinehart, and Winston, 1972).

capital. In contrast, an equivalent business-risk *unlevered* firm is one that, in principle, is 100% equity financed. This firm type classification is helpful to understanding the economic profit calculation because EVA is measured by subtracting a company's dollar cost of capital—a reflection of its weighted average cost of debt *and* equity capital in a sources of financing approach—from its *unlevered* net operating profit after taxes, NOPAT. With this distinction, the firm's EVA can be expressed as:

$$EVA = NOPAT - \$COC$$

NOPAT is used in the basic EVA formulation for two reasons: First, an economic profit emphasis on this term serves as a modern-day reminder that a company largely receives profits from the desirability, or lack thereof, of its overall products and services. In turn, the risk or uncertainty of NOPAT is a reflection of every firm's inherent business risk. Secondly, since most firms have some form of business debt outstanding, they receive a yearly interest tax subsidy—measured by the corporate tax rate times a company's interest expense—that is already reflected in the dollar cost of capital (\$COC) calculation.

As we'll shortly see, an incorrect focus by managers or investors on the levered firm's net operating profit after taxes, LNOPAT, rather than its unlevered net operating profit, NOPAT, would lead to an *upward* bias in the company's economic profit. By recognizing the possible "double counting" of a firm's yearly debt-interest tax subsidy, the manager or investor avoids imparting a *positive* bias in the firm's EVA, and, ultimately, its enterprise value and stock price.

HOW TO ESTIMATE BASIC EVA

Let's now unfold basic EVA into its two essential ingredients—namely, NOPAT, the unlevered net operating profit after taxes, and \$COC, the dollar cost of invested capital. We'll begin with NOPAT.[2]

In the absence of any EVA accounting adjustments, the firm's unlevered net operating profit after taxes can be expressed in terms of its tax-adjusted earnings before interest and taxes, EBIT, according to:

---

[2] A discussion of basic EVA is also provided by Thomas P. Jones, "The Economic Value Added Approach to Corporate Investment," in *Corporate Financial Decision Making and Equity Analysis*, ICFA (Charlottesville, VA: Association for Investment Management and Research, 1995).

We'll look at some of the standard accounting adjustments to estimating EVA (and CFROI) in Chapter 9. For an exhaustive discussion of EVA-based accounting adjustments, see G. Bennett Stewart III, *The Quest for Value* (Harper Collins, New York: 1991).

$$NOPAT = EBIT \times (1 - t)$$
$$= (S - COGS - SG\&A - D) \times (1 - t)$$

In this expression, EBIT $\times$ $(1 - t)$ is the unlevered firm's net operating profit after tax. This basic EVA term is a reflection of the firm's earnings before interest and taxes, EBIT, less *unlevered* business taxes—measured by EBIT less t times EBIT.[3] Likewise, the terms, S, COGS, and SG&A in the NOPAT specification refer to the firm's sales; cost of goods sold; and selling, general, and administrative expenses, respectively. In principle, the depreciation term, D, should be a charge that reflects the *economic* obsolescence of the firm's assets. In Chapter 10, we'll take a look at the EVA importance of economic depreciation versus accounting depreciation. We'll also look at the EVA role of negative depreciation arising from intangibles (goodwill arising from mergers and acquisitions, etc.) that lead to an increase in the firm's enterprise value.

In turn, the firm's dollar cost of capital, $COC, can be expressed as:

$$\$COC = COC \times C$$

In this expression, COC is the weighted average cost of debt *and* equity capital (expressed as a required rate in decimal form), and C is the firm's total net operating capital.[4] In turn, the weighted average capital cost, COC, is given by:

$$COC = \text{After-tax debt cost} \times \text{Debt weight}$$
$$+ \text{Equity cost} \times \text{Equity weight}$$

Taken together, these financial developments show that the firm's EVA can be expressed in *basic* terms as:

$$EVA = NOPAT - \$COC$$
$$= EBIT \times (1 - t) - COC \times C$$
$$= [S - COGS - SG\&A - D] \times (1 - t) - COC \times C$$

---

[3] In effect, "t" is an unlevered tax rate because NOPAT (in the *first* expression) equals EBIT less unlevered cash taxes.

[4] It is important to note that we are now focusing on the EVA calculation for an "ongoing" company. In this context, the dollar cost of capital can be expressed as the amount of invested capital, C, *times* the cost of capital, COC. This contrasts with the earlier capital cost expression used in the two-period Fisherian wealth model whereby capital costs at period 2 were expressed as $C \times (1 + COC)$ to reflect both interest and principal on the maturing loan.

Hence, the preceding formula shows that a firm's EVA is equal to its unlevered net operating profit after taxes *less* the dollar cost of all capital employed within the firm. In the next section, we'll look at a simple income statement and balance sheet to show how to measure a firm's "economic value added." The manager or investor who is already familiar with the process of estimating economic profit in a *basic* setting may prefer to read Chapter 9 for an explanation of EVA accounting adjustments and other real-world measurement challenges.

OK BEVERAGE COMPANY (OKB)

Let's now estimate basic EVA for a hypothetical firm called, "OK Beverage Company." Exhibits 4.1 and 4.2 show the income statement and balance sheet for OKB at an established point in time.

Looking at OK Beverage Company's financial statements from a traditional accounting perspective, one sees that the firm appears to be a profitable beverage producer. Based on the income statement shown in Exhibit 4.1, the firm reports *positive* net income and earnings per share, at $8,213 and $1.31, respectively. In addition, with stockholder's equity at $96,600 the beverage company's rate of return on equity (ROE) is positive, at 8.5% ($8,213/$96,600 × 100). Moreover, this accounting ROE figure results from multiplying OKB's return on assets, ROA at 5.4%, by its equity multiplier (assets/equity) of 1.57.[5]

EXHIBIT 4.1   OK Beverage Company Income Statement

	Status Quo Position
Sales	$125,000
COGS	86,000
SG&A	22,000
Interest Expense	3,312
Pretax Profit	13,688
Taxes (at 40%)	5,475
Net Income	$8,213
Shares Outstanding	6,250
EPS	$1.31

[5] The breakdown of ROE into ROA and financial leverage components is explained in greater detail in Chapter 8.

EXHIBIT 4.2   OK Beverage Company Balance Sheet

Cash	$7,000	Accounts Payable	$10,000
U.S. Govt. securities	8,000	Wages Payable	2,000
Accounts Receivable	14,000	Tax Accruals	2,000
Inventory	53,000	Current Liabilities	14,000
Current Assets	82,000	(*non*-interest bearing)	
Property	4,000	Long-term Debt	41,400
Net Plant	15,000	(8% Coupon)	
Net Equipment	51,000		
Net Fixed Assets	70,000	Common Stock at Par (par value $.10; 6250 shares auth./outstanding)	625
		Addit. Paid in Capital	14,375
		Retained Earnings	81,600
		Stockholder's Equity	96,600
		Liabilities and	
Total Assets	$152,000	Stockholders Equity	$152,000

OKB's Economic Profit

To see if OK Beverage Company is truly a profitable company—that is, a wealth creator with (discounted) positive EVA—we'll first calculate the firm's *unlevered* net operating profit after taxes, NOPAT. Upon substituting the firm's sales, cost of goods sold, selling, general, and administrative, and tax rate figures into the NOPAT formulation, we obtain:[6]

$$\text{NOPAT} = [S - COGS - SG\&A] \times (1 - t)$$
$$= [\$125,000 - \$86,000 - \$22,000] \times (1 - 0.4)$$
$$= \$17,000 \times 0.6 = \$10,200$$

In order to estimate OKB's projected *dollar* cost of capital, the manager or investor needs to know something about (1) the after-tax cost of debt, (2) the estimated cost of equity capital, (3) the "target" debt weight, *if any*, in the firm's capital structure, and (4) the amount of operating capital employed in the beverage business. With respect to the

---

[6] For convenience, we'll assume that depreciation is included in the SG&A account of OK Beverage Company. We'll take a detailed look at the EVA role of depreciation (economic *versus* accounting depreciation) in a later chapter.

first requirement, OKB's after-tax cost of debt can be estimated according to:

$$\text{After-tax debt cost} = \text{Pretax debt cost} \times (1 - t)$$
$$= 0.08 \times (1 - 0.4)$$
$$= 0.048 \text{ or } 4.8\%$$

In this expression, the pretax debt cost, at 8%, is taken as the firm's average coupon rate on the balance sheet (for simplicity, we'll assume that the firm's bonds are trading at face value). OKB's pretax borrowing cost of 8% can also be obtained by dividing the firm's interest expense, $3,312, by the face value of its long term debt, at $41,400.

In turn, we'll use the capital asset pricing model (developed by William Sharpe, *et al.*)[7] to estimate OKB's cost of equity capital. With a risk-free interest rate of 6.5%, a market-driven equity risk premium of 6%, and a common stock beta of 1.0, the firm's CAPM-based cost of equity capital becomes:[8]

$$\text{CAPM} = R_f + MRP \times \text{Beta}$$
$$= 0.065 + 0.06 \times 1.0$$
$$= 0.125 \text{ or } 12.5\%$$

Moreover, if we assume that OKB's "target" debt-to-capital ratio is, say, 30%, the firm's overall cost of capital can be measured according to:

$$\text{COC} = \text{After-tax debt cost} \times \text{Debt weight}$$
$$+ \text{Equity cost} \times \text{Equity weight}$$
$$= 0.048 \times (0.3) + 0.125 \times (0.7)$$
$$= 0.102 \text{ or } 10.2\%$$

Repackaging the Balance Sheet

With knowledge of OKB's operating capital it is possible to calculate the dollar cost of invested capital, $COC. In this context, it is helpful to

---

[7] See, for example, William F. Sharpe, "Capital Asset Prices: A Theory of Market Equilibrium under Conditions of Risk," *Journal of Finance* (September 1964).

[8] The "just right" way of calculating a firm's cost of equity capital has come under several empirical challenges in recent years. For example, see Eugene F. Fama and Kenneth R. French, "The Cross Section of Expected Stock Returns," *Journal of Finance* (June 1992). However, it should be emphasized that the validity of the EVA model does *not* require that security prices are set according to the single- (beta) factor CAPM.

recognize that the firm's balance sheet can be "repackaged" in a way that shows the *equivalency* of the firm's operating and financing capital. Exhibit 4.3 illustrates this result.

Exhibit 4.3 shows that OKB's operating *and* financing capital is $138,000. The operating capital (left hand side of balance sheet) is equal to net working capital plus net plant, property and equipment. Likewise, in the absence of EVA accounting adjustments, the financing capital is just long-term debt plus stockholders' equity. Hence, the firm's overall dollar-cost of capital can be calculated by applying the weighted average cost of capital, at 10.2%, to either the firm's tangible operating capital or its equivalent financing source of invested capital. Whatever side of the EVA balance sheet is chosen, OKB's *dollar* cost of capital is $14,076:

$$
\begin{aligned}
\$COC &= COC \times C \\
&= 0.102 \times \$138{,}000 \\
&= \$14{,}076
\end{aligned}
$$

More importantly, since OKB's dollar cost of financing, $COC, is higher than its unlevered net operating profit after taxes, NOPAT, the firm has *negative* economic profit:

$$
\begin{aligned}
EVA &= NOPAT - \$COC \\
&= \$10{,}200 - \$14{,}076 \\
&= -\$3{,}876
\end{aligned}
$$

EXHIBIT 4.3   OK Beverage Company Operating and Financial Capital (Aggregate Results)

Operating Capital:		Financing Capital:	
Net Working Capital			
Current Assets	$82,000		
Current Liabilities	(14,000)		
(*non*-interest bearing)			
	68,000	Long Term Debt	$41,400
Net Fixed Assets	70,000	Stockholder's Equity	96,600
Totals:	$138,000		$138,000

While OKB *looks* like a profitable beverage producer from a traditional accounting perspective, the basic EVA insight reveals that the firm is a (potential) wealth destroyer.[9] This happens because the firm's operating profitability is not sufficient enough to cover the overall dollar cost of invested capital.

OKB's Residual Return on Capital (RROC)

We can also show that OKB has negative EVA because its underlying "residual (or surplus) return on capital," RROC, is negative. This wealth-wasting situation occurs when a firm's after-tax return on invested capital, ROC, falls short of the weighted average capital cost, COC. To illustrate this, simply define RROC as the firm's EVA-to-Capital ratio. At –2.8%, one sees that OKB's adverse *surplus* return on capital is caused by its negative economic profit:

$$
\begin{aligned}
RROC &= EVA/Capital \\
&= -\$3,876/\$138,000 \\
&= -0.028 \text{ or } -2.8\%
\end{aligned}
$$

Likewise, since EVA can be expressed as the firm's initial capital, C, times the residual return on capital, RROC, this same result is obtained by focusing on the *spread* between the firm's after-tax return on invested capital, ROC, and its weighted average cost of debt and equity capital, COC:

$$
\begin{aligned}
RROC &= ROC - COC \\
&= 0.074 - 0.102 = -0.028 \\
&= -0.028 \text{ or } -2.8\%
\end{aligned}
$$

In this expression, ROC, at 7.4%, results from dividing NOPAT, $10,200, by the firm's invested capital, $138,000.[10] The COC is the now familiar cost of capital percentage of 10.2%.

OKB's Interest Tax Subsidy

As we noted before, when looking at a firm's economic profit, it is important to use its unlevered net operating profit after taxes, NOPAT in the first step of the EVA calculation. This is important because the dollar cost of invested capital (step two in the EVA calculation) already reflects the interest tax subsidy (if any) received on the firm's outstand-

---

[9] We'll see in a later section that persistently adverse EVA leads to negative net present value.

[10] The spread between ROC and COC is commonly referred to as the "EVA spread."

ing debt obligations. By double counting this debt-induced tax subsidy, the manager or investor would not only overestimate the firm's operating profit, but he or she would also impart a positive bias in the firm's enterprise value and its stock price.

To show the source of bias, it is helpful to note that the levered firm's net operating profit after taxes, LNOPAT, can be expressed in terms of the equivalent business-risk unlevered firm's net operating profit, NOPAT, *plus* a yearly interest tax subsidy. Looking at OKB in this levered (with debt) and unlevered (without debt) context yields:

$$
\begin{aligned}
\text{LNOPAT} &= \text{NOPAT} + t \times \text{Interest} \\
&= \$10{,}200 + 0.4 \times \$3{,}312 \\
&= \$11{,}525
\end{aligned}
$$

In this expression, $t \times$ Interest (at \$1,325), is the yearly interest tax subsidy that OKB receives as a levered firm, as opposed to a debt-free company. However, this *same* interest tax benefit is already reflected in the firm's dollar capital cost via the reduced cost of corporate debt financing.

To show this, recall that OKB's after tax cost of debt was previously expressed as:

$$
\begin{aligned}
\text{After-tax debt cost} &= \text{Pretax debt cost} \times (1 - t) \\
&= 0.08 \times (1 - 0.4) \\
&= 0.048 \text{ or } 4.8\%
\end{aligned}
$$

In this formulation, the firm's pretax cost of debt, 8%, is reduced by 320 basis points due to the tax benefit that OKB receives from deductibility of its debt interest expense. Expressing this leverage-induced reduction in the firm's dollar cost of capital yields the same yearly interest tax benefit that is already reflected in the beverage company's levered operating profit:

$$
\begin{aligned}
\$\text{COC tax subsidy} &= t \times (\text{Pretax debt cost}) \times \text{Debt} \\
&= 0.4 \times [\$3{,}312/\$41{,}400] \times \$41{,}400 \\
&= \$1{,}325
\end{aligned}
$$

Thus, to avoid positive bias, OKB's economic profit must be calculated by *first* estimating what its net operating profit after taxes, NOPAT, would be as an equivalent business-risk unlevered firm— namely, an "OKB like" company with no business debt—and *then* subtracting the dollar cost of debt and equity capital from this unlevered net operating profit figure.

OKB's EVA on a Pretax Basis

If the manager or investor were inclined to calculate OK Beverage Company's EVA on a pretax basis, then the beverage producer's unlevered net operating profit before taxes, at $17,000, would be used in conjunction with the pretax dollar cost of capital.[11] The only complication here is that the after-tax cost of equity capital needs to be "grossed up" by one *minus* the business tax rate to convert it to a pretax financing rate. To see how this works, note that OKB's weighted average cost of capital can be expressed on a before tax basis as:

$$\begin{aligned}
\text{Pretax COC} &= \text{Debt weight} \times \text{Pretax debt cost} \\
&\quad + \text{Equity weight} \times \text{Pretax equity cost} \\
&= 0.3 \times 0.08 + 0.7 \times [0.125/(1-0.4)] \\
&= 0.17 \text{ or } 17\%
\end{aligned}$$

In this formulation, the firm's *pretax* cost of equity capital is 20.8%, and its pre-tax cost of capital is 17%. With this development, OKB's *pretax* EVA is:

$$\begin{aligned}
\text{Pre-tax EVA} &= \text{EBIT} - \text{Pretax COC} \times \text{C} \\
&= \$17,000 - 0.17 \times \$138,000 \\
&= -\$6,460
\end{aligned}$$

Likewise, the firm's pre-tax EVA is equal to its after-tax EVA "grossed up" by one *minus* the business tax rate, *t*:

$$\begin{aligned}
\text{Pretax EVA} &= \text{After-tax EVA}/(1-t) \\
&= -\$3,876/(1-0.4) \\
&= -\$6,460
\end{aligned}$$

OKB's Growth Opportunities

Given that OK Beverage Company has negative economic profit, the firm has a clear incentive to find a *positive* growth opportunity. In this context, let's suppose that the firm's managers discover (finally!) that they can invest $20,000 in a new product distribution system that will perma-

---

[11] The pretax approach to estimating a firm's economic profit is helpful because the manager or investor focuses directly on the unlevered firm's operating profit without getting tangled up with tax issues arising from depreciation and other accounting complexities. However, tax considerations *do* arise when converting the after-tax cost of equity capital (CAPM or otherwise) to a pretax required rate of return, as introduced in the illustration that follows.

nently increase sales by $40,000. In turn, suppose that OKB's cost of goods sold and selling, general, and administrative expense accounts will rise by $25,000 and $5,000 per year, respectively. With these assumptions, the firm's estimated annual NOPAT will go up by $6,000:

$$
\begin{aligned}
\Delta \text{NOPAT} &= \Delta(S - \text{COGS} - \text{SG\&A}) \times (1 - t) \\
&= (\$40,000 - \$25,000 - \$5,000) \times (1 - 0.4) \\
&= \$6,000
\end{aligned}
$$

Since the firm's operating capital rises by $20,000 to support the higher sales forecast, OKB's estimated (annual) capital costs rise by $2,040:

$$
\begin{aligned}
\Delta\$\text{COC} &= \text{COC} \times \Delta C \\
&= 0.102 \times \$20,000 \\
&= \$2,040
\end{aligned}
$$

Taken together, the changes in NOPAT and $COC reveal that OKB's growth opportunity is a desirable investment for its shareholders. With these figures, OKB's EVA rises by $3,960 per annum:

$$
\begin{aligned}
\Delta \text{EVA} &= \Delta \text{NOPAT} - \Delta\$\text{COC} \\
&= \$6,000 - \$2,040 \\
&= \$3,960
\end{aligned}
$$

As a result of OK Beverage Company's investment opportunity, it is interesting to see that the firm has moved from a wealth destroyer to a wealth-neutral position. Among other things, this implies that the firm's revised return on invested capital, 10.3% ($16,200/$158,000), is now close to the overall cost of capital, 10.2%. Likewise, in this wealth-neutral situation, the firm's residual return on capital, RROC, is nearly zero. Of course, with further growth opportunities, OKB has the *potential* to become a wealth creator with *discounted* positive economic profit. In the next section, we'll look at the basic valuation consequences of OKB's growth opportunities, including an estimate of its enterprise value and stock price.

BASIC VALUATION CONSIDERATIONS

Up to this point, we used the income and balance sheets for OK Beverage Company to calculate economic profit (EVA) in a basic financial setting. However, nothing was said at that point about the market value of

OKB as an ongoing company. Without getting into extensive valuation considerations here, some simple pricing insights are obtained by assuming that investors pay an NPV (net present value) multiple of, say, *10-times* the estimated EVA of "OKB-like" companies.[12] In the ensuing development, we'll express the firm's enterprise value, V, as the sum of (1) the total operating capital employed in the business, C, plus, (2) the net present value (NPV = MVA[13]) from the firm's existing assets and future growth opportunities:

$$V = C + NPV$$

With an EVA multiplier of ten times OKB's revised aggregate EVA of \$84 (–\$3,876 + \$3,960), the firm's estimated market value added is \$840. Upon adding this NPV figure to its revised operating capital (*with* the \$20,000 growth opportunity), one obtains:

$$\begin{aligned} V &= C + NPV \\ &= \$158,000 + \$840 \\ &= \$158,840 \end{aligned}$$

Summarizing these basic valuation findings: With a positive EVA growth opportunity, OKB has moved from a wealth destroyer to a wealth neutral position. The firm's zero-expected *total* EVA is generated by a return on invested capital, ROC, that now approximately equals the weighted average cost of capital—even though ROC is higher than the firm's pre- and posttax cost of debt financing. Because of OKB's wealth-neutral position, the firm's enterprise value-to-capital (or, in more popular terms, the price-book ratio) is near unity. Incidentally, at this point, OKB's profitability index ratio (ROC/COC) is close to one.

Estimating OKB's Stock Price

OKB's stock price can always be viewed as its equity capitalization divided by total shares outstanding. Although simple enough in concept, the stock price calculation is complicated by the fact that the beverage producer will have to issue *more* shares in order to finance the positive growth opportunity. Let's begin the share valuation process by assuming that the \$20,000 investment opportunity will be financed according to OKB's target capital structure proportions, assumed at 30% debt and 70% equity, respectively.

---

[12] We'll cover EVA and related discounted cash flow valuation models in Chapters 6 and 7.
[13] MVA, for Market Value Added, is the popular equivalent of NPV. As noted before, these value added terms are used interchangeably in the EVA literature.

$$\Delta C = \Delta D + \Delta E$$
$$= w_d \times \Delta C + (1 - w_d) \times \Delta C$$
$$= 0.3 \times \$20,000 + 0.7 \times \$20,000$$
$$= \$20,000$$

In this financing expression, ΔC is the change in the firm's operating capital due to the proposed investment opportunity, and w_d (at 30%) is OKB's presumed *target* debt weight in its capital structure. As shown, the amount of new debt, ΔD, is \$6,000 and the equity capital, ΔE, requirement is \$14,000.

The amount of new equity, ΔE, raised by OK Beverage Company to finance the growth opportunity can be viewed as the number of new OKB shares issued, n^*, *times* the estimated price per share. In turn, the *intrinsic* worth of the stock can be estimated by dividing the firm's aggregate equity capitalization (with the growth opportunity taken into account) by total shares outstanding—including the original 6,250 shown on the balance sheet *plus* new shares issued. With these considerations, the equity financing formula becomes:

$$\Delta E = n^* \times \text{Stock price}$$
$$= n^* \times [(V - D)/(6,250 + n^*)]$$

Substituting the known values for ΔE, V, and D into the above expression yields:

$$\$14,000 = n^* \times [(\$158,840 - \$47,400)/(6,250 + n^*)]$$

Upon solving the equity financing formula for n^*, one obtains 898 shares of common stock (rounded). With 7,148 total shares outstanding, OKB's stock price—with the *positive* NPV opportunity—is \$15.59.

$$\text{Stock price} = \text{Equity capitalization}/\text{Total shares}$$
$$= \$111,440/(6,250 + n^*)$$
$$= \$111,440/7,148$$
$$= \$15.59$$

Not surprisingly, OKB's estimated stock price is close to the new book value of its outstanding common stock. At \$15.47, this figure is obtained by dividing the firm's revised book capital, at \$110,600 (\$96,600 *plus* \$14,000), by the 7,148 common shares outstanding. In economic terms, OKB's stock price is close to book value per share because the firm's overall net present value—due to the nearly zero-total expected EVA—is now close to zero. In the absence of any further changes in OKB's growth opportunities (whereby ROC exceeds COC), the firm's price-to-book ratio should rise in the marketplace from 0.72 (shown in the next section) to *unity*; and remain at that relative figure until any further economic changes.

At this point, it should be noted that corporate actions that merely give OKB's shareholders the "illusion of value creation"—such as arbitrarily splitting the firm's stock, or possibly swapping the outstanding shares for more debt to give a falsely higher EPS or ROE signal—will still lead to a stock price that returns to the *intrinsic* value associated with the firm's wealth-neutral position. That is, in a well-functioning capital market, only real growth opportunities—whereby firms have positive *residual* capital returns—will cause the enterprise value of the firm and its outstanding (debt and) equity shares to rise in the marketplace.

DISCOVERING REAL VALUE

Let's look again at OKB to find the source of "real value" in this beverage company. In the status quo, or no-growth position, it was discovered that the firm's existing assets generated negative EVA. Assuming that investors pay an EVA multiple of *ten times* for "OKB-like" companies—specifically, in the *range* where EVA is either positive or negative—that places the firm's initial enterprise value at $99,240:

$$V = C + NPV$$
$$= \$138,000 + 10 \times (-\$3,876)$$
$$= \$99,240$$

In this negative EVA situation, OKB's value-to-capital ratio (or price-to-book ratio) is less than unity:

$$V/C = 1 + NPV/C$$
$$= 1 + (-\$38,760/\$138,000)$$
$$= 0.72$$

This relative value finding is interesting because conventional investor wisdom holds that "value stocks" have *low* price relatives, along with high dividend yields. In OKB's case though, its enterprise value (as well as its stock price) seems low when measured relative to earnings and/or book value because the firm's enterprise value *should* be low. Although investor wisdom might view the outstanding equity as a "value stock" investment, the underlying beverage company is hardly a real value opportunity in its *status quo* position with negative NPV.

EXHIBIT 4.4   OKB's Real-Value Opportunities

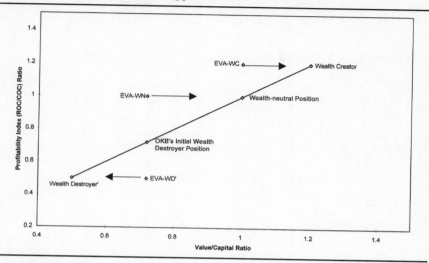

Active Value Opportunities

However, when OKB's growth opportunity is factored into the valuation analysis, the stock can be viewed as a real-value stock with *positive* earnings (EVA) momentum. If investors are generally slow in either discovering or reacting to these economic changes, then the firm's shares could be an active *buy* opportunity for some period of time. In this context, Exhibit 4.4 shows the research benefit of making a distinction between a value stock *per se*—like OKB in its status quo position—and an active value opportunity, whereby, investors have not fully discounted the firm's wealth-creating EVA potential.

Specifically, we know that OKB is a wealth destroyer if it simply remains as is. In this static situation, the firm's after-tax return on invested capital (ROC) is *not* sufficiently high enough to cover the cost of capital, at 10.2%. Consequently, the firm's negative (average) EVA produces an enterprise value-to-capital ratio that is justifiably *less* than unity. By conventional standards, OKB might be considered a value stock because of the low price-to-book ratio, at 0.72. In contrast, the economic profit insight reveals—due to the *adverse* EVA projection—that OKB has a low relative valuation because it *should* have.[14]

---

[14] It should be noted that cyclical behavior in a company's economic profit might also lead to a low price-to-book (and price-to-earnings) ratio. Discerning the source of a company's low (or high) price relative is particularly important for active-minded investors.

With the positive EVA-growth opportunity, at $3,960, OKB's profitability index (measured by the ROC/COC) should rise to *one*. If the capital market were efficient—in the sense of *fully* reflecting the beverage producer's NPV opportunities—then the firm's price-to-book ratio would instantly rise to unity. Based on the previous assumptions (primarily, the EVA-multiplier of *ten times*), OKB's existing market value would rise from $99,240 to $158,840, and its stock price would soar from $9.25, ($99,240 – $41,400)/6,250, to around $15.59.

On the other hand, if the capital market were slow to react to OKB's real growth opportunity, then its outstanding stock (and possibly bonds) would be an active value opportunity for *informed* investors. The firm's delayed price response could be caused by various inefficiencies, including the possibility that investors were unfamiliar with the practical aspects of EVA valuation analysis, or that given OKB's track record, they were *unwilling* to believe that the beverage firm would ever experience any meaningful future growth.

Exhibit 4.4 provides at least *two* reasons why OKB may be considered an active value opportunity. The beverage company is a potential buy opportunity because its estimated profitability index ratio—*with* the positive growth opportunity—is higher than the required PI ratio for a wealth destroying firm having a value-to-capital ratio of 0.72. Alternatively, with a projected profitability index ratio of unity (shown as EVA-WN), the exhibit reveals that the stock would be attractive to informed investors because the actual or *status quo* price-to-book ratio falls short of the required value-to-capital ratio for wealth neutral firms. In the absence of a timely pricing response, OKB would be undervalued in the capital market.

Exhibit 4.4 also reveals *dynamic* pricing implications that are consistent with the principles of shareholder wealth maximization. Suppose, for instance, that after becoming a wealth neutral firm—with an average profitability index and value/capital ratio of unity—OKB announces a *second* growth opportunity such that the PI ratio rises from *one* to 1.2 (see EVA-WC point in the exhibit). Again, in the absence of an instantaneous price response, the firm's equity (and possibly risky debt) securities would be a buy opportunity for active minded investors. This happens because OKB's estimated profitability index ratio, 1.2, would now be consistent with the PI ratio for a wealth creating firm. Therefore, its value-to-capital ratio should rise in the marketplace by some 20% to reflect the firm's movement from a wealth neutral (with the first positive NPV opportunity) to a wealth-enhancing firm (with the second growth opportunity).[15]

---

[15] For simplicity, linearity is assumed in Exhibit 4.4. Later on, we'll explore the non-linear characteristics of EVA drivers and enterprise value.

In contrast, if OKB were to announce a *negative* NPV project at, say, the firm's *initial* wealth destroyer position in Exhibit 4.4, then the firm's price-book ratio would fall in the capital market in response to adverse EVA happenings (see EVA-WD in the exhibit). With pricing delays, the firm's outstanding securities (both equity and debt) would be viewed as a sell or short-sell opportunity for active investors. On balance, the basic EVA insights show that security prices can rise *and* fall in response to fundamental changes in a firm's real growth opportunities—whereby its future returns on invested capital exceed or fall short of the projected COC.

WAYS TO INCREASE EVA

Based on the previous considerations, we see that basic EVA is helpful for managers and investors because it provides a transparent look at the key features of economic profit measurement. In this context, basic EVA reveals that a company is not economically profitable until it covers its usual operating expenses and all of its financial capital costs—including the dollar cost of debt *and* equity capital. In this fundamental sense, EVA is, in principle, superior to traditional accounting profit measures such as EBIT, EBITDA and net operating income. Additionally, we can use basic EVA to gain some strategic insight on the steps that managers must take to permanently improve the economic profit outlook and, thereby, shareholder wealth.

There are several ways that a company can improve its economic profit outlook.[16] In this context, the basic EVA formulation suggests that wealth conscious managers should take steps to:

- Increase business revenue
- Reduce operating expenses where prudent
- Use less capital to produce the same amount of goods and services
- Use more capital in the presence of *positive* growth opportunities
- Reduce the cost of capital

Expanding a firm's market share is, of course, captured by rising sales level in the basic EVA formula. Other things the same (operating expenses and capital costs), higher revenue means higher economic profit. Also, it should be no surprise that reducing a company's operat-

---

[16] The first four ways to improve economic profit are consistent with those emphasized by Tully. See, Shawn Tully, "The Real Key to Creating Wealth," *Fortune*, September 20, 1993.

ing expenses via cost cutting and/or achieving tax efficiency enhances economic profit because the SG&A and cash tax accounts go down. However, if using cost cutting as a tool to improve the EVA outlook, managers must be cautioned that too much cost cutting "cuts" the fabric of the firm's future economic profit—and in so, reduces the enterprise value of the firm and its outstanding shares.

Note, too, that if EVA is to be taken seriously as an improvement over traditional accounting profit measures, then it must do *more* than just show that increasing revenue and/or reducing operating expenses will improve the firm's enterprise value and its stock price. Fortunately, this is where economic profit and traditional accounting profit measurement depart since EVA fully "accounts" for the dollar cost of capital in terms of both the amount of operating capital employed in a business and the opportunity cost of that invested capital.

EVA emphasizes the role of invested capital as can be seen in the basic EVA formulation. Clearly, anything that managers can do to (1) improve inventory and Net PP&E (net plant, property, and equipment) turnover ratios on the balance sheet, and (2) reduce business uncertainty (as reflected in a decline in NOPAT volatility) will have beneficial cost of capital implications via the impact on C and COC, respectively. Moreover, we used the basic EVA formula to show that investing more capital (rather than less capital) in positive economic profit growth opportunities is really what shareholder value creation is all about.

Finally, EVA links the income statement and balance sheets with a value-based focus on net operating profit (NOPAT, from adjusted income statement) and invested capital (C, from adjusted balance sheet). Unlike accounting profit, EVA measures the dollar cost of capital by multiplying the amount of invested capital by the overall cost of capital. Hence, EVA measures economic profit in the classical economists view of "profit" because the business owners' normal return on invested capital is fully reflected in the profit calculation. Since accounting profit accounts only for the dollar cost of debt financings, via interest expense, it completely misses the dollar cost of equity capital. This cost of financing omission is especially important for companies that typically finance their growth opportunities with equity capital—such as firms in the technology and health care fields.

SUMMARY

In this chapter, we looked at how to estimate economic profit in a basic setting. The goal here was to abstract from the conventional plethora of

EVA accounting adjustments to illustrate the unique features of economic profit measurement. Simply put, EVA is NOPAT less the dollar cost of invested capital, $COC. It is consistent with the classical economists notion of "profit" because it measures profitability net of both the usual operating expenses of running a business and the opportunity cost of invested capital. Also, with its emphasis on NOPAT less dollar COC, EVA—more aptly, the discounted value thereof—is a direct measure of the economic value that managers contribute to the firm's invested capital.

Before moving on, it should be emphasized that economic profit measurement does *not* imply that accounting profit measurement is irrelevant. Indeed, several accounting items such as sales, cost of goods sold, and selling, general, and administrative expenses are included in the estimation of any company's NOPAT. Also, accounting profit does—albeit imprecisely, as we will see in a later chapter—include the after-tax interest cost on the firm's debt. However, this is where the similarities between EVA and accounting profit end, since, EVA links both the income statement and balance sheet in a way that fully reflects the dollar cost of *all* sources of financial capital, particularly the dollar cost of equity capital.

This conceptual difference in profit measurement is particularly poignant for companies in sectors like technology and health care that tend to finance their growth opportunities with equity rather than debt. For these growth sectors, the basic EVA formula can be used to show that the weighted average cost of debt and equity capital, COC, is the cost of equity capital. Surely, equity capital is not a "free" source of financing capital as accounting profit measures such as EBIT, EBITDA, and net operating earnings mistakenly suggest.

CHAPTER 5

Financial Characteristics of Wealth Creators (*and* Destroyers)

The NPV model presented in Chapter 2 reveals that wealth-creating firms have discounted positive economic profit. This "good news" for the shareholders occurs when the firm's managers invest in real assets having an after-tax return on capital (ROC) that on average exceeds the weighted average cost of capital (COC). Moreover, that managers can make wealth-maximizing investment decisions for all of the shareholders by following the NPV rule is one of the major "Separation Principles" of modern corporation finance.[1]

Conversely, the NPV model presented in Chapter 2 reveals that wealth-destroying companies have discounted negative economic profit. This "bad news" for the shareholders occurs when the firm's managers invest in real assets having an after-tax return on capital that on average falls short of the weighted average cost of capital. In this chapter we'll look at the empirical relationship between MVA and EVA with an eye

---

[1] A rigorous treatment of the famous "Separation Principles" of corporation finance can be found in Eugene F. Fama and Merton H. Miller, *The Theory of Finance* (New York: Holt, Rinehart, and Winston, 1972). Separation Principle I suggests that operating and financing decisions are separable. This principle has corporate-wide EVA implications because it implies that—in a perfect capital market—the cost of capital is independent of the method of financing.

Likewise, Separation Principle II indicates that corporate investment decisions can be made independently of shareholder "tastes" for present and future consumption. Accordingly, positive NPV (or discounted positive EVA) projects are wealth increasing for *all* of the firm's owners, while negative NPV projects destroy shareholder wealth.

toward understanding the financial characteristics of wealth creators and wealth destroyers. We'll begin the empirical journey with a look at the recent MVA and EVA experiences of large U.S. wealth creators (ranked by MVA) followed by an empirical assessment of the MVA-EVA characteristics of well-known U.S. companies that have recently destroyed shareholder value.

MVA AND EVA: TOP-TEN U.S. WEALTH CREATORS

Focusing on companies that have in fact created wealth can provide some real world insight on the process of wealth creation. In this context, Exhibit 5.1 presents the MVA and EVA characteristics of the "top-ten" U.S. wealth creators that were listed in the Stern Stewart Performance 1000 Universe at year-end 2000. The exhibit suggests that wealth creators (ranked by MVA) have large enterprise valuations because *they should have*. With the notable exceptions of Cisco Systems and American International Group, the exhibit shows that eight of the top-ten U.S. companies had contemporaneously positive MVA and EVA at year 2000. The positive association between the two measures of financial success suggests that the currently favorable EVA conveys positive news to shareholders about the firm's underlying ability to generate economic profit for the future.

EXHIBIT 5.1   Top Ten Wealth Creators in Performance Universe at Year-End 2000

Company	MVA (in U.S. $ Millions)	EVA (in U.S. $ Millions)	Return on Capital (%)	Cost of Capital (%)
General Electric Co.	426,616	5,943	20.43	12.11
Cisco Systems Inc.	272,131	−365	12.02	13.11
Microsoft Corp.	217,235	5,919	39.06	14.29
Wal-Mart Stores	206,187	1,596	12.76	9.99
Merck & Co.	203,689	4,836	24.00	8.62
Oracle Corp.	174,589	1,039	34.08	12.88
American International Group	169,982	−786	9.76	11.16
Citigroup Inc.	169,640	4,646	19.03	12.74
Pfizer Inc.	167,646	942	10.65	9.40
Intel Corp.	163,586	5,032	30.52	13.08

*MVA = Market value of the firm less invested capital.

Exhibit 5.1 shows that General Electric, Cisco Systems, and Microsoft Corporation were at the top of the 2000 wealth creator list with MVA values of $426,616 million, $272,131 million, and $217,235 million respectively. This means that the enterprise value of these U.S. wealth creators exceeded the capital employed in the respective businesses by a substantial amount. As reported, General Electric, Cisco Systems, and Microsoft also occupied the top MVA slots in the Performance Universe for 1999—this time, with Microsoft boasting an NPV value of $629,470 million (!), and General Electric and Cisco Systems having MVA values of $471,786 million and $348,442 million. Moreover, Exhibit 5.1 shows that General Electric outdistanced Pfizer Inc. and Intel Corporation (MVA ranks 9 and 10 for year 2000) by some $260,000 million in market value added.

Exhibit 5.1 also points to some possible anomalies in the MVA and EVA relationship for large wealth creators. In particular, Intel's 2000 EVA, at $5,032 million, is among the highest reported EVA figures for the top-ten U.S. wealth creators. In contrast, the semiconductor firm's reported MVA, at $163,586 million, is considerably lower than that observed for General Electric (*especially*) and Microsoft. In principle, this could mean that investors were somewhat less optimistic about Intel's ability to generate substantially positive EVA for the future. On the other hand, it could mean that the enterprise value of the semiconductor company was relatively undervalued in the capital market at year-end 2000.

More importantly, Exhibit 5.1 shows that positive MVA is *not* always associated with currently positive EVA. In this context, the exhibit shows that Cisco Systems and American International Group had currently negative EVA in the presence of their positive MVA, at $272,131 million and $169,982 million. Two possible explanations seem consistent with this finding: Regarding Cisco, investors may have been correctly optimistic about the networking firm's ability to generate positive economic profit for the future. On the other hand, the contemporaneously negative association between the two financial measures suggests that Cisco's outstanding securities were *overvalued* at year-end 2000.[2]

ROC and COC: Top-Ten Wealth Creators

The underlying source of the positive EVA for the top-ten U.S. wealth creators is shown in Exhibit 5.2. Not surprisingly, the exhibit shows that powerful wealth creators have an after-tax return on capital that bests the weighted average cost of capital. For example, large wealth creators like General Electric, Microsoft, Merck, and Oracle Corpora-

---

[2] A similar argument would apply to the outstanding equity *and* debt securities of any company with positive MVA in the presence of negative (expected) EVA.

tion support this observation with after-tax return on capital ratios that are considerably higher than their respective cost of capital estimates. Indeed, the 2000 EVA spread (ROC *less* COC) for the four U.S. wealth creators were 8.32%, 24.77%, 15.38%, and 21.20% respectively.

Exhibit 5.2 also shows that the return on capital for Microsoft, Oracle, and Intel for year 2000 is considerably higher than the corresponding ROC ratios for General Electric, Wal-Mart, and Pfizer. This capital return differential occurs because the technology companies were generating high returns on a relatively small amount of invested capital. For instance, Oracle's 2000 return on capital, at 34.08%, was earned on an *average* operating capital base of just $4,900 million!

Microsoft and Intel generated capital returns for year 2000 in excess of 30% on average operating capital bases of $23,890 million and $28,853 million respectively. On the other hand, General Electric reported a 20.43% after-tax return on $71,421 million of average capital employed in the business. Moreover, Wal-Mart's return on capital for 2000 was generated on a relatively large operating capital base of $57,778 million, while Pfizer's 10.65% ROC was earned on an average (and volatile) operating capital base of $75,637.[3]

EXHIBIT 5.2   Return on Capital versus Cost of Capital: Top-Ten Wealth Creators in Performance Universe at 2000

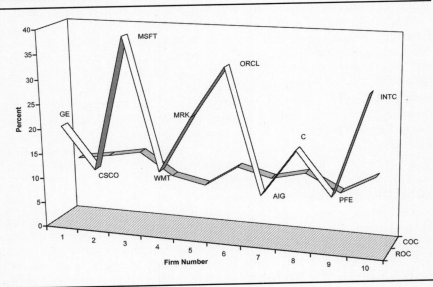

---

[3] Indeed, Stern Stewart reports that Pfizer's operating capital ranged from $16,939 million at the start of 2000 to $134,335 at the end of that year.

A closer look at Exhibit 5.2 suggests that fluctuations in EVA estimates among the top-ten U.S. wealth creators in the 2001 Performance Universe is determined primarily by the volatility in after-tax return on capital ratios (ROC). In this context, the individual COC figures are relatively stable around the *cross-sectional* average rate of 11.74%. In contrast, the after-tax capital return figures for the top-ten wealth creators fluctuate sharply about the cross-sectional average of 21.23%. Moreover, the standard deviation on the ten reported ROC ratios is 10.45%, while cross-sectional volatility in COC ratios for the ten U.S. wealth creators was 1.86%.

MVA AND EVA: 50 LARGE WEALTH CREATORS

Exhibit 5.3 expands the wealth creator focus by showing the relationship between the MVA-to-Capital and EVA-to-Capital ratios for the 50 largest U.S. wealth creators in the Performance Universe at year-end 2000. As shown, the exhibit indicates that a positive relationship exists between the relative value-added measures for top performing U.S. companies. That is, when the EVA-to-Capital ratio is positive, the corresponding MVA-to-Capital ratio is also positive. Conversely, when the EVA-to-Capital ratio is low and sometimes negative for wealth creators, the MVA-to-Capital ratio is also low among wealth creators.

EXHIBIT 5.3   MVA-to-Capital versus EVA-to-Capital Ratio: 50 Largest Wealth Creators in Performance Universe at Year-End 2000

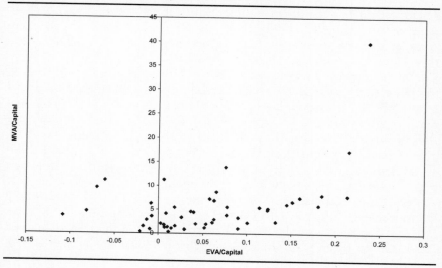

EXHIBIT 5.4   Regression Statistics for 50 Largest Wealth Creators in Performance
Universe: Year-End 2000

$$\text{MVA/Capital} = 3.36 + 35.93 \, \text{EVA/Capital}$$
$$(t\text{-value}) \quad (3.49) \quad (3.53)$$

$$\text{Adjusted } R^2 = 19\%$$

$$N = 50 \text{ Firms}$$

Another look at Exhibit 5.3 reveals that 40 of the 50 (or 80%) largest U.S. wealth creators at year-end 2000 had jointly positive MVA and EVA-to-Capital ratios. This finding indicates that the firm's most recently announced EVA makes a positive (presumably, a surprise) contribution to the firm's overall enterprise valuation, as measured empirically by the MVA-to-Capital ratio. This positive EVA momentum is clearly "good news" for the shareholders as it conveys windfall capital gains on the firm's outstanding equity and debt securities (via credit upgrades on the risky corporate bonds).

The 10 out of 50 large "wealth creators" in the exhibit with positive MVA-to-Capital ratios in the presence of their currently negative EVA-to-Capital ratios suggests that future growth opportunities play a *doubly* meaningful role in the valuation of these large capitalization firms. That is, if the capital market were efficient at year-end 2000, then investors were also optimistic about the ability of the ten companies with currently negative EVA to generate economic profit for the future. Conversely, if the market were inefficient due to misplaced investor optimism, the securities of these supposed wealth creators would be overvalued at that time.

The empirical observations shown in Exhibit 5.3 are reinforced by the regression statistics shown in Exhibit 5.4. In particular, Exhibit 5.4 reports the linear association between the MVA-to-Capital ratio (dependent variable) and the EVA-to-Capital ratio (explanatory variable) for the 50 largest U.S. wealth creators at year-end 2000. With an EVA "beta" (slope coefficient) of 35.93, and a t-statistic of 3.53, the exhibit shows that the EVA-to-Capital ratio for large U.S. wealth creators is a highly significant variable in the MVA equation.

The cross-sectional regression statistics for 2000 reveal that 19% of the movement in the MVA-to-Capital ratio among top-ranked U.S. companies is explained by contemporaneous variations in the EVA-to-Capital factor. On the other hand, the EVA-based regression suggests that 81% of the cross movement in any specific wealth creator's MVA (-to-Capital ratio) is determined by other factors—presumably *future* EVA considerations. As explained in an upcoming section, the adjusted R^2 in the MVA and EVA relationship for the top-50 U.S. wealth creators is quite variable over time. For example, over the 1996–2000 period, the adjusted R^2 values for top-ranked U.S. wealth creators ranged from a low of 0% in 1999 up to highs of 72% and 93% for 1996 and 1997 respectively.[4]

ROC and COC: 50 Large Wealth Creators

Exhibit 5.5 reveals the source of the positive relationship between MVA and EVA measures shown in the previous exhibit. Specifically, Exhibit 5.5 presents a comparison of the after-tax return on capital (ROC) and the cost of capital (COC) for the 50 largest U.S. "wealth creators" in the Performance Universe at year-end 2000. As expected, the exhibit reveals that wealth-creating firms have positive "market value added" because their after-tax return on capital exceeds the weighted average cost of capital. In other words, large wealth creators have a mostly positive residual (or surplus) return on capital where ROC is higher than COC.

EXHIBIT 5.5 ROC versus COC: 50 Largest Wealth Creators in Performance Universe at Year-End 2000

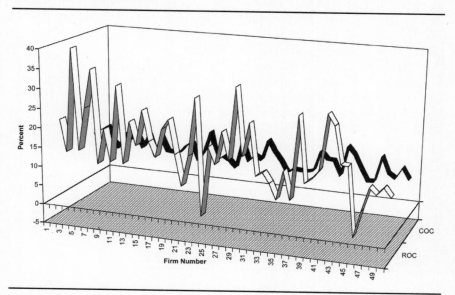

[4] Moreover, the high R^2 values in the MVA and EVA relationship for top-ranked U.S. wealth creators can be influenced by "outliers."

EXHIBIT 5.6 Multiple Regression Statistics for 50 Largest Wealth Creators in Performance Universe: Year-End 2000

$$\text{MVA/Capital} = -4.31 + 75.90 \, \text{COC} + 28.61 \, [\text{ROC} - \text{COC}]$$
$$(t\text{-value}) \quad\quad (-1.29) \quad (2.47) \quad\quad (3.02)$$

$$\text{Adjusted } R^2 = 22\%$$

$$N = 50 \text{ Firms}$$

Taken together, the positive residual return on capital given by the ROC and COC findings in Exhibit 5.5 is the reason for the positive EVA-to-Capital ratios shown in Exhibit 5.3. In turn, this positive EVA-to-Capital information is clearly "good news" to the shareholders as it leads to an improvement in the enterprise value of the firm. In this context, the cross-sectional findings for large U.S. wealth creators are consistent with the theoretical predictions of the NPV model—whereby, the firm's EVA is positive when the anticipated residual return on capital (ROC *minus* COC) is greater than zero.

The empirical connection between the MVA-to-Capital ratio and the residual return on capital for the 50 largest U.S. wealth creators in the Performance Universe at year-end 2000 is reinforced by the multiple regression statistics reported in Exhibit 5.6. With a slope coefficient of 28.61, and t-statistic of 3.02, the residual return on capital factor has a significantly positive impact on the firm's MVA-to-Capital ratio.

The multiple regression results for 2000 also reveal that *cross-sectional* variation in the cost of capital among U.S. "wealth creators" is a statistically significant factor in explaining why these firms are characterized as wealth creators in the first instance. In particular, the cross-sectional significance of the COC factor may result because companies operating in wealth-creating sectors of the economy such as technology have a relatively high cost of (equity) capital, especially when compared to wealth-creating companies operating in the industrial sector. In the cross section, the high cost of (equity) capital may be "signaling" companies that have relatively attractive EVA growth opportunities.

A STATISTICAL LOOK AT WEALTH CREATORS OVER TIME

In view of the empirical findings for top U.S. wealth creators for 2000, it is helpful to see if the MVA- and EVA-to-Capital relationship is statistically significant for other years. In this context, Exhibit 5.7 presents a time series display of the regression statistics that were estimated between the two measures for top U.S. wealth creators over the five years 1996–2000. The sample portfolios used in the regression analyses consist of the 50 largest wealth creators listed in the 2001 Performance Universe, after adjustment for any MVA and EVA data omissions.

Exhibit 5.7 provides *yearly* estimates of the percentage of MVA-to-Capital variation explained (adjusted R^2), the EVA-beta (slope), and the *t*-statistic respectively that emerged in linear regressions over the five-year reporting interval. The exhibit reveals that the percentage of MVA variation explained by the EVA-to-Capital factor for U.S. wealth creators varies quite substantially over time—with adjusted R^2 values fluctuating from 72% and 93% in 1996 and 1997 on down to virtually *nothing* in 1999, then up to 19% in year 2000. At 45%, the average R^2 value for top-50-firm portfolios during the 1996–2000 period reveals that the size-adjusted EVA measure is a significant factor for U.S. wealth creators.

Exhibit 5.7 also shows that the EVA betas ranged from about 35 in 1996 and 1997, up to a highly significant MVA multiple of 66 in 1998, respectively. The five-year average on the reported slope measures was 38 (rounded) over the 1996–2000 period. On average, this means that a unit increase in the EVA-to-Capital ratio leads to a 38-fold increase in the MVA-to-Capital ratio for wealth creating companies. Moreover, this view that the MVA and EVA-to-Capital relationship for large U.S. wealth creators is an empirically robust one is supported by the average *t*-statistic of 9.5 on the estimated EVA betas.

EXHIBIT 5.7   MVA- and EVA-to-Capital Regression Statistics: 50 Largest Wealth Creators in Performance Universe: 1996–2000

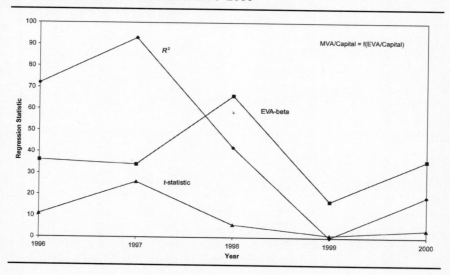

Additionally, Exhibit 5.8 reports the regression statistics for the 50 largest U.S. wealth creators observed in regression analyses of the *unadjusted* MVA and EVA variables during the 1996–2000 period. These regressions reveal that while the EVA betas (slope measures) for top U.S. companies are statistically meaningful in the "raw regressions," the percentage of yearly MVA variation explained by the dollar-based EVA factor is somewhat lower than the adjusted R^2 figures observed in Exhibit 5.7— especially during the early years of the comparative regression surveys.

Specifically, the *t*-statistics on the EVA-betas in the unadjusted regressions were 7.7 and 5.6 in 1996 and 1997, compared with *t*-values of 11 and 26 in the capital-adjusted "MVA on EVA" regressions. The *t*-statistics on the EVA betas for 1999 and 2000 were 4.0, while *t*-values of 1.0 and 4.0 (rounded) were observed for top U.S. wealth creators in the size-adjusted regressions. The five-year average *t*-value in the dollar-based MVA and EVA regressions is 4.8 (with an average EVA-beta of 19), compared with an average *t*-statistic of 9.5 (with an average EVA beta of 38) observed in the capital adjusted regressions.

Moreover, the percentage of MVA variation explained by the *unadjusted* EVA factor ranged from a low of 13% in 1998 to a high of 54% in 1996. On average, the dollar-based EVA variable explains about 31% of the cross-sectional variability in the unadjusted MVA for large U.S. wealth creators. This too is statistically significant, but somewhat lower than the average R^2 value of 45% obtained in the MVA-to-Capital and EVA-to-Capital regressions.

EXHIBIT 5.8 MVA and EVA Regression Statistics: 50 Largest Wealth Creators in Performance Universe: 1996-2000

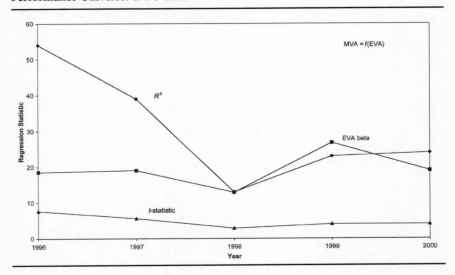

FINANCIAL CHARACTERISTICS OF WEALTH DESTROYERS

As with wealth creators, the NPV model of corporate finance has some powerful implications for wealth wasters. Specifically, the model predicts that firms having persistently negative EVA will ultimately destroy shareholder value. The wealth loss to the shareholders is caused by the firm's negative anticipated EVA spread. In this unfortunate situation, the firm's average return on capital is less than the weighted average cost of capital. Indeed, the two-period NPV model explained in Chapter 2 suggests that *seemingly* profitable companies in a traditional accounting realm can destroy wealth even though their after-tax return on capital is more than sufficient to cover the after-tax cost of debt.[5]

Knowledge of the financial characteristics of wealth destroyers can be particularly helpful to corporate managers and investors. Armed with a clear understanding of the MVA and EVA linkage for firms that have in fact destroyed wealth, corporate managers can use this information to avoid the kind of managerial mistakes that gives rise to troubled firms in the first instance. Likewise, with a refocused eye toward economic profit, managers of troubled companies can see why their relatively low capital return investments (positive ROC that falls below COC) have led to the currently adverse MVA situation.

In the absence of a concerted effort by the managers of troubled firm to generate a positive residual return on capital (RROC), the firm's debt and equity capitalization will remain far below the firm's wealth-maximization potential. Indeed, without a clear focus on how to measure economic profit, the troubled firm's managers may inadvertently invite a hostile "tender offer" bid from a more wealth conscious (that is, MVA-oriented) management team. Either way—restructuring for positive change or corporate takeover—a negative EVA situation cannot persist indefinitely lest a company meet its ultimate demise.[6]

Information about a firm's EVA situation is also important for investors. By focusing research efforts on economic profit, securities analysts or portfolio managers can gain pricing insight on the likely

---

[5] It is important to emphasize—yet again—that EVA is positive when the after-tax return on capital is higher than the weighted average cost of debt *and* equity capital. Firms having consistently positive after-tax capital returns that lie below the cost of capital will destroy wealth, even though their capital returns are sufficient enough to cover the anticipated after-tax cost of debt. This corporate finance consideration is at the heart of what the "EVA revolution" is really all about.

[6] It is important to emphasize that negative MVA (NPV) will, in principle, be associated with negative expected EVA. It is quite possible though that a firm's current EVA (as opposed to its long-term EVA) outlook might be in cyclical decline due a recession in the general economy.

direction of *both* the firm's risky debt and equity securities. In particular, the NPV model predicts that troubled firms having negative EVA momentum will see their bond and stock prices decline over time. Stock price declines because the negative EVA outlook results in a reduction in the *intrinsic value* of the firm's future stream of real earnings. In turn, bond prices fall because the negative EVA outlook leads to "credit downgrades" in the firm's risky debt. The investment and portfolio importance of looking at firms having both positive and negative EVA characteristics is further explained in Chapter 13. For now, it is time to gain some empirical understanding of the MVA and EVA linkage for companies that have—in retrospect—destroyed shareholder value.

MVA AND EVA: TOP-TEN U.S. WEALTH DESTROYERS

Exhibit 5.9 presents MVA and EVA findings for the ten largest wealth destroyers listed in the 2001 Performance 1000 Universe. Among the findings for year-end 2000, the exhibit shows that wealth destroyers (again, ranked by MVA) have currently low enterprise valuations because *they should have*. In particular, the exhibit shows the U.S. wealth destroyers had currently negative EVA in the presence of their adverse MVA figures. In numerical terms, the negative MVA figures ranged from –$6,703 million for VeriSign Inc. down to –$31,808 and –$87,206 million of cumulative wealth destruction for WorldCom and AT&T.[7]

While the after-tax return on capital figures are consistently positive in Exhibit 5.9, these firms can be viewed as wealth destroyers because their capital returns fall below the weighted average cost of capital.[8] For instance, the negative MVA values for 3Com Corp. and General Motors (at –$8,287 million and –$29,171 million) result in part because their after-tax return on capital ranges from only 52% to 86% of the reported cost of capital for these large capitalization firms. This brings to mind a few key observations in the identification of a wealth destroyer. Specifically, wealth destroyers can mistakenly look "profit-

---

[7] It is again interesting to note that WorldCom had grossly negative MVA (and EVA) at year-end 2000 even if one includes the earnings bias due to accounting fraud. Given its persistently negative EVA during the 1990s, the firm was "bust" from an EVA perspective long before the accounting scandals that surfaced in late 2001 and 2002.
[8] Is important to reemphasize that MVA is the present value of EVA. Hence, the magnitude or sign of EVA for a particular year is neither a necessary or sufficient condition to determine whether a company is a wealth creator or destroyer. However, consistently negative EVA is a defining characteristic of a wealth destroyer and persistently positive EVA is a defining characteristic of a wealth creator.

able" because they have a positive return on invested capital. Secondly, wealth destroyers can mistakenly look profitable because the return on capital is not only positive but also exceeds the after-tax cost of debt. However, the true test of a wealth creator or destroyer involves a comparison of the (expected) return on capital with the weighted average cost of debt *and* equity capital. Regarding this point, all ten U.S. companies in Exhibit 5.9 fail to meet this basic wealth creator test.[9]

Additionally, it should be noted that it is possible for a company to have negative MVA and positive EVA. We'll see this in an upcoming section when we look at the MVA and EVA characteristics of the bottom-50 companies listed in the Performance Universe at year-end 2000. When this happens, the apparent anomaly in the MVA and EVA relationship has two competing explanations—the efficient market explanation and the inefficient market explanation. With currently negative MVA and positive EVA, the efficient market argument would hold that investors are highly pessimistic about the firm's ability to generate positive economic value added for the future. On the other hand, if the capital market were inefficient, then the disjoined MVA and EVA situation would indicate that the risky debt and equity securities of such companies are undervalued in the capital market. When this happens, astute investors with an EVA research platform can take advantage of the mispriced securities.

EXHIBIT 5.9   Bottom-Ten Companies in Performance Universe at Year-End 2000

Company	MVA* (in U.S. $ Millions)	EVA (in U.S. $ Millions)	Return on Capital (%)	Cost of Capital (%)
VeriSign, Inc.	−$6,703	−1,713	0.24	15.81
Kmart Corp.	−$7,155	−943	3.19	7.99
3Com Corp.	−$8,287	−538	5.53	10.56
Xerox Corp.	−$8,411	−1,602	3.37	8.15
Bank of America Corp.	−$9,860	−1,420	10.19	11.92
First Union Corp.	−$16,130	−1,508	5.31	11.36
Lucent Technologies Inc.	−$18,771	−6,469	4.79	13.70
General Motors Corp.	−$29,171	−1,065	5.73	6.70
WorldCom Inc.	−$31,808	−5,387	6.33	11.45
AT&T Corp.	−$87,206	−9,972	4.47	9.29

*MVA = Market value of the firm less invested capital.

---

[9] Again, this is a basic wealth-creator test because we are only looking at EVA for one particular year. MVA is the discounted value of EVA.

ROC and COC: Top-Ten Wealth Destroyers

Exhibit 5.10 shows a visual comparison of the after-tax return on capital (ROC) versus the cost of capital (COC) for the top-ten wealth destroyers in the Performance Universe at year-end 2000. The findings in this exhibit are important for two reasons. First, the U.S. wealth destroyers shown here have grossly negative net present values even though the return on capital ratios are all positive. In this context, the ten largest wealth wasters in the Performance Universe for 2000 had an average capital return of only 4.92%. Meanwhile, the average cost of capital for the ten U.S. companies averaged 10.69% at that time.

For recent wealth wasters—like AT&T, WorldCom, and General Motors—the financial chain of events goes like this:[10] At –5.77%, the negative average residual return on capital (10.69%–4.92%) leads to the negative average EVA for the ten firms shown in Exhibit 5.10. In turn, the current EVA announcement presumably conveys negative information to investors about the firm's future ability to generate economic profit. If correct, then the adverse EVA anticipation results in a dramatic decline in the market value of the firm. This explanation is, in part, the economic reasoning behind the large negative MVA figures for the wealth destroyers shown in Exhibit 5.9.

EXHIBIT 5.10   Return on Capital versus Cost of Capital: Bottom-Ten Companies in Performance Universe at Year-End 2000

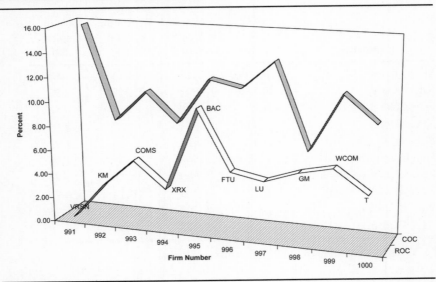

---

[10] Barring from the discussion, the fraudulent accounting behavior at WorldCom!

Second, the reported findings suggest that the cross-sectional differences in the EVA estimates for the ten largest wealth destroyers at year-end 2000 were due to cross variability in both the after-tax return on capital and the cost of capital. With a cross standard deviation of 2.55%, the return on capital estimates fluctuate about the average ROC of only 4.92% for the ten firms reported in Exhibit 5.10. With a cross standard deviation of 2.78%, the cost of capital estimates fluctuate about the average COC of 10.69%. Looking forward, findings like this implore managers and investors to jointly assess the capital return and capital cost picture in the identification of wealth creating and wealth destroying firms.

MVA AND EVA: 50 LARGE WEALTH DESTROYERS

In view of the empirical findings for the ten largest U.S. wealth wasters, it is helpful for managers and investors to see if the negative MVA and EVA association is present in a larger sample of firms. In this context, Exhibit 5.11 graphs the MVA-to-Capital and EVA-to-Capital ratios for the 50 largest U.S. wealth destroyers in the Performance Universe at year-end 2000.[11]

EXHIBIT 5.11   MVA-to-Capital versus EVA-to-Capital Ratio: Bottom 50
Companies in Performance Universe for 2000

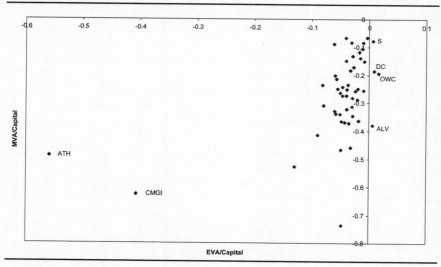

[11] Notably, the bottom 50 companies in the Performance Universe at year-end 2000 had negative MVA.

Not surprisingly, the exhibit reports consistently negative MVA-to-Capital ratios in the presence of mostly negative EVA. In this context, 46 of the 50-paired MVA and EVA-to-Capital ratios occur at negative points in Exhibit 5.11. This pervasive negative finding for wealth destroyers is interesting because it suggests that the currently adverse EVA announcement has negative information content about the firm's future growth opportunities. If correct, the economic source of the negative EVA impact on NPV and (therefore) enterprise value must in some sense be due to shareholder's longer-term assessment of a negative EVA spread—whereby, the after-tax return on capital largely falls short of the weighted average cost of capital.

By default, Exhibit 5.11 shows that only four companies had positive EVA-to-Capital ratios in the presence of their currently negative MVA-to-Capital ratios. At year-end 2000, the four companies were Sears Roebuck & Co. (S), Dana Corporation (DCN), Owens Corning Corporation (OWC), and Autoliv Inc. (ALV), respectively. Taken together, Exhibit 5.11 suggests that wealth wasters have low corporate valuations because *they should have*. In effect, the negative expected EVA leads to negative MVA and a concomitant decline in shareholder value.

Comparisons with Wealth Creators

The empirical findings for wealth destroyers are especially interesting when compared to the previously reported wealth creator findings. In Exhibit 5.3, it was shown that while the MVA and EVA relationship is empirically robust for wealth creators, some 20% (10 out of 50) of the sample companies had negative EVA-to-Capital ratios in the presence of contemporaneously positive MVA. This seemingly anomalous finding for U.S. wealth creators was explained (in an efficient market context) by saying that investors were confident about the future ability of these firms to generate positive economic value—even though the current EVA-to Capital ratios were negative.

In contrast, Exhibit 5.11 points to a potential pricing asymmetry in the way that investors value the currently announced EVA for wealth creators and wealth destroyers. In numerical terms, the exhibit shows that only 8% (four out of 50) of the firms in the so-called wealth destroyer sample had contemporaneously positive EVA-to-Capital and negative MVA-to-Capital ratios. On the other hand, some 20% of the top-50 U.S. wealth creators had contemporaneously negative EVA-to-Capital and positive MVA-to-Capital ratios. Alternatively stated, 92% of the 50 largest U.S. wealth destroyers at year-end 2000 had contemporaneously negative EVA and MVA-to-Capital ratios, while 80% of the wealth creator sample had jointly positive MVA and EVA-to Capital ratios.

Taken together, these findings are consistent with pricing asymmetry whereby, (1) the firm's *currently* announced EVA conveys a greater pricing signal for wealth destroyers than it does for wealth creators, and (2) the capital market is far more willing to take a chance on the *future* EVA abilities of wealth creating firms with currently negative EVA in comparison with that of wealth-destroying firms showing currently positive EVA. In the case of negative MVA firms like Sears Roebuck & Co., Dana Corporation, Owens Corning, and Autoliv Inc. (Exhibit 5.11), it seems fair to say that their presumed managerial steps toward generating positive EVA have fallen on investors' deaf ears.[12]

Moreover, it may be that troubled firms suffer from an abundance of adverse "managerial noise." In effect, the clattering of conflicting financial sounds down in "wealth-destroyer land" can prevent investors from either hearing, or worse yet, believing, the firm's present efforts at generating consistently positive economic value-added. Hence, corporate managers in companies facing serious financial difficulties *must* therefore make a concerted effort at convincing shareholders about the hopefully positive managerial actions that they are taking to enhance the firm's economic profit outlook going forward.

Statistical Results for 50 Large Wealth Destroyers

The strength of the statistical association between the MVA and EVA for the 50 largest U.S. wealth destroyers in the 2001 Performance Universe is shown in Exhibit 5.12. As with the regression statistics shown previously for U.S. wealth creators, the exhibit reports the EVA-beta (slope measure), t-statistic, and the adjusted R^2 value in the MVA-to-Capital and EVA-to-Capital regression.

EXHIBIT 5.12 Regression Statistics for 50 Largest Wealth Destroyers in Performance Universe at Year-End 2000

$$\text{MVA/Capital} = -0.23 + 0.74 \text{ EVA/Capital}$$
$$(t\text{-value}) \quad (-11.2) \quad (3.81)$$

$$\text{Adjusted } R^2 = 22\%$$

$$N = 50 \text{ Firms}$$

---

[12] The author in earlier studies has noted this view that a potential pricing asymmetry exists between wealth creators and destroyers.

With a slope measure of 0.74 (EVA-beta) and t-statistic at 3.81, Exhibit 5.12 shows that the EVA-to-Capital factor has a statistically significant impact on the MVA-to-Capital ratio for the 50 U.S. wealth destroyers at year-end 2000. However, in light of the noticeably wide scatter of negative MVA- and EVA-to-Capital points shown in Exhibit 5.11, it appears that the 22% percent of MVA variation explained for the bottom-50 companies in the Performance Universe is biased by a few outliers. Evidence of suspected bias in the size-adjusted MVA and EVA relationship is evident in Exhibit 5.13, which shows the presumed linear fit through the widely dispersed MVA-to-Capital and EVA-to-Capital pairs for wealth destroyers at year-end 2000.

While on the surface the adjusted R^2 values are about the same for the top-50 wealth creators *and* destroyers in the 2001 Performance Universe (19% versus 22%), the EVA-beta of 0.74 that emerges in the cross section for large U.S. wealth destroyers is *dramatically* lower than the 35.93 sensitivity estimate observed for the 50 comparable wealth creators. The reduced responsiveness in the size-adjusted MVA and EVA ratios for wealth destroyers is presumably due to the above-mentioned conflicting and "noisy markets" argument for troubled firms.

EXHIBIT 5.13 Regression Line for Bottom 50 Companies in Performance Universe at Year-End 2000

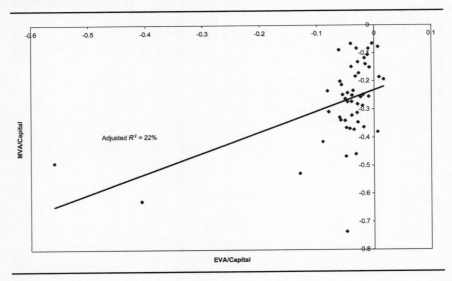

ROC and COC: 50 Large Wealth Destroyers

Exhibit 5.14 provides another look at the MVA and EVA characteristics of wealth wasters. The exhibit provides a visual display of the after-tax return on capital (ROC) versus the cost of capital (COC) for the 50 largest U.S. wealth destroyers at year-end 2000. Among the findings, the exhibit shows that wealth destroyers such as At Home Corporation (ATHM) and CMGI—with grossly negative capital returns—and wealth destroyers such as AT&T and General Motors—with positive yet low invested capital returns—have a consistently negative EVA spread in the cross section.

In percentage terms, Exhibit 5.14 confirms that 92% (46 out of 50) of the largest U.S. wealth destroyers at year-end 2000 had after-tax capital returns that fell short of the capital costs. From an efficient market perspective, these adverse EVA spreads conveyed negative information to investors about the ability of the bottom-50 companies at year-end 2000 to generate positive EVA for the future. If correct, the negative EVA signal led to a lowering of the market value of the firm and its risky debt and equity securities. As noted before, Owens Corning, Sears Roebuck & Co., Dana Corporation, and Autoliv Inc. stand out among the bottom-50 companies in the Performance Universe as exceptions to the rule that wealth destroyers have a currently negative residual return on capital. Having said that, it seems fair to say that wealth destroyers have generally low capital returns when measured against the cost of capital.

EXHIBIT 5.14   Return on Capital versus Cost of Capital: Bottom 50 Companies in Performance Universe for 2000

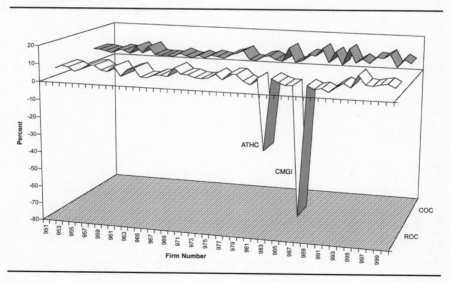

MVA AND EVA: DECILE CHARACTERISTICS OF THE PERFORMANCE UNIVERSE

Moving forward, it is helpful for managers and investors to have knowledge of the MVA and EVA relationship across the general spectrum of companies reported in the Performance 1000 Universe. This empirical perspective can be obtained by looking at the pricing characteristics of portfolios of firms that have created wealth, firms that are presumably striving to create wealth, and those companies that have in fact destroyed shareholder value. In this context, Exhibit 5.15 reports the linear regression results for the ten MVA deciles (100 companies in each decile) of the Performance Universe at year-end 2000.

The portfolio regressions are interesting in a number of respects. In particular, Exhibit 5.15 shows that the "EVA-beta" in the regression of the EVA-to-Capital ratio on the MVA-to-Capital ratio generally declines as one moves from first decile companies in the Performance Universe on down to tenth decile firms. In this context, the EVA-betas fluctuate from 15.52 to 14.78 for first and second decile companies on down to virtually *nothing* for ninth and tenth decile firms. Moreover, the EVA breaking point occurs between the fifth and sixth deciles when the EVA-beta drops from 6.53 down to around zero for sixth through tenth decile firms.

EXHIBIT 5.15   Regression Statistics for Deciles in Performance 1000 Universe at Year-End 2000

$$MVA/Capital = Alpha + Beta \times EVA/Capital$$

Decile No.	Intercept	EVA–Beta	t-Statistic	Adjusted R^2 (%)
1	5.25	15.52	1.33	0.76
2	3.62	14.78	3.91	12.60
3	2.46	13.24	22.12	83.14
4	2.73	11.56	4.52	16.44
5	1.60	6.53	5.75	24.44
6	1.17	0.34	0.24	0.00
7	0.76	−0.10	−0.18	0.00
8	0.21	0.29	1.46	1.12
9	−0.04	0.09	0.80	0.00
10	−0.21	0.58	4.41	15.69
Average	1.76	6.28	4.43	0.15

Exhibit 5.15 also shows that the EVA-betas are generally significant for the first five deciles of the Performance Universe. Along this line, the "*t*-statistics" on the EVA-betas are higher than the critical *t*-value of "2," with the notable—and surprising—exception of first decile companies.[13] Along this line, the *t*-statistics range from about 4 to 6 (rounded) for second, fourth and fifth deciles up to a high of 22 for third decile companies in the 2001 Performance Universe. In contrast, the *t*-statistics are generally insignificant (meaning less that the number 2) for companies in the bottom five deciles, with the notable exception of the tenth decile.

Exhibit 5.15 shows that the highest R^2 values are concentrated in the top-five deciles in the Performance Universe. In this context, the R^2 values range from a high of 83% for third decile companies down to about 1%–0% for companies in deciles six to nine. The exhibit also shows that the cross decile average EVA-beta is 6.28, the average *t*-statistic is 4.43, and the average R^2 is nearly zero across all deciles in the 2001 Performance Universe. However, the average regression results across the ten deciles mask the fundamental differences among wealth creators and wealth destroyers in the Performance Universe.

ROC and COC: A Closer Look at the "Middle of the Road" Firms

Finally, Exhibit 5.16 provides a display of the after-tax return on capital versus the cost of capital for large capitalization U.S. firms reported in the sixth decile of the Performance Universe at year-end 2000. This "middle of the road" portfolio with an eclectic mix of positive *and* negative residual capital returns (RROC) is interesting, especially when compared to the return on capital and cost of capital findings for wealth creators and destroyers.

On balance, the cross-decile characteristics of firms listed in the Performance 1000 Universe are consistent with the predictions of the classic NPV model. Wealth creators have mostly positive residual capital returns, while wealth destroyers have a preponderance of after-tax capital returns that—while generally positive—fall below the weighted average cost of capital. Moreover, "middle of the road firms," like those companies reported in the sixth decile of the Stern Stewart Performance Universe have residual capital returns (RROC) that largely fluctuate about the wealth-neutrality position of *zero*.

---

[13] This finding contrasts with a statistically significant finding observed earlier by the author for first decline companies in the Performance Universe.

EXHIBIT 5.16   Return on Capital versus Cost of Capital: Sixth Decile of
Performance Universe for 2000

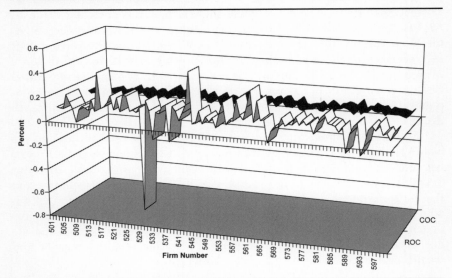

SUMMARY

This chapter looks at the empirical relationship between MVA and EVA
for wealth creators *and* destroyers. While the initial focus is on companies that have created wealth, the purpose here is to assess the *maximum* pricing strength of the contemporaneous EVA factor on MVA. If
the EVA factor were found to be insignificant among wealth creators,
then there would be little reason to hold this metric out to the financial
community as a value-based measure of corporate success. On the other
hand, if the EVA metric is a significant factor in explaining both the sign
and volatility in a firm's market value added, then managers and investors alike should pay close attention to the information content of this
financial performance measure.

The empirical findings over the 1996–2000 period reveal that the
EVA-to-Capital factor explains about 45% of the cross-sectional variation in the MVA-to-Capital ratios for the 50 largest U.S. wealth creators. However, the adjusted R^2 values are quite variable fluctuating
from 93% in 1997 to *virtually* nothing in 1999, then back up to 19% in
2000. The regression results for wealth creators are also sensitive to
possible "outliers" in the contemporaneous MVA and EVA relationship.

The chapter also focuses on the financial characteristics of firms that have in retrospect destroyed wealth. Knowledge of the MVA and EVA characteristics of wealth wasters is important for corporate managers because it provides some meaningful insight on what *not to do* when making real investment decisions for the future. On this score, the empirical evidence for troubled firms provide managers with a clear message about the NPV implications of investing in negative EVA-generating activities. Specifically, wealth is destroyed when managers invest in projects having after tax capital returns that fall short of the weighted average cost of debt and equity capital.

Knowledge about the financial characteristics of wealth destroyers is also important to investment managers. In principle, wealth-destroying firms having negative EVA announcements will see that their stock *and* bond prices are falling in the capital market as the "bad news" conveys windfall capital losses to the firm's security holders. Stock prices fall because of the reduced economic profit outlook, while bond prices decline due to "credit downgrades" on the firm's risky debt securities. For wealth creators, the opposite sequence of EVA pricing events should occur in the capital market.

The empirical results for wealth destroyers are especially interesting when compared to the findings of wealth creators. In this context, some 92% of the bottom-50 MVA-ranked firms in the Performance Universe at year-end 2000 had negative EVA-to-Capital ratios. In the wealth creator sample, 80% of the 50 firms had *contemporaneously* positive MVA- and EVA-to-Capital ratios. Other things the same, this implies a pricing asymmetry whereby the currently negative EVA announcement for wealth destroyers is more meaningful to investors than the currently positive EVA announcement for wealth creators. Moreover, with a predominately negative association between MVA and EVA for wealth destroyers, it appears that troubled firms are plagued by an abundance of adverse "managerial noise." Indeed, the presumably positive steps that managers at companies such as Sears Roebuck & Co. and Owens Corning (Exhibit 5.11) were taking to turn the negative EVA situation around may have fallen on investors' clogged ears.

CHAPTER 6

Enterprise Valuation I: Free Cash Flow Model

There are of course several approaches that can be used to estimate the market value a company and its outstanding stock. These approaches range from the traditional dividend discount and free cash flow models to the modern economic profit (EVA) approach to enterprise valuation. While several valuation models exist, the overriding principle to keep in mind is that the value of the firm is, after all, the value of the firm! That is, at any given moment in time, the firm's market value is based on a discounted stream of cash flows generated by its existing and antici-pated future growth assets. Regardless of how one packages these cash flows—as dividends, free cash flow, or even economic profit—the firm's enterprise value and its warranted stock price must be consistent across *all* approaches to enterprise valuation.[1]

In this chapter, we'll focus on the traditional free cash flow model. We'll emphasize the pricing aspects of free cash flow for several reasons: (1) Most managers and investors utilize or are at least familiar with the concept of free cash flow; (2) free cash flow recognizes that a company must make periodic investments in order to maintain existing assets and to grow a company's revenue and earnings stream; and (3) it is a simple and natural transition to go from discounted free cash flow to the EVA approach to enterprise valuation described in the next chapter.

---

[1] The pricing equivalence of discounted cash flow models is an outgrowth of the risk-adjusted equal rate of return principle explained by Fama and Miller. See Eugene F. Fama and Merton H. Miller, *The Theory of Finance* (Holt, Rinehart and Winston, Inc., 1972).

Towards the end of this chapter, we'll look at the classic dividend discount model (DDM). While dividends are in principle the ultimate source of investor value, it is often difficult to see how a dividend stream relates to the real investment decisions made by corporate managers in large companies with multiple divisions and subsidiaries. Unlike dividend valuation, this real-world limitation is less so for free cash flow and economic profit valuation approaches.[2] Indeed, dividend valuation is a rather fruitless exercise for many of today's companies—such as health care and technology firms—that retain most of their earnings for—hopefully—positive future growth.

This chapter begins with a review of discounted cash flow concepts with an eye toward understanding the basics of enterprise valuation. We'll then look at how to forecast free cash flow over a horizon period where managers or investors have a comfort level in forecasting cash flow. We'll also see how to estimate the value of a firm during the residual or "continuing" period. Upon combining the valuation results from horizon and residual periods, we'll understand how to estimate the firm's enterprise value and its warranted stock price.

Additionally, we'll see how variations in a company's discount rate or cost of capital can impact its enterprise value in a meaningful way. We'll then take a look at the general structure of the classic dividend discount model (DDM). In the next chapter, we'll look at the relationship between free cash flow and economic profit, and we'll examine the differences between these traditional and modern approaches to enterprise valuation.

OVERVIEW OF CASH FLOW MODELS

According to financial theory, the market value of any company can be expressed as a discounted stream of future cash flows. In formal terms, we can express the enterprise value of the firm as:[3]

$$EV = \sum_{t=1}^{\infty} CF_t / (1+r)^t$$

[2] We'll look at the classic dividend discount model (DDM) after covering the free cash flow approach to enterprise valuation.
[3] Consistent with the title to this chapter (*and* the next one), the firm's enterprise value is now more formally noted as EV.

In this expression, EV denotes enterprise value, CF_t is the firm's estimated (free[4]) cash flow at period t, and r is the discount rate or cost of capital.[5] While the generalized cash flow model is helpful in seeing how a company derives its overall market value, the model must be simplified in order to be useful in practice.

Two simplifications are often made to the general discounted cash flow (DCF) model: (1) The market value of the firm is viewed as the present value of cash flows estimated over a horizon period and residual period; and (2) the firm's estimated value is obtained using simplifying assumptions about how cash flows are growing over time—specifically, either constant growth in cash flow or variable growth in cash flows. We'll begin with a two-stage cash flow model where the life of the firm is split up into two components: a horizon period, which represents the period which managers or investors feel comfortable forecasting a set of cash flows, and a residual or "continuing period," which provides an estimate of the firm's cash flow stream during the posthorizon period.

Along this line, the firm's enterprise value with horizon and residual period assumptions can be expressed as:

$$
\begin{aligned}
EV &= \sum_{t=1}^{T} CF_t/(1+r)^t + 1/(1+r)^T[RV_T] \\
&= \sum_{t=1}^{T} CF_t/(1+r)^t + 1/(1+r)^T[CF_{(T+1)} \times RV/CF] \\
&= \sum_{t=1}^{T} CF_t/(1+r)^t + 1/(1+r)^T[CF_{(T+1)}/(r-g_{LT})]
\end{aligned}
$$

In the first EV expression, the first term on the right-hand side is the firm's estimated horizon value, HV, while the second term represents the firm's *current* residual value, RV. In the latter expression, RV_T denotes the firm's residual or continuing value at the end of the horizon period.

In the second EV expression, the firm's residual value is viewed as an RV multiple of the *one-step-ahead* cash flow (or normalized cash

---

[4] From this point on, the words "cash flow" should be taken to mean "free cash flow." In a nutshell, free cash flow is net operating profit after taxes (NOPAT) *less* net investment for any given time period. We'll look at how to measure and value free cash flow at a later point.

[5] For now, we'll use "r" instead of "COC" to denote the discount rate in our basic discussion of enterprise valuation. Later on, we'll revert back to the familiar COC in the detailed application of the free cash flow approach to estimating enterprise value and stock price.

flow estimate) at period $T + 1$. Also, in the third EV expression, the firm's residual value is based on the assumption that the firm's cash flows are growing at a long-term, or competitive, growth rate during the post horizon period. Of course, the last enterprise value expression only makes sense when g_{LT} is *less* than the discount rate, r.

BASICS OF ENTERPRISE VALUATION

We can frame the basics of enterprise valuation with the following example. Suppose, that a company anticipates a $100 "free cash flow" for the next ten years, followed by $20 each year, forever.[6] There are two steps to estimating the firm's enterprise value based on these cash flow assumptions:

Step 1: Calculate the horizon value, HV, or present value of the estimated cash flows for years 1 to T:

This first step can be accomplished by recognizing that the present value of a $1 annuity for T years at rate r, PVIFA(r,T), is equal to:

$$PVIFA(r, T) = 1/r[1 - 1/(1 + r)^T]$$
$$= 1/r[1 - PVIF(r, T)]$$

In this expression, PVIFA(r,T) is the present value of a $1 annuity. In turn, PVIF(r,T) is the present value of $1 promised T periods from now at a discount rate, r. With a $100 cash flow annuity for ten years and a discount rate of, say, 10%, the firm's estimated horizon value, HV, equals $614.00:

$$HV = \$100 \times PVIFA(10\%, 10)$$
$$= \$100 \times (1/0.1)[1 - 0.386]$$
$$= \$100 \times 6.14 = \$614.00$$

Step 2: Calculate the residual value, RV, or discounted value of the estimated residual value at the end of the horizon period.

There are two substeps to estimating the firm's *current* residual value, RV(0):

---

[6] We could of course make the present value application more realistic by assuming, say, $ thousands or $ millions.

Step 2.a: Calculate the firm's residual value at year T, $RV(T)$.

This is equal to the present value of the estimated cash flows during the posthorizon years. Based on the simplifying perpetuity assumption regarding CF_{T+1}, we obtain:

$$
\begin{aligned}
RV(10) &= CF_{11}/r \\
&= \$20/r \\
&= \$20 \times 10 = \$200
\end{aligned}
$$

Step 2.b: Calculate the current worth of the estimated residual value:

$$
\begin{aligned}
RV(0) &= PV(10\%, 10) \times RV(10) \\
&= 1/(1 + 0.1)^{10} \times RV(10) \\
&= 0.386 \times \$200 = \$77.20
\end{aligned}
$$

We can now "roll-up" the results to obtain the firm's estimated enterprise value, EV at \$691.20. This consists of the estimated horizon value, HV at \$614.00, plus the estimated residual value, RV at \$77.20.

$$
\begin{aligned}
EV &= HV + RV \\
&= \$614.00 + \$77.20 \\
&= \$691.20
\end{aligned}
$$

It is now a simple matter to estimate the firm's stock price. For instance, with 100 shares of common stock outstanding and *no* interest-bearing debt, the estimated value of the stock is \$6.91:

$$
\begin{aligned}
\text{Stock price} &= [\text{Enterprise value} - \text{Debt}]/\text{Shares} \\
&= [\$691.20 - 0]/100 \\
&= \$6.91
\end{aligned}
$$

GROWTH MODELS

Rather than estimating a set of cash flows during horizon and residual years, growth models can be employed as a convenient way to simplify the discounted cash flow process. In this regard, there are two well-known cash flow models that are used in practice: (1) the constant cash flow growth model (or the "Gordon Model"), and (2) the variable growth cash flow model. We'll begin with the constant growth model.

The constant cash flow growth model makes the simplifying assumption that the estimated one-step-ahead cash flow—in this case, CF(1)—is growing at a competitive or long term growth rate of g per period. In the constant growth cash flow model, the firm's enterprise value, EV, can be expressed as:

$$EV = CF(1)/(r - g)$$

In this expression, CF(1) is the estimated cash flow one year from the current period, and g is the *annualized* constant growth rate. If not given, the constant growth rate can be estimated by using the starting and ending figures from a historical series of cash flows—such as CF(0) back to CF(−J)—according to:

$$g = [CF(0)/CF(-J)]^{1/J} - 1.0$$

Constant Growth Example

As an application of the constant growth cash flow model, suppose that a company's one-step-ahead cash flow, *CF(1)* of $100, is expected to grow at a rate of 3% each year, forever. With long-term constant growth, the firm's enterprise value, EV, is equal to $1,428.57.

$$EV = \$100/(0.1 - 0.03)$$
$$= \$100/0.07 = \$1,428.57$$

Note that the estimated market value of the firm with constant growth is considerably higher than a perpetuity result of $1,000 [equal, $100/r]. Notice too that the estimated enterprise value obtained with the constant growth model is also higher than the value that we obtained before with simplifying annuity assumptions during horizon and residual periods. These differences in valuation arise because of the 3% cash flow growth assumption in the constant growth model. Moreover, in terms of DCF terminology, the term $(r - g)$ in the constant cash flow growth model can be interpreted as the cash flow "cap rate," while 14.29 [equal, $1/(r - g)$] can be viewed as the cash flow multiplier, or capitalization factor.

Variable Growth Model

The variable cash flow growth model is yet another form of the discounted cash flow model. In the variable growth model, there are multiple growth rates that serve to capture the pattern of cash flows during horizon and residual periods. In this context, it is common to assume that cash flow is growing at a relatively high rate during the horizon years, while cash flow growth settles down to a mature or competitive growth rate during the residual years.[7] We can make a simple change to the cash flow assumption in the previous constant growth example to see how this model works.

Specifically, suppose that a company's estimated one-step-ahead cash flow, CF(1) of $100, is expected to grow at 5% for (just) one year, followed by a long-term or mature growth rate of 3%. In this case, there are *two* steps to estimating the firm's enterprise value with variable growth assumptions:

Step 1: Calculate the present value of the estimated cash flows generated during the first cash flow growth phase—using our previous terminology, we'll interpret this result as the horizon value, HV.

Step 2: Calculate the present value of the cash flows earned during the mature growth phase—as before, we'll interpret this result as the *current* value of the firm's estimated future residual value.

With variable growth, the present value of the cash flows during the horizon years can be expressed as:

$$HV = \sum_{t=1}^{T} CF(1) \times (1 + g_{NT})^{T-1} / (1 + r)^T$$

In this expression, CF(1) is the one-step-ahead cash flow, g_{NT} is the *near*-term growth rate in cash flow during the horizon period, and r is the familiar discount rate or cost of capital. With just two cash flow periods during the horizon period, we can express the horizon value function as:

$$HV = CF(1)/(1 + r) + CF(2)/(1 + r)^2$$
$$= CF(1)/(1 + r) + CF(1)(1 + g_{NT})/(1 + r)^2$$

Thus, the present value of the estimated cash flows for the two-year horizon period is $177.69:

$$HV = \$100/(1.10) + \$100(1.05)/(1.1)^2$$
$$= \$90.91 + \$105 \times 0.8264$$
$$= \$177.69$$

---

[7] In practice, some managers and investors might use a "three-stage" growth model, with a transitional or decay rate of cash flow growth between horizon and residual stages.

In turn, the firm's residual value at the end of period 2, RV(2), can be calculated by recognizing that (1) the cash flow forecast for period 3 can be viewed as CF(2) growing at the *long*-term growth rate; and (2) the one-step-ahead forecast for period 3 is growing at the mature or competitive growth rate, g_{LT}. With these assumptions, the *one-step-ahead* cash flow, CF(3), can be estimated according to:

$$
\begin{aligned}
CF(3) &= CF(2)(1 + g_{LT}) \\
&= CF(1)(1 + g_{NT})(1 + g_{LT}) \\
&= \$100(1.05)(1.03) = \$108.15
\end{aligned}
$$

Next, the firm's residual value at the end of the two-year horizon period can be expressed as:

$$
RV(2) = CF(3)/(r - g_{LT})
$$

Upon substituting the estimated cash flow for period 3, CV(3) equal $108.15, into the above expression yields RV(2), at $1,545:

$$
\begin{aligned}
RV(2) &= \$108.15/(0.1 - 0.03) \\
&= \$108.15/0.07 \\
&= \$1,545.00
\end{aligned}
$$

Moreover, upon combining the results for horizon and residual periods, we obtain the estimated enterprise value, at $1,454.55:

$$
\begin{aligned}
EV &= \text{Horizon value} + \text{Residual value} \\
&= \$177.69 + [1/(1 + r)^2] \times RV(2) \\
&= \$177.69 + 0.8264 \times \$1,545 \\
&= \$1,454.55
\end{aligned}
$$

Notice that the variable growth value of $1,454.55 differs by a *small* amount from the 3% constant growth model result of $1428.57.[8] This minor difference in enterprise value results because we only assumed a 5% rate of growth in the cash flow for year 2. All other cash flow values were assumed to be growing at 3%, as in the previous constant growth example.

---

[8] In practice, a variable growth model can produce an answer that is *substantially* different from that obtained with a constant growth model. However, the goal in this application is simply to show that the present value dynamics of a variable growth model are in fact different from that of a constant growth procedure.

TRADITIONAL FREE CASH FLOW MODEL

Let's now build on our DCF foundation by taking a detailed look at the traditional free cash flow model.[9] As before, the enterprise value of the firm can be viewed as the present value of the anticipated cash flow stream generated by the firm's existing assets and its expected future growth assets not currently in place. In general terms, the FCF model can be expressed as:

$$EV = \sum_{t=1}^{\infty} \frac{FCF_t}{(1 + COC)^t}$$

In this expression, EV is the firm's enterprise value, FCF_t is the assessed free cash flow at year t, and COC (note change in discount rate notation *from r to COC*) is the familiar weighted average cost of debt and equity capital.[10]

In turn, the firm's assessed free cash flow at year t, FCF_t, can be viewed as the anticipated net operating profit after tax, NOPAT, *less* the annual net investment, IN, to support the firm's growth. In formal terms, we have:

$$FCF_t = NOPAT_t - IN_t$$

Before proceeding, it should be noted that we can make a distinction between *gross* investment, IG, and *net* investment, IN. Specifically, gross investment refers to: (1) capital spending required to maintain the economic productivity of the firm's existing assets; (2) working capital additions to support a growing revenue and earnings stream; and (3) any new investments made by the firm's managers in—hopefully—positive

---

[9] For an early application of the free cash flow model, see Alfred Rappaport, "Strategic Analysis for More Profitable Acquisitions," *Harvard Business Review* (July/August 1979). Recent insight on how to apply the free cash flow model can be found in (1) Thomas Copeland, Timothy Koller, and Jack Murrin, *Valuation: Measuring and Managing the Value of Companies, Third Edition* (New York: John Wiley & Sons, 2001), and (2) Frank J. Fabozzi and James L. Grant, *Value Based Metrics: Foundations and Practice* (eds.) (New Hope, PA: Frank J. Fabozzi Associates, 2000).

[10] Anyone who has had a basic course in finance is familiar with the cost of capital. We'll explore the pricing implications of COC changes at a later point in this chapter. We also explore how to estimate this key EVA factor in Chapter 11.

NPV projects. On the other hand, *net* investment, IN, refers to gross investment *less* (in principle) economic depreciation.[11]

Summarizing these results, in the traditional free cash flow model, the firm's enterprise value is equal to the present value of its expected free cash flow stream, where the expected free cash flow at period *t* can be expressed as NOPAT less the corresponding *net* investment. As mentioned above, net investment refers to gross capital expenditures at year *t* less the required maintenance expenditures (measured by economic depreciation) on the firm's existing assets.[12] As with gross investment, net investment includes the required change in working capital (period change in operating current assets less the associated change in operating current liabilities) to support a growing revenue and earnings base.

Estimating Free Cash Flow: NOPAT Approach

While several forecasting approaches can be used to estimate a company's free cash flow, we'll use the traditional revenue forecasting approach described by Rappaport.[13] In this context, the free cash flow estimate for any given year is based on forecasted *sales* net of *both* operating expenses and capital expenditures. In this approach, operating and investment expenditures are typically expressed as a fraction of a growing revenue stream. Hence, the free cash flow forecast for any given period is conditioned on the forecast of revenue. A robust sales forecasting approach that can be used to produce a free cash flow estimate for any given period *t* is given by:

$$\begin{aligned} \text{FCF}_t &= S_{t-1}(1+g)p(1-t_u) - (w+f)(S_t - S_{t-1}) \\ &= \text{EBIT}_t(1-t_u) - (w+f)(S_t - S_{t-1}) \\ &= \text{NOPAT}_t - \text{Net investment}_t \end{aligned}$$

In this expression, $S(t-1)$ is the firm's base revenue, g is the anticipated revenue growth rate, p is the pretax operating margin (EBIT/Sales), and w and f are working capital and *net* investment fractions, respectively. These investment-related fractions are applied to the estimated year-

[11] Stephen O'Byrne sheds some fascinating insight on how to measure depreciation in an economic profit context. See Stephen F. O'Byrne, "Does Value-Based Management Discourage Investment in Intangibles?" Chapter 5 in *Value-Based Metrics: Foundations and Practice*. Also, we'll examine the EVA importance of economic depreciation versus straight-line depreciation in Chapter 10.

[12] This chapter generally defines free cash flow as NOPAT less *net* investment. In a moment, we'll see that free cash flow can equivalently be expressed as gross operating profit after taxes (GOPAT) less *gross* investment.

[13] See Rappaport, "Strategic Analysis for More Profitable Acquisitions."

over-year change in sales to obtain net investment, IN. To see how this works, we'll make the following assumptions to obtain an estimate of free cash flow for year 1:

- Base Revenue = $100 (*or 100% of any given base*)
- Revenue growth rate = 15%
- Pretax operating margin (EBIT/Sales) = 20%
- *Net* capital investment = 20% of *increased* sales
- Change in Working Capital = 10% of *increased* sales
- Unlevered tax rate = 35%[14]

Based on these assumptions, the free cash flow estimate for period 1 is given by:

$$
\begin{aligned}
\text{FCF}(1) &= \text{NOPAT}(1) - \text{IN}(1) \\
&= \$115 \times 0.2 \times 0.65 - [0.2 + 0.1][\$115 - \$100] \\
&= \$14.95 - \$4.50 = \$10.45
\end{aligned}
$$

Notice that in the free cash flow model, the primary focus is on the firm's net operating profit after tax (NOPAT) *less* the net investment (IN) required to maintain existing assets and to support a growing revenue and earnings stream. Notice too that in second FCF expression, NOPAT can be expressed as tax adjusted EBIT less net investment.[15] Thus, free cash flow makes sense from a valuation perspective because the firm cannot expect to produce the NOPAT estimate of $14.95 in future years, let alone grow that figure without a supporting investment at period 1.

Exhibit 6.1 shows a ten-year stream of free cash flow estimates that were produced by the revenue-forecasting model. For any given year, free cash flow is equal to NOPAT less net annual investment, IN. In the next section, we'll look at the equivalent gross operating profit after taxes (GOPAT) approach to estimating free cash flow, as some managers and investors prefer to work with gross cash flow and gross investment figures rather than net cash flows. We'll then "roll up" the results using the assessed NOPAT, net investment, and resulting free cash flow figures to estimate the enterprise value of the firm and warranted stock price.

---

[14] It is standard practice to use an unlevered tax rate when estimating NOPAT because any tax benefits associated with debt financing (including operating leases) should already be reflected in the firm's weighted average cost of capital, COC.

[15] Specifically, in the *second* FCF expression, the first term is tax-adjusted EBIT, at $115 \times 0.2 \times 0.65 = \$14.95$.

EXHIBIT 6.1 Estimating Free Cash Flow: NOPAT Approach

Period	1	2	3	4	5	6	7	8	9	10
Sales	$115.00	$132.25	$152.09	$174.90	$201.14	$231.31	$266.00	$305.90	$351.79	$404.56
Op. Exp.	92.00	105.80	121.67	139.92	160.91	185.04	212.80	244.72	281.43	323.64
EBIT	23.00	26.45	30.42	34.98	40.23	46.26	53.20	61.18	70.36	80.91
Taxes	8.05	9.26	10.65	12.24	14.08	16.19	18.62	21.41	24.63	28.32
NOPAT	14.95	17.19	19.77	22.74	26.15	30.07	34.58	39.77	45.73	52.59
NCapInv.	3.00	3.45	3.97	4.56	5.25	6.03	6.94	7.98	9.18	10.55
Work Cap	1.50	1.73	1.98	2.28	2.62	3.02	3.47	3.99	4.59	5.28
Net Inv.	4.50	5.18	5.95	6.84	7.87	9.05	10.41	11.97	13.77	15.83
FCF	10.45	12.02	13.82	15.89	18.28	21.02	24.17	27.80	31.97	36.76

116

Free Cash Flow: GOPAT Approach

Since some managers and investors prefer to work with gross cash flows and gross investment, it is helpful to show the equivalence of free cash flow using both net *and* gross cash flow figures. In this context, Exhibit 6.2 shows that the firm's free cash flow can also be expressed in the context of its gross operating profit after taxes, GOPAT, less annual gross capital additions (including working capital additions). To estimate the firm's free cash flow this way, we simply add back depreciation to both NOPAT and annual net investment according to:

$$
\begin{aligned}
\text{FCF}_t &= \text{GOPAT}_t - \text{GI}_t \\
&= (\text{NOPAT}_t + D_t) - (\text{IN}_t + D_t) \\
&= (\text{NOPAT}_t - \text{IN}_t)
\end{aligned}
$$

Upon *adding* back depreciation, we see that the firm's yearly free cash flow can be expressed in terms of its gross operating profit after taxes, GOPAT, less *gross* capital investment at t, GI_t. The equivalent GOPAT approach to estimating the firm's free cash flow during the horizon years is shown in Exhibit 6.2. Not surprisingly, we obtain the same set of free cash flow estimates whether we use a net cash flow approach or a gross cash flow approach.

FREE CASH FLOW VALUATION

As explained before, when using a DCF model one often sees the value of the firm split up into two components, namely (1) the value of free cash flow estimates generated over the "horizon" years and (2) the present worth of free cash flow generated during the "residual" or "continuing" years. In this two-way breakout, the horizon years capture that portion of the firm's life where the manager or investor feels comfortable projecting free cash flows on a periodic basic. In our case, we'll use the ten years of free cash flow estimates produced by the revenue-forecasting model to assess the horizon value of the firm. We'll then look at how the firm's derives a significant portion of its enterprise value and warranted stock price from free cash flow generated during the post-horizon or residual years.[16]

---

[16] The fact that residual value often makes up a sizable component of a company's market value should *not* be interpreted to mean that existing assets are of little or no consequence in the valuation process. Indeed, the cash flow from existing assets carries over to the residual period, quite often in a perpetual manner.

EXHIBIT 6.2 Estimating Free Cash Flow: GOPAT Approach

Period	1	2	3	4	5	6	7	8	9	10
Sales	$115.00	$132.25	$152.09	$174.90	$201.14	$231.31	$266.00	$305.90	$351.79	$404.56
Op. Exp.	92.00	105.80	121.67	139.92	160.91	185.04	212.80	244.72	281.43	323.64
EBIT	23.00	26.45	30.42	34.98	40.23	46.26	53.20	61.18	70.36	80.91
Taxes	8.05	9.26	10.65	12.24	14.08	16.19	18.62	21.41	24.63	28.32
NOPAT	14.95	17.19	19.77	22.74	26.15	30.07	34.58	39.77	45.73	52.59
Deprec.	0.90	1.04	1.19	1.37	1.57	1.81	2.08	2.39	2.75	3.17
GOPAT	15.85	18.23	20.96	24.11	27.72	31.88	36.66	42.16	48.49	55.76
G.CapInv.	3.90	4.49	5.16	5.93	6.82	7.84	9.02	10.37	11.93	13.72
Work Cap	1.50	1.73	1.98	2.28	2.62	3.02	3.47	3.99	4.59	5.28
Gross Inv	5.40	6.21	7.14	8.21	9.44	10.86	12.49	14.36	16.52	19.00
FCF	10.45	12.02	13.82	15.89	18.28	21.02	24.17	27.80	31.97	36.76

FCF Valuation: Horizon Years

Exhibit 6.3 shows how to "roll up" the ten years of free cash flow estimates for the horizon years. The exhibit reports NOPAT, net annual investment, free cash flow, the present value of free cash flow for any given year, and the *cumulative* present value of the free cash flow estimates over the horizon period.[17] Using a "cost of capital" (discount rate) of 10%, we see that the $10.45 free cash flow estimate for year 1 has a currently assessed market value of $9.50.

Upon calculating the present value of the ten years of free cash flow estimates and cumulating these values, we see that the firm's warranted horizon value is $116.98. With long-term debt at, say, $12, and five shares of common stock outstanding, the warranted horizon value of each share of stock would be $21.00.

Horizon-year stock price
= (Horizon-year enterprise value – LT debt)/Equity shares
= ($116.98 – $12)/5 = $21.00

However, stopping here in the enterprise valuation process would be unduly conservative because it presumes that the firm is unable to generate discounted positive free cash flow beyond the horizon period. Such an unfortunate state of affairs might exist for a company's shareholders if (1) the firm's existing capital assets at that time (year-end 10 in our

EXHIBIT 6.3 Free Cash Flow Valuation

Year	NOPAT	Net Invest	FCF	Pres.Val. 10%	Cum. PV
1	$14.95	$4.5	$10.45	$9.50	$9.50
2	17.19	5.18	12.01	9.93	19.43
3	19.77	5.95	13.82	10.38	29.81
4	22.74	6.84	15.9	10.86	40.67
5	26.15	7.87	18.28	11.35	52.02
6	30.07	9.05	21.02	11.87	63.88
7	34.58	10.41	24.17	12.40	76.29
8	39.77	11.97	27.8	12.97	89.26
9	45.73	13.77	31.96	13.55	102.81
10	52.59	15.83	36.76	14.17	116.98

---

[17] We'll look at the free cash flow approach to residual period valuation in the next section.

case) were completely obsolete; and if (2) the NPV on all future investments were zero (equivalently, the marginal return on future investments were unable to best the cost of capital, COC).

FCF Valuation: Residual Years

While several assumptions can be made about free cash flow generation during the posthorizon years,[18] we'll make the simplifying (and economically consistent) assumption that the marginal return on the *net* investment at the end of the horizon period (and beyond) earns a cost of capital return. This is tantamount to saying that (1) free cash flow for posthorizon years is equal to the one-period ahead estimate of NOPAT; and (2) that economic profit generated by the end-of-horizon period net investment (and the EVA on any future net investment) is precisely equal to zero. With this zero-NPV assumption, the firm's residual (or "continuing") value at year T can be expressed in simple terms as:

$$RV_T = NOPAT_{T+1}/COC$$

While the resulting perpetuity is a convenient way out of any complex pricing process, we still need to estimate the *one-period-ahead* NOPAT as of the end of the horizon period.[19] Fortunately, we can obtain this one-step-ahead forecast with knowledge of (1) the firm's "plowback" or net investment-to-NOPAT ratio and (2) the marginal return on invested capital, MROC. With this information, we can express the firm's growth in NOPAT, g_N, as:

$$g_N = PBR \times MROC$$

In this expression, g_N is the estimated year-over-year growth rate in NOPAT from the end of the horizon period, PBR is the plowback ratio, measured by *net* investment during the last year of the horizon period over the end-of-horizon period net operating profit after taxes, $NOPAT_T$, and MROC is the marginal return on net invested capital.[20]

---

[18] Such possibilities include constant growth in free cash flow beyond year T (at a growth rate *less* than COC) to some form of competitive "decay" in the estimated free cash flow during the residual years.

[19] We'll see under what condition the one-step-ahead NOPAT perpetuity formula applies at a later point in the chapter.

[20] The growth in NOPAT, g_N, can be expressed as the product of the net investment plowback ratio *times* the marginal return on net invested capital, MROC, because (1) PBR measures net investment over NOPAT (at end of the horizon period in our case); and (2) MROC equals the *change* in NOPAT over net investment.

Assuming that the net investment at year 10, at $15.83 (see Exhibit 6.3) earns a cost of capital return, COC equal 10%, we obtain an estimated NOPAT growth rate for the residual or continuing period of 3%.

$$g_N = (\$15.83/\$52.59) \times 0.10$$
$$= 0.3010 \times 0.10 = 0.0301 \ (\text{or } 3.01\%)$$

It is now a simple matter to estimate the one-step-ahead NOPAT forecast according to:

$$NOPAT_{11} = NOPAT_{10} \times (1 + g_N)$$
$$= \$52.59 \times 1.0301 = \$54.17$$

Thus, the firm's residual value at year 10 is equal to $541.73. This is obtained by discounting the one-step-ahead NOPAT perpetuity by the 10% cost of capital. Equivalently, this residual value figure is obtained by multiplying the estimated NOPAT perpetuity of $54.17 by a price-to-NOPAT "multiplier" of 10 (equal to 1/COC).

$$RV_{10} = \$54.17/0.10$$
$$= \$54.17 \times 10 = \$541.73$$

Moreover, upon discounting the residual value (at year 10) back ten periods, we obtain the warranted value, at $208.86, of the free cash flow generated during the residual or continuing years. As summarized in Exhibit 6.4, we see that the enterprise value of the firm is $325.84. This value consists of $116.98 in horizon value *plus* $208.86 of current residual value. With long-term debt at $12, and five shares of common stock outstanding, the warranted stock price is *now* $62.77.

Before proceeding, it is interesting to see that the current residual value, at $208.86, makes up some 64% of the firm's warranted enterprise value. This large residual value impact is a common finding when using discounted cash flow approaches—including DDM, free cash flow, and even economic profit approaches—to estimate enterprise value and stock price. In the real world, the residual value impact is especially pronounced for growth-oriented companies[21] (example, companies in technology and health care sectors of the economy) since most of their

---

[21] The term "growth-oriented companies" is taken to mean companies that can earn substantially positive EVA on future investment opportunities. They do so because the after-tax rate of return on future investment opportunities exceeds the COC in a substantial way.

EXHIBIT 6.4   FCF Valuation: Horizon and Residual Years

Year	NOPAT	Net Invest*	FCF	Pres.Val. 10%	Cum. PV
1	$14.95	$4.50	$10.45	$9.50	$9.50
2	17.19	5.18	12.01	9.93	19.43
3	19.77	5.95	13.82	10.38	29.81
4	22.74	6.84	15.90	10.86	40.67
5	26.15	7.87	18.28	11.35	52.02
6	30.07	9.05	21.02	11.87	63.88
7	34.58	10.41	24.17	12.40	76.29
8	39.77	11.97	27.80	12.97	89.26
9	45.73	13.77	31.96	13.55	102.81
10	52.59	15.83	36.76	14.17	116.98
11 plus*	54.17				
		Residual Value		541.73	208.86
		Corporate Value			325.84
		LT Debt			12.00
		Equity			313.84
		Share OS			5.00
		Price			62.77

* Net investment at year 10 (and any net investment thereafter) earns a cost of capital return.

enterprise value comes from distant—and often very difficult to predict—free cash flows generated by future R&D investments.

A CLOSER LOOK AT RESIDUAL VALUE

In the previous section, we assumed that the firm's *net* investment during the residual period earned a cost of capital return, COC. This convenience allowed us to model the firm's residual value as a one-step-ahead perpetuity on its net operating profit after taxes, namely $NOPAT_{T+1}/COC$. To see why this simplification works, note that we could always express the firm's residual value in terms of the constant growth free cash flow model according to:

$$RV(T) = FCF_{T+1}/(COC - g)$$

In turn, the firm's free cash flow at period $T + 1$ can be expressed in terms a one-step-ahead NOPAT forecast according to:

$$FCF_{T+1} = NOPAT_{T+1}(1 - PBR)$$

In this expression, $NOPAT_{T+1}$ is the firm's estimated one-step-ahead net operating profit after taxes, and PBR is the fraction of NOPAT (at period T) that is invested back into the firm—that is, PBR is the net investment to NOPAT ratio. Since, the firm's growth rate—expressed in terms of NOPAT growth, g_N—can be expressed as the marginal return on net invested capital, MROC, times the net investment plowback ratio, PBR, we can rewrite the residual value function as:[22]

$$RV(T) = [NOPAT_{T+1}(1 - PBR)]/(COC - g_N)$$
$$= [NOPAT_{T+1}(1 - g_N/MROC)]/(COC - g_N)$$

Assuming for convenience (or actuality) that the after-tax return on the net investment at period T (and all future net investment) earns a cost of capital return, that is, MROC equals COC, we obtain:

$$RV(T) = [NOPAT_{T+1}(1 - g_N/COC)]/(COC - g_N)$$
$$= [NOPAT_{T+1}(COC - g_N)/COC]/(COC - g_N)$$
$$= NOPAT_{T+1}/COC$$

As before, the firm's residual value at period T can always be modeled as NOPAT perpetuity under the assumption that the net present value (equivalently, discounted economic profit[23]) on net investment during the residual years is equal to zero. In other words, the residual value of the firm is unaffected by neutral NPV investments that neither create wealth nor destroy it.

---

[22] Specifically, since growth in NOPAT equals MROC times PBR, we can express the net investment plowback ratio as g_N/MROC. For further insight and application, see Copeland, Koller, and Murrin, *Valuation: Measuring and Managing the Value of Companies*.

[23] We'll see how this works in an EVA context in Chapter 7. Simply put, if MROC equals COC, then the rise in NOPAT is precisely offset by the added capital cost associated with the prior period's (or beginning of current period's) net investment. Hence, *both* the "EVA spread" and the resulting NPV on the marginal investment that occurs at the end of the horizon period are equal to zero.

CHANGES IN COC

While managers and investors spend a justifiable amount of time estimating free cash flow, they sometimes miss the pricing significance of variations in the cost of capital. This is understandable given the amount of time required to produce a time series of estimates on NOPAT and net capital investment. We can see the pricing importance of COC changes by returning to our previous illustration. Note that when the firm's free cash flow figures were discounted at 10%—a standard rate used in many present value applications—we found that the firm's enterprise value was $325.84. Exhibits 6.5 and 6.6 (table and graph, respectively) show what happens to the firm's estimated market value when the cost of capital rises and falls in increments of 50 basis points from a base rate of 10%.

The corporate pricing relationships shown in these exhibits are consistent with financial theory in a number of interesting respects. First, Exhibit 6.5 shows that an *inverse* relationship exists between the firm's estimated enterprise value and the weighted average cost of capital. For example, when the cost of capital rises from 10% to 11% (a 100 basis point increase), the firm's estimated market value declines from $325.84 to $284.92. Conversely, if the firm's cost of capital were to decline from 10% to 9%, the firm's warranted value would rise from $325.84 to $376.98. In practice, the underlying source of such COC changes can be attributed to (1) unanticipated changes in the risk-free rate of interest, and, just as importantly, (2) fundamental changes in the business risk premium required by the firm's investors.

Second, it is interesting to see the *convex* relationship between enterprise value and the cost of capital. Exhibit 6.6 shows that when the cost of capital rises by 100 basis points, the estimated market value of the firm falls by 12.56%. In contrast, when the discount rate falls by 100 basis points—from 10% to 9%—the market value of the firm rises by 15.69%. Likewise, an asymmetric pricing response occurs when the cost of capital rises or falls by 200 basis points. These enterprise valuation findings are consistent with well-known pricing relationships in the fixed income market. In effect, the "convexity" in the enterprise value-cost of capital relationship reveals that firm values are more sensitive to cost of capital declines than to equivalent basis-point increases in the weighted average cost of capital.

EXHIBIT 6.5 FCF Model: Cost of Capital Sensitivity Analysis

Rate %	Basis Pt. Change	Horiz. Val.	NOPAT T+1*	Resid.Val. at T	PV of Resid.Val.	EV	Stock Price	% Change EV
8.0	-200	$130.45	$53.86	$673.21	$311.82	$442.28	$86.06	35.73
8.5	-150	126.89	53.94	634.54	280.65	407.54	79.11	25.07
9.0	-100	123.46	54.01	600.16	253.52	376.98	73.00	15.69
9.5	-50	120.16	54.09	569.41	229.76	349.93	67.59	7.39
10.0	0	116.98	54.17	541.73	208.86	325.84	62.77	0.00
10.5	50	113.92	54.25	516.69	190.37	304.29	58.46	-6.61
11.0	100	110.97	54.33	493.92	173.95	284.92	54.58	-12.56
11.5	150	108.13	54.41	473.13	159.31	267.44	51.09	-17.92
12.0	200	105.39	54.49	454.08	146.20	251.59	47.92	-22.79

* Assume net investment at T (and beyond) earns the relevant cost of capital.

EXHIBIT 6.6   Enterprise Value and the Cost of Capital: FCF Model

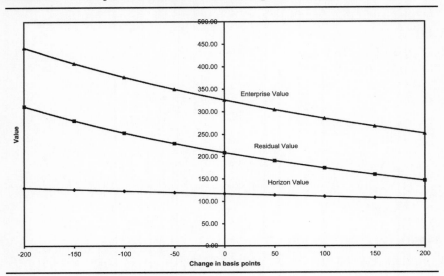

Additionally, Exhibit 6.6 shows that the residual value function is considerably more sensitive to cost of capital changes than the horizon-value function. This is also consistent with known present value relationships in that long *duration* assets (or cash flows) are more sensitive to interest rate changes than short duration assets. In effect, the residual value function is a present value reflection of distant cash flows generated in the post horizon years, periods $T + 1$ to infinity. Consequently, the firm's residual value is like a long duration asset that is highly sensitive to cost of capital changes. In contrast, the firm's horizon value can be viewed as a relatively short duration asset, and thereby less sensitive to COC changes. These pricing differences can be seen in Exhibit 6.5 (or 6.6). For example, when the firm's cost of capital declines by 100 basis points, the firm's estimated residual value rises by 21.38%, while its horizon value increases by a much smaller percentage, at 5.54%.

DIVIDEND DISCOUNT MODEL (DDM)

While our focus thus far has been on estimating enterprise value in the context of the traditional free cash flow model, it should be clear that we could model the firm's stock price in the context of a discounted stream of dividends per share. In this regard, the classic DDM can be expressed as:

$$P = \sum_{t=1}^{\infty} \text{Dividend per share}_t / (1 + r_e)^t$$

As with the free cash flow model, the dividend discount model can be unfolded into (1) a constant growth version, and (2) a variable-growth version. The constant growth dividend discount model (DDM) can be expressed as:

$$P = d(1)/(r_e - g)$$

In this pricing expression, $d(1)$ is the *one-step-ahead* dividend per share forecast, g is the long-term dividend (and earnings) growth rate, and r_e is equity discount rate, or the cost of equity capital (a prominent component of COC).

A Look at the Two-Phase DDM

Likewise, practitioners of the two-stage DDM often employ the horizon and residual value framework that we examined before for the traditional free cash flow model. In this context, the variable growth DDM can be used to estimate the stock price of a dividend paying company according to:

$$P = \sum_{t=1}^{T} d_t/(1 + r_e)^t + 1/(1 + r_e)^T [P_T]$$

$$= \sum_{t=1}^{T} d_t/(1 + r_e)^t + 1/(1 + r_e)^T [d_{(T+1)}/(r_e - g_{LT})]$$

In the two phase dividend discount model, P_T is the residual or continuing value of the stock at the end of the horizon period T. Upon summing up the present value of dividends during horizon and residual years, one obtains a DDM estimate of the warranted value of a company's stock.

CAVEATS

Before moving on, it should be noted that if the DDM is applied consistently, then it must produce the same warranted stock price and enterprise value as that obtained from the free cash flow model. In principle, it really doesn't matter whether one expresses the value of the firm and its stock as a discounted stream of dividends, free cash flow, or even economic profit (EVA). Having said that, there are practical benefits of using the free cash flow model (and by extension, the EVA model) over the classic dividend discount model.

The practical benefits of using a free cash flow approach to enterprise valuation over a DDM approach are based on the following considerations: (1) Many of today's companies have either opted to reduce or not pay dividends—therefore, they plow earnings back into the company for future growth; (2) unlike dividends, free cash flow provides a *transparent* look at how a company actually receives and invests funds—via NOPAT and capital expenditures; and, for our purposes, (3) it is a simple and natural transition to move from free cash flow valuation to economic profit (EVA) valuation—a measurement and valuation direction that we now turn.

CHAPTER 7

Enterprise Valuation II:
Economic Profit Model

This chapter builds on the previous one by providing a foundation on the economic profit (EVA) approach to enterprise value. In this context, we'll see that NPV is equal to a discounted stream of economic profit. Along the way, we'll see that the EVA model provides the *same* discounted cash flow estimate of enterprise value and warranted stock price as that obtained using the traditional free cash flow model. With a joint emphasis on discounted cash flow concepts, the FCF and EVA linkage is important for managers and investors who are either unfamiliar with economic profit measurement and valuation, or for critics (especially) who *incorrectly* perceive that EVA is a shortsighted measurement tool.

Based on the discussion in Chapter 6, we know that free cash flow is a step in the right direction because it looks at net operating profit after taxes (NOPAT) *less* the required net investment (IN) to support a growing revenue and earnings stream. In turn, economic profit reinforces free cash flow measurement because it provides a *direct* measure of wealth creation. In this regard, EVA makes a periodic assessment of whether a company's after tax return on invested capital, ROC, exceeds the weighted average cost of capital, COC. As explained before, the sign of the "EVA spread" is a key determinant of whether the firm's NPV is positive—a reflection of wealth-creating investment decisions—or possibly, negative—a reflection of investment decisions that, unfortunately, waste shareholder value.

ECONOMIC PROFIT MODEL

The EVA model differs from the free cash flow model because it provides a direct measure of the value added to invested capital.[1] The wealth added to invested capital is called net present value. As introduced in Chapter 2, the firm's NPV is equal to the present value of the anticipated economic profit stream generated by its existing and anticipated future assets. We can begin our examination of the EVA model by recognizing that the firm's enterprise value can be expressed as:

$$EV = C + NPV$$

In this expression, EV is enterprise value, C is invested capital, and NPV is net present value.[2]

In turn, the firm's NPV can be expressed as a discounted stream of economic profit according to:

$$NPV = \text{Present value of EVA}$$

$$= \sum_{t=1}^{\infty} \frac{EVA_t}{(1 + COC)^t}$$

In the above formula, EVA is the estimated economic profit at time period t, and COC is the familiar weighted average cost of capital. Other things the same, we see that managers create wealth by making discounted positive economic profit—and therefore, positive NPV—decisions.[3] They destroy wealth by making discounted negative EVA decisions.

As explained in Chapter 2, economic profit is positive when the estimated after-tax return on invested capital, ROC, exceeds the cost of capital, COC. That is, EVA is positive when the "EVA spread" is positive. On the other hand, economic profit—and its discounted NPV equivalent—is negative when corporate managers invest in assets (both tangible and intangible) having an after-tax return that, on balance, falls short of the COC.

---

[1] As noted before, this does *not* mean that the EVA approach to enterprise valuation gives a better answer than that obtained from other valuation models, including dividend discount models (DDMs) and free cash flow approaches.

[2] As explained in Chapter 9, invested capital, or "EVA capital," can be obtained using an *equivalent* assets or financing approach.

[3] When evaluating companies, managers and investors *must* be keenly aware of economic profit influences from industry, sector, and general market effects.

EVA Link with Free Cash Flow

There are two things to keep in mind when exploring the relationship between the traditional free cash flow model and the economic profit model. The first is obvious—namely, both FCF and EVA models *must* produce the same warranted value of the firm and its stock price. In this theoretical sense, the two discounted cash flow approaches are equivalent. Having said that, it is worth reemphasizing that the EVA model provides managers and investors with a *direct* measure of how the firm derives its overall net present value.

The second thing to keep in mind regarding FCF and EVA valuation pertains to the capital charge on invested assets. Specifically, in the free cash flow model, the present value of the capital charge on the firm's periodic investment is *implicitly* recognized in the same year that the capital expenditure is incurred. In contrast, in the economic profit approach to enterprise valuation an *explicit* capital charge on the beginning of year net invested capital is assessed each year.

To see how this investment equivalence works, suppose—as in our free cash flow application at year 1—that a company spends $4.50 in net capital improvement during a particular year. In the free cash flow model, the entire net investment would be subtracted from NOPAT in the year incurred. As mentioned above, this is equivalent to recognizing the present value of the yearly capital charge that would normally be assessed in the economic profit model. Assuming that the capital charge can be expressed as perpetuity, yields:

$$
\begin{aligned}
IN(1) &= \$4.50 \\
&= COC \times \$4.50/COC = \$4.50
\end{aligned}
$$

Notice that the free cash flow model subtracts the entire net investment of $4.50 from NOPAT. In the EVA approach, the periodic capital charge of $0.45 (assuming a 10% cost of capital) would be deducted from each year's NOPAT, beginning in the first year *following* the capital expenditure. Of course, the investment expenditure (initially, at $4.50) is added to the end of year 1 capital base to arrive at BOY capital for the second year.

Forecasting Economic Profit

With this FCF-EVA relationship in mind, let's now see how economic profit can be estimated using the revenue forecasting approach that we examined in Chapter 6. In this context, Exhibit 7.1 shows how to estimate the firm's EVA over the ten-year "horizon period." With NOPAT(1) at $14.95, initial (net[4]) capital of $40, and a cost of capital of 10%, we see that the firm's assessed economic profit for year 1 is $10.95:[5]

$$EVA(1) = NOPAT(1) - COC \times C(0)$$
$$= \$14.95 - 0.10 \times \$40.00 = \$10.95$$

Likewise, at $12.74, economic profit for year 2 is just NOPAT less the assessed capital charge on net invested capital at the end of year 1 (or the BOY capital at year 2).

$$EVA(2) = NOPAT(2) - COC \times C(1)$$
$$= \$17.19 - 0.10 \times \$44.50 = \$12.74$$

At $44.50, the net invested capital at the start of year 2 is a reflection of the initial capital, C(0) of $40.00, plus the net annual investment of $4.50 that occurred during year 1.

EXHIBIT 7.1   Forecasting Economic Profit (EVA)

Year	Yearly Net Inv.*	Total Net Capital	NOPAT	Capital Charge	Economic Profit
0		$40.00			
1	$4.50	44.50	$14.95	$4.00	$10.95
2	5.18	49.68	17.19	4.45	12.74
3	5.95	55.63	19.77	4.97	14.80
4	6.84	62.47	22.74	5.56	17.18
5	7.87	70.34	26.15	6.25	19.90
6	9.05	79.39	30.07	7.03	23.04
7	10.41	89.8	34.58	7.94	26.64
8	11.97	101.77	39.77	8.98	30.79
9	13.77	115.54	45.73	10.18	35.55
10	15.83	131.37	52.59	11.55	41.04
11 plus			54.17	13.14	41.04

* Assume net investment at year 10 (and all future net investment) earns a cost of capital return (or zero EVA).

---

[4] Since we are using NOPAT from the EVA income statement, we must use *net* (of accumulated depreciation) operating assets from the EVA balance sheet—recall Chapter 6. We could use gross operating profit after tax (GOPAT) and gross investment to obtain the same EVA results.

[5] Again, the dollar units assumed in the illustration are a matter of detail rather than substance.

In a similar manner, Exhibit 7.1 shows how to estimate economic profit for the rest of the horizon period, covering years 3 to 10. Notice that the estimated economic profit for year 11 is $41.04. This figure equals the assessed NOPAT for year 11, at $54.17, less the capital charge, at $13.14, on the beginning of year 11 (or end of year 10) net invested capital. Moreover, the one-step-ahead EVA figure for the residual period results because of our *simplifying* assumption in Chapter 6 that the marginal return on net invested capital, MROC, at the end of the horizon period equals the (marginal) cost of invested capital COC. Equivalently, the economic profit (and resulting NPV) on net invested capital at year 10 equals zero, such that the overall projected EVA remains unchanged, at $41.04.[6]

VALUATION OF ECONOMIC PROFIT

Exhibit 7.2 shows how to "roll up" the economic profit estimates into the NPV generated during the horizon years and the NPV generated during the residual period. The sum of these two NPV figures is the total net creation of wealth that has been added to the firm's invested capital. Holding market forces constant, this is a reflection of the wealth that has been created (or destroyed) by the firm's internal and external (via corporate acquisitions, etc.) investment decisions.

Exhibit 7.2 shows that the cumulative present value of the estimated economic profit stream during the horizon period is $127.63. This figure can be interpreted as the NPV generated from economic profit during the horizon years. In turn, with economic profit perpetuity of $41.04 commencing in year 11, we see that the firm's residual EVA value (or NPV at year 10) is $410.40 (*rounded*). With our simplifying assumptions, this NPV figure is calculated according to:

$$
\begin{aligned}
NPV(10) &= \text{Present value at Year 10 of future EVA} \\
&= EVA(11)/COC \\
&= \$41.04/0.10 = \$410.40
\end{aligned}
$$

Upon discounting the residual EVA value back to the current period, we obtain the NPV of the economic profit stream generated during the residual years, at $158.21. Also, upon adding up the NPV of economic profit generated during horizon *and* residual years, we obtain

---

[6] In other words, if MROC equals COC, then the *change* in EVA from period T to $T + 1$ is zero because the *change* in NOPAT, at $1.58, is equal to the dollar capital charge on the end-of-horizon period net investment of $15.83.

the firm's overall net creation of wealth from existing and anticipated future assets not currently in place.

$$NPV(0) = NPV(\text{Horizon years}) + NPV(\text{Residual years})$$
$$= \$127.63 + \$158.21 = \$285.84$$

With an initial capital base of $40.00, the firm's estimated enterprise value is thus $325.84:

$$EV = C + NPV$$
$$= \$40.00 + \$285.84 = \$325.84$$

Moreover, with long-term debt at $12 and five shares of common stock outstanding, the firm's warranted stock price is:

$$\text{Warranted stock price} = [EV - Debt]/Shares$$
$$= [\$325.84 - \$12]/5 = \$62.77$$

EXHIBIT 7.2   Valuation of Economic Profit

Year	EVA	Pres.Val. 10%	Cum. PV
1	$10.95	$9.95	$9.95
2	12.74	10.53	20.48
3	14.80	11.12	31.60
4	17.18	11.73	43.34
5	19.90	12.36	55.69
6	23.04	13.00	68.70
7	26.64	13.67	82.37
8	30.79	14.36	96.73
9	35.55	15.08	111.81
10	41.04	15.82	127.63
	Residual Value	410.36	158.21
	NPV		285.84
	Capital		40.00
	Corp.Val		325.84
	LT Debt		12.00
	Equity		313.84
	Share OS		5.00
	Price		62.77

Not surprisingly, the enterprise value and the warranted stock price are the same figures that we obtained before using the traditional free cash flow approach (see Chapter 6). As explained above, the EVA approach to enterprise valuation provides managers and investors with a *direct* assessment of the wealth that is being added (*via* discounted economic profit on existing and anticipated future growth assets) to the firm's invested capital.

INVESTMENT OPPORTUNITIES

In the EVA model, the firm's enterprise value is defined as invested capital *plus* aggregate net present value. With a simple rearrangement to the model, we can look at that part of the firm's enterprise value that is attributed to economic profit generated by existing assets *and* the EVA contribution due to future investment (or growth) opportunities. Taken together, the two economic profit sources determine the firm's aggregate net present value.

In this context, the firm's enterprise value can be split into two components: (1) the present value of a NOPAT perpetuity generated by existing assets, NOPAT/COC, and (2) the net present value of the firm's anticipated investment opportunities, G_f according to:[7]

$$EV = NOPAT/COC + G_f$$

The obvious question at this point is how to estimate the NPV contribution of the firm's anticipated investment opportunities, G_f. While several discounted cash flow approaches exist to estimate the market value of future investment opportunities, we'll look at a simplified version of the "T-period" EVA model.[8]

T-Period EVA Model

In the T-period EVA model, the investor makes an assessment of the *number* of periods that the firm can generate *positive* economic profit on its anticipated future assets. This boils down to an estimate of the number of positive EVA periods that managers and investors perceive that

---

[7] The enterprise valuation model presented here is based on the classic "Investment Opportunities Approach to Valuation" described by Fama and Miller—see Eugene F. Fama and Merton H. Miller, *The Theory of Finance* (New York: Holt, Rinehart and Winston, Inc., 1972).

[8] For an insightful discussion of the T-period EVA model, see G. Bennett Stewart III, *The Quest for Value* (New York: Harper Collins, 1991).

the firm can invest in real assets having an after-tax return on invested capital that exceeds the expected COC. In formal terms, the T-period economic profit model can be expressed as follows:

$$G_f = (\text{AEP} \times T)/\text{COC}(1 + \text{COC})$$

In this expression. AEP is the average economic profit (or annualized EVA) on new investments, while T is the estimated number of positive EVA periods.

For simplicity, let's make the assumption that (1) economic profit earned during the horizon years is attributed entirely to existing assets,[9] while (2) any economic profit generated during the residual period is due to future assets *not* currently in place.[10] Also, let's make the simplifying assumption that the estimated economic profit for year 11, at $41.04, can be used to proxy the average economic profit generated during the residual years. Based on these simplifications, the T-period EVA model suggests that a large portion of the firm's NPV and enterprise value can be determined by estimating the number of periods that it can generate positive economic profit during the residual years.

For example, with no restriction on the number of years that the firm can earn economic profit of $41.04 during the residual period, we found that the firm's estimated NPV at year 10 was $410.40 [$41.04/0.10, *rounded*]. This residual EVA value has a current NPV of $158.21. Notice too that in the absence of economic profit growth during the residual years that the NPV of $158.21 is the maximum *current* value of the firm's estimated EVA stream during the posthorizon years. This, in turn, sets upper limit values on both the firm's aggregate NPV and its warranted enterprise value. Drawing values from before, we have $285.84 and $325.84, respectively.

In general, the T-period EVA model presumes that a firm's opportunity to earn positive economic profit during the residual period is limited by technological obsolescence and/or competition in the market for goods and services. If correct, then managers and investors must make an assessment of the number of periods that a company can *realistically* earn positive economic profit for the future. By implication, we can say that investors will not "pay" for negative EVA generated during the residual period covering years "$T + 1$" to infinity.

---

[9] This simplification presumes that the firm's existing capital is worthless at the end of the ten-year horizon period.

[10] In the previous EVA illustration, we assumed *no* future investment opportunities beyond the horizon period. While we utilize the same numbers in the T-period EVA illustration that follows, the goal here is to shed some basic insight on EVA investment opportunities (or periods) without getting bogged down in detailed formulas that model the firm's investment opportunities.

With these considerations, Exhibit 7.3 shows how the NPV of the firm's future growth opportunities varies as the number of positive EVA periods goes from five to 100 years. At $410.40, the exhibit shows the upper limit value of the economic profit stream generated during the residual period. Notice how the residual value changes as "T" varies from five to 100 years of positive economic profit. Based on present value dynamics, we see (not shown graphically) that the residual value function *asymptotically* approaches a line that represents the present value of the EVA perpetuity.

Exhibit 7.3 shows that with just five years of positive EVA during the residual years, the NPV of future EVA opportunities is only $59.97 (see RV(0)). Stating this finding in terms of the firm's enterprise value and its warranted stock price, we obtain $227.61 and $43.12 respectively. In contrast, with 20 and 30 years of positive economic profit during the residual period, the NPV values of future EVA opportunities are $134.69 and $149.14. Exhibit 7.3 also shows that with "T" of 20 and 30 years, the firm's enterprise values are $302.33 and $316.78. The corresponding stock price estimates are $58.07 and $60.96 respectively.

EXHIBIT 7.3 T-Period EVA Model

COC	10%
Horizon Years	10

Residual Period	Annuity	RV(T)	RV(0)	NPV(0)*	EV	Stock Price	Price Ratio %
5	$41.04	$155.56	$59.97	$187.61	$227.61	$43.12	68.70
10	41.04	252.15	97.21	224.85	264.85	50.57	80.56
20	41.04	349.36	134.69	262.33	302.33	58.07	92.51
30	41.04	386.84	149.14	276.78	316.78	60.96	97.11
40	41.04	401.29	154.72	282.35	322.35	62.07	98.89
50	41.04	406.86	156.86	284.50	324.50	62.50	99.57
60	41.04	409.01	157.69	285.32	325.32	62.66	99.83
70	41.04	409.84	158.01	285.64	325.64	62.73	99.94
80	41.04	410.16	158.13	285.77	325.77	62.75	99.98
90	41.04	410.28	158.18	285.81	325.81	62.76	99.99
100	41.04	410.33	158.20	285.83	325.83	62.77	100.00
Infinite	$41.04	$410.36	$158.21	$285.84	$325.84	$62.77	100.00

* NPV(0) reflects present value of EVA during horizon and residual years

With *unlimited* positive economic profit in the residual years, we see that the firm's estimated enterprise value is $325.84 and its warranted stock price is $62.77. These are the values that we initially obtained before. Notice that with five years of positive EVA in residual years that the estimated stock price is only 69% ($43.12/$62.77) of the price obtained with unlimited positive economic profit. With 20 and 30 years of positive economic profit in posthorizon years, the warranted stock prices are 93% and 97%, respectively, of the price obtained with unlimited positive economic profit.[11] Thus, managers and investors must make an accurate assessment of the number of periods that a company can earn economic profit for the future in order to have a *realistic* view of enterprise value and stock price.

Market-Implied Investment Period

The generalized T-period EVA model can be rearranged to solve for the market-implied number of years of positive economic profit on future investment opportunities. The following inputs are required to solve for market-implied T that is imbedded in a firm's NPV and enterprise value:

- Enterprise value (outstanding debt plus equity values)[12]
- NOPAT perpetuity (or annualized equivalent of periodic NOPAT on existing assets)
- Average economic profit on new investments
- Cost of capital (COC)

Upon solving for the market implied number of growth periods, T, that the firm expects to earn positive economic profit, we obtain:

$$T = \left[EV - \frac{NOPAT}{COC}\right] \times \frac{COC(1 + COC)}{AEP}$$

Upon calculating market implied T, managers and investors can then assess whether this figure is consistent with a company's "warranted" number of periods to earn positive economic profit on future investments.

Based on our previous illustration, if the actual number of positive EVA periods was, say, ten years rather than 30 years, then the firm's enterprise value and stock price would be *overvalued* in the capital market. Based on the figures supplied before, the firm's stock price would fall over time from $60.96 to $50.57—unless of course the firm's managers could preempt the decline by surprising investors positively about the number of periods that the firm could earn positive economic profit for the future. Conversely, a company's stock would be *undervalued* if investors incorrectly perceived that the number of positive EVA periods was, say, ten years when in fact the warranted EVA period was longer.

OVERVIEW OF COST OF CAPITAL EFFECTS

As with future growth opportunities, the cost of capital is yet another EVA factor that is central to enterprise valuation. While Chapter 11 is devoted to cost of capital measurement, we'll see here how *seemingly* small changes in COC can have a large impact on enterprise value and warranted stock price. Specifically, Exhibits 7.4 and 7.5 (table and graph, respectively) show what happens to the key components of enterprise value—including the NPV of economic profit generated during the horizon and residual years—and the warranted stock price when the cost of capital rises by 100 basis points (due to rising interest rates or heightened business uncertainty) or falls by 100 basis points (due to declining interest rates or reduced business uncertainty).[13]

With a 10% cost of capital, we found that the firm's enterprise value was $325.84. This figure includes the initial $40 capital investment *and* the NPV of economic profit generated during the horizon and post-horizon years—at $127.63 and $158.21, respectively. At that discount rate, the firm's warranted stock price is $62.77. However, Exhibits 7.4 and 7.5 also reveal that if the cost of capital were to decline from 10% to 9%—due perhaps to a general decline in interest rates or a decline in the required business risk premium—then the firm's enterprise value and warranted stock price would rise to $376.98 and $73.00. This 100-basis-point change in COC translates into a 15.69% rise in the firm's enterprise value.[14]

---

[13] Indeed, one would expect a dramatic rise in the equity risk premium (a component of the cost of equity) due to the tragic events of September 11, 2001. If correct, this would go a long way in helping to explain the sharp decline in stock prices that occurred in the aftermath of "9/11."

[14] This, of course, is the same percentage response to a change in COC that we observed before using the free cash flow model—see Chapter 6.

EXHIBIT 7.4 Cost of Capital Sensitivity Analysis: EVA Model

Rate %	Basis Pt. Change	NPV(H)	EVA T+1*	RV(T)	RV(0)	NPV(0)	Tot. Cap.	EV	Stock Price	% Change EV
8	−200	$151.30	$43.35	$541.84	$250.97	$402.28	$40.00	$442.28	$86.06	35.73
8.5	−150	144.99	42.77	503.17	222.54	367.54	40.00	407.54	79.11	25.07
9	−100	138.95	42.19	468.79	198.02	336.98	40.00	376.98	73.00	15.69
9.5	−50	133.17	41.61	438.04	176.75	309.93	40.00	349.93	67.59	7.39
10	0	127.63	41.04	410.36	158.21	285.84	40.00	325.84	62.77	0.00
10.5	50	122.32	40.46	385.32	141.97	264.29	40.00	304.29	58.46	−6.61
11	100	117.24	39.88	362.55	127.68	244.92	40.00	284.92	54.58	−12.56
11.5	150	112.36	39.30	341.76	115.07	227.44	40.00	267.44	51.09	−17.92
12	200	107.69	38.73	322.71	103.90	211.59	40.00	251.59	47.92	−22.79

* Assume net investment at T (and beyond) earns the relevant cost of capital.

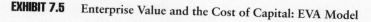

EXHIBIT 7.5 Enterprise Value and the Cost of Capital: EVA Model

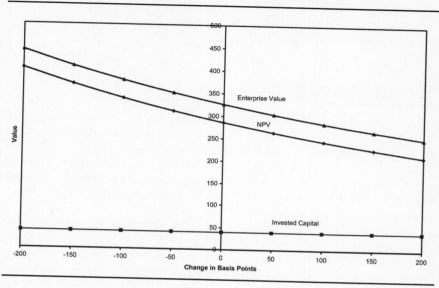

On the other hand, if the firm's cost of capital were to rise by 100 basis points—from 10% to 11%—then the two exhibits show that the firm's enterprise value and warranted stock price would decline to $284.92 and $54.58 respectively. This in turn represents a 12.56% decline in the firm's warranted enterprise value. As with the present value impact of changes in a company's future investment opportunities, we again see (recall Chapter 6) that enterprise value and warranted stock price are impacted in a nonlinear way by fluctuations in the firm's cost of capital.

Pricing Implications

The investment opportunities and cost of capital illustrations provides some strategic pricing insight for managers and investors. First, it appears that uncertainty about the number of years that a firm can generate positive economic profit on new investments and/or uncertainty about the firm's *true* cost of capital can have a material impact on both its enterprise value and its warranted stock price. Second, there are changes in T and COC that can produce the same impact on the price of any company's stock. For example, the warranted stock price—see Exhibits 7.3 and 7.4, respectively—drops from $62.77 to about $51 when T declines to 10 years or the cost of capital, COC, rises to

11.5%.[15] Hence, anything that managers can do to either increase the positive EVA investment period and/or decrease the weighted average cost of capital will surprise investors *positively* and have a meaningful impact on both enterprise value and stock price.

RECONCILIATION OF EVA MODELS

While examining the EVA model, we focused on two standard formulations for the firm's enterprise value. In this context, we said that the firm's enterprise value is equal to (1) invested capital, C, *plus* aggregate NPV and, (2) the present value of a NOPAT perpetuity on existing assets *plus* the NPV of all future investment opportunities—as captured by G_f. We can now reconcile these equivalent expressions for the firm's warranted enterprise value as follows:

To begin, note that NOPAT can be expressed as a capital charge earned on the firm's existing assets *plus* the EVA generated by existing assets already in place. From this, we can see why the firm's enterprise value is equal to invested capital, C, plus the NPV of all future economic profit arising from both existing assets, EVA/COC, and expected future assets, G_f, according to:

$$
\begin{aligned}
EV &= NOPAT/COC + G_f \\
   &= [COC \times C + EVA]/COC + G_f \\
   &= C + [EVA/COC + G_f] \\
   &= C + NPV
\end{aligned}
$$

As before, the firm's enterprise value is in fact equal to invested capital *plus* aggregate NPV. In turn, the firm's aggregate net present value is equal to the present value of all future economic profit.

Based on the preceding developments, we see that a company's NPV has two primary sources: (1) the present value of economic profit generated by the firm's existing assets, namely EVA/COC, and (2) the NPV contribution attributed to economic profit "improvement" from anticipated future assets not currently in place as captured by G_f in the enterprise valuation model. Moreover, economic profit—whether earned on existing or future assets—is positive *if and only if* the firm invests in real assets having an after-tax return on invested capital that on average exceeds the weighted average cost of capital.

---

[15] Specifically, if T falls from infinity to ten years, or COC rises from 10% to 11.5%, then the stock price declines from $62.77 to about $51—actually, the price is $50.57 with T at ten years, and $51.09 with COC at 11.5% separately.

SUMMARY

The EVA model has several attractive features and—like all DCF models—some limitations. On the positive side, the economic profit model provides a *direct* means by which managers and investors can assess the NPV contribution from existing assets as well as future growth opportunities. In this context, the firm's total creation of wealth—as measured by its NPV—is equal to the present value of all future economic profit generated by existing assets and anticipated future assets (or growth opportunities) not currently in place. With discounted positive economic profit a company is a wealth creator, while with discounted negative economic profit a company is—unfortunately—a wealth destroyer.

While EVA valuation is intuitively appealing, managers and investors need to realize that the resulting estimates of enterprise value and warranted stock price are *highly* sensitive to the model inputs. We found that a seemingly small change in the firm's anticipated future investment period and/or its cost of capital can have a meaningful impact on the value of the firm and its outstanding shares. Moreover, with uncertainty about model inputs, it is clear that managers must do everything within their responsibility and control to (honestly!) surprise investors *positively* about key economic profit parameters such as the EVA investment period and the cost of capital, COC.

CHAPTER 8

Traditional Measures of Profitability and Success

This chapter focuses on how to evaluate companies using traditional measures of profitability and success. In this context, we'll examine the benefits and limitations of using traditional metrics—such as return on equity (ROE)—to evaluate companies before moving on to a detailed investigation of how to evaluate companies, industries, and even market economies from an economic profit perspective. While *numerous* financial measures are available, a manager or investor is often left wondering which metrics—albeit, traditional or EVA based—are most important to emphasize from a shareholder value perspective. This chapter sheds light on traditional measures that are available to evaluate companies while the rest of this book focuses on how to analyze companies in an economic profit context.[1]

OVERVIEW OF FINANCIAL RATIOS

Traditional measures of efficiency and profitability can be split up into several categories of ratios. These broad categories include activity ratios, liquidity ratios, interest coverage ratios, debt ratios, and profitability ratios. Activity ratios measure the ability of a firm to efficiently turn its assets, including inventory and receivables. Liquidity ratios such as the current ratio and quick ratio provide an assessment of a firm's

---

[1] Numerous textbooks exist on traditional measures of profitability and success. The goal of this chapter is to review traditional metrics such as ROE as a background for comparison with the EVA approach to company analysis.

ability to meet its short-term financial obligations. In turn, coverage ratios measure the firm's ability to cover fixed charges such as interest expense, lease obligations, and even preferred stock dividends via the fixed interest payment coverage ratio. Likewise, managers and investors to assess whether a firm is over or under-leveraged relative to a perceived "target" mix of debt and equity use corporate leverage ratios including the debt-to-equity ratio and debt-to-capital ratio.

From the investor or shareholder's perspective (a focus that we'll emphasize in this chapter), emphasis is placed on growth rates and profitability ratios, measured either over time or in a cross section with other comparable companies. Moreover, in practice, growth rates and profitability ratios are often juxtaposed with company valuation measures—such as the price-to-earnings and price-to-book value ratios—to assess the relative attractiveness of a company's common stock. A partial list of traditional growth and profitability measures include:

- Growth in Revenue
- Growth in Earnings (or Cash Flow)
- Growth in Book Value
- Return on Equity
- Return on Capital
- Return on Assets

Likewise, a part listing of traditional valuation measures used by managers and investors to assess the attractiveness of a company's stock include:

- Price/Revenue Ratio
- Price/Cash Flow Ratio
- Price/Earnings Ratio
- Price/Book Value Ratio
- Value/Replacement Cost Ratio (Tobin's Q)[2]
- Dividend Yield

---

[2] Tobin's Q is defined as the ratio of market value of assets to replacement cost of assets. Given the availability of accounting data, we'll focus in this chapter on the price/book value ratio as opposed to the more complex enterprise value-to-replacement cost of assets. For an interesting discussion of the conceptual and practical application of this economic valuation ratio, see Pamela P. Peterson and David R. Peterson, *Company Performance and Measures of Value Added*, The Research Foundation of the Institute of Chartered Financial Analysts (Charlottesville, VA: AIMR, 1996).

We'll begin with a review of traditional measures of profitability and success by looking at how to estimate revenue and earnings growth rates. Next, we'll focus on the "Dupont formula,"[3] with its emphasis on decomposition of a company's return on equity (ROE) into several underlying financial ratios. In practice, managers and investors use this formula to highlight the information content of a company's return on assets (among other ratios) and financial leverage. We'll then see how to evaluate profitability ratios in the context of traditional valuation measures such as price-to-earnings and the price-to-book value ratios, and we'll see how traditional profitability measures can be "rolled up" into a fundamental stock return (FSR) for comparison with other companies along the Securities Market Line. The latter development is important because traditional metrics alone are rather meaningless without a reconciliation of company fundamentals with the investor's (or shareholder's) required return on invested capital.[4]

FOREWORD ON TRADITIONAL PERFORMANCE MEASURES

Managers and investors often speak in terms of revenue, earnings, and cash flow growth, as well as a firm's rate of return on equity and capital. Although revenue is *not* profit, a company must still produce and market a meaningful product in order to show positive accounting earnings (let alone positive economic earnings). Likewise, a company's revenue must grow over time for it to show sustainable profit growth. For excessive cost cutting and a dearth of capital investment simply to show higher profits will eventually have a negative impact on the firm's long-term revenue and earnings growth capabilities. These adverse profit and investment considerations also apply to the firm's need to generate a solid return on equity. After all, it is the shareholders who are the firm's ultimate owners, and it is their financial capital that is at most risk when a company makes imprudent short-term decisions that adversely impact the firm's long-term growth prospects.

---

[3] The traditional "Dupont formula" is explained in most any textbook on finance and investments. Also, the decomposition of return ratios into profit margin and turnover ratios is attributed to E.I. duPont de Nemours & Company (American Management Association 1960).
[4] Reconciliation of asset or capital returns with the cost of invested capital is, after all, the essence of economic profit (EVA) approach to company analysis.

GROWTH RATES

To illustrate the role of growth in traditional company analysis, we'll use selected financial information from the 2001 Annual Report of State Street Corporation. Specifically, in the 2001 Letter to Shareholders (see Exhibit 8.1), Chairman and CEO David Spina emphasizes the strategic financial goals of the banking and financial services company in terms of (1) sustainable *real* revenue (and earnings) growth of 12.5%, and (2) a *reaffirmed* target return on equity (ROE) goal of 18% for years 2000 to 2010.[5]

To see whether State Street's *actual* performance is consistent with its strategic financial goals, Exhibit 8.2 reports selected income and balance sheet items obtained from the bank's Annual Report for the 1997–2001 period. These items include revenue, net operating income, per share (operating) earnings and dividends from the income statement followed by equity and assets from the balance sheet.

State Street's 2001 operating revenue, $3,914 million, can always be viewed as the future value (FV) of the 1997 revenue of $2,342 million. In this context, the bank's 2001 revenue results from *four* years of compounding the initial present value figure of $2,342 according to:

$$FV = PV^*(1 + g_r)^4$$

EXHIBIT 8.1 State Street Corporation 2001 Letter to Shareholders

"We continue to differentiate ourselves by stating a goal for revenue growth. We have reaffirmed our goal of achieving 12.5% real compound annual growth from 2000 to 2010, although, as has been true in the past, we do not expect to achieve that rate every year in the ten-year period.

Our supporting goal for return on stockholders' equity is to achieve 18% annually. In 2001, we exceeded that goal by delivering operating ROE of 18.2%.

> *David A. Spina*
> *Chairman and*
> *Chief Executive Officer*

Source: State Street 2001 Annual Report, page 7.

---

[5] State Street's revenue *and* earnings growth targets for the 1990s were 12.5% in real terms. The bank's past ROE target of 18% is also projected for the decade 2000 to 2010. Financial information for State Street Corporation is obtained from the 2001 Annual Report. See *www.statestreet.com*.

EXHIBIT 8.2   State Street Corporation Selected Income and Balance Sheet Information (U.S. $Millions, *Except* Per Share Figures)

Year	2001	2000	1999	1998	1997	4-Year Growth	4-Year Real Growth*
Operating Revenue	$3,914	$3,615	$3,119	$2,765	$2,342	0.1370	0.1129
Operating Earnings	661	595	489	436	380	0.1484	0.1243
Operating EPS	2.00	1.81	1.49	1.33	1.16	0.1459	0.1218
Dividends per share	0.405	0.345	0.30	0.26	0.22	0.1648	0.1407
Stockholders' Equity	3,845	3,262	2,652	2,311	1,995	0.1783	0.1542
Total Assets	$69,896	$69,298	$60,896	$47,082	$37,975	0.1648	0.1407

* Based on 2.41% annualized inflation rate, as reported by the U.S. Department of Labor, Bureau of Labor Statistics. See *www.bls.gov.*
Source: State Street 2001 Annual Report, page 7. See *www.statestreet.com.*

Upon inserting the bank's revenue figures into the future value (FV) expression, and solving for the four-year annualized growth rate, g_r, we obtain:

$$g_r = (FV/PV)^{\frac{1}{4}} - 1.0$$
$$= (\$3,914/\$2,342)^{0.25} - 1.0$$
$$= 0.1370 \text{ or } 13.7\%$$

Additionally, State Street's four-year operating earnings growth, g_e, can be determined in a similar manner. At 14.84%, the annualized nominal earnings growth is calculated according to:

$$g_e = (\$661/\$380)^{0.25} - 1.0$$
$$= 0.1484 \text{ or } 14.84\%$$

Moreover, in order to obtain the *real* growth rates for State Street Corporation—per State Street's strategic financial objectives—we need to *subtract* the four-year annualized inflation rate from the nominal revenue and earnings growth rates. With annualized inflation running at 2.41% for the December 1997 to December 2001 years, the real revenue and earnings growth rates for the bank were 11.29% and 12.43%, respectively.[6] Since these percentages are near the 12.5% real growth target set by State Street's Board of Directors, the actual revenue and earnings growth figures are largely consistent with the stated financial goals of the bank.

Indeed, State Street Corporation's name changes in recent years—from State Street Bank and Trust Company to State Street Boston to its present name—were largely designed to emphasize the global growth orientation of its financial services operations. This is consistent with the company's growing dominance in the nonlending and fee-generating areas of global master trust/custody, securities processing, foreign exchange trading, global securities lending and, especially, global asset management (SSgA). The 2001 Annual Report also reveals that State Street Corporation derives about 72% (2,832/3,914) of its 2001 operating revenue from such consistent-growth and relatively stable fee income sources.[7]

---

[6] Inflation data used in this illustration is obtained from the U.S. Department of Labor (Bureau of Labor Statistics) Web site. See *www.bls.gov*.

[7] Indeed, Exhibit 8.2 shows that equity and assets at State Street Corporation were growing in *real* terms at 15.42% and 14.07%, respectively.

ROE INSIGHTS FROM THE DUPONT FORMULA

Let's now look at the information content of return on equity (ROE) as a traditional measure of financial success. From an accounting perspective, return on equity is *simply* net (operating) income divided by stockholder's equity.[8] The Dupont formula expands this definition by showing that the firm's return on equity can be obtained by *multiplying* return on assets (ROA) by a corporate leverage factor—typically measured by the ratio of total assets to stockholder's equity, A/E. In turn, the firm's return on assets (ROA) is measured by dividing net (operating) income by total assets (NI/A), or equivalently, by multiplying the net profit margin (Net Income/Sales or NI/S) *times* the asset turnover ratio (Sales/Assets or S/A). In more formal terms:

$$\begin{aligned} ROE &= ROA \times Leverage \\ &= NI/A \times A/E \\ &= [NI/S \times S/A] \times A/E \end{aligned}$$

Consider Exhibit 8.3. It is interesting to see that State Street's operating return on equity, save year 2001, is consistent with its stated ROE target of 18% for the 1990s and the century turn.[9] To the unsuspecting investor, this finding might seem surprising, especially since the company's operating return on assets (ROA) ranges from about 0.8% to 1.0%. For example, the operating return on assets for State Street Corporation for year 2001 was 0.95%.

EXHIBIT 8.3 State Street Corporation: Selected Financial Ratios and ROE Breakdown

Year	2001	2000	1999	1998	1997
Net Operating Margin	0.1689	0.1646	0.1568	0.1577	0.1623
Asset Turnover	0.0560	0.0522	0.0512	0.0587	0.0617
Operating ROA	0.0095	0.0086	0.0080	0.0093	0.0100
Operating ROE	0.1719	0.1824	0.1844	0.1887	0.1905
Implied FLM*	18.18	21.24	22.96	20.37	19.04

* ROE/ROA

---

[8] We'll use net operating income in the ROE calculation for State Street. This is consistent with State Street's earnings focus in the 2001 Annual Report.

[9] State Street *boasts* operating ROE of 18.2% for year 2001. On the conservative side, operating ROE is 17.19% if one divides net operating income, at $661 million, by stockholders' equity ($3,845 million, as reported in "Selected Financial Data" of the 2001 Annual Report). The latter ROE is consistent with the 17.2% figure for 2001 reported by Value Line.

$$ROA = NI/A$$
$$= 661/69,896 = 0.0095 \text{ or } 0.95\%$$

However, the seemingly low ROA for State Street can be interpreted in at least two ways. First, we see that in 2001 State Street earned $661 million on a relatively large asset base of $69,896 million. Second, the seemingly low return on operating assets for that year can be attributed to a fairly attractive net profit margin (NPM), at 16.89%, multiplied by a very *low* asset turnover ratio of 0.056:

$$ROA = NPM \times S/A$$
$$= [661/3,914] \times [3,914/69,896]$$
$$= [0.1689] \times [0.056] = 0.0095 \text{ or } 0.95\%$$

In turn, the Dupont formula can be used to explain the large difference between the ROE of State Street and its underlying ROA. Exhibit 8.3 shows that the bank's 2001 ROE is 17.19% while its operating ROA is only 0.95%. With these ratios, the *implied* leverage factor for State Street Corporation must be 18.18. That is, according to the Dupont formula, implied leverage is just the ratio of return on equity to return on assets. For year 2001, we obtain:

$$\text{Implied leverage} = ROE/ROA$$
$$= 0.1719/0.0095 = 18.18$$

Moreover, another look at State Street's 2001 Annual Report (selected items in Exhibit 8.2) reveals that Stockholder's Equity was $3,845 million, while total assets equals $69,896 million. These equity and asset figures yield a leverage factor of 18.18 that is, of course, consistent with the implied leverage factor.

Rolling up the Results

The Dupont formula reveals that State Street Corporation's seemingly low return on assets, around 0.8% to 1% per year, is generally "geared up" by a leverage factor that is consistent with the 18% ROE target of the bank. These ratio findings are shown in Exhibit 8.3. With a financial leverage factor over 18, it should be apparent that anything the bank's managers can do to improve its operating efficiency—either through improved operating margins or asset turns—will have a multiplied ROE effect many times over. Taken together, we see that ROE is related to the net profit margin, the asset turnover ratio, and the leverage multiplier according to:

$$
\begin{aligned}
\mathrm{ROE} &= \mathrm{ROA} \times \mathrm{Leverage} \\
&= (\mathrm{NPM} \times \mathrm{AT}) \times [\mathrm{A/E}] \\
&= (\mathrm{NI/S} \times \mathrm{S/A}) \times [1/(1 - \mathrm{DR})]
\end{aligned}
$$

In this ROE expression, ROA is expressed as the net profit margin (net income over sales) *times* the asset turnover ratio—measured by the sales-to-assets ratio. Moreover, the last expression in the ROE formulation shows that the leverage factor, A/E, can be written as the *inverse* of one-*minus* the debt ratio (DR). The debt ratio in the traditional Dupont formula results from *dividing* total liabilities (including a firm's current liabilities) by total assets.

COKE'S CLASSIC "ROE FORMULA"

Before proceeding to examine some traditional valuation measures, let's contrast State Street's 2001 ROE with that of Coca-Cola in the soft drinks and beverages sector.[10] At 34.92% ($3,969 million/11,366 million), Coke's 2001 return on equity is not only considerably higher than State Street's—due to higher growth opportunities—but the "packaging" of the ROE figures is *noticeably* different. In contrast with the bank, Coca-Cola's 2001 return on assets (ROA) and financial leverage multiplier were 17.71% and 1.972, respectively. With these figures, Coke's classic "ROE-formula" for 2001 consists of:

$$
\begin{aligned}
\mathrm{ROE} &= \mathrm{ROA} \times \mathrm{Leverage} \\
&= [3,969/22,417] \times [22,417/11,366] \\
&= 0.1771 \times 1.972 = 0.3492 \text{ or } 34.92\%
\end{aligned}
$$

Coca-Cola's high return on equity largely results from its ROA of 17.71%. This robust figure is due to Coke's ability to generate solid profits on its assets—as evidenced by a net profit margin of 19.75% ($3,969/$20,092) in the presence of an asset turnover ratio of 0.8963 ($20,092/$22,417). From a comparative perspective, Coke's "classic" ROE, at 34.92%, is attributed to its *high* return on assets, while State Street's lower—yet still attractive—ROE figure of 17.19% is due to favorable profits being earned on a relatively *small* amount of bank equity capital—in the presence of their worldwide asset base of $69,896 million.

---

[10] Financial data for Coca-Cola is obtained from the company's 2001 Annual Report. See *www.coca-cola.com*.

TRADITIONAL VALUATION MEASURES

In the traditional realm of determining whether a stock is mispriced, investors look at relative valuation measures such as the price/earnings, price/cash flow, and price/book value ratios. This relative approach to company valuation is thought productive because investors should (1) look unfavorably at stocks of companies that are selling at *excessively* high multiples of earnings and book value, while (2) they should look favorably at companies that have *unjustifiably* had their stock price driven down too far and too fast relative to the firm's underlying earnings potential. In other words, stocks of companies with abnormally high earnings/price, book/price and dividend yields may be attractive buy opportunities, while stocks of companies having excessively low earnings and book yields may be sell or shorting candidates.[11]

To examine these price relative (or yield) concepts we'll again use information from the 2001 Annual Report of State Street Corporation. The annual report to shareholders provides summary data that can be used to calculate some key valuation measures. The relevant per share figures for the banking and financial services company are shown in Exhibit 8.4. Likewise, with knowledge of State Street's 2001 closing stock price, at $52.25, we can convert the per share figures to key valuation measures and yields as shown in Exhibit 8.5.

EXHIBIT 8.4   State Street Corporation: Selected Per Share Information (Year-End 2001)

Revenue Per Share[a]	$11.84
Earnings Per Share	$2.00
Dividends Per Share	$0.405
Book Value Per Share	$11.63
Closing Stock Price	$52.25

[a] Using the "fully diluted shares" figure in the 2001 Annual Report gives State Street's Operating Revenue Per Share of $11.84 ($3,914 million/330.5 million shares).
Source: State Street 2001 Annual Report

---

[11] Unlike traditional valuation metrics, one of the major benefits of the EVA approach to securities analysis is that a manager or investor knows *why* a company has a low price-to-earnings or price-to-book value ratio. This is because the price-to-book ratio, for example, is a function of the firm's ability to generate positive of negative NPV.

EXHIBIT 8.5   State Street Corporation: Price Relatives and Yields (Year-End 2001)

Price/Revenue Ratio	Revenue Yield
4.413×	22.7%
Price/Earnings Ratio	Earnings Yield
26.125	3.8%
Price/Dividend Ratio	Dividend Yield
129.012×	0.8%
Price/Book Ratio	Book Yield
4.493×	22.3%

Data for calculations: State Street 2001 Annual Report

The obvious issue at this point is how to interpret the price relative and yield information shown in Exhibit 8.5. To address this question, the manager or investor should ask whether State Street's stock *should* be selling for 26 times earnings, as well as multiple of 129 times its per share dividend. At first glance, these price relatives seem out of line since Value Line, for example, reports that bank stocks during 2001 were selling for about 19 times earnings with a dividend yield of around 3% (equivalently, a price-to-dividend multiple of 33.33).[12] If one views State Street as a typical "bank," then the stock was obviously overvalued in the traditional realm due to excessive price multiples and (therefore) abnormally low yields. A decline in stock price would therefore lead to a concomitant fall in the price-to-earnings ratio and a rise in the dividend yield.

On the other hand, the 2001 Annual Report for State Street Corporation reveals that about 72% ($2,832 million/$3,914) of its revenue is generated from the consistent-growth "fee revenue" side of the business as opposed to revenue generation from traditional forms of lending.[13] These fee revenue sources include master trust/custody, securities processing, foreign exchange trading, global securities lending, and global asset management (SSgA). From this perspective, the seemingly high price relatives and low yields (dividend or earnings' yields) were a sign that investors were optimistic—although not necessarily overly so— about the firm's *future* growth opportunities in servicing financial assets worldwide.

Also, it is noteworthy that State Street's 2001 loan-to-asset ratio is *only* 7.6% (down from 15.2% in 1995), while Value Line reports an

[12] *Value Line Investment Survey* (New York, NY) May 31, 2002, p. 2101.
[13] To affirm its strategic focus on servicing financial assets worldwide, State Street sold its commercial banking business in 1999.

average loan-to-asset ratio of about 46% for firms they cover in the banking sector. Hence, the seemingly high price relatives and low yield figures reported for State Street Corporation in Exhibit 8.5 may be a *fundamental* way of saying that the company is not simply your typical "bank."

FUNDAMENTAL STOCK RETURN (FSR)

Up to this point we have looked at several traditional measures of profitability and success—including ROE, ROA and relative valuation measures such as the price-to-earnings and price-to-book value ratios. However, we have said little if anything about how these metrics relate to the underlying ability of a company to generate a return on its outstanding stock. In this regard, a measure called the "fundamental stock return (FSR)"[14] is helpful in assessing the expected return that a company could potentially earn based on its fundamentals. Specifically, the fundamental stock return (FSR) is equal to the sum of the assessed dividend yield (dy) and the expected internal capital generation rate, $icgr$.[15] In turn, the capital generation rate is equal to the earnings "plowback" ratio, PBR, times the expected return on equity, ROE. In more formal terms, a company's fundamental stock return can be expressed as:

$$FSR = dy + icgr$$
$$= d/p + (1 - DPR) \times ROE$$
$$= d/p + PBR \times ROE$$

In this expression, DPR is the firm's dividend payout ratio, and d/p is the dividend yield on its outstanding common stock. Also, PBR is the plowback ratio, measured by one *minus* DPR.

Since PBR is the fraction of earnings that are retained by a company for internal investment in real assets, the fundamental stock return

---

[14] Fabozzi and Grant explain the concept of "rolling up" company ratios into a fundamental stock return. See, Frank J. Fabozzi and James L. Grant, *Equity Portfolio Management* (New Hope, PA: Frank J. Fabozzi Associates, 1999).

[15] If one makes the simplifying assumption that a firm's dividends and earnings grow at a constant rate each year, then the "fundamental stock return" is analogous to the "internal rate of return (IRR)" on a company's stock. With variable growth, the IRR formula is a more complete representation of the implied return on a firm's stock, as it reflects that rate which sets the present value of anticipated cash flows (dividends, free cash flow, etc.) equal to the firm's current stock price. We'll cover valuation models at a later point.

shows that capital growth is related to financial happenings at the company level. That is, the firm's internal capital generation rate, *icgr*, derives its value from the product of the fraction of earnings retained for future investment, PBR, (which is a reflection of added equity capital resulting from reinvestment of the firm's accounting profit) *times* the estimated return that the firm's managers can generate on those retained funds. ROE in the traditional realm of company analysis is that likely return of accounting profit on shareholders' equity. Hence, there are several reasons why managers and investors have viewed return on equity as a "pillar" of traditional financial analysis.

FSR APPLICATIONS

Let's look again at State Street Corporation to see how a manager or investor could assess the fundamental stock return (*FSR*) with knowledge of ROE and a few other financial ratios. We'll first estimate the internal capital generation rate for year 2001. The pertinent figures for this calculation are shown in Exhibit 8.6. In particular, the 2001 internal capital generation rate for State Street can be expressed as the product of the bank's[16] plowback ratio, at 0.7975 (alternatively, one *minus* DPR of 0.2025), *times* the operating return on owner's equity (ROE) of 17.19%:

$$icgr = PBR \times ROE$$
$$= 0.7975 \times 0.1719 = 0.1371 \text{ or } 13.71\%$$

EXHIBIT 8.6   State Street Corporation: Internal Capital Generation Rate and Fundamental Stock Return

Year	2001	2000	1999	1998	1997
Dividend yield	0.0078	0.0056	0.0082	0.0074	0.0076
DPR	0.2025	0.1906	0.2013	0.1955	0.1897
Plowback ratio	0.7975	0.8094	0.7987	0.8045	0.8103
Operating ROE	0.1719	0.1824	0.1844	0.1887	0.1905
Internal cap gen rate	0.1371	0.1476	0.1473	0.1518	0.1544
FSR	0.1449	0.1532	0.1555	0.1592	0.1619
Stock Price	$52.25	$62.11	$36.53	$35.06	$29.09
Rule of 72*	4.97	4.70	4.63	4.52	4.45

* 72/FSR %.

[16] The author continues to say "bank" for State Street Corporation out of habit.

Additionally, since ROE is the product of return on assets (ROA) *times* the leverage factor, the bank's internal capital generation rate, *icgr*, can also be expressed as:

$$icgr = PBR \times [ROA \times (A/E)]$$
$$= 0.7975 \times [0.0095 \times 18.18] = 0.1371$$

In turn, the internal capital generation rate can be combined with the State Street's annual dividend per share and year-end stock price to arrive at the fundamental return on the stock for 2001:[17]

$$FSR = dy + icgr$$
$$= 0.405/52.25 + 0.1371$$
$$= 0.0078 + 0.1371 = 0.1449 \text{ or } 14.49\%$$

Thus, the 2001 Annual Report of State Street Corporation reports some interesting traditional financial measures—including ROE, leverage, the internal capital generation rate, and the dividend payout ratio. There is, however, no attempt by the bank to show the formal linkage between company accounting data and the *fundamental* rate of return (FSR) on the stock. The concept of a fundamental stock return is an added insight that must be provided by a manager or investor. Moreover, given the EVA perspective of this book, there is little if any formal attempt by many companies to "roll up" their underlying company ratios—such as dividend yield, PBR, and ROE—into a return that is specific to the firm let alone make a comparison of such a return with the required return on invested capital.[18]

Coke's Fundamental Stock Return

The same procedure can be used to link Coca-Cola's return on equity with its fundamental stock return. For example, during 2001 the beverage firm's dividend yield was 1.53% ($0.72/$47.15), while the plowback and ROE ratios were 54.9% (1 – 0.451) and 34.92%, respectively.[19] With these figures, Coke's internal capital generation rate, *icgr*, for year 2001 was 19.17%:

$$icgr = PBR \times ROE$$
$$= 0.549 \times 0.3492 = 0.1917 \text{ or } 19.17\%$$

---

[17] Technically speaking, a BOY stock price or average price for the year should be used in the calculation of the dividend yield.

[18] Notice that up to this point, we have explored traditional ratios without any reference to the investor's required return on invested capital. This is an unfortunate void in traditional financial analysis that we'll address in an upcoming section.

[19] Again, these figures were obtained from the 2001 Annual Report of Coca-Cola.

Additionally, upon adding the dividend yield, 1.53%, to the firm's estimated internal growth rate, we obtain Coke's 2001 fundamental stock return of 20.7%:

$$\text{FSR} = dy + icgr$$
$$= 0.0153 + 0.1917 = 0.2070 \text{ or } 20.7\%$$

With a solid ROE and internal capital generation rate, we see that Coke's fundamental stock return is quite attractive. If an investor could actually earn a 20.7% return on the stock, then an investment in Coca-Cola would presumably double in approximately 3.5 years (72/20.7). This compares with an investment double in State Street stock of roughly five years (72/14.49). Of course industry and economy-wide developments (as well as other economic profit considerations) could cause these projections to vary by a considerable amount.

TRADITIONAL OMISSION OF THE REQUIRED RETURN

One of the major problems[20] with the traditional approach to company analysis is that it doesn't make a formal connection between the required return on a stock and its inherent risk. For example, State Street's 2001 Annual Report provides investors with meaningful information about the company's ROE and internal capital generation rate, *icgr*. Yet, nothing is shown in the report about how this information can be used by managers or investors to see if the firm's fundamental stock return (*FSR*) is greater than some preestablished benchmark, as measured by the expected or *required* return on its outstanding common stock. This omission is important because the fundamental stock return is based on underlying company accounting data—such as plowback ratio and ROE—while the investors' required return is based (or *should* be) on an equilibrium model of expected return and risk.[21]

---

[20] Aside from the many EVA accounting issues to estimate a company's net operating profit after tax (NOPAT).

[21] Moreover, in view of the benefits of the traditional approach to security analysis, the manager or investor must realize that one of its major limitations is that there is *no* formal mechanism that describes the *equilibrium* relationship between expected return and risk. Without this, the manager or investor is left in a quandary about the appropriate benchmark that a measure like ROE or even the fundamental stock return (FSR) should be compared to see if a stock provides an appropriate "risk-adjusted" return in the marketplace.

As we have seen before, a simple approach to estimating the required return on common stock is obtained by using the capital asset pricing model (CAPM).[22] In this context, the required return on stock is estimated according to:

$$ER = R_f + MRP \times Beta$$

In this expression, R_f is the risk-free rate of interest, MRP is the expected market risk premium, and beta measures the systematic or relative risk of the firm's stock. According to CAPM, if beta is higher than unity—as in the case of *growth* stocks—the expected or required return on the stock is higher than that projected for the market portfolio. Conversely, when beta is less than one—most notably for so-called *value* stocks—the required or expected stock return, ER, falls short of the anticipated return on the market portfolio.[23]

For example, with a risk-free rate of 6.5%, and a market risk premium of 6%, the expected return on the market portfolio is 12.5%. This results because the beta of the market is *one*. With these assumptions, State Street Corporation has a CAPM expected return of 14.9%. The higher than market required return on State Street stock results because the beta, at 1.4, is higher than unity. Although the bank's fundamental stock return, at 14.49%, exceeds the anticipated market return, the 2001 *FSR* of State Street falls *below* the CAPM required return. While State Street looks like a fairly attractive company with a 2001 ROE of 17.19% and a fundamental stock of 14.49%, the equity risk adjustment—via the FSR-CAPM linkage—reveals that State Street stock barely meets the investors return requirement.[24]

Most importantly, we see that traditional metrics such as ROE, the internal capital generation rate, and the fundamental stock return must be joined with the investor's opportunity cost of invested capital. This synthesis of accounting profit fundamentals and equity risk considerations—using CAPM or some other risk-pricing model—must occur

---

[22] A more robust approach to estimating the required return on stock is obtained with a fundamental factor model. However, factor models in use today are typically based on accounting based measures of profit such as EPS, ROE, and traditional valuation measures such as the price-to-earnings and price-to-book ratios. We'll look at an EVA-based factor model approach to estimating the required return on common stock at a later point in this book.

[23] We'll examine the meaning of growth stocks and value stocks from an economic profit (EVA) perspective in a later chapter.

[24] On the other hand, Coca-Cola with a noticeably lower beta of 0.85 has a CAPM required return of 11.6%. Since Coke's 2001 FSR is 20.7%, the beverage producer easily bests both the expected market return and the required rate of return.

before a meaningful assessment can be made regarding the attractiveness (or unattractiveness) of a company's stock.[25] As emphasized in this book, this leads to a critical distinction between accounting profit measurement and economic profit (EVA) measurement. Unlike accounting earnings, EVA reflects the adjustments that are necessary to go from accounting profit to cash operating profit, and it also "fully reflects" the dollar opportunity cost of invested capital—measured by COC *times* the amount of invested capital employed in a business.

ROLE OF THE SECURITIES MARKET LINE

Exhibit 8.7 provides a display of the 2001 fundamental stock return versus CAPM for selected companies in the financial services and beverage sectors. The financial services companies include State Street Corporation, JP Morgan/Chase, and Bank of New York, while the beverage producers include Coca-Cola and PepsiCo, Inc. In this exhibit, the "y-axis" shows the FSR and CAPM for the banking and soft drink companies as well as the projected return on a market index fund. The "x-axis" shows the relative risk, or beta, measures for the respective companies and the market index (at unity). Also, the line labeled SML, for Securities Market Line, represents *unlevered* and *levered* combinations of the risk-free asset and the market portfolio, measured in expected return and beta-risk space.

EXHIBIT 8.7   FSR versus CAPM: Selected Companies for Year 2001

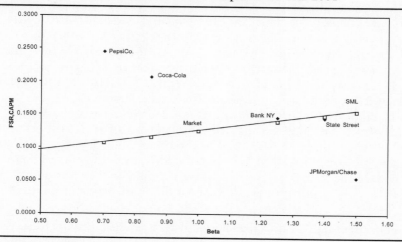

25 Even still, managers and investors *must* recognize that accounting earnings are not economic earnings.

In principle, securities with fundamental stock returns (FSR) that exceed the Securities Market Line (SML) are attractive opportunities because the underlying companies have the potential to earn a return—based on company fundamentals—that exceeds the opportunity cost of equity capital. Likewise, any stock whose *FSR* falls below the CAPM benchmark is considered unattractive in this security selection framework. This happens because the sum of a company's expected dividend yield and internal capital generation rate is not sufficiently high enough for the fundamental stock return to lie either on or above the Securities Market Line.

In effect, the FSR-CAPM relationship indicates that investors should buy securities of firms having a fundamental stock return that lies above the CAPM line, as their projected returns seem high when evaluated in terms of the firm's accounting earnings capabilities.[26] In contrast, investors should consider selling or shorting the shares of companies with FSR's that fall below the Securities Market Line, because their projected returns seem low when measured by the firm's dividend yield and anticipated internal growth opportunities. By inference, stocks that lie on the SML are priced "just right," in the sense that their fundamental return could be *synthetically* replicated by leveraging down or up the market fund.

Exhibit 8.7 shows that State Street Corporation and Bank of New York have fairly attractive fundamental stock returns. In particular, State Street's FSR is 14.49%, while Bank of New York's FSR is 14.59%. Also, the fundamental stock returns for the two banks exceed the projected market return of 12.5%. However, these cross-sectional comparisons are limited because the fundamental stock return must be compared to a required return that "fully reflects" the inherent risk of the security. Specifically, the FSR's can be compared to the required return *à la* CAPM.[27] Notably, when a manager or investor "accounts" for equity risk, the fundamental stock returns for State Street and Bank of New York are close to the Securities Market Line.

Bank of New York, with a FSR of 14.59%, bests the CAPM of 14.00% by a small percentage, while State Street's FSR falls short of the CAPM requirement of 14.90%. On the other hand, JP Morgan/Chase, with FSR of only 5.49% falls below the SML by a substantial amount. Again, we see that the cost of equity—via the concomitant equity risk adjustment—is central to the determination of attractive or unattractive

---

[26] Before raising the flag here on traditional analysis, it is important to reemphasize that we are dealing with accounting earnings rather than cash or economic earnings.
[27] This of course presumes that CAPM is the appropriate measure of the cost of equity.

investment opportunities. In effect, the betas for State Street and Bank of New York—at 1.4 and 1.25—serves as a risk adjustment to what *otherwise* looks like attractive companies using traditional financial metrics such as ROE, internal capital generation rate, and the "rolled up" fundamental stock return.[28]

In the beverage sector, Coca-Cola and PepsiCo have attractive FSR's, at 20.7% and 24.48%, for year 2001. The two beverage producers are also attractive because of their relatively low equity risk. According to Value Line, Coke has a beta of 0.85 and PepsiCo's beta is only 0.7.[29] Comparatively speaking, PepsiCo seemed to be the better investment opportunity during 2001 because its fundamental stock return was not only higher than Coke's, but its relative risk (as measured by beta) was lower than that observed for Coca-Cola. Again, when comparing companies either within or across industries, the risk adjustment is key: On a comparative basis, the lower equity risk makes the beverage producers seem even *more* attractive than might otherwise be surmised by just looking at accounting profit ratios as all too frequently happens in traditional financial analysis.

TRADITIONAL ROLE OF LEVERAGE

As explained in Chapter 3, managers and investors often look at corporate leverage ratios—such as debt-to-equity, debt-to-capital and debt-to-asset ratios—when evaluating the likely performance and risk of a company and its outstanding securities. In the traditional model, leverage is thought to be value increasing because higher levels of corporate debt lead to higher ROE and per-share-earnings.[30] However, astute managers and investors are aware that excessive amounts of debt—beyond some presumed company *target* level—may be wealth destroying for the shareholders. This negative side of debt is generally due to abnormal earnings volatility associated with a rising probability of corporate bankruptcy and default.

Let's look again at Coca-Cola to show how debt financing impacts the return on equity (ROE). Based on our previous discussion, we know that Coke's financial leverage ratio can be expressed as:

---

[28] Notice that JP Morgan/Chase looked unattractive during 2001 due to a low FSR and a high CAPM beta, at 1.5.

[29] *Value Line Investment Survey* (New York, NY) May 10, 2002.

[30] With debt financing, levered companies receive a yearly interest tax subsidy relative to unlevered companies.

$$\text{Leverage} = \text{ROE/ROA}$$
$$= 0.3492/0.1771 = 1.972$$

In turn, we can unfold the leverage ratio into the "debt ratio"—where debt is viewed broadly to mean current liabilities, long-term debt, deferred income taxes, and other liabilities[31]—according to:

$$\text{Leverage} = 1/(1 - DR)$$

From this, we see that Coca-Cola's "debt ratio" (again, broadly speaking) for year 2001 must be:

$$\text{Debt ratio} = [\text{Leverage} - 1]/\text{Leverage}$$
$$= [1.972 - 1.0]/1.972$$
$$= 0.4929 \text{ or } 49.29\%$$

Thus, the 2001 return on equity for Coca-Cola implies that the company is financed with 49% total debt. Let's now see what happens to Coke's ROE (for a *given* ROA) if the debt ratio were to vary from, say, 30% of assets up to 60% of assets. If Coke's total debt rises to 60% of assets, we have:

$$\text{ROE} = \text{ROA} \times [1/(1 - DR)]$$
$$= 0.1771 \times [1/(1 - 0.6)]$$
$$= 0.4428 \text{ or } 44.28\%$$

In this case, the increase in debt leads to a noticeably higher return on equity (ROE), from 34.92% to 44.28%. Conversely, if Coke's debt-to-asset ratio were to decline to 30%, then ROE would fall from 34.92% down to 25.3%.

$$\text{ROE} = \text{ROA} \times [1/(1 - DR)]$$
$$= 0.1771 \times [1/(1 - 0.3)]$$
$$= 0.253 \text{ or } 25.3\%$$

At this point, the obvious question that arises is why doesn't Coke's management simply increase the proportion of debt to total assets? If higher ROE really leads to higher stock prices, then a mere change in

---

[31] Recall that the leverage ratio is assets over equity (A/E). Therefore the difference between assets and equity on a company's balance sheet must include all forms of debt, including current liabilities, long-term debt, deferred income taxes, other liabilities and the like.

the debt ratio would seem a "free lunch" approach to increasing the stock price (therefore, shareholder value).

The answer to this question depends on whether there exists an "optimal" capital structure mix of debt relative to assets. As explained in Chapter 3, the capital structure question is a complex one in the theory of finance because there are several explanations on this issue—ranging from the "traditionalists" position on capital structure to the Modigliani-Miller position. According to the traditionalist position, if Coca-Cola's debt-to-asset ratio were lower than the industry debt-to-asset ratio, then Coke would have an incentive to increase the mix of debt relative to assets to generate a concomitant rise in ROE and share price.

Conversely, if Coke's debt-to-asset ratio were higher than that observed for industry peers, then Coke's share price would decline if debt were increased even though ROE would rise in line with the predictions of the Dupont formula. On the other hand, if the "MM" view of capital structure is an apt description of real world capital markets, then Coca-Cola's share price would be *invariant* to the corporate leverage decision, even though ROE would rise and fall with higher or lower levels of debt. As explained in Chapter 3, the invariance of share price to corporate leverage (debt-equity, debt-capital, and debt-asset) ratios arises because the opportunity cost of invested capital is *directly* related to the leverage ratio.[32]

Finally, consider Exhibit 8.8: This exhibit shows the 2001 debt-to-capital ratio[33] for Coca-Cola, PepsiCo, and the soft drinks industry[34] respectively. Notice that in the traditional view, Coke has a large "debt capacity" since its debt-to-capital ratio, at 10%, is considerably lower than the debt-to-capital ratio for the beverage industry, at 41%. A similar debt-to-capital interpretation applies to PepsiCo, although Pepsi's debt burden is higher than that observed for Coca-Cola. In the traditional realm, Coca-Cola and Pepsi could easily boost ROE (again, for a *given* ROA) and presumably stock price by simply increasing the capital structure mix of debt relative to capital. However, the forceful "MM" argument suggests that Coke's shareholders would be better served if the firm's managers devoted their time to finding positive NPV (equivalently, discounted positive EVA) opportunities rather than wasting time and resources on capital structure decisions that give investors an illusion of value creation.

---

[32] In a CAPM context, beta is *linearly* related to the debt/equity ratio. Again, we see that the required return is a key ingredient to shareholder value. This is fully recognized by the EVA approach to enterprise valuation.

[33] The debt-to-capital ratio is typically defined as long-term debt divided by "total capital." In this context, capital is viewed as long-term debt *plus* equity.

[34] *Value Line Investment Survey* (New York, NY) "Soft Drinks Industry Report," May 10, 2002, p. 1546.

EXHIBIT 8.8   Capital Structure Proportions for Soft Drink Industry: Year 2001 ($ Millions)

	Coca-Cola	PepsiCo.	Soft Drink Industry
LT Debt	$1,219	$2,651	$21,600
Equity	11,366	8,648	31,350
Capital	12,585	11,299	52,950
Debt/Cap	0.0969	0.2346	0.4079

Source: Value Line Investment Survey, May 10, 2002, p. 1546.

SUMMARY

This chapter reviews and applies traditional measures of profitability and success. Financial measures like growth in revenue, earnings, and book value—as well as return on equity (ROE) and return on assets (ROA)—are at the heart of the traditional approach to company analysis. Along this line, the "Dupont formula" is often used to show how profitability and leverage changes at a company can impact—either positively or negatively—the shareholder's return on equity (ROE). Also, managers and investors to see if a company's internal growth opportunities are correctly "priced" in the marketplace use traditional valuation measures such as price/earnings and price/book value ratios. In this regard, active investors should avoid overpaying for the firm's perceived future growth opportunities, while they should consider buying those securities where stock price has been incorrectly driven down to a level that is inconsistent with a firm's fundamental earning potential.

We found that with knowledge of a company's ROE and earnings plowback ratio (PBR), it is possible to estimate the internal capital generation rate, *icgr*. Upon adding this projected growth figure to a company's estimated dividend yield, the manager or investor obtains the fundamental rate of return on common stock (FSR). From a traditional viewpoint, it was argued that if the FSR is greater than the (CAPM) required return, then stock price seems low when measured relative to the firm's revenue and earnings growth capabilities. On the other hand if the fundamental stock return falls short of the required return, then the stock appears to be overvalued. Consequently, the investor should consider selling or shorting the presumed mispriced shares of stock. In this framework, the firm's common stock is thought to be priced "just right" when the projected FSR equals the required rate of return.

We also reviewed the traditional role of corporate debt policy. In general, the traditional view holds that pricing gains are available to stockholders of firms that are moving toward their "optimal" capital structure, while share price declines may be imposed on shareholders when the firm moves away from the "just right" mix of debt and equity capital. A word of caution should be issued to managers and investors when examining the pricing role of corporate debt policy *per se*. In this context, we noted that managers and investors need to figure out whether a seemingly favorable change in ROE is due to changes in the firm's real growth opportunities, or possibly due to an illusionary share-holder benefit from rising corporate debt—*especially* when the firm's corporate leverage goes beyond the presumed "target" level (to the extent that one exists).

On balance, its seems reasonable to say that a "value-enhancing" return on equity results from increased profitability on the firm's existing (*and* future) assets in the presence of a relatively stable leverage ratio. The source of beneficial return on assets (ROA) comes from a higher expected net profit margin (NPM) and asset turnover ratio. Depending on where the firm is currently positioned relative to its target capital structure, question-able ROE and per share earnings occurrences may be associated with increases (or decreases) in a variety of corporate debt ratios, including debt-to-equity, debt-to-capital, and debt-to-asset ratios respectively. Given the benefits of traditional financial analysis, managers and investors must also take note of the major limitation of this approach to company analy-sis (aside from EVA accounting adjustments). That is, traditional financial analysis is incomplete because of an *inadequate* recognition and treatment of the required return on invested capital.

CHAPTER 9

EVA Accounting Adjustments

In Chapter 4, we looked at how to estimate basic economic profit. The goal of that chapter was to highlight the benefit of EVA measurement over accounting profit measurement *without* getting tangled up in a plethora of EVA-based accounting adjustments. In this chapter, we'll tackle the standard accounting adjustments that are necessary to estimate NOPAT and invested capital in practice. These NOPAT adjustments—including accounting for changes in LIFO reserve and accumulated goodwill accounts and the implied interest expense on operating leases—are generally made to convert accrual numbers to cash-based operating profit, and to remove the effects of financing decisions from operating results.

In our EVA treatment of accounting adjustments, we'll see that NOPAT should reflect the cash operating taxes that would normally be paid by an unlevered company. This adjustment is necessary because the beneficial effects of leverage (if any) show up in the after-tax cost of debt component of the weighted average cost of capital, COC. From an EVA tax perspective, we'll adjust reported income taxes by changes in the deferred income tax account, and we'll add back the various interest tax subsidies received by a company to reported income taxes.

We'll also see that accounting adjustments to arrive at NOPAT have corresponding adjustments to obtain invested capital on the EVA balance sheet. After that, we'll look at a detailed application on how to estimate economic profit with standard accounting adjustments. We'll close the chapter with a look at how standard accounting adjustments impact another prominent economic profit metric, namely Cash Flow Return on Investment (CFROI).

STANDARD ACCOUNTING ADJUSTMENTS

Stewart provides a "generally accepted" boilerplate of accounting adjustments that are necessary to estimate a company's NOPAT and invested capital in practice.[1] In this context, he shows the equivalent "bottom-up *and* top-down" approaches to estimating a company's net operating profit after taxes, along with the equivalent "asset *and* financing" approaches to estimating invested capital. We'll begin with a discussion of EVA accounting adjustments to estimate NOPAT and then follow with a discussion of the companion adjustments to estimate invested capital. Exhibit 9.1 shows the standard accounting adjustments that are used in the equivalent bottom up *and* top down approaches to estimating NOPAT.

NOPAT Estimation

In the *bottom-up approach* to estimating NOPAT, the manager or investor begins with net operating profit before taxes. As noted in Chapter 4, this is just the familiar earnings before interest and taxes (EBIT) figure on a company's income statement.[2] To this amount, several EVA-based accounting adjustments are made to move toward a better representation of the firm's pretax cash operating profit. For examples, the increase in LIFO reserve account is added back to operating profit to adjust for the overstatement of cost of goods sold—due to an overstatement of product costing—in a period of rising prices, while the *net* increase in research and development expenditures is added back to pretax operating profit to recognize that R&D expenditures should be capitalized (meaning put on the EVA balance sheet) because they generate a *future* stream of benefits.[3]

---

[1] See G. Bennett Stewart III, *The Quest for Value* (New York: Harper Collins, 1991).

[2] Net operating profit *before* taxes (EBIT) is also the same as operating profit *after* depreciation and amortization as shown in Exhibit 9.1.

[3] In other words, R&D expenditures should be capitalized and amortized over a useful time period such as five years—rather than expensed in the current year as if these expenditures have no future cash flow benefits. For example, if R&D expenditures for a given year were $100,000, then $80,000 would be placed on the balance sheet (at year end) and the remaining $20,000 would be charged to income. Assuming the entire R&D investment were already included in a selling, general and administrative expenses account, then the *net* R&D increase of $80,000 would get added back to obtain the EVA amortization of R&D expenditures, at $20,000.

A similar EVA adjustment applies to other accounting items such as bad debt expense. To arrive at cash operating taxes one also must consider adjustments to reported income taxes when making these EVA changes.

EXHIBIT 9.1   Calculation of NOPAT from Financial Statement Data

A. Bottom-up approach
Begin:
   Operating profit after depreciation and amortization
Add:
   Implied interest expense on operating leases
   Increase in LIFO reserve
   Increase in accumulated goodwill amortization
   Increase in bad-debt reserve
   Increase in capitalized research and development
   *Increase in cumulative write-offs of special items**
Equals:
   Adjusted operating profit before taxes
Subtract:
   Cash operating taxes
Equals:
   NOPAT

B. Top-down approach
Begin:
   Sales
Subtract:
   Cost of goods sold
   Selling, general, and administrative expenses
   Depreciation
Add:
   Implied interest expense on operating leases
   Increase in equity reserve accounts (see above listing)
   Other operating income
Equals:
   Adjusted operating profit before taxes
Subtract:
   Cash operating taxes
Equals:
   NOPAT

---

* To the extent that write-offs are included in operating results rather than an extraordinary or unusual item.
Exhibit based on information in G. Bennett Stewart III, *The Quest for Value* (New York: Harper Collins, 1991).

Likewise, the increase in accumulated goodwill amortization is added back to pretax cash operating profit to reflect the fact that goodwill is a form of capital investment that needs to earn a cost of capital return just like expenditures on physical capital. Also, the *net* increase in bad debt reserve is added back to pretax operating profit to more accurately reflect a company's expected default experience per period. Additionally, the implied interest expense on operating leases is added back to operating results to remove the effects of debt-related financing decisions. Also, the rise in reengineering and restructuring expenditures is added back to pretax operating profit because these expenditures are viewed in an EVA framework as reengineering or restructuring "investments."

In the *top-down* approach (again, see Exhibit 9.1) to estimating NOPAT, the manager or investor begins with Sales and then adds the *increase* in several equity reserve accounts including the LIFO reserve and accumulated goodwill accounts, the bad debt reserve account, and the rise in other equity reserve accounts noted above. As with the *bottom-up* approach to estimating NOPAT, the implied interest expense on operating leases is added to the EVA-based income statement. Information on LIFO (and other) reserve and leasing accounts is generally found in the footnotes to accounting statements. Moreover, in the top down approach, the manager or investor subtracts the usual accounting income statement items such as cost of goods sold (COGS), selling, general, and administrative expenses (SG&A), and depreciation. Also, other operating expenses shown on the income statement are subtracted in the calculation of pretax cash operating profit while other operating income is added back.

Cash Operating Taxes

Taxes on pretax cash operating profit—as opposed to reported income taxes—must be subtracted from pretax cash operating profit to arrive at NOPAT. The arrival at NOPAT assumes that there are no further EVA adjustments needed because of, say, after-tax operating items that were previously deemed to be after-tax nonoperating items. The general steps involved in the calculation of cash operating taxes are shown in Exhibit 9.2. In the EVA tax calculation, the manager or investor begins with reported income tax expense from the income statement. To this amount, one subtracts (adds) the increase (decrease) in the deferred income tax account obtained from the balance sheet.

Exhibit 9.2 shows that the tax benefit received from interest expense (tax rate × interest expense) and the tax benefit received from implied interest expense on operating leases must be added to reported income

EXHIBIT 9.2   Cash Operating Taxes

Begin
Reported income taxes
Subtract:
   Increase in deferred income tax account
   Taxes on *nonoperating* income
Add:
   Tax subsidy on interest expense
   Tax subsidy on implied interest expense on operating leases
Equals:
   Cash operating taxes

taxes to remove the tax benefit (if any) obtained from debt-related financing decisions. Also, taxes on nonoperating income (or tax benefits received from nonoperating expenses) must be subtracted from (added to) accounting income taxes to obtain an accurate measure of cash operating taxes. Upon subtracting cash operating taxes from pre-tax net operating profit (from either the bottom-up *or* top-down approach), one obtains NOPAT.

Invested Capital

Exhibit 9.3 shows the EVA accounting adjustments that are necessary in the equivalent asset and financing approaches to estimating invested capital. In the *assets approach*, the manager or investor begins with net short term operating assets (basically, net working capital). This reflects moneys tied up in current assets such as accounts receivables and inventories as well as a normal amount of cash needed for operations.[4] Current liabilities such as accounts payable, accrued expenses, and income taxes payable are, of course, netted from the short term operating asset accounts. Short-term notes payable (a current liability account) are excluded because they represent a source of debt financing. As we'll shortly see, interest-bearing debt is reflected in the sources of financing approach and the debt-interest tax subsidy is reflected in the calculation of a company's (dollar) cost of capital.

---

[4] Estimates of a normal amount of cash required for operations vary by industry—such as 0.5% to 2% of net sales. Also, one can make a distinction between invested capital and operating capital. Operating capital is generally viewed as invested capital net of excess cash and marketable securities *and* goodwill-related accounts. We will focus on invested capital in the EVA illustration that follows.

EXHIBIT 9.3   Calculation of Capital Using Accounting Financial Statements

A. *Asset approach*
Begin:
    Net (short term) operating assets
Add:
    Net plant, property, and equipment
    Intangibles
    Other assets
    LIFO reserve
    Accumulated goodwill amortization
    Bad-debt reserve
    Capitalized research and development
    Cumulative write-offs of special items
    Present value of operating leases
Equals:
    Capital

B. *Sources of financing approach*
Begin:
    Book value of common equity
Add equity equivalents:
    Preferred stock
    Minority interest
    Deferred income tax
    Equity reserve accounts (see above listing)
Add debt and debt equivalents:
    Interest-bearing short-term debt
    Current portion of long-term debt
    Long-term debt
    Capitalized lease obligations
    Present value of operating leases
Equals:
    Capital

Exhibit based on information in G. Bennett Stewart III, *The Quest for Value* (New York: Harper Collins, 1991).

Net plant, property and equipment, intangibles (presumably goodwill arising from mergers and acquisitions), and other assets are then added to net short term operating assets. As shown in Exhibit 9.3, several equity reserve accounts are added to this basic invested capital figure including LIFO Reserve, accumulated goodwill amortization, net capitalized research and development, cumulative bad debt reserve, and the cumulative write-off of special items such as reengineering and restructuring costs. Also, the present value of operating leases is added back to arrive at invested capital on the EVA balance sheet.

In the *sources of financing approach* (again, Exhibit 9.3), the manager or investor begins with the book value of common equity. This is just the familiar Common at Par and Retained Earnings amounts on the balance sheet. To this sum, one adds several "equity equivalent" accounts including those already listed on a company's balance sheet, such as preferred stock, minority interest, and deferred income taxes, as well as the companion equity reserve accounts mentioned in the assets approach to estimating invested capital, namely LIFO reserve, accumulated goodwill amortization, net capitalized research and development, bad debt reserve, and the cumulative write-offs of special items.

Debt and debt equivalents are then added to arrive at an EVA-based figure for invested capital. These debt-related accounts include those listed on the balance sheet—including interest bearing short-term debt, current portion of long-term debt, long-term debt, and capitalized lease obligations—as well as "off balance sheet" items such as the present value of operating leases.[5] With the engagement of several EVA accounting adjustments, we see that the asset *and* financing approaches to estimating invested capital produce a robust measure (at least compared with basic EVA capital explained in Chapter 4) of economic capital that is actually tied up in a business.

EVA Application with Accounting Adjustments

Now that we have seen the standard accounting adjustments that are necessary to estimate a company's NOPAT and invested capital, we'll look at a detailed application of these EVA concepts. In this context, Exhibit 9.4 presents an income statement for a hypothetical company called "Fix-It-Yourself Company," while Exhibit 9.5 presents the conventional balance sheet. We'll begin the EVA discussion and analysis with the income statement.

A quick perusal of the income statement for Fix-It-Yourself Company shows familiar items like net sales, cost of goods sold (COGS), selling, general, and administrative expenses (SG&A), depreciation, and *unadjusted* operating profit before taxes (EBIT). Some obvious income statement accounts that can be recast in an economic profit framework include interest expense, nonoperating expenses and reported income taxes.

---

[5] The EVA recognition of "off balance sheet" debt brings up an interesting issue. While EVA accounting uses information that is deemed accurate from a company's *published* financial reports—including income statement, balance sheet, and relevant footnotes (an "off balance" sheet item), EVA cannot possibly reflect "off balance sheet" debts arising from hidden liabilities or fraudulent accounting transactions as in the notorious case of Enron.

EXHIBIT 9.4 Income Statement: Fix-It-Yourself Company ($ thousands)

	Current Year	Previous Year
Net sales	$120,378	$102,755
Cost of goods sold	60,245	52,822
Gross profit	60,133	49,933
Selling, general & administrative	42,351	35,840
Operating profit before depreciation	17,782	14,093
Depreciation	5,125	4,177
Operating profit (EBIT)	12,657	9,916
Interest expense	1,379	1,342
Nonoperating expense (net)	2,789	2,435
Pretax profit	8,489	6,139
Income taxes	2,971	2,149
Net Income	$5,518	$3,990
Shares Outstanding	5,225	5,225
Earnings per share	$1.06	$0.76

Since we are trying to assess the after-tax operating profit of Fix-It-Yourself Company as an unlevered firm, the reported tax figure shown on the income statement has EVA bias due to several reasons. Specifically, the tax figure is biased upward due to the rise in deferred income taxes, while cash taxes actually paid by Fix-It-Yourself Company as an unlevered firm are biased downward due to (1) the tax subsidies received on debt and debt equivalents (operating leases) and (2) the tax benefit received on nonoperating expenses.[6]

Suppose that upon inspection of the footnotes to Fix-It-Yourself Company's financial statements along with further company research we find the following EVA-related information:[7]

---

[6] In the illustration, it was assumed that deferred taxes went up over the year's course.

[7] In order to reduce the volume of EVA accounting adjustments, R&D "investment" is omitted in the text application that follows. A basic explanation of the EVA treatment of R&D expenditures is provided in a previous note.

Also, managers or investors should *not* use the illustration that follows to gauge either the magnitude or priority of EVA accounting adjustments that can be made in practice. The magnitude of EVA accounting adjustments is often company specific, while the prioritizing of such adjustments is often manager or investor specific. For example, some investors feel that EVA adjustments for restructuring expenditures and R&D investments *should* take priority over the EVA treatment of LIFO reserves and deferred income taxes.

Fix-It-Yourself Company: Footnotes and company research ($ thousands):

Present value of operating leases (year-end):	$4,292*
Implied interest expense on operating lease (current year):	370*
Accumulated LIFO reserve (year-end):	1,225
Year-over-year change in LIFO reserve:	−110
Accumulated goodwill amortization:	4,550
Change in accumulated goodwill amortization:	425
Cumulative restructuring charges:	3,975
Change in cumulative restructuring charges (pretax):	375**
Operating cash requirement: 2% of net sales (industry standard)	

*Operating lease calculations are explained in a later section.
**Change in cumulative restructuring charges reflected in selling, general and administrative expense account on income statement.

EXHIBIT 9.5   Balance Sheet: Fix-It-Yourself Company ($ thousands)

	Current Year	Previous Year
Current Assets		
Cash and cash equivalents	$2,542	$2,312
Accounts receivable	32,721	28,657
Inventory	20,448	16,310
Other current assets	2,076	1,902
Total Current Assets	$57,787	$49,181
Net plant, property & equipment	27,230	25,602
Intangibles, net	300	265
Other assets	89	47
Total Assets	$85,406	$75,095
Current Liabilities		
Accounts payable	8,210	6,426
Accrued expenses	3,378	2,978
Taxes payable	7,789	6,572
Notes payable	2,994	2,543
Total Current Liabilities	22,371	18,519
Long-term debt	17,240	16,492
Deferred income tax	565	372
Minority Interest	210	210
Common stock	10,000	10,000
Retained earnings	35,020	29,502
Common Equity	45,020	39,502
Total Liabilities and Equity	$85,406	$75,095

With this information, we'll make several EVA accounting adjustments to pretax operating profit (EBIT) of Fix-It-Yourself Company. These bottom-up accounting adjustments include: (1) the implied interest expense on operating leases (calculation explained in a later section); (2) the decrease in LIFO reserve due presumably to falling material prices; (3) the increase in accumulated goodwill amortization; and (4) the increase in cumulative restructuring charges—which, in the EVA view, are more aptly treated as period restructuring or reengineering "investments." Upon making these standard EVA accounting adjustments, we see that Fix-It-Yourself Company's adjusted pretax operating profit rises from \$12,657 to \$13,717 as shown below.[8]

Fix-It-Yourself Company: Operating Profit Adjustments (\$ thousands): (*Bottom-Up Approach*)

Item:	Amount	Source/Calculation
Operating Profit (EBIT)	\$12,657	Income statement
Add (Subtract):		
Implied interest expense on operating leases	370	$0.08 \times 4,631^*$
Increase (decrease) in LIFO reserve	(110)	LIFO reserve change
Increase in Goodwill amortization	425	Accumulated goodwill change
Increase in Cumulative restructuring charges	375	Change in restructuring charges
Adjusted Operating Profit	\$13,717	

* Average of present value of operating lease at beginning and end of year. Detail explained in a later section.

The next item for EVA consideration is the cash operating taxes paid by Fix-It-Yourself Company as an unlevered firm. As mentioned before, we must adjust Fix-It-Yourself Company's reported income taxes downward to account for the year-over-year increase in deferred income taxes shown on the balance sheet. Also, if Fix-It-Yourself Company were, in fact, an unlevered company, it would not receive the interest tax subsidy on the company's debt, nor would it receive the implied tax subsidy on the interest expense on operating leases. Moreover, interest tax subsidies (if any) are reflected in the firm's dollar cost of capital.

Thus, we must add back the debt-induced tax benefits to Fix-It-Yourself Company's reported income tax. Also, we must add back the tax benefit that Fix-It-Yourself Company receives on nonoperating expenses as

---

[8] Unless otherwise noted, all dollar figures are in thousands.

well as the tax benefit that it received by including (the assumed) period restructuring charges in selling, general, and administrative expenses. We make these adjustments because we are looking for a reliable operating profit figure for Fix-It-Yourself Company as an *on-going* concern. With these EVA adjustments, the adjusted cash operating taxes of Fix-It-Yourself Company were $4,498. This is noticeably higher than the reported income tax figure, at $2,971, on the income statement shown as follows:

Fix-It-Yourself Company: Cash Operating Taxes:

Reported Income Taxes	$2,971	Income statement
Subtract:		
Increase in deferred taxes	193	Balance sheet
Add:		
Tax subsidy from interest expense	483	0.35 × $1,379
Tax subsidy from implied interest	130	0.35 × $370
Tax benefit from nonoperating expense	976	0.35 × $2,789
Tax benefit from restructuring charge	131	0.35 × $375
Cash Operating Taxes	$4,498	

Taken together, we see that Fix-It-Yourself Company's net operating profit after tax (NOPAT) is $9,219. This figure results from subtracting the cash operating taxes, at $4,498, from the adjusted pretax operating profit, at $13,717, that we estimated before:

Fix-It-Yourself Company: Net Operating Profit After Taxes (NOPAT)

Adjusted Operating Profit	$13,717
Subtract:	
Cash operating taxes	4,498
NOPAT	$9,219

We can obtain the same NOPAT results using a top-down approach. In this context, we begin with net sales. To this figure, we add the implied interest expense on operating leases, increase (decrease) in LIFO reserve, increase in accumulated goodwill amortization, and the rise in cumulative restructuring charges. We then subtract the traditional income statement items including cost of goods sold, selling, general, and administrative expenses and a period charge for wear and tear of the company's assets (measured in principle by *economic* depreciation rather than reported accounting depreciation).[9]

With these EVA adjustments, we again see that Fix-It-Yourself Company's adjusted operating profit were $13,717. Upon subtracting cash operating taxes, at $4,498, from adjusted operating profit, we obtain Fix-It-Yourself's Company's NOPAT of $9,219:

Fix-It-Yourself Company: Operating Profit Adjustments ($ thousands):
(*Top-Down Approach*)

Net Sales	$120,378
Add (subtract):	
Implied interest expense on operating leases	370
Increase (decrease) in LIFO reserve	(110)
Increase in Accumulated goodwill amortization	425
Increase in Cumulative restructuring charges	375
Subtract:	
Cost of goods sold	60,245
Selling, general & administrative expenses	42,351
Depreciation	5,125
Adjusted Operating Profit	$13,717
Subtract:	
Cash Operating Taxes	$4,498
NOPAT	$9,219

Capital Adjustments

One of the benefits of economic profit measurement is that it links the income statement with the balance sheet. In this context, we must not only look at how "top line" revenue leads to "bottom line" profit (NOPAT in our case), but we must also assess a company's profitability relative to capital employed in a business. Also, from an EVA accounting perspective, we must recognize that for every income statement adjustment, we must also make a corresponding balance sheet adjustment to arrive at invested capital. At this point, it is helpful to review Exhibit 9.5, which shows a conventional balance sheet for Fix-It-Yourself Company.

While the balance sheet is helpful in our goal of measuring Fix-It-Yourself Company's operating capital—since it includes short-term operating assets and liabilities along with net plant, property and equip-

---

[9] We'll examine the complicated issue of economic versus accounting depreciation in Chapter 10. For now, we'll use reported depreciation on the income statement.

ment—it does not reflect all the EVA capital adjustments that go along with the income statement that we made before. Specifically, Fix-It-Yourself Company's balance sheet does not reflect the invested capital amounts arising from "off balance sheet" items like LIFO reserve, accumulated goodwill amortization, cumulative restructuring charges, and the present value of operating leases.

Given these omissions, we'll adjust the balance sheet to more closely approximate invested capital. Using the "assets approach" to estimating invested capital for Fix-It-Yourself Company we obtain the following results:

Fix-It-Yourself Company: Calculation of Invested Capital (Assets Approach)

Net short-term operating assets	$38,410	Current assets *less* noninterest bearing current liabilities
Net Plant, Property and Equipment	27,230	
Intangibles, net	300	
Other assets	89	
LIFO reserve	1,225	
Accumulated goodwill amortization	4,550	
Cumulative restructuring charges	3,975	
Present value of operating leases	4,292	
Invested Capital	$80,071	

Based on EVA capital adjustments, we see that Fix-It-Yourself Company's invested capital is $80,071. This figure consists of the reported balance sheet items—including net short-term operating assets (current assets less noninterest bearing current liabilities) plus net plant, property, and equipment, net intangibles, and other assets—and the standard EVA accounting adjustments—including LIFO reserve, accumulated goodwill amortization, cumulative restructuring charges, and the present value of operating leases (among others). At $14,042, the EVA accounting adjustments make up 18% ($14,042/$80,071) of Fix-It-Yourself Company's invested capital. It is also possible to make a distinction between operating capital and invested capital.[10]

---

[10] As noted before, operating capital excludes excess cash and marketable securities and goodwill-related accounts. In our illustration, Fix-It-Yourself Company's cash and cash equivalents account is about 2% of net sales so we need only adjust invested capital for the intangibles (presumed net goodwill) and the accumulated goodwill amortization. Therefore, Fix-It-Yourself Company's invested capital is $80,071 while its operating capital is $75,221 ($80,071 − $300 − $4,550).

We can of course arrive at the same amount of invested capital using the "sources of financing" approach. As shown, we begin with book value of common equity. To this amount, we add equity equivalents including those already listed on the balance sheet—such as preferred stock (if any), minority interest, and (cumulative) deferred income tax—as well as the equity reserve accounts that were cited before—including LIFO reserve, accumulated goodwill amortization, and cumulative restructuring charges (among others). Taken together, these equity and equity equivalents for Fix-It-Yourself Company sum up to $55,545:

**Fix-It-Yourself Company: Calculation of Invested Capital
(Sources of Financing Approach)**

Book value of common equity	$45,020
Add: Equity equivalents	
Preferred stock	0
Minority interest	210
Deferred income tax	565
LIFO reserve	1,225
Accumulated goodwill amortization	4,550
Cumulative restructuring charges	3,975
Equity and equity equivalents	55,545
Short-term debt (notes payable)	2,994
Long-term debt	17,240
Present value of operating leases	4,292
Debt and debt equivalents	24,526
Invested Capital	$80,071

Next, we add the debt and debt equivalents. This figure includes the debt-related items already listed on the balance sheet—including short-term debt (notes payable) and long-term debt—as well as debt equivalents—such as the present value of operating leases that we mentioned before. Taken together, the debt and debt equivalents for Fix-It-Yourself Company sum up to $24,526. Not surprisingly, upon adding equity-and-debt-related amounts using a sources of financing approach, we obtain the firm's invested capital of $80,071.

Cost of Capital Application

We can use the results obtained in the sources of financing approach to obtain the capital structure mix of debt and equity. Specifically, we see that Fix-It-Yourself Company's debt and debt equivalents make up 31% of invested capital, while equity and equity equivalents make up the balance, at 69%. We'll use these capital structure proportions as input to the cost of capital, COC. But first, we must estimate the after-tax cost of debt and the after-tax cost of equity:

Fix-It-Yourself Company: Capital Structure Proportions

	Amount	Weight
Debt and debt equivalents	$24,526	0.31
Equity and equity equivalents	55,545	0.69
Invested Capital	$80,071	1.00

With an 8% pretax yield on Fix-It-Yourself Company's outstanding debt and a corporate tax rate of 35%, we obtain an after-tax debt cost of 5.2%. Furthermore, with a 5% risk-free interest rate, a 5% market risk premium, and a beta of 0.8, we obtain a CAPM-based required return on equity of 9%.[11] Upon combining the capital structure weights with the after-tax expected return estimates, we obtain a 7.82% cost of capital for Fix-It-Yourself Company. This percentage is the "hurdle rate" that capital investments at Fix-It-Yourself Company must meet in order to produce a sustainable positive economic profit as shown below.[12]

Fix-It-Yourself Company: Cost of Capital Estimation

Estimated after-tax cost of debt:
Pretax debt cost = 8%
After-tax cost of debt = 8% × (1 − 0.35) = 5.20%

Estimated of cost of equity:
CAPM* = R_f + MRP% × Beta = 5% + 5% × 0.8 = 9%

Estimated cost of capital (COC):
COC = 0.31 × 5.20 + 0.69 × 9.00 = 7.82%

* Risk-free rate (R_f) *and* expected market risk premium (MRP) assumed at 5%.

---

[11] While CAPM is a convenient method for calculating a company's cost of equity, there are several limitations to this traditionally celebrated model. CAPM limitations are generally attributed to (1) instability in market risk premium (MRP) and the systematic risk (beta), and (2) the empirical recognition that nonsystematic risk factors also influence expected security returns. We'll look at estimation issues associated with the cost of equity capital (a key component of the cost of capital) in Chapter 11.
[12] While the theory of EVA is robust, an obvious practical limitation arises with the choice of "book" versus market weights in the calculation of the cost of capital and therefore economic profit more generally. For a rigorous discussion of EVA measurement (and valuation) limitations, see Pablo Fernández, *Valuation Methods and Shareholder Value Creation* (London: Academic Press, 2002).

We can now "roll-up" the calculations to obtain Fix-It-Yourself Company's economic profit. Upon subtracting the capital charge, at $6,262 (COC × Invested Capital) from previously estimated NOPAT, we obtain the firm's current (operative word here) EVA at $2,957. From a valuation perspective, if Fix-It-Yourself Company could generate this figure as perpetuity, then the company's existing assets would make a $37,813 (EVA/COC = $2,957/0.0782) contribution to invested capital. In this context, Fix-It-Yourself Company is a wealth creator with discounted positive economic profit (that is, positive NPV) as shown in the table below. (In Chapter 7, we explored the enterprise valuation side of economic profit in much greater detail.)

Fix-It-Yourself Company: Estimated EVA ($ thousands)

	Current Year	
NOPAT	$9,219	
Capital charge	6,262	COC × Invested Capital
EVA	$2,957	

Moreover, we can obtain economic profit by multiplying the "EVA spread" or residual return on capital (ROC-COC) by invested capital. With a return on invested capital of 11.51% and a cost of capital (COC) of 7.82%, we obtain an EVA spread of 3.69%. Upon multiplying Fix-It-Yourself Company's residual return on capital by invested capital, at $80,071, we again obtain the estimated dollar EVA of $2,957 (difference due to rounding).

Fix-It-Yourself Company: EVA Spread Approach

ROC = NOPAT/Invested Capital
     = $9,219/$80,071
     = 11.51%

COC = 7.82%

EVA Spread = ROC – COC = 3.69%

EVA = EVA Spread × Invested Capital
     = 0.0369 × $80,071 = $2,957 (rounded)

Operating Leases: A Closer Look

In our previous discussion on how to estimate NOPAT, we were provided with estimates on the implied interest expense on operating leases and the present value of operating leases. Let's now look at how these figures can be obtained in practice. Specifically, suppose that Fix-It-Yourself Company's leasing footnote shows that a $1,075 rental payment is due each year (taken to mean from the end of the current year) for the next five years along with an overall total leasing commitment (unadjusted for present value effects) of $10,750 thereafter. Assuming that Fix-It-Yourself Company's pretax yield on debt is 8%, we find that the discounted value of the 5-year rental commitment is $4,292. This figure is the present value of operating leases as of the *end* of the current year.

If we step back to the beginning of the current year and assume a 6-year rental commitment at that time, we obtain a present value lease estimate of $4,970. The average of these two present value figures is $4,631. Next, upon multiplying the average present value of operating leases by the 8% pretax yield on corporate debt, we obtain an estimate of the implied interest expense on operating leases of $370 (0.08 × $4,631). The calculation of the present value of operating leases and the resulting implied interest expense are as follows:

Fix-It-Yourself Company: Capitalization of Operating Leases

Leasing footnote: Operating leasing payment of $1,075 for five years. Leasing payments beyond year 5 total $10,750.

Capitalization of Operating Leases:
5-year operating lease payments = $1,075
Pretax debt yield = 8%

Present Value of 5-Year Operating Lease Commitments:
(From *End* of Current Year)

Year Relative	Lease Payment	Present Value
1	$1,075	$995
2	1,075	922
3	1,075	853
4	1,075	790
5	1,075	732
Total		$4,292

Cont.

Present value of 6-year operating lease commitments:

(from *beginning* of current year)   Total $4,970

                                           Average   *$4,631*

Implied interest on operating lease = 0.08 × $4,631 = $370

Before proceeding, it is interesting to note that if the $1,075 rental payment were to last for an indefinite time period (that is, if lease payment were made in perpetuity), then the capitalized value of the operating rental commitments would be $13,438 ($1,075/0.08). This figure is $9,146 higher than the (year-end) present value figure that results with a 5-year leasing horizon![13]

Moreover, at $1,075 (0.08 × $13,438), the implied interest charge on the leasing perpetuity is noticeably higher than the $370 average figure that we estimated before. It goes without saying that managers and investors must be aware of the economic profit differences arising from varying assumptions about the maturity of operating leases.[14] Also, it should now be clear where we obtained the capitalized value of the 5-year operating leasing commitment (at $4,292, for use in the *end* of current year capital adjustment) and the associated implied interest charge (at $370) for use on the EVA balance and income statements, respectively.

ROC DECOMPOSITION

We can now unfold the after-tax return on invested capital (ROC) into some meaningful financial ratios. Specifically, the following analysis table shows a decomposition of Fix-It-Yourself Company's ROC into a NOPAT margin—measured by the ratio of NOPAT to net sales—and a invested capital turnover ratio—measured by net sales over invested capital. While this EVA ratio analysis might look similar to a more traditional breakdown of return on assets (ROA) and return on equity (ROE), managers and investors should be aware that ROC is a noticeable improvement

---

[13] However, if the operating leasing commitment were in perpetuity, then the present value of rental commitments would be close to the market value of the underlying asset. That kind of lease would presumably already be shown on a company's balance sheet as capitalized lease obligations.

[14] Pamela Peterson also emphasizes this point in an insightful EVA illustration for McDonald's Corporation. See Pamela Peterson, "Value-Based Measures of Performance," Chapter 4 in Frank J. Fabozzi and James L. Grant (eds.), *Value-Based Metrics: Foundations and Practice* (New Hope PA: Frank J. Fabozzi Associates, 2000).

over these traditional measures. This is because (1) ROA and ROE do not "account" for the EVA accounting adjustments that we made before; and (2) ROE is contaminated by debt-related financing decisions.[15]

Fix-It-Yourself Company: ROC Decomposition

ROC = NOPAT/Capital = $9,219/$80,071 = 11.51%
NOPAT Margin = NOPAT/Net sales = $9,219/$120,378 = 7.66%
Capital Turnover Ratio = Net sales/Capital = $120,378/$80,071 = 1.50
ROC = NOPAT Margin × Capital Turnover Ratio = 7.66 × 1.50 = 11.51%

At 11.51%, we see that Fix-It-Yourself Company's ROC is estimated by multiplying NOPAT margin, at 7.66%, by the invested capital turnover ratio of 1.50. Other things the same, it should be clear that anything that management can do to increase the NOPAT margin—for example, by obtaining reasonable cost savings on a given amount of revenue—and the invested capital turnover ratio—via improved capital efficiencies resulting from a lower net working capital to sales ratio and/ or a lower net plant, property and equipment to sales ratio—will result in improved returns on invested capital.[16] Such operating and capital-based improvements should impact economic profit and, ultimately, stock price in a favorable way.

Real-World Illustration

As a real-world application, Wolin and Klopukh provide an interesting breakdown of return on invested capital for Dayton Hudson Corporation.[17] Their EVA ratio application is shown in Exhibit 9.6. In this

---

[15] According to the traditional Dupont formula (see Chapter 8), ROE can be calculated by multiplying ROA—or net profit margin times asset turnover ratio—by the equity multiplier—assets over equity. In this context, ROC looks similar to ROA. However, both ROE and ROA have limited value because of the omitted EVA accounting adjustments. Moreover, the equity multiplier (as part of ROE) is contaminated by corporate leverage, since this ratio can also be expressed as 1/(1-DR), where DR is the total debt to assets ratio.

[16] Since the invested capital turnover ratio is net sales over invested capital, we can express this ratio as the *inverse* of the sum of (1) net working capital to sales ratio, (2) plant, property, and equipment to sales ratio, and (3) other assets to sales ratio. Looking at ROC this way shows that economic profit proponents are concerned with *both* top line revenue generation and bottom line economic profit (measured net of a firm's dollar cost of invested capital).

[17] See Jason L. Wolin and Steven Klopukh, "Integrating EVA® into the Portfolio Management Process," Chapter 6 in *Value-Based Metrics: Foundations and Practice.*

exhibit, we see a cross-sectional comparison of the NOPAT margin and invested capital turnover ratios for Dayton Hudson and its competitors—including Costco, K-Mart, and Wal-Mart—as well as a time-wise comparison of Dayton's one-year invested capital return versus a three-year average. Exhibit 9.6 also shows how income statement and balance sheet margins—such as gross profit margin and the net working capital margin (net working capital/sales) can be "rolled up" into a NOPAT margin and invested capital turnover ratio.

EXHIBIT 9.6   EVA Ratio Analysis for Dayton Hudson Corp. EVA-Based Financial Ratio Tree

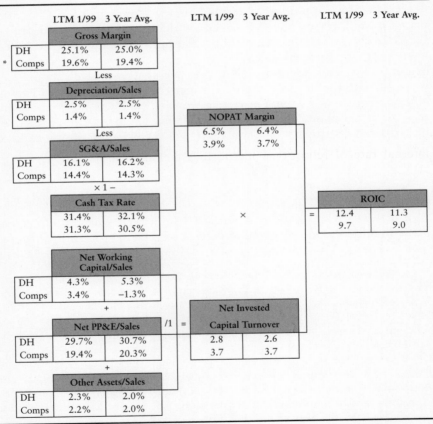

* Comparisons include Costco, K-Mart, and Wal-Mart. Competitor firm results are based on the mean ratio.
Source: Jason L. Wolin and Steven Klopukh, "Integrating EVA® into the Portfolio Management Process," Chapter 6 in *Value-Based Metrics: Foundations and Practice* (New Hope PA: Frank J. Fabozzi Associates, 2000).

Exhibit 9.6 shows that at the time of the report that Dayton Hudson's return on invested capital was noticeably higher than that of its close competitors. By inspection, we see that the upscale retailer had attractive capital returns because its NOPAT margin bested that of competitor firms. However, it seems that Dayton Hudson could generate even higher after-tax returns on invested capital if it could increase the invested capital turnover ratio. According to Wolin and Klopukh, this EVA improvement would require an examination of the firm's inventory policies and the economic profit consequences of the retailer's longer-term strategy of trying to best competitors by investing more capital on new stores.

CFROI ESTIMATION

Before moving on, we'll look at some prominent accounting adjustments associated with another prominent economic profit metric—namely, Cash Flow Return on Investment (CFROI). While in theory, EVA and CFROI can be used to derive the *same* answer for a company's economic profit, the twin metrics differ in practice in several important ways. Specifically, EVA is a dollar-based measure of economic profit while CFROI is an internal rate of return-type metric that measures the expected rate of return over the average life of a company's existing assets. Unlike EVA, CFROI uses gross cash flow and gross capital investment measures and the resulting IRR is measured in real terms as opposed to nominal terms.

Without getting into all the details,[18] the following five steps can be used to estimate a company's CFROI:

- Compute the average life of a company's existing assets
- Compute the gross cash flow
- Compute the gross investment
- Compute the sum of nondepreciating assets
- Solve for the CFROI (or internal rate of return)

In the first step, the average life of a company's existing assets can be measured by dividing gross depreciable assets by depreciation expense. Next, gross cash flow is equal to net income adjusted for financing expenses—such as interest expense and operating rental payments--and noncash operating expenses such as depreciation and amortization and the change in deferred taxes.

[18] For a rigorous explanation of CFROI, see Bartley J. Madden, *CFROI Valuation: A Total Systems Approach to Valuing the Firm* (Woburn, MA: Butterworth-Heinemann, 1999).

In turn, gross investment includes *gross* plant, property, and equipment and the EVA capital adjustments that we looked at before—including LIFO reserve, accumulated goodwill amortization, cumulative restructuring charges, and the present value of operating leases (among others). Also, in the CFROI calculation, nondepreciating assets include net short-term operating assets (current assets less noninterest bearing current liabilities), land and other assets. Following this five-step procedure, managers and investors can estimate a company's nominal CFROI.[19] The resulting IRR figure is then compared to the cost of capital to determine whether a company's has positive or negative economic profit.

CFROI Application

Let's return to the income statement and balance sheet (Exhibits 9.4 and 9.5) for Fix-It-Yourself Company to illustrate the accounting adjustments that are necessary to estimate CFROI in practice. We'll begin with the average life of the firm's existing assets. Assuming, for convenience, that gross plant, property, and equipment on the balance sheet equals $51,250, we find that the estimated life of the firm's existing assets is ten years. This figure is calculated as follows:

Fix-It-Yourself Company: Average Life of Existing Assets

Gross plant, property & equipment = $51,250
Depreciation expense (income statement) = $5,125

Average life of existing assets   = Gross PP&E/Depreciation
$51,250/$5,125 = 10 years

Next, the gross cash flow for Fix-It-Yourself Company is obtained by adding the following items to net income: depreciation and amortization, interest expense, rental (lease) expense and the increase in deferred taxes. The resulting gross cash flow figure is $13,290:

Fix-It-Yourself Company: Gross Cash Flow ($ thousands)

Net income (before extraordinary items)	$5,518
Depreciation and amortization	5,125
Interest expense	1,379
Rental expense	1,075 (operating leases)
Increase in deferred taxes	193
Gross Cash Flow	$13,290

[19] For simplicity, we'll look at nominal as opposed to real CFROI.

Starting with gross plant, property and equipment, net intangibles, and adding the EVA capital adjustments that we made before, provides estimate of gross cash investment for Fix-It-Yourself Company. Upon making these capital adjustments, we find that Fix-It-Yourself Company's Gross Cash Investment is $65,592:

Fix-It-Yourself Company: Gross Cash Investment ($ thousands)

Gross plant, property & equipment	$51,250
Goodwill, net	300
LIFO Reserve	1,225
Accumulated Goodwill Amortization	4,550
Cumulative Restructuring Charges	3,975
Present Value of Operating Leases	4,292
Gross Cash Investment	$65,592

Also, assuming that net plant, property and equipment consist of $8,000 in land, we can estimate the nondepreciating assets for Fix-It-Yourself Company.[20] At $46,499, this amount is calculated as follows:

Fix-It-Yourself Company: Nondepreciating Assets ($ thousands)

Net short-term operating assets	$38,410
Land	8,000
Other assets	89*
Nondepreciating assets	$46,499

*Assumed nondepreciating.

We can now "roll-up" the previous calculations to obtain an estimate of CFROI. Based on the above considerations, the (nominal) CFROI for Fix-It-Yourself Company is 19.09%. Using a standard IRR procedure, this percentage return is calculated as follows:

Fix-It-Yourself Company: CFROI

FV = Sum of nondepreciating assets = $46,499
PV = Gross cash investment = $65,592
Payment = Gross cash flow = $13,290
N = Average life of existing assets = 10 years

IRR = (nominal) CFROI = 19.09%

[20] For simplicity, the nondepreciating "land" account is not netted from the GPP&E account.

If for convenience we use the previously estimated COC of 7.82% as the company-wide "hurdle rate" for capital investments,[21] we again see that Fix-It-Yourself Company is a potential wealth creator.[22] This favorable NPV result occurs because the after-tax return on existing assets (in this instance, cash flow return on investment) exceeds the weighted average cost of capital.

SUMMARY

In this chapter, we looked at standard EVA accounting adjustments that can impact a company's economic profit in practice. The standard income statement adjustments include *changes* in the following accounts: LIFO reserve, accumulated goodwill amortization, net capitalized research and development, net bad debt expense, and cumulative restructuring charges. The implied interest expense on operating leases must also be reflected on the EVA income statement. In turn, with each income statement adjustment we found that a companion accounting adjustment was necessary to estimate invested capital on the EVA balance sheet.

We can then estimate economic profit with knowledge of a company's net operating profit after tax (NOPAT) and the dollar cost of capital. While the EVA calculated with standard accounting adjustments should provide a better approximation to true economic profit, it goes without saying that there may be several other adjustments that could impact a firm's economic profit in a meaningful way. At some point, however, the manager or investor must decide the "just right" number of EVA accounting adjustments for the company at hand. Presumably, the ideal set of adjustments occurs where the marginal benefit of making another EVA (or CFROI) accounting adjustment is just offset by the marginal cost of making the income statement and balance sheet change.

We also looked at standard accounting adjustments that are necessary to calculate a company's cash flow return on investment. Like EVA, there are many accounting adjustments that can be made to estimate a company's CFROI in practice. While it was shown in Chapter 2 that these metrics are theoretically equivalent measures of economic profit, EVA and CFROI dif-

---

[21] Due to empirical limitations associated with CAPM, Holt Value Associates prefers an internally-generated cost of capital for the firm. Moreover, in practice, the CFROI and hurdle rate are measured in real as opposed to nominal terms. See Madden, *CFROI Valuation: A Total Systems Approach to Valuing the Firm.*

[22] As with EVA, the operative word here is "potential" wealth creator. We still need to know something about the expected return on future assets not currently in place measured relative to the cost of invested capital.

fer in some important ways. Unlike EVA, CFROI is (1) an IRR-based measure of economic profit, (2) measured over the estimated life of a company's existing assets, and (3) estimated in real terms as opposed to nominal terms. Practically speaking though, the two economic profit measures are similar in the sense that if *on balance* CFROI or EVA-based ROC exceed the relevant cost of capital, COC, then a company is a wealth creator. Conversely, if CFROI or ROC falls below the cost of invested capital, then a company is a wealth destroyer. We'll explore the valuation side of economic profit measurement as we move forward in this book.

APPENDIX A
EVA ESTIMATION: MICROSOFT CORPORATION

Based on the standard accounting adjustments explained in Chapter 9, Appendix A provides a real-world illustration of how to estimate NOPAT and Invested Capital for Microsoft Corporation—a well-known wealth creator.[23] The following exhibits (*with footnotes*) are relevant to the 2000 NOPAT and Invested Capital calculations for Microsoft Corporation:

Exhibit	Item
9.A.1	2000 Income Statement
9.A.2	1999-2000 Balance Sheet
9.A.3	2000 NOPAT: Bottom-up Approach
9.A.4	2000 NOPAT: Top-down Approach
9.A.5	2000 Invested Capital: Assets Approach
9.A.6	2000 Invested Capital: Financing Approach
9.A.7	2000 Economic Value Added

On balance, the 2000 NOPAT estimate for Microsoft Corporation using the standard accounting adjustments explained in this chapter is consistent with the more customized NOPAT estimate obtained by Stern Stewart. The similarity of NOPAT estimates (with accounting adjustments) is a more general finding obtained by the author on industrial companies that comprise the Dow Jones Industrial Average. However, the resulting independent EVA estimates for companies may differ due to varying assumptions about the risk-free rate of interest, the estimate of systematic risk (beta), the market risk premium, and weights (book *versus* market) used in the cost of capital estimation process.

[23] Consistent with the fundamental nature of a wealth creator, the independent EVA estimates obtained by the author and Stern Stewart on Microsoft were *positive* for year 2000.

EXHIBIT 9.A.1 Microsoft Corporation—Income Statement ($ Millions, Except per Share Figures)

	Jun-00 Historical	Jun-99 Historical
Sales	$22,956.00	$19,747.00
Cost of Goods Sold	2,334.00	2,331.00
Selling, General, and Administrative Expense	8,925.00	6,890.00
Operating Income Before Depreciation	11,697.00	10,526.00
Depreciation and Amortization	668.00	483.00
Interest Expense	0.00	0.00
Nonoperating Income (Expense) and Special Items	3,246.00	1,848.00
Pretax Income	14,275.00	11,891.00
Income Taxes - Total	4,854.00	4,106.00
Minority Interest	0.00	0.00
Income Before Extraordinary Items	9,421.00	7,785.00
Extraordinary Items and Discontinued Operations	0.00	0.00
Net Income (Loss)	9,421.00	7,785.00
Earnings Per Share (Primary)– Excluding Extraordinary Items	1.81	1.54
Earnings Per Share (Primary)– Including Extraordinary Items	1.81	1.54
Common Shares Used to Calculate Primary EPS	5,189.00	5,028.00
Earnings Per Share (Fully Diluted)– Excluding Extraordinary Items	1.7	1.42
Earnings Per Share (Fully Diluted)– Including Extraordinary Items	1.7	1.42

Source: Compustat.

EXHIBIT 9.A.2   Microsoft Corporation—Balance Sheet ($ Millions)

	Jun-00	Jun-99
ASSETS		
Cash and Short-Term Investments	$23,798.00	$17,236.00
Receivables	3,250.00	2,245.00
Inventories - Total	0.00	0.00
Prepaid Expense	0.00	0.00
Other Current Assets	3,260.00	752.00
Total Current Assets	$30,308.00	$20,233.00
Property, Plant, and Equipment - Total (Gross)	4,314.00	3,516.00
Depreciation, Depletion, and Amortization (Accumulated)	2,411.00	1,905.00
Property, Plant, and Equipment - Total (Net)	$1,903.00	$1,611.00
Investments and Advances - Equity Method	0.00	4,162.00
Investments and Advances - Other	17,726.00	10,210.00
Intangibles	0.00	0.00
Deferred Charges	0.00	0.00
Other Assets	2,213.00	940.00
TOTAL ASSETS	$52,150.00	$37,156.00
LIABILITIES		
Debt - Due in One Year	0.00	0.00
Notes Payable	0.00	0.00
Accounts Payable	1,083.00	874.00
Income Taxes Payable	585.00	1,607.00
Accrued Expense	557.00	396.00
Other Current Liabilities	7,530.00	5,841.00
Total Current Liabilities	$9,755.00	$8,718.00
Long-Term Debt - Total	0.00	0.00
Deferred Taxes	1,027.00	0.00
Investment Tax Credit	0.00	0.00
Minority Interest	0.00	0.00
Other Liabilities	0.00	0.00
EQUITY		
Preferred Stock - Redeemable	0.00	0.00
Preferred Stock - Nonredeemable	0.00	980.00
Total Preferred Stock	0.00	980.00
Common Stock	0.07	0.06
Capital Surplus	23,194.93	13,843.94
Retained Earnings	18,173.00	13,614.00
Less: Treasury Stock - Total Dollar Amount	0.00	0.00
Total Common Equity	$41,368.00	$27,458.00
TOTAL STOCKHOLDERS' EQUITY	$41,368.00	$28,438.00
TOTAL LIABILITIES AND STOCKHOLDERS' EQUITY	$52,150.00	$37,156.00
COMMON SHARES OUTSTANDING	5,283.00	5,109.00

Source: Compustat.

EXHIBIT 9.A.3   Microsoft Corporation—2000 NOPAT: Bottom-up Approach
(\$ Millions)

Begin:		
Operating Profit After Depreciation	\$11,029.00	
Add:		
Implied interest on Operating Leases	40.73	(note 1)
Increase/(Decrease) in LIFO Reserves	—	(note 2)
Increase/(Decrease) in Capitalized R&D	693.00	(note 3)
Equals:		
Adjusted Operating Profit Before Taxes (A)	11,762.73	
Begin:		
Income Tax Expense	4,854.00	
Add:		
Tax on Interest Expense	—	
Tax on Implied interest on Operating Leases	14.26	
Change in Deferred Taxes (Balance Sheet)	(1,027.00)	(note 4)
Tax on Special Items	(1,136.10)	(note 5)
Equals:		
Cash Operating Taxes (B)	2,705.16	
NOPAT (A-B)	9,057.57	

EXHIBIT 9.A.4   Microsoft Corporation—2000 NOPAT: Top-Down Approach
(\$ Millions)

Begin:		
Sales	\$22,956.00	
Less:		
Cost of Goods sold	2,334.00	
Selling, General and Administrative expenses	8,925.00	
Depreciation	668.00	
Add:		
Implied interest on Operating Leases	40.73	(note 1)
Increase/(Decrease) in LIFO Reserve	—	(note 2)
Increase/(Decrease) in Capitalized R&D	693.00	(note 3)
Other Operating Income	—	
Equals:		
Adjusted Operating Profits Before Taxes (A)	11,762.73	
Income Tax Expense	4,854.00	
Add:		
Tax on Interest Expense	—	
Tax on Implied interest on Operating Leases	14.26	
Change in Deferred Taxes (Balance Sheet)	(1,027.00)	(note 4)
Tax on Special Items	(1,136.10)	(note 5)
Equals:		
Cash Operating Taxes (B)	2,705.16	
NOPAT (A-B)	9,057.57	

EXHIBIT 9.A.5 Microsoft Corporation—2000 Invested Capital: Assets Approach (BOY capital, $ Millions)

Begin:		
Current Assets net of Current Liabilities	$11,515.00	(Current Liabilities exclude Notes Payable and Short-term Debt)
Add:		
Net Property, Plant and Equipment	1,611.00	
Intangibles	—	
Other Assets	15,312.00	
LIFO Reserves	—	(note 2)
Unamortized R&D	2,814.00	(note 3)
Present Value of Operating Leases	436.39	(note 1)
Equals:		
Invested Capital	$31,688.39	

EXHIBIT 9.A.6 Microsoft Corporation—2000 Invested Capital: Financing Approach (BOY capital, $ Millions)

Begin:		
Book Value of Common Equity	$27,458.00	
Add: Equity Equivalents		
Preferred Stock	980.00	
Minority Interest	—	
Deferred Income Taxes	—	
Unamortized R&D	2,814.00	(note 3)
LIFO Reserves	—	(note 2)
Total Equity	$31,252.00	
Add:		
Debt and Debt Equivalents		
Interest Bearing short-term debt	—	
Long-term Debt	—	
Other Liabilities	—	
PV of Operating Leases	436.39	(note 1)
Total Debt	$436.39	
Equals:		
Invested Capital	$31,688.39	

EXHIBIT 9.A.7   Microsoft Corporation 2000 Economic Value Added ($ Millions)

		Weights
Total Debt ($ millions)	$436.39	1.38% wd
Total Equity ($ millions)	$31,252.00	98.62% we
Total Capital ($ millions) – (A)	$31,688.39	
Levered Stock Beta (Valueline)	1.20	
Cost of Debt (rd)	6.00%	
Tax Rate (t)	35.00%	
Post-tax Cost of Debt {(1 – t) × rd}	3.90%	
Risk Free Rate	5.00%	
Risk Premium	6.00%	
Cost of Equity (using CAPM) – (re)	12.20%	
WACC [{(1 – t) × rd × wd} + {re × we}] – (B)	12.09%	
Cost of Capital ($ millions) – {(B) × (A)}	3,829.76	
NOPAT ($ millions) – (C)	9,057.57	
EVA ($ millions) – [(C) – {(B) × (A)}]	$5,227.81	Wealth Creator!

Microsoft Corporation: Notes to NOPAT and Capital Calculations

1. The Present Value of Operating Leases for 2000 and 1999 were $679 million and $436 million respectively. The interest rate implicit in the leases is assumed to be 6%. Accordingly the charge for 2000 is $679 × 6%.
2. LIFO Reserves for 2000 and 1999 were $ nil million and $ nil million respectively.
3. R&D Expenses are assumed to be capitalized when incurred and then amortized ratably over three years. Therefore, R&D amortization for 2000 is 1/3 of the aggregate expenditure on R&D during each of three years 1998, 1999, and 2000.

   Following similar logic, Unamortized R&D for 2000 is 2/3 of the expenditure in 2000 and 1/3 of the expenditure in 1999. Note also that, by the end of 2000, the balance of unamortized R&D from 1998 will be nil. Given below is the year-wise expenditure on R&D:

   1997 – $1,925 million
   1998 – $2,502 million
   1999 – $2,970 million
   2000 – $3,775 million

Hence, R&D expense for 2000 is 1/3 of ($2,502 + $2,970 + $3,775) = $3,082. Likewise, Unamortized R&D at the beginning of year 2000 will be 2/3 of expenditure in 1999 and 1/3 of expenditure in 1998—namely, 2/3 × $2,970 + 1/3 × $2,502 = $2,814. Balance at the end of 2000 is $ 3,507, making for an increase of $693.

4. A decrease in Deferred Tax Liabilities represents a higher cash payout for taxes. Similarly, an increase in Deferred Tax Assets represents a higher cash payout for taxes.

5. Special Items or Nonoperating Items are treated as nonrecurring items. Therefore, to insulate the EVA calculations from the effects of these items, we exclude them from our calculation of Adjusted Profits. To keep the calculations consistent, we must also insulate the calculation of taxes from the effects of these items. If Special Items were a net income, it would mean that the company's tax liability is higher to the extent of the net income effect whereas if the Special items were a net expense, the company's tax liability would be lower to the extent of the net expense.

6. The figures for Accumulated Goodwill written-off were not available in Compustat. Furthermore, under current U.S. GAAP, goodwill is no longer required to be amortized and hence the adjustment to capital is not needed.

APPENDIX B
EVA ESTIMATION: GENERAL MOTORS CORPORATION

Appendix B provides a real-world illustration of how to estimate NOPAT and Invested Capital for General Motors Corporation—unfortunately, a recent wealth destroyer.[24] The following exhibits (*with footnotes*) are relevant to the 2000 NOPAT and Invested Capital calculations for General Motors Corporation:

Exhibit	Item
9.B.1	2000 Income Statement
9.B.2	1999–2000 Balance Sheet
9.B.3	2000 NOPAT: Bottom-up Approach
9.B.4	2000 NOPAT: Top-down Approach
9.B.5	2000 Invested Capital: Assets Approach
9.B.6	2000 Invested Capital: Financing Approach
9.B.7	2000 Economic Value Added

[24] Consistent with the fundamental nature of a wealth destroyer, the independent EVA estimates obtained by the author and Stern Stewart on General Motors were *negative* for year 2000.

As with Appendix A, the resulting 2000 NOPAT estimate for General Motors using the standard accounting adjustments explained in Chapter 9 is consistent with the more customized NOPAT estimate obtained by Stern Stewart. The similarity of NOPAT estimates is a general finding obtained by the author on industrial companies that comprise the Dow Jones Industrial Average. However, as noted before, the resulting independent EVA estimates for companies may differ due to varying assumptions about the risk-free rate of interest, the estimate of systematic risk (beta), the market risk premium, and weights (book *versus* market) used in the cost of capital estimation process.

EXHIBIT 9.B.1 General Motors Corporation Income Statement ($ Millions, Except per Share Figures)

	Dec-00 Historical	Dec-99 Historical
Sales*	$180,557.00	$174,694.00
Cost of Goods Sold	130,830.00	128,095.00
Selling, General, and Administrative Expense	22,252.00	18,845.00
Operating Income Before Depreciation	27,475.00	27,754.00
Depreciation and Amortization	13,411.00	12,318.00
Interest Expense	9,552.00	7,750.00
Nonoperating Income (Expense) and Special Items	2,333.00	1,036.00
Pretax Income	6,845.00	8,722.00
Income Taxes - Total	2,393.00	3,118.00
Minority Interest	0.00	28.00
Income Before Extraordinary Items	4,452.00	5,576.00
Extraordinary Items and Discontinued Operations	0.00	426.00
Net Income (Loss)	4,452.00	6,002.00
Earnings Per Share (Primary)– Excluding Extraordinary Items	6.80	8.70
Earnings Per Share (Primary)– Including Extraordinary Items	6.80	9.36
Common Shares Used to Calculate Primary EPS	582.00	643.00
Earnings Per Share (Fully Diluted)– Excluding Extraordinary Items	6.68	8.53
Earnings Per Share (Fully Diluted)– Including Extraordinary Items	6.68	9.18

* Figure reflects the latest available on Compustat.
Source: Compustat.

EXHIBIT 9.B.2 General Motors Corporation Balance Sheet ($ Millions)

	Dec-00	Dec-99
ASSETS		
Cash and Short-Term Investments	$10,284.00	$10,442.00
Receivables	110,788.00	94,788.00
Inventories - Total	16,704.00	16,316.00
Other Current Assets	8,388.00	9,006.00
Total Current Assets	$146,164.00	$130,552.00
Property, Plant, and Equipment - Total (Gross)	120,815.00	119,418.00
Depreciation, Depletion, and Amortization (Accumulated)	42,972.00	43,798.00
Property, Plant, and Equipment - Total (Net)	$77,843.00	$75,620.00
Investments and Advances - Equity Method	3,497.00	1,711.00
Investments and Advances - Other	17,317.00	14,275.00
Intangibles	14,795.00	14,847.00
Deferred Charges	20,184.00	16,100.00
Other Assets	23,300.00	21,625.00
TOTAL ASSETS	$303,100.00	$274,730.00
LIABILITIES		
Debt - Due in One Year	19,018.00	15,677.00
Notes Payable	59,933.00	53,266.00
Accounts Payable	25,725.00	21,516.00
Income Taxes Payable	1,016.00	1,445.00
Accrued Expense	24,840.00	24,723.00
Other Current Liabilities	1,971.00	1,001.00
Total Current Liabilities	$132,503.00	$117,628.00
Long-Term Debt - Total	65,843.00	62,963.00
Deferred Taxes	6,451.00	6,656.00
Investment Tax Credit	0.00	0.00
Minority Interest	707.00	596.00
Other Liabilities	67,421.00	66,243.00
EQUITY		
Preferred Stock - Redeemable	0.00	0.00
Preferred Stock - Nonredeemable	0.00	0.00
Total Preferred Stock	$0.00	$0.00
Common Stock	914.00	1,033.00
Capital Surplus	21,108.00	13,808.00
Retained Earnings	8,153.00	5,803.00
Less: Treasury Stock - Total Dollar Amount	0.00	0.00
Total Common Equity	$30,175.00	$20,644.00
TOTAL STOCKHOLDERS' EQUITY	$30,175.00	$20,644.00
TOTAL LIABILITIES AND STOCKHOLDERS' EQUITY	$303,100.00	$274,730.00
COMMON SHARES OUTSTANDING	548.18	619.41

Source: Compustat.

EXHIBIT 9.B.3   General Motors Corporation—2000 NOPAT: Bottom-up Approach ($ Millions)

Begin:		
Operating Profit After Depreciation	$14,064.00	
Add:		
Implied interest on Operating Leases	104.32	(note 1)
Increase/(Decrease) in LIFO Reserves	39.00	(note 2)
Increase/(Decrease) in Capitalized R&D	(500.00)	(note 3)
Equals:		
Adjusted Operating Profit Before Taxes (A)	13,707.32	
Begin:		
Income Tax Expense	2,393.00	
Add:		
Tax on Interest Expense	3,343.20	
Tax on Implied interest on Operating Leases	36.51	
Change in Deferred Taxes (Balance Sheet)	205.00	(note 4)
Tax on Special Items	(816.55)	(note 5)
Equals:		
Cash Operating Taxes (B)	5,161.16	
NOPAT (A-B)	8,546.16	

EXHIBIT 9.B.4   General Motors Corporation—2000 NOPAT: Top-down Approach ($ Millions)

Begin:		
Sales	$180,557.00	
Less:		
Cost of Goods sold	130,830.00	
Selling, General and Administrative expenses	22,252.00	
Depreciation	13,411.00	
Add:		
Implied interest on Operating Leases	104.32	(note 1)
Increase/(Decrease) in LIFO Reserve	39.00	(note 2)
Increase/(Decrease) in Capitalized R&D	(500.00)	(note 3)
Other Operating Income	—	
Equals:		
Adjusted Operating Profits Before Taxes (A)	13,707.32	
Begin:		
Income Tax Expense	2,393.00	
Add:		
Tax on Interest Expense	3,343.20	
Tax on Implied interest on Operating Leases	36.51	
Change in Deferred Taxes (Balance Sheet)	205.00	(note 4)
Tax on Special Items	(816.55)	(note 5)
Equals:		
Cash Operating Taxes (B)	5,161.16	
NOPAT (A-B)	8,546.16	

EXHIBIT 9.B.5 General Motors Corporation—2000 Invested Capital: Assets Approach (BOY capital, $ Millions)

Begin:		
Current Assets net of Current Liabilities	$81,867.00	(Current Liabilities exclude Notes Payable & other short term debt)
Add:		
Net Property, Plant and Equipment	75,620.00	
Intangibles	14,847.00	
Other Assets	53,711.00	
LIFO Reserves	1,890.00	(note 2)
Unamortized R&D	7,167.00	(note 3)
Present Value of Operating Leases	1,865.00	(note 1)
Equals:		
Invested Capital	$236,967.00	

EXHIBIT 9.B.6 General Motors Corporation—2000 Invested Capital: Financing Approach (BOY capital, $ Millions)

Begin:		
Book Value of Common Equity	$20,644.00	
Add: Equity Equivalents		
Preferred Stock	—	
Minority Interest	596.00	
Deferred Income Taxes	6,656.00	
Unamortized R&D	7,167.00	(note 3)
LIFO Reserves	1,890.00	(note 2)
Total Equity	$36,953.00	
Debt and Debt Equivalents		
Interest Bearing short-term debt	68,943.00	
Long-term Debt	62,963.00	
Other Liabilities	66,243.00	
PV of Operating Leases	1,865.00	(note 1)
Total Debt	$200,014.00	
Equals:		
Invested Capital	$236,967.00	

EXHIBIT 9.B.7 General Motors 2000 Economic Value Added ($ Millions)

		Weights
Total Debt ($ millions)	$200,014.00	84.41% wd
Total Equity ($ millions)	$36,953.00	15.59% we
Total Capital ($ millions) – (A)	$236,967.00	
Levered Stock Beta (Valueline)	1.10	
Cost of Debt (rd)	6.00%	
Tax Rate (t)	35.00%	
Post-tax Cost of Debt {(1 – t) × rd}	3.90%	
Risk Free Rate	5.00%	
Risk Premium	6.00%	
Cost of Equity (using CAPM) – (re)	11.60%	
WACC [{(1 – t) × rd × wd} + {re × we}] – (B)	5.10%	
Cost of Capital ($ millions) – {(B) × (A)}	12,087.09	
NOPAT ($ millions) – (C)	8,546.16	
EVA ($ millions) – [(C) – {(B) × (A)}]	(3,540.94)	Wealth Destroyer!

General Motors Corporation: Notes to NOPAT and Capital Calculations

1. The Present Value of Operating Leases for 2000 and 1999 were $1,738 million and $1,865 million respectively. The interest rate implicit in the leases is assumed to be 6%. Accordingly the charge for 2000 is $1,738 × 6%.
2. LIFO Reserves for 2000 and 1999 were $1,929 million and $1,890 million respectively.
3. R&D Expenses are assumed to be capitalized when incurred and then amortized ratably over three years. Therefore, the R&D amortization for 2000 is 1/3 of the aggregate expenditure on R&D during each of three years 1998, 1999, and 2000.

   Following similar logic, Unamortized R&D for 2000 is 2/3 of the expenditure in 2000 and 1/3 of the expenditure in 1999. Note also that, by the end of 2000, the balance of unamortized R&D from 1998 is nil. Given below is the year-wise expenditure on R&D:

   1997 – $8,200 million
   1998 – $7,900 million
   1999 – $6,800 million
   2000 – $6,600 million

Hence expenses for 2000 are ($6,600 + $6,800 + $7,900)/3 = $7,100

Unamortized R&D at the beginning of 2000
= 2/3 × $6,800 + 1/3 × $7,900 = $7,167

Unamortized R&D at the end of 2000
= 2/3 × $6,600 + 1/3 × $6,800 = $6,667

Net Change in Unamortized R&D is thus ($500.00)

4. A decrease in Deferred Tax Liabilities represents a higher cash payout for taxes. Similarly, an increase in Deferred Tax Assets represents a higher cash payout for taxes.

5. Special Items or Nonoperating Items are treated as nonrecurring items. Therefore, to insulate the EVA calculations from the effects of these items, we exclude them from our calculation of Adjusted Profits. To keep the calculations consistent, we must also insulate the calculation of taxes from the effects of these items. If Special Items were a net income, it would mean that the company's tax liability is higher to the extent of the net income effect whereas if the Special Items were a net expense, the company's tax liability would be lower to the extent of the net expense.

CHAPTER 10

Role of Economic Depreciation

In Chapter 9, we examined the standard EVA accounting adjustments that are necessary to estimate a company's net operating profit after taxes (NOPAT) and its invested capital. In practice, there are even more sophisticated refinements that a manager or investor could make to arrive at a company's economic profit. Following the pioneering work of Ehrbar and O'Byrne, these EVA adjustments include the advanced treatment of accounting items such as depreciation, acquisition good-will, strategic investments, short-term operating assets, and even environmental liabilities.[1] In this chapter, we'll look at how the concept of economic depreciation—both positive *and* negative depreciation—can sharpen analyst estimates of NOPAT, invested capital, and economic profit.

We'll first look at the inconsistency of using straight-line depreciation in the measurement of economic profit. In this regard, we'll see how economic depreciation helps to resolve the straight-line depreciation bias in the return on invested capital. Next, we'll examine the role of negative economic depreciation—namely, assets with appreciating cash flows—in providing improved capital return and EVA estimates for companies that pursue strategic growth opportunities via internal R&D investments and/or corporate acquisitions.

---

[1] Stephen O'Byrne provides a rigorous discussion of several "EVA on EVA" accounting refinements including economic depreciation, acquisition goodwill, short-term operating assets, and environmental liabilities. See Stephen F. O'Byrne, "Does Value-Based Management Discourage Investment in Intangibles?" Chapter 5 in *Value-Based Metrics: Foundations and Practice* (New Hope, PA: Frank J. Fabozzi Associates, 2000). Al Ehrbar's insightful discussion of EVA accounting issues can be found in *EVA: The Real Key to Creating Wealth* (New York: John Wiley and Sons, 1998).

ROC BIAS USING STRAIGHT-LINE DEPRECIATION

For convenience, let's return to Fix-It-Yourself Company (recall Chapter 9). Suppose the popular home supply company has the opportunity to invest in a fleet of bulk lifting machines that will improve in-store distribution of products and save on labor costs. Further, suppose that each machine costs $32,000 and generates a pretax dollar-based operating margin—earnings before interest, taxes and depreciation (EBITD)—of $15,000 for four years. Exhibit 10.1 shows a yearly breakdown of Fix-It-Yourself Company's *unadjusted* NOPAT and invested capital on a per machine basis.

With straight-line depreciation, the annual capital recovery is $8,000 per lifting machine. Also, with EBITD of $15,000 each year, we see that Fix-It-Yourself Company's net operating profit after tax (NOPAT)—assuming a 35% tax rate—is constant at $4,550 per year. Likewise, the firm's yearly free cash flow estimates—NOPAT less *net* annual investment—are also constant at $12,550. As presented in Exhibit 10.1, these cash flow estimates do not give a manager or investor any reason to believe that the returns per lifting machine are improving or deteriorating with the passage of time.

Yet, Exhibit 10.1 shows that the after-tax return on invested capital is rising quite dramatically over time. At 56.88% for year 4, the return on invested capital (ROC) is noticeably higher than the after-tax capital

EXHIBIT 10.1 ROC Bias Using Straight Line Depreciation

Year	0	1	2	3	4
EBITD		$15,000	$15,000	$15,000	$15,000
Depr.		8,000	8,000	8,000	8,000
EBIT		7,000	7,000	7,000	7,000
Taxes		2,450	2,450	2,450	2,450
NOPAT		4,550	4,550	4,550	4,550
Net Invest	$32,000	−8,000	−8,000	−8,000	−8,000
FCF		12,550	12,550	12,550	12,550
IRR%	20.80%				
Capital	32,000	24,000	16,000	8,000	0
ROC%*		14.22%	18.96%	28.44%	56.88%

* ROC% = [NOPAT/BOY Capital] × 100.

return of 14.22% for year 1. The obvious culprit in the matter is the constant decline in invested capital caused by straight-line depreciation of $8,000 per year. That is, while NOPAT—as well as free cash flow—for the lifting machine is constant each year, the denominator of the return on invested capital ratio continues to fall.

Managers and investors must of course we wary of projects that give the "illusion" of dramatically improving capital returns. That is not to say that capital investment opportunities cannot give great returns. However, in the case at hand, we'll see that the after-tax capital returns on the proposed lifting machines are not only constant each year, but they are also equal to an (adjusted) after-tax internal rate of return of 20.10%. As O'Byrne points out, there are two key steps to show such financial results: (1) calculate the economic depreciation on the proposed capital investment, and (2) rework the NOPAT and invested capital figures to arrive at the correct after-tax return on invested capital.[2]

Estimation and Benefit of Economic Depreciation

Exhibit 10.2 shows how to estimate economic depreciation on Fix-It-Yourself Company's proposed lifting machines. In a nutshell, economic depreciation is viewed as the return of principal (or capital recovery) on an amortized loan such as a mortgage or automobile loan. With knowledge of the investment cost (at $32,000) and the pretax dollar operating margin (EBITD at $15,000 for four years), we can calculate the pretax internal rate of return (IRR) on the proposed lifting machine, at 30.92%. We can quantify this present value of annuity relationship as:

$$\$32,000 = \$15,000 \times \text{Annuity factor (IRR, 4 years)}$$
$$= \$15,000 \times [1/\text{IRR} \times (1 - 1/(1 + \text{IRR})^4)]$$

In this expression, IRR is the pretax internal rate of return on one of Fix-It-Yourself Company's proposed lifting machines. As noted before, each machine costs $32,000 and has an estimated 4-year pretax dollar operating margin of $15,000. Also, with knowledge of the pretax IRR, at 30.92%, we can now calculate the yearly "interest" return and capital recovery (economic depreciation) on the proposed lifting machine. Exhibit 10.2 shows the yearly breakdown of "interest" and return of "principal," as well as the invested capital balance at the end of each year. In effect, we are splitting up the annual project EBITD of $15,000 into economic depreciation (capital recovery) and EBIT components.

---

[2] See O'Byrne, "Does Value-Based Management Discourage Investment in Intangibles?"

EXHIBIT 10.2   Economic Depreciation on New Project

Year	0	1	2	3	4
Capital*	$32,000	$26,894	$20,210	$11,459	$2
Level payment (project EBITD)		15,000	15,000	15,000	15,000
Pretax IRR%	30.92%				
$ Interest return** (project EBIT)		9,894	8,316	6,249	3,543
Capital recovery (project depreciation)		5,106	6,684	8,751	11,457

*Year 4 capital difference from zero due to rounding.
**$ Interest return = Pretax IRR × BOY Capital.

EXHIBIT 10.3   Correction of ROC Bias Using Economic Depreciation

Year	0	1	2	3	4
EBITD		$15,000	$15,000	$15,000	$15,000
Depr.		5,106	6,684	8,751	11,457
EBIT		9,894	8,316	6,249	3,543
Taxes		3,463	2,911	2,187	1,240
NOPAT		6,431	5,405	4,062	2,303
Net Invest	$32,000	−5,106	−6,684	−8,751	−11,457
FCF		11,537	12,089	12,813	13,760
After-tax IRR%	20.10%				
Capital*	32,000	26,894	20,210	11,459	2
ROC%		20.10%	20.10%	20.10%	20.10%

*Year 4 capital difference from zero due to rounding.
Note: After-tax IRR of 20.10% is also equal to $(1 - t)$ Pretax IRR:
$(1 - 0.35) \times 30.92\% = 20.10\%$.

We are now ready to calculate the revised NOPAT, invested capital, and after-tax return on capital figures for Fix-It-Yourself Company's proposed lifting machine. With economic depreciation, we see in Exhibit 10.3 that the projected NOPAT estimates are declining each year in the presence of companion declines in the amount of invested capital. Interesting enough though, the yearly decline in NOPAT and invested capital is such that the after-tax return on invested capital is constant at 20.10%. Moreover, at this rate, the after-tax return on invested capital (ROC) is equal to the after-tax internal rate of return.

The EVA importance of this illustration for managers and investors should be crystal clear. First, managers and investors should take a good look at invested capital returns to see if they are in fact increasing or decreasing. Incorrect capital budgeting decisions by managers and/or incorrect stock selection decisions by investors can result without a proper assessment of invested capital returns. Second, we know that investment opportunities should be evaluated in the context of an internal rate of return (after-tax return on invested capital using economic depreciation) measured relative to the cost of capital.

In terms of Fix-It-Yourself Company's investment opportunity, the proposed lifting machine is acceptable as long as the weighted average cost of capital is *less* than the firm's after-tax capital return (IRR) of 20.10%. While it is likely that the home supply company's "hurdle rate" is less than this rate, one should note that if straight-line depreciation were used in assessing EVA, the project would be rejected if the cost of capital were above 14.22% (ROC for year 1 in Exhibit 10.1). In effect, the proposed lifting machines will create value for Fix-It-Yourself Company's shareholders as long as the after-tax cost of capital is less than 20.10%. Otherwise, shareholder value will be destroyed at this company—or any real world company in a similar position—as reflected in a declining stock price.

NEGATIVE DEPRECIATION (ACQUISITIONS AND R&D INVESTMENTS)

While the concept of positive economic depreciation can be used to address an "old assets versus new assets problem," the concept of negative economic depreciation—with appreciating cash flows and asset values—can be used to improve capital return and economic profit estimates for acquisitions and internal R&D investments.[3] These strategic investments generally have sizable "back-loaded" cash flows. To illustrate this EVA refinement, let's assume that Fix-It-Yourself Com-

---

[3] In the previous section, we looked at how positive economic depreciation eliminates bias in capital returns that results from straight-line depreciation. However, it should be evident that if a manager or investor were looking at a rising stream of returns on existing assets, he or she might be misled into thinking that the "old assets" were quite attractive with little need for replacement. This faulty EVA thinking could severely limit the firm's future growth opportunities.

pany is contemplating the purchase of an Internet-based hardware store called "Why Wait Supply Company." For convenience, we'll use the cash flow and enterprise valuation results from Chapter 6 in explaining the benefits of using negative economic depreciation over the "conventional" EVA approach.[4]

Exhibit 10.4 shows the first five (out of ten) years of capital return estimates for Why Wait Supply Company. In this exhibit, we see two measures of invested capital return: (1) the forecasted return on existing operating capital, and (2) the standard EVA return on acquisition capital. The favorable return estimates on operating capital are obtained by dividing the firm's net operating profit after tax (NOPAT) by the amount of operating capital. In contrast, the *meager* returns on acquisition capital shown in Exhibit 10.4 are based on the assumption that Fix-It-Yourself Company acquires the internet supply company for its assessed DCF value of $325.84 (recall Chapter 6).[5]

However, if Fix-It-Yourself Company pays the present value of the free cash flow estimates that we estimated before for Why Wait Supply Company, then the proposed acquisition will neither create value nor destroy any value. In this context, shareholders of Fix-It-Yourself Company would be no better or no worse off if the acquisition capital were returned and placed in a similar risk (a similar beta) portfolio opportunity earning 10% per annum.[6] Equivalently, if Fix-It-Yourself Company pays the DCF value of $325.84 for Why Wait Supply Company, then the net present value of the proposed acquisition must be zero. Moreover, the adjusted economic profit earned each year will also be zero since the *adjusted* return on acquisition capital must equal the cost of invested capital.

---

[4] The major economic profit players—including CS First Boston, Goldman Sachs, and Stern Stewart & Co.—have provided tremendous insight on the many accounting adjustments that can impact NOPAT and invested capital. Their (now) conventional EVA adjustments include the treatment of LIFO reserves, goodwill, operating leases, deferred taxes and the like.

However, the major EVA players seem to have missed the measurement benefit of using negative economic depreciation over GAAP-pronounced straight-line depreciation—perhaps, because of the complexities that go with economic depreciation estimation.

[5] With a DCF value of $325.84 and existing capital of $40, it is interesting to note that acquisition goodwill makes up 88% of the assumed acquisition price. At that price, the bidding firm (Fix-It-Yourself Company) is paying 21.8 times first year's NOPAT of $14.95. This is typical of an internet-based acquisition where the target firm (Why Wait Supply Company) is presumed to derive most of its enterprise value from "back loaded" cash flows.

[6] We assumed a cost of capital of 10% in the initial calculation of enterprise value shown in Chapter 6.

EXHIBIT 10.4 Acquisition Forecast (Portion of 10-Year Forecast)

Period	0	1	2	3	4	5
NOPAT		$14.95	$17.19	$19.77	$22.74	$26.15
Operating Capital	$40	44.5	49.68	55.63	62.47	70.34
Return on						
Operating Capital %		37.38	38.63	39.79	40.88	41.86
Book Capital with Acquisition*	325.84	330.34	335.52	341.47	348.31	356.18
Return on Book Acquisition Capital %		4.59%	5.20%	5.89%	6.66%	7.51%
Cost of Capital %**		10%	10%	10%	10%	10%
Capital Charge		32.58	33.03	33.55	34.15	34.83
Acquisition EVA (unadjusted)		−17.63	−15.84	−13.78	−11.41	−8.68

* Book Capital with Acquisition = Acquisition purchase price plus yearly operating investment.
** Cost of capital assumption = 10%.

Another look at Exhibit 10.4 reveals the nature of EVA measurement problem at hand. Notice that the conventional EVA acquisition returns are less than the (assumed) cost of capital of 10%. Also, we see the logical inconsistency of simply measuring NOPAT over unadjusted acquisition capital as the economic profit on an otherwise zero net present value opportunity is negative in each and every year. The negative economic profit in the standard approach to measuring acquisition capital is incorrect because there is no companion adjustment to NOPAT and invested capital for the appreciation in enterprise value due to a rising series of "back loaded" cash flows. This is a common occurrence for capital budgeting opportunities like corporate acquisitions and R&D investments. These strategic investments have low free cash flow and (NOPAT) earnings yield in the early years followed by substantial operating profit and capital returns thereafter.[7]

---

[7] For example, the cash yield (FCF at year 1/purchase price) on the acquisition is only 3.2% ($10.45/$325.84 × 100).

EXHIBIT 10.5 Acquisition EVA Using Economic Depreciation (Portion of 10-Year Forecast)

Period	0	1	2	3	4	5
Free Cash Flow		$10.45	$12.02	$13.82	$15.89	$18.28
Less:						
Return on Enterprise Value		32.58	34.80	37.08	39.40	41.75
Equal:						
Decline in Enterprise Value		−22.13	−22.78	−23.26	−23.51	−23.47
Plus:						
Investment		4.5	5.18	5.95	6.84	7.87
Equal:						
Economic Depreciation		−17.63	−17.60	−17.31	−16.67	−15.60
Adjusted NOPAT		32.58	34.79	37.08	39.41	41.75
Adjusted Capital	$325.84	347.97	370.75	394.01	417.52	440.99
Adjusted ROC%		10%	10%	10%	10%	10%
Cost of Capital*		10%	10%	10%	10%	10%
Adjusted Capital Charge		32.58	34.80	37.08	39.40	41.75
Adjusted Economic Profit**		0.00	−0.01	0.00	0.01	0.00

* Cost of capital assumption = 10%.
** Difference from zero due to rounding.

Exhibit 10.5 shows how to adjust NOPAT and invested capital to a cost of capital return on acquisition capital. Without getting into all the details, the yearly appreciation in enterprise value gets added back to the DCF acquisition price of $325.84, while the *negative* economic depreciation is added back to NOPAT. In this context, consider the adjustments to NOPAT and invested capital for year 1. At −$22.13, the negative decline in enterprise value—or the appreciation in enterprise value from year 0 to 1—can be expressed in one of two ways: (1) the change in present value of free cash flow estimates (provided in Chapter 6) that occurs between years 0 and 1, or (2) the dollar-based cash yield for year 1—free cash flow estimate of $10.45 for year 1—less the total dollar return earned on enterprise value (at $32.58, which equals 10% of the acquisition price of $325.84).

The decline in enterprise value can be expressed this second way because the total dollar return is equal to the dollar-based cash yield plus the overall change in market value[8]—whereby positive economic depreciation represents a decline in enterprise value and negative economic depreciation represents an appreciation in enterprise value. Moreover, upon adding the new investment of $4.50 (at year 1) to the negative decline in enterprise value of –$22.13, we obtain the economic depreciation figure for the proposed acquisition.

As revealed in Exhibit 10.5, the negative economic depreciation for year 1 is –$17.63. Upon adding (the negative of) this figure to the unadjusted NOPAT of $14.95, we obtain the adjusted after-tax operating profit of $32.58. Also, upon calculating the year 1 capital charge of $32.58 (10% of the acquisition purchase price of $325.84), we obtain the adjusted NOPAT and invested capital figures at year 1 that provide a zero economic profit on the acquisition. Repeating this rather complex—yet informative—procedure produces the desired economic profit results. That is, the yearly economic profit figures on the proposed acquisition equal zero.

In general, the utilization of negative economic depreciation for a *value-neutral* investment yields the following EVA results: (1) the adjusted NOPAT is equal to the yearly dollar capital charge; (2) the adjusted return on acquisition capital equals the percentage cost of capital; and (3) the forecasted economic profit—adjusted NOPAT less adjusted dollar capital charge—is equal to zero in every year. These EVA results arise because of the initial value-neutral—or zero NPV—assumption whereby, say, a bidding firm pays the full DCF value of the target firm. The EVA particulars—NOPAT versus dollar COC or adjusted ROC versus COC—would be different if the strategic investment opportunity were value creating or value destroying.

SUMMARY

There are sophisticated refinements that a manager or investor can make to the standard approach to estimating economic profit. In this chapter, we examined the concept of *positive* economic depreciation to show how to adjust for the inherent bias in invested capital returns that

---

[8] In notation form, we have:

$$\$R = FCF + \Delta EV$$

In this expression, $\$R$ is the total dollar return on the firm for any given year, FCF is the corresponding free cash flow, and ΔEV is the year-over-year change in enterprise value. Upon solving for the negative (of the) change in enterprise value yields the desired result:

$$-\Delta EV = FCF - \$R$$

result when using straight-line depreciation in the standard EVA calculation (recall Chapter 9). We noted that economic depreciation results in capital returns that are consistent with the internal rate of return on a company's capital investments. This is a desirable property of invested capital returns from a capital budgeting perspective.

We also looked at how the concept of *negative* economic depreciation can provide managers and investors with better capital return estimates on strategic investments such as acquisitions and internal R&D investments. Whether or not managers or investors take the time to make such detailed refinements depends on a cost-benefit analysis. At the very least, managers and investors should be aware of the fact that even after making several conventional EVA accounting adjustments to NOPAT and invested capital that bias may still be present in invested capital returns. Unfortunately, faulty investment decisions can result from such omissions.

Having said that, it is important to keep a focus on the "big picture" aspect of economic profit measurement.[9] Despite the complexities that are involved when estimating a company's EVA in practice—dollar return on capital less dollar cost of capital—we are making a conscious effort to measure corporate financial success in a way that is *directly* linked to wealth creation. In addition to the numerous problems that are associated with traditional accounting profit measures—such as "bottom line" net income and percentage-based return on equity— accounting profit does not provide investors with a profit measure that fully "accounts" for the required return (debt *and* equity capital combined) on invested capital.

---

[9] This EVA point is strongly emphasized by Grant and Abate. See James L. Grant and James A. Abate, *Focus on Value: A Corporate and Investor Guide to Wealth Creation* (New York: John Wiley & Sons, 2001).

CHAPTER 11

Estimating the Cost of Capital

In the free cash flow and EVA valuation models presented in Chapters 6 and 7, we found that variations in the cost of capital have a significant impact on the enterprise value of the firm and its stock price. Consequently, it is important for managers and investors to have a clear understanding of how to estimate the cost of capital—*particularly*, the cost of equity capital.[1] To help fill a remaining void on how to estimate the cost of capital, we'll look in this chapter at both traditional and emerging EVA approaches to cost of capital estimation.

We'll begin with a look at the benefits and limitations of the Capital Asset Pricing Model. Next, we'll examine other traditional approaches to estimating the cost of capital—including the DDM or Gordon Growth Model and the Arbitrage Pricing Theory approaches to cost of capital estimation. We'll then look at two EVA-based approaches to estimating the cost of capital including (1) an EVA risk scoring approach, based on market and company specific happenings, and (2) a fundamental factor model approach using EVA risk factors. By providing a foundation on alternative cost of capital approaches, managers and investors should depart this chapter with a solid understanding of how to estimate the cost of capital in practice.

---

[1] While estimating the cost of debt is important too, we'll look in this chapter at traditional and EVA-based approaches to estimating the cost of equity capital.

TRADITIONAL APPROACHES TO ESTIMATING THE COST OF CAPITAL

There are four widely used approaches to estimating the cost of equity capital in a traditional realm.[2] The expected return models include:

- CAPM
- Gordon Growth Model
- APT (factor models)
- Bond Yield Buildup

Arguably, the CAPM is the most commonly used approach to estimating the cost of equity capital.[3] However, as with any risk-pricing model, there are benefits *and* limitations that go along with an equilibrium-expected return model that purports to represent reality.

On the plus side, CAPM evolves out of Modern Portfolio Theory. In this context, capital market theory—*à la* Markowitz and Sharpe—asserts that there exists a linear relationship between the expected return on a security and its level of "systematic (or beta) risk" in the marketplace. Second—and critically important to the cost of capital discussion at hand—CAPM presumably captures the *linear* association between the expected return on levered stock and the debt-to-equity ratio. As emphasized in Chapter 3, this was an important cost-of-capital consideration in our comparison of the traditional versus Modigliani-Miller views on corporate debt policy. Indeed, both the Capital Asset Pricing Model and the "MM" theories on capital structure are based on the assumption of a perfect capital market.

In more formal terms, the CAPM-based expected return on common stock is, *first*, linearly related to the level of systematic risk and, *secondly*, linearly related to the debt-to-equity ratio. With respect to the first condition, the CAPM cost of equity capital is given by:

$$r_e = r_f + (r_m - r_f)B_{e,m}$$

[2] As noted before, the focus of this chapter is on how to estimate the cost of equity capital—a central component of the weighted average cost of capital. The traditional approaches to estimating the cost of equity are also covered by Stowe, Robinson, Pinto, and McLeavey. See John Stowe, Thomas Robinson, Jerald Pinto, and Dennis McLeavey, *Analysis of Equity Investments: Valuation* (Charlottesville, VA: Association for Investment Management and Research, 2002).
[3] For examples, Stern Stewart, Goldman Sachs, and CS First Boston use CAPM-based approaches to estimating the cost of equity capital.

In this expression, r_e is the expected return on common stock, r_f is the risk-free rate of interest, $(r_m - r_f)$ is the expected market premium, and $B_{e,m}$ is the beta or systematic risk of stock in the marketplace. According to CAPM, high beta stocks—such as "growth stocks"—*should* have high expected returns, while low beta stocks—such as so-called "value stocks"—*should* have relatively low expected returns. Also, CAPM has a desirable cost of capital feature because risk—via the beta—is built directly into the formation of expected returns.

Another CAPM-based cost of capital benefit evolves from the second linearity condition. In this context, the single-factor model captures the presumed *linear* relationship between the expected return on a security and the debt-to-equity ratio. As explained in Chapter 3, leverage capture is central to the operational efficiency of MM Proposition II. Indeed, Hamada proved that beta risk is linearly related to the debt-to-equity ratio.[4] As corporate leverage goes up, the "levered beta" goes up in response to the higher level of financial risk. In turn, the higher beta leads to an increase in the required rate of return on common stock. This CAPM-linked interpretation of MM Proposition II can be used to (re)establish the notion that the weighted average cost of capital and, therefore, economic profit and enterprise value are invariant to the corporate debt decision.

Specifically, the beta of the levered stock is linearly related to the debt-to-equity ratio according to:

$$B_{e,m} = B_{u,m}(1 + D/E)$$

In this expression, $B_{e,m}$ is the beta of the levered stock, $B_{u,m}$ is the beta of the unlevered stock (or the beta of the unlevered firm), and D/E is the debt-to-equity ratio.[5] With CAPM substitution into the general weighted average cost of capital formula, it can be shown that the cost of capital for the levered firm is again *equal* to the cost of capital of the equivalent business-risk unlevered firm. According to Hamada, the levered COC is equal to the unlevered COC because the beta of the levered firm, $B_{l,m}$, is equal to the beta of the unlevered firm, $B_{u,m}$. Accordingly, the cost of capital in an MM-CAPM linked formulation can be expressed as:

---

[4] Robert S. Hamada, "Portfolio Analysis, Market Equilibrium, and Corporation Finance," *Journal of Finance* (March 1969).

[5] Hamada's beta formulation is also similar in a world with corporate taxes and *no* deductibility of debt interest expense. In principle, the tax issue boils down to the cost of capital consequences of deductibility of debt interest expense. However, if Miller's 1977 debt tax argument is applicable, then Hamada's beta formula applies in a world with *and* without deductibility of debt interest expense.

$$COC_l = COC_u$$
$$= r_f + (r_m - r_f)B_{u,m}$$

In this expression, the beta of the levered firm is equal to the beta of the unlevered firm, $B_{u,m}$. Consequently, in the combined MM-CAPM view, corporate debt policy has *no* impact on the levered firm's cost of capital and, therefore, *no* effect on economic profit and enterprise value.

CAPM Limitations

While CAPM is a widely used risk-pricing model, several empirical studies show that beta alone does *not* fully account for the observed average returns on common stocks. For example, in a long-term study of common stock returns over the 1941–1990 period, Fama and French conclude that the traditionally celebrated CAPM relationship between average returns and beta risk is "weak," and "perhaps nonexistent."[6] Moreover, they argue that "two easily measured variables," including size (equity capitalization) and book-to-price ratio provide a "simple and powerful characterization of the cross-section of average stock returns for the 1963–1990 period."

Although disagreement exists about why CAPM does not fully account for average returns on common stocks, most empirical studies uncover several challenges to the single factor expected return model. These empirical findings are problematic from a cost of capital—and economic profit—perspective because the expected return on common stock is a critical component of the weighted average cost of capital. Indeed, the cost of equity capital for growth companies operating in the technology sector *is* the cost of capital. Moreover, even if the Capital Asset Pricing Model were an apt description of equilibrium expected returns, the model is complicated by the fact that the "market risk premium" is not static, and appears to change in a dynamic way with the business cycle.[7]

TRADITIONAL ALTERNATIVES TO CAPM

There are of course other traditional approaches to estimating the cost of equity capital.[8] These CAPM alternatives include (1) the Gordon

---

[6] Eugene Fama and Kenneth French, "The Cross Section of Expected Stock Returns," *Journal of Finance* (June 1992).

[7] In effect, the market risk premium—a central risk-pricing component of CAPM—goes down as the economy moves into an expansionary phase, while the market premium goes up during business contraction.

[8] We'll look at EVA-based approaches to estimating the cost of equity in an upcoming section.

Growth Model explained in Chapter 6, (2) the Arbitrage Pricing Theory or factor model approach, and (3) a simple bond yield buildup approach. While each of these cost of equity approaches is described elsewhere, we'll look at the basics of these CAPM alternatives.[9] First, the DDM or Gordon Growth Model.

In the Gordon Growth Model, an estimate of the required return on common stock is obtained by solving for the discount rate that equates the market price of the stock with the expected one-step-ahead dividend per share and the long-term growth rate according to:

$$r_e = d(1)/P + g$$

In this expression, r_e is the required return on common stock (equivalently, the cost of equity from a company's perspective), $d(1)$ is the expected one-step-ahead dividend, and g is the long-term or constant growth rate in dividends, earnings, and (even) market price.[10] For example, if the expected dividend yield on the stock market were 1.5% (expected dividend/price) and the constant market growth rate were 7%, then the required return on the average stock in the market (beta equal unity) would be 8.5%. Additionally, with a risk free rate of interest of, for example, 5%, the projected market risk premium would be 3.5%. With market efficiency, the Gordon Growth Model is a simple, yet meaningful approach to estimating the cost of equity capital.

Arbitrage Pricing Theory (APT)

The Arbitrage Pricing Theory is a robust—yet more time consuming and more costly—approach to estimating the cost of equity capital. While the APT is internally consistent with the CAPM, the model seems more informative in the sense that it attributes the expected return on common stock to a set of risk premiums that are driven by pervasive macroeconomic factors in the economy. In general terms, the APT model can be expressed as:

$$r_e = b_0 + b_1F_1 + b_2F_2 + b_3F_3 + \dots + b_nF_n$$

In this model, r_e is (again) the required return on common stock, b_0 is the short-term risk-free rate, b_i measures the sensitivity of the stock to the ith systematic factor, and F_i denotes the risk premium associated

---

[9] See Stowe, Robinson, Pinto, and McLeavey, *Analysis of Equity Investments. Valuation.*

[10] It goes without saying that the required return on equity in the Gordon Growth Model only makes sense if the capital market is price efficient.

with the ith macro risk factor. Burmeister, Ibbotson, Roll and Ross provide an empirical representation of the APT.[11] In the BIRR representation of the U.S. economy, there are five pervasive macroeconomic risk factors including:

- Confidence risk
- Time horizon risk
- Inflation risk
- Business-cycle risk
- Market-timing risk

Briefly, confidence risk is captured by the unanticipated change in the return difference between 20-year corporate and government bonds. When investor confidence is high, investors presumably require a lower return for bearing this risk. Conversely, when investor confidence is low, investors require a high return for bearing confidence risk. In the BIRR model, time horizon risk is measured by the unanticipated yield spread between 20-year government bonds and 30-day Treasury bills. With a small- or narrow-term premium, investors are presumably more willing to invest in long-term financial instruments such as common stocks.

Inflation risk is measured by the unanticipated change in the inflation rate. Not surprisingly, most common stocks have a negative return sensitivity to this factor. In the BIRR model, business-cycle risk is captured by the unanticipated change in macroeconomic activity. Additionally, market-timing risk measures the portion of the overall stock market (S&P 500) that is not captured by the first four macroeconomic factors. As a "pure" market play, most stocks have a positive sensitivity to market timing risk.

Exhibit 11.1 shows how to estimate the required return on common stock in the multifactor BIRR model. As shown, the required return on stock—at 12.9% in the illustration—is obtained by multiplying each factor sensitivity by the associated risk premium, then "summing up" the macro-risk contributions (or products). Further discussion and application of the BIRR model—with estimated factor sensitivities and risk premiums—can be seen at *www.birr.com*. Moreover, Fama and French have developed a multifactor risk model to estimating the cost of equity capital based on traditional fundamental factors such as beta, size (equity capitalization), and book-to-price ratio.[12]

---

[11] For a description and illustration of the BIRR model, see *www.birr.com*.

[12] Eugene Fama and Kenneth French, "Common Risk Factors in the Returns on Stocks and Bonds" *Journal of Financial Economics*, Vol. 33, No. 1 (1993).

EXHIBIT 11.1 Calculation of Required Return on Common Stock in the BIRR Model

Factor	Stock Sensitivity	Risk Premium %
Confidence Risk	0.25	2.59
Time Horizon Risk	0.55	−0.66
Inflation Risk	−0.40	−4.32
Business-cycle Risk	1.65	1.49
Market-timing Risk	0.95	3.61

Short term risk free rate = 5%.
Required return on stock (cost of equity):

$$r_e = 5 + (0.25 \times 2.59) - (0.55 \times 0.66) - (-0.40 \times 4.32)$$
$$+ (1.65 \times 1.49) + (0.95 \times 3.61)$$
$$= 12.9\%$$

Bond Yield Buildup Approach

The bond yield buildup approach is a much simpler approach to estimating the cost of equity capital. In this approach, the long-term yield on a company's traded bonds is used as the base rate, upon which a judgmental-based (more or less) equity premium is added to obtain the required return on common stock. The yield to maturity on a company's bonds incorporates the term premium on long-term government bonds as well as yield compensation for default risk.

For example, if a company's bonds were yielding 7%, and the estimated equity risk premium on the stock were 4.5%, then the required return on the common stock would be 11.5%. Upon combining the after-tax bond yield—7% net of any debt tax subsidy—and the cost of equity—at 11.5%—with the target capital structure "weights," one could easily obtain the weighted average cost of capital for risk benchmarking and valuation purposes.

EVA APPROACH TO COST OF CAPITAL ESTIMATION

We'll now look at two EVA-based approaches to estimating the cost of capital. We'll first look at the EVA risk-scoring approach of Abate,[13] and

[13] The EVA risk-scoring model was initially presented in Exhibit 4 in James A. Abate, Frank J. Fabozzi, and James L. Grant, "Equity Analysis using Value-Based Metrics," Chapter 9 in T. Daniel Coggin and Frank J. Fabozzi (eds.), *Applied Equity Valuation* (New Hope, PA: Frank J. Fabozzi Associates, 1999). The base market premium in this proprietary EVA model is based on the risk premium to the "least risky" equity in the marketplace.

then the EVA factor model approach developed by Grant and Abate.[14] In the Abate model, a company's required return on common stock is determined by an EVA risk buildup (or scoring) approach that incorporates (1) the risk free rate of interest; (2) a market-driven premium to the *lowest* risk equity; (3) known fundamental factors such as size and leverage; *and* (4) growth and stability in a company's economic profit over time. Holding constant the first three equity risk pricing considerations, companies that have demonstrated stability (or consistency) in their company-specific EVA growth rate are assigned a *lower* cost of capital than companies having otherwise substantial firm-specific volatility in their economic profit.

Exhibit 11.2 provides a snapshot of how the required return on equity capital is estimated in the Abate model. As shown, the model begins with a risk-free interest rate and a base equity risk premium. To this, a company specific risk premium is added to account for fundamental factors such as size and leverage, as well as a firm specific risk premium obtained from a proprietary scoring measure on the volatility of economic profit. The lower the company-specific EVA volatility score, the lower the required return on equity capital. Conversely, the higher the EVA risk score, the higher the assessed cost of equity capital.

EXHIBIT 11.2   Required Return versus Company Specific Risk Score

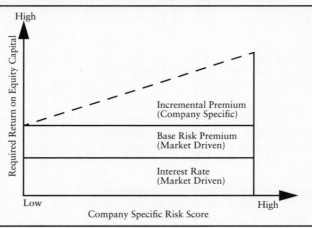

Source: See Exhibit 4, p. 157 in James A. Abate, Frank J. Fabozzi, and James L. Grant, "Equity Analysis Using Value-Based Metrics," Chapter 9 in *Applied Equity Valuation,* T. Daniel Coggin and Frank J. Fabozzi (eds.) (New Hope, PA: Frank J. Fabozzi Associates, 1999).

---

[14] Grant and Abate develop the EVA factor model approach in *Focus on Value.* See James L. Grant and James A. Abate, *Focus on Value: A Corporate and Investor Guide to Wealth Creation* (New York: John Wiley & Sons, 2001).

One important implication of the expected return model shown in Exhibit 11.2 is that a growth company with consistent economic profit growth (low company-specific risk score) will be assigned a lower cost of equity capital than a similarly positioned growth company (that is, similar size, leverage, and industry designation) with substantial volatility (high company-specific risk score) in its EVA growth rate. With this foundation, let's now look at the basics of an EVA factor model approach to estimating the cost of equity capital.

EVA FACTOR MODEL APPROACH TO COST OF EQUITY

As mentioned before, there are multifactor risk models that can be used in lieu of the single (beta) factor CAPM. Fundamental factors models like Fama-French and BARRA have been used to build forecasts of equity returns based on beta, size, book-to-price ratio, earnings yield, and earnings momentum—among other "common factors"—that influence expected security returns.[15] Also, macroeconomic factor models—such as Burmeister, Ibbotson, Roll, and Ross as well as Salomon RAM (Risk Attribute Model)—have been used in practice to estimate the expected return on common stock in the context of interest rate and economy-wide changes in corporate profits, among other macro risk-pricing factors. In this section, we'll look at a factor-based EVA model that can be used to shed added insight on the estimation of expected returns, beyond the single factor CAPM, and multifactor risk models that are based solely on traditional fundamental factors.

An EVA factor model with a systematic market factor (captured by the CAPM beta) and three systematic nonmarket (or fundamental) factors can be expressed as:

$$r_e = \text{CAPM} + b_1\text{Size} + b_2\text{NPV/Capital} + b_3\text{SD}_{\text{EVA}}$$

In this expression, r_e is the expected return on common stock. CAPM is the familiar Capital Asset Pricing Model.[16] Additionally, there is a traditional fundamental factor—namely, size (equity capitalization)—and two fundamental EVA factors—including the NPV-to-Capital ratio and the standard deviation of economic profit (all factors standardized relative to

---

[15] From an economic profit perspective, one obvious limitation of using traditional fundamental factor models to estimate the required return on equity is that the risk factors are often based on accounting measures of profit and leverage

[16] Grant and Abate, *Focus on Value: A Corporate and Investor Guide to Wealth Creation.*

reference index). In the EVA factor model, the "b_i" coefficients represent the risk premia associated with the respective fundamental factors.[17]

Firm size is included in the EVA risk-pricing model for consistency with Fama-French. In practice, the model incorporates the empirical findings of Jensen, Johnson, and Mercer who suggest that equity size (especially, for small cap stocks) may be endogenous to pervasive macroeconomic factors that include interest rate developments and monetary policy.[18] Also, following empirical research of the author,[19] and Yook and McCabe,[20] the EVA risk-pricing model incorporates the NPV-to-Capital ratio to capture the extra market risk (or extra market covariance) associated with the behavior of troubled firms.[21] Notably, the NPV-to-Capital ratio is a measure of a company's ability (*or lack thereof*) to invest in wealth creating projects. It is therefore a measure of company strength or resilience.

Indeed, wealth creators have a high NPV-to-Capital ratio, while wealth destroyers have a low to negative NPV-to-Capital ratio—due to their fundamental inability to invest in projects having an after-return on capital that exceeds the weighted average cost of capital. Consequently, the EVA factor model recognizes that risk averse investors require high-expected returns for investing in the stocks of troubled firms—namely, companies with low to negative NPV—while comparatively low expected returns for investing in the stocks of robust firms—that is, companies with positive NPV. Moreover, the EVA risk-pricing model includes the (standardized) standard deviation of economic profit, SD_{EVA}, to account for the market-adjusted volatility in a company's economic profit.

---

[17] In the EVA factor model discussion that follows, the heretofore factor sensitivity term, b_i, will be referred to as a risk premium. In this regard, the contribution of a factor (EVA or otherwise) to the cost of equity is equal to the standardized factor value times the respective factor risk premia.

[18] Gerald Jensen, Robert Johnson, and Jeffrey Mercer, "The Inconsistency of Small-Firm and Value Stock Premiums," *Journal of Portfolio Management* (Winter 1998).

[19] For examples, see: (1) James L. Grant, "Foundations of EVA for Investment Managers," *Journal of Portfolio Management* (Fall 1996), (2) the first edition of this book, and (3) the empirical evidence presented in this writing.

[20] Ken C. Yook and George M. McCabe, "An Examination of MVA in the Cross-Section of Expected Stock Returns," *Journal of Portfolio Management* (Spring 2001).

[21] In the EVA factor model, the NPV-to-Capital ratio is used in place of the (Fama-French) price-to-book value ratio for two reasons: (1) the price/book ratio is plagued by accounting problems due to book value, and, most importantly, (2) NPV is a *direct* measure of wealth creation.

EXHIBIT 11.3   Standardization of Volatility of EVA Factor in Unit Normal Distribution

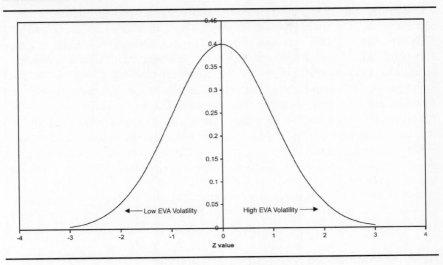

Factor Standardization Procedure

In a factor model, the factor values are standardized in terms of the "unit normal distribution." This means that if the factor value for a common stock were consistent with the average factor value for the representative stock in the marketplace, then the stock's standardized factor value would be zero. Atypical factor values can then be conveniently assigned in terms of standard deviation units from zero. Exhibit 11.3 shows how the standardization procedure works for the volatility of economic profit factor, SD_{EVA}.

Exhibit 11.3 shows that if a company has abnormally high volatility of economic profit, then its standardized factor value would be located to the right of zero in the unit normal distribution. Recall that a standardized factor value of zero is associated with the average firm in a market index. On the other hand, if a company had relatively stable EVA, then its standardized volatility of economic profit measure would be less than zero—a sign of stability in the marketplace. Moreover, this same kind of logic can be applied to other common factors including the size factor and the standardized NPV-to-Capital ratio. Exhibit 11.4 shows the standardized factor values for the stocks of two companies.

In the illustration, Companies A and B have a market capitalization that is consistent with that of the average stock in a market index. This is because their standardized size indicators equal zero. However, the two companies are fundamentally different in their ability to create wealth.

Indeed, Company A is a powerful wealth creator, while Company B looks like a wealth destroyer. Specifically, Company A's standardized NPV-to-Capital ratio is *plus* two standard deviations from the average company in the marketplace. Conversely, Company B's standardized NPV-to-Capital ratio is *minus* two standard deviations from the average company. All else constant, the EVA risk-pricing model would assign a relatively low expected return on the common stock of Company A, and a correspondingly high expected return on the stock of Company B.

Exhibit 11.4 also suggests that Company A is a wealth creator with relatively low volatility in its economic profit. In this context, Company A's standardized EVA volatility factor is negative. In contrast, Company B has a relatively high degree of economic profit uncertainty as captured by a standardized EVA volatility that is greater than zero. Taken together, the standardized NPV-to-Capital ratio and EVA volatility factors suggest that Company A is a powerful *and* consistent wealth creator, while Company B is a risky, troubled firm that in turn has a high expected return on its common stock.

Factor Model Illustration of Expected Return on Equity

Let's now "roll up" the individual factor contributions to estimate the required return on the common stocks of Companies A and B. As shown before, each factor contribution is the product of the factor risk premia (the relevant "b_i") and the standardized factor value. Given that relative NPV strength and EVA stability are two common factors that are rewarded in real world financial markets, we'll assume that the NPV risk premia is negative, while the required premium on EVA volatility is positive.[22] Drawing from the previous illustration, the standardized factor values and assumed risk premiums are shown in Exhibit 11.5, along with the factor model assessment of the expected return on the stocks of companies A and B.

EXHIBIT 11.4 Standardized Factor Values for Stocks of Two Companies

Factor	Company A	Company B
Size (*equity cap*)	0.0	0.0
NPV/Capital ratio (*strength*)	2.0	−2.0
EVA Volatility (*stability*)	−1.0	1.0

---

[22] For convenience, the risk premia on the standardized NPV-to-Capital ratio and the EVA standard deviation were set at −0.01 and 0.01, respectively. This means that wealth creators with stable economic profit are assigned a relatively low cost of equity (relative to CAPM), while wealth destroyers with volatile EVA happenings are assigned a relatively high cost of equity capital.

EXHIBIT 11.5   EVA Factor Model Estimates of Required Return on Common Stock

Company A: *Wealth Creator:*
Required Return on Stock of Company A:

$$r_{e,A} = 10\%^a + (-0.5\%) \times 0.0 + (-1.0\%) \times 2.0 + 1.0\% \times (-1.0) = 7\%$$

Company B: *Wealth Destroyer:*
Required Return on Stock of Company B:

$$r_{e,B} = 10\%^a + (-0.5\%) \times 0.0 + (-1.0\%) \times (-2.0) + 1.0\% \times (1.0) = 13\%$$

^{a}CAPM $= r_f + (r_m - r_f)B_{e,m} = 5\% + (5\%)1.0 = 10\%$

Exhibit 11.5 shows that the required return on Company A's stock, at 7%, is considerably lower than the required return on Company B's stock, at 13%. This implies that the overall cost of capital for Company A is lower than the cost of capital for Company B. In effect, the EVA risk-pricing model suggests that wealth-creating firms are jointly rewarded for their relative strength (measured by a *positive* standardized NPV-to-Capital ratio) and their EVA stability (measured by a *negative* standardized EVA standard deviation). The combination of these beneficial risk-pricing considerations is reflected in a comparatively low cost of capital. In turn, the EVA-based factor model implies that risky, troubled companies should be penalized by a high cost of capital for both their inconsistent economic profit generation and their fundamental inability to create wealth.

EVA FACTOR MODEL APPLICATION: DOW JONES INDUSTRIAL COMPANIES

Before moving on, it is helpful to shed some light on how the EVA factor model works in the real world. In this context, Exhibit 11.6 provides a graphical display of the estimated cost of equity using the EVA factor model *versus* the CAPM for 27 industrial (nonfinancial) companies in the Dow Jones Industrial Average.[23,24] The exhibit shows that the factor

[23] In the EVA factor model on the Dow Industrials, the NPV-to-Capital ratio was estimated on each company at year-end 2000, while the standard deviation of economic profit was estimated using five years of EVA data. Also, in the cost of equity estimation process, the risk premiums on the standardized NPV and EVA factors were again set at –0.01 and 0.01, respectively. Clearly, large-scale empirical research is warranted to obtain accurate estimates of EVA risk premia.

[24] For those interested in the details, "raw betas" were used as input in the cost of equity estimates shown in Exhibit 11.6. The relative positioning of the equity cost estimates—EVA factor model versus CAPM—for the Dow Industrials is similar using the less diverse beta estimates produced by Value Line.

model estimates of the cost of equity for companies like AT&T and Intel Corporation were noticeably higher than the comparable estimates obtained using the traditional CAPM. This happened because at year-end 2000, AT&T had a negative standardized NPV-to-Capital ratio combined with a sharply positive standardized five-year EVA-volatility estimate. While Intel's standardized NPV-to-Capital ratio was close to zero among Dow Industrials, the chipmaker experienced abnormal EVA volatility over the five-year period ending in December 2000.

In contrast, Exhibit 11.6 shows that Minnesota, Mining & Manufacturing (3M), Eastman Kodak, and Honeywell International had EVA factor model estimates of the cost of equity that fell below the CAPM. This happened because their standardized NPV-to-Capital ratios were generally greater than zero, and their standardized EVA volatility estimates fell below zero (a sign of relative economic profit stability among Dow Industrials). Notably, if the EVA factor model were an apt description of reality, then stocks with factor model equity costs that plot *above* the CAPM line—like AT&T and Intel Corporation at 2000— would be relatively overvalued from an economic profit risk perspective (that is, if the lower rate cost of equity produced by the CAPM were used to discount cash flows instead of the EVA factor model).

EXHIBIT 11.6   EVA Factor Model versus CAPM: Dow Industrials at Year-End 2000

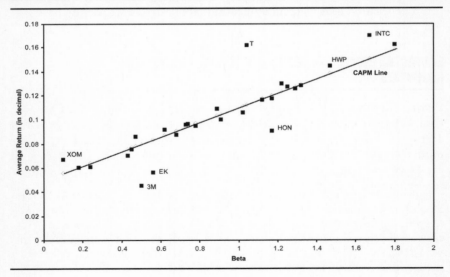

Conversely, stocks with EVA factor model estimates of the cost of equity that plot *below* the CAPM line—such as 3M and Honeywell International at 2000—would be relatively undervalued from an EVA risk standpoint (this time, if the higher rate cost of equity produced by the CAPM were used to discount cash flows instead of the EVA factor model).[25] Going forward, the comparative cost of equity analysis presented in this chapter—the EVA factor model versus CAPM and other traditional models—points to the need for further empirical research and a *much* fuller understanding by managers and investors of the extreme complexity of the cost of equity capital.

---

[25] In fairness to CAPM, it is interesting to see (Exhibit 11.6) that most of the EVA cost of equity estimates lie close to the CAPM line. Indeed, at year-end 2000, the average difference between the EVA and CAPM cost of equity estimates for the Dow Industrials was zero.

CHAPTER 12

Estimating MVA with Published Financial Reports

As explained before, the EVA approach to enterprise valuation makes an *explicit* connection with how wealth is truly created in an efficient capital market. This pricing benefit happens because the intrinsic worth of the anticipated EVA stream produces a direct estimate of the firm's *net present value*. Managerial decisions (via internal growth opportunities or corporate acquisitions) that enhance the firm's market value added (MVA) lead to an increase in shareholder wealth, while corporate actions that cause negative net present results actually destroy it. Unfortunately, when estimating MVA in practice, the published data that investors and managers need to estimate the firm's market value added is rarely in a form that is conducive to making the EVA valuation approach a simple task.

In this chapter, we'll look at how to use published financial data to estimate MVA in the context of a two-stage EVA growth model. The two-step DCF procedure (or pricing template) used to estimate the firm's net present value seems easy enough if one has in hand the relevant EVA estimates. In practice, the *four* parameters of a two-stage EVA growth model—including the one-step-ahead EVA forecast, EVA(1), the near-term EVA growth rate, g_{NT}, the long-term EVA growth rate, g_{LT}, and the cost of capital, COC—need to be estimated from financial reports that may look both challenging and vague to managers and investors. In an attempt to illustrate—and hopefully overcome—some of the real world difficulties that may arise, we'll use a Value Line report for Merck & Co. to see how published financial data can be used to energize the firm's market value added. But first, we'll examine how to estimate MVA in the context of a two-stage EVA growth model.[1]

TWO-STAGE EVA GROWTH MODEL

Since the firm's economic growth varies over time, a simple constant growth model has some serious practical limitations. In particular, the constant-growth EVA model requires that the growth rate in the firm's economic profit is not only constant for all future time periods, but that it also lies *below* the firm's weighted average cost of capital, COC. This long-term growth condition is clearly inconsistent with the corporate profit experiences of many growth-oriented firms that operate in economic sectors like beverages, health care, and technology.

Fortunately, a company's pricing precision can be improved by unfolding its economic profit potential into multiple stages of EVA growth. For instance, in the two-stage EVA growth model—with abnormal growth in economic profit followed by mature growth to infinity—the firm's market value-added (MVA) can be expressed in present value terms as:

$$MVA(0) = \sum_{t=1}^{T} EVA(t)/(1+COC)^t + PVIF_{COC,\,T}[MVA(T)]$$

$$= \sum_{t=1}^{T} EVA(1)(1+g_{NT})^{t-1}/(1+COC)^t + PVIF_{COC,\,T}[EVA(T+1)/(COC-g_{LT})]$$

The first term on the right-hand side of the two-stage EVA growth model is the intrinsic value of the firm's expected EVA during the near-term growth phase. During these years, the firm's one-step-ahead EVA forecast, $EVA(1)$, is presumably growing at an abnormally high (or possibly low) rate of, say, g_{NT}. However, because of competition and/or technological considerations within the industry, the growth rate in the firm's economic profit settles down to g_{LT} for the long term.[2] Thus, the MVA(T) term in the above expression represents the residual (or continuing) value of the firm's market value added at the end of the abnormal EVA growth phase.

---

[1] In Chapter 7, we looked at how to estimate MVA with horizon and residual periods. The two-stage EVA growth model described here is similar in interpretation, with the notable exception that we'll use a near-term EVA growth rate and a long-term EVA growth rate to estimate MVA during horizon and residual years, respectively. Also, the horizon and residual periods chosen will be consistent with the reporting of financial data on a Value Line report.

[2] Indeed, given competitive forces, the long-term EVA growth rate might be zero.

Moreover, the second term in the two-stage EVA growth model reveals that the firm derives its market value added at period T from the anticipated EVA at period $T + 1$, discounted back to that time by the long-term EVA "capitalization rate," $(COC - g_{LT})$. In turn, the present value interest factor, $PVIF = 1/(1 + COC)^T$, is used to discount the firm's expected market value added at T, $MVA(T)$, back to the current time period (zero). Upon adding the two EVA-based pricing expressions to the firm's capital investment, $C(0)$, one obtains the enterprise value of the firm, $V(0)$. The intrinsic value of the stock is then obtained by subtracting debt (and debt equivalents) from estimated enterprise value and dividing the difference by the number of shares of common stock outstanding.

ILLUSTRATION OF THE TWO-STAGE EVA GROWTH MODEL

As a numerical illustration of the two-stage EVA growth model, suppose that the firm's estimated EVA at period 1 is $15 million. Further suppose that EVA(1) is expected to grow at a near-term rate of, say, 10% for three years. Following this abnormal growth phase (where, g_{NT} is assumed equal to the cost of capital, COC) the firm's EVA growth rate is expected to decline to 2.5% for all future years thereafter. Exhibit 12.1 shows how the firm's market value-added at period *zero* can be estimated with a convenient pricing *template* for the two-stage EVA growth model.

Combining the MVA Results

The MVA pricing template (Exhibit 12.1) reveals that the firm's *total* net present value is the sum of (1) the market value added from the near-term EVA growth opportunity, and (2) the MVA contribution from the firm's long-term (or mature) economic profit strategy. Upon adding the financial results shown, the two-step MVA procedure yields the firm's total market value added at time period zero:

$$
\begin{aligned}
MVA(0) &= \textit{Step A plus Step B} \\
&= \$54.56 + \$186.41 \\
&= \$240.97
\end{aligned}
$$

At $340.97 million, the firm's estimated enterprise value is the sum of the capital employed in the business (taken as $100 million) and the aggregate net present value—measured in the illustration by MVA(0). This enterprise pricing development can be expressed as:

$$
\begin{aligned}
EV(0) &= C(0) + MVA(0) \\
&= \$100 + \$240.97 \\
&= \$340.97
\end{aligned}
$$

EXHIBIT 12.1   Pricing Template: Two-Stage EVA Growth Model

Step A: Calculate the MVA contribution from the estimated EVA stream during the *abnormal* growth stage: This portion of the pricing template shows the estimated EVA for years one through four, followed by their present values when discounted at a 10% cost of capital.

Market Value Added from the Firm's Near-Term EVA Growth Opportunity ($ Millions)

Period	0	1	2	3	4
EVA$(t)^*$	—	15.00	16.50	18.15	19.97
PVIF$_{10,\,t}$		0.909	0.826	0.751	0.683
PVIF$_{10,t} \times$ EVA(t)		13.64	13.64	13.64	13.64

$*$ EVA(t) = EVA$(t-1)[1 + g_{NT}]$, for $t = 2$ to 4

MVA(0) from Near-Term Growth Opportunity: $\$54.56 = \Sigma^4 EVA(t)/(1.1)^t$

Step B: Calculate the MVA contribution from the estimated EVA stream generated during the long term or *mature* growth phase. This section of the pricing template shows how to calculate the present value at period *zero* of the firm's estimated MVA at time period *T*.

Market Value-Added From the Firm's Long-Term Growth Opportunities ($ Millions)

$$\begin{aligned} EVA(5) &= EVA(4)[1 + g_{LT}] \\ &= \$19.97(1.025) \\ &= \$20.47 \end{aligned}$$

$$\begin{aligned} MVA(4) &= EVA(5)/(COC - g_{LT}) \\ &= \$20.47(0.10 - 0.025) \\ &= \$272.93 \end{aligned}$$

$$\begin{aligned} MVA \text{ (0) from Long-Term Growth Opportunities} &= PVIF_{10,\,4} \times MVA(4) \\ &= 0.683 \times \$272.93 \\ &= \$186.41 \end{aligned}$$

Upon subtracting the (assumed) $100 million in long-term debt from the estimated enterprise value, one obtains the firm's equity capitalization, at $240.97 million. Also, with 10 million common shares outstanding, the intrinsic (present) worth of the stock is $24.10. Interestingly, the near-term EVA growth opportunity leads to a 20% ($4.10/$20) improvement in the company's stock price when compared to the price obtained with a simple constant-growth EVA model.[3]

In the two-stage EVA growth model, it should be apparent that the firm derives it total net present value (NPV) from both the near-term EVA outlook and the longer-term economic profit (EVA) forecast. With these pricing developments in mind, it is possible to see why some wealth creators (recall, Chapter 5) have positive market value added (MVA) in the presence of their currently negative EVA outlook. In a nutshell, investors must be largely optimistic about the firm's *long-term* ability to generate future economic profit.

Moreover, in seemingly anomalous situations where wealth destroyers have a currently favorable EVA outlook—recall some of the wealth destroyers shown in Chapter 5—the efficient market argument implies that investors must be exceedingly *pessimistic* about the EVA outlook over the long haul. If this were not the case, then the debt and equity securities of so-called "wealth destroyers" having currently positive EVA would be undervalued in the capital market. Stocks like these would represent an active "buy opportunity" for astute investors.

LINKAGE WITH THE CLASSIC NPV MODEL

The wealth implications of the *two-stage* EVA growth model can be illustrated graphically in the context of the *two-period* NPV model described in Chapter 2. In this context, it is important to recognize that the firm's *residual cash flow* (RCF) in the forthcoming year is a reflection of, (1) the intrinsic value at period 1 of the firm's near-term EVA stream, and (2) the present value of the long-term EVA growth opportunities when discounted back to that time.

For ease of calculation, it is helpful to note that the firm's residual cash flow at period 1, RCF(1), can also be expressed in terms of the firm's market value added (MVA) at period zero *times* one plus the

---

[3] The firm's enterprise value with constant EVA growth of 2.5% is $300 million. This consists of $200 million in market value added ($15/0.075) *plus* the initial capital investment. Upon subtracting $100 million in long-term debt from enterprise value and dividing by 10 million shares, one obtains an estimate of stock price at $20 per share.

weighted average cost of capital. At \$265.07 million, the firm's residual cash flow (RCF) is derived from:

$$RCF(1) = \sum_{t=1}^{T} EVA(t)/(1 + COC)^{t-1} + PVIF_{COC,\,T-1}[MVA(T)]$$
$$= [MVA(0)](1 + COC)$$
$$= [240.97](1.1)$$
$$= \$265.07$$

Upon inserting the MVA(0) and RCF(1) figures—at \$240.97 and \$265.07 respectively—into the NPV graph shown in Exhibit 12.2, one sees the desired results. In particular, the classic *two-period* NPV model shows that the firm's aggregate market value added is equal to the present value of the *one-step ahead* anticipated residual cash flow. The firm's RCF at year 1 or MVA(1) is in turn equal to the discounted value at that time of the firm's near-term EVA outlook *and* the assessed valuation (at period 1) of its long-term ability to generate economic value added.

At \$375.07 million, the two-period NPV graph also shows the firm's estimated enterprise value at time period 1. The company's overall value at that time is obtained by growing its currently estimated enterprise value, at \$340.97 million, by the 10% cost of capital for one year. By extension, the two-period (NPV) wealth findings shown in Exhibit 12.2 suggest that EVA is a theoretically robust financial metric in *any* multiperiod framework.

EXHIBIT 12.2   NPV Illustration of the Variable Growth EVA Model

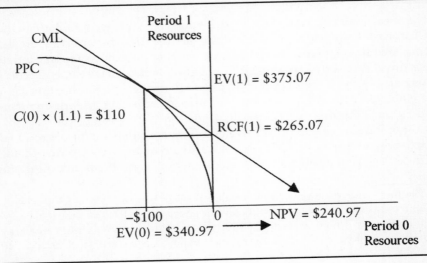

ESTIMATING EVA: THE CASE OF MERCK & CO.

We are now in a position to apply the two-stage EVA growth model in a real-world setting. In this context, Exhibit 12.3 shows some pertinent sections of the April 26, 2002 Value Line report for Merck & Co. As shown, the published financial report does not provide any direct EVA information that can be used to estimate the firm's market value added. Specifically, the *unlevered* net operating profit after taxes (NOPAT) and the (dollar) weighted average cost of capital (COC) figures are *absent* from the Value Line report. These data omissions represent the two major items that are necessary to calculate the firm's economic value added. Likewise, without the cost of capital, COC, there is no direct way of estimating the "residual return on capital (RROC)" for this well-known pharmaceutical company.

Fortunately, a closer look at the Value Line report for Merck & Co. reveals that it does provide many subsidiary metrics for calculating key drivers of the firm's "ex ante" EVA. In this context, Value Line lists by year the anticipated sales, the operating profit margin (OPM), and the annual depreciation amount. According to Value Line, the operating profit margin is calculated by dividing EBITDA (rather than EBIT) by sales. In turn, these financial estimates can be "rolled up" into a basic measure of the firm's unlevered net operating profit after taxes (NOPAT).

Likewise, the Value Line report provides some helpful information for estimating Merck's weighted average cost of capital. In this context, the report provides information that can be used to assess the pretax cost of debt and the potential "target debt weight" in the firm's capital structure. Also, the Value Line "beta" can be used as the *relative* risk input when calculating the firm's CAPM-based cost of equity capital. With this background, let's now see how the Value Line report can be used to estimate the major components of the two-stage EVA growth model.

Then, the research focus can turn to how the reported data can be used to calculate the market value added (MVA) for Merck & Co. The enterprise value application at hand will be examined in the context of (1) Merck's EVA forecast for 2003; (2) the near-term EVA growth rate; (3) the long-term EVA growth rate; and (4) Merck's weighted average cost of debt and equity capital. Based on the Value Line format, it is assumed that the enterprise value of the firm and its outstanding shares are being evaluated at *year-end* 2002.

EXHIBIT 12.3   Value Line Report: Merck & Co.

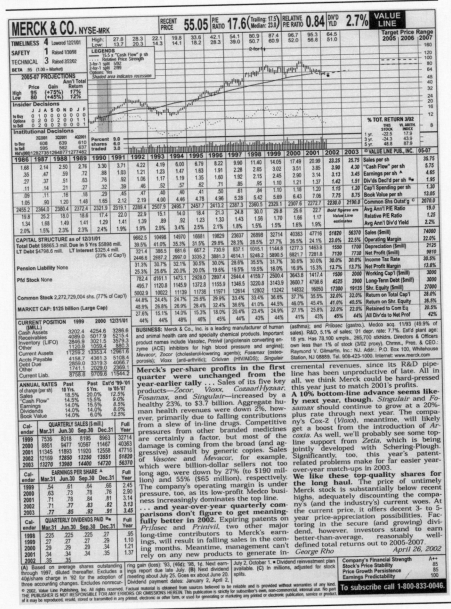

Source: *Value Line Investment Survey* (New York, NY), April 26, 2002.

The One-Step Ahead EVA Forecast

One of the helpful inputs to the two-stage EVA growth model is the firm's estimated economic value added for the forthcoming year. This *one-step ahead* EVA forecast is important in the model because it can be combined with knowledge of the near-term EVA growth rate, g_{NT}, to provide estimates of the EVA stream during the presumed abnormal growth period. Since Value Line does not provide EVA estimates, this figure has to be inferred (*and* augmented with information external to the report) from the financial information provided on their company report.

The first component of the one-step-ahead EVA forecast is the firm's *unlevered* net operating profit after taxes (NOPAT). In basic terms (recall, Chapter 4[4]), this component of the firm's economic value added (EVA) for any given year can be expressed as:

$$NOPAT = EBIT(1 - t)$$

In this expression, EBIT is the firm's estimated earnings before interest and taxes (EBIT) and t is the unlevered tax rate.

A quick look at Exhibit 12.3 reveals that Value Line does *not* list the yearly EBIT or cash tax rate figures. However, Merck's estimated earnings before interest and taxes (EBIT) for 2003 can be estimated by subtracting depreciation from the reported EBITDA. EBITDA is obtained by multiplying the estimated sales figure, at $56,370 million, by the Value Line operating margin of 22.5%. Upon subtracting the estimated 2003 Depreciation, at $1,700 million, from the estimated EBITDA, one obtains the firm's anticipated EBIT for 2003:

$$
\begin{aligned}
EBIT(2003) &= EBITD - D \\
&= [Sales \times OPM] - D \\
&= [\$56,370 \times 0.225] - \$1,700 \\
&= \$10,983 \text{ million}
\end{aligned}
$$

With knowledge of the 2003 EBIT figure, and an estimated (unlevered) tax rate of 35%, it is possible to calculate a *one-step ahead* forecast of Merck's net operating profit after taxes according to:

$$
\begin{aligned}
NOPAT(2003) &= EBIT(1 - t) \\
&= \$10,983(1 - 0.35) \\
&= \$7,139 \text{ million}
\end{aligned}
$$

---

[4] In the chapter at hand, the focus is on how real-world estimates of EVA can be used to map MVA (or NPV). In this regard, one can use basic EVA estimates like those obtained in this chapter using a Value Line report, or more "sophisticated" EVA estimates based on the value-based accounting adjustments that were explained before.

Estimating the Cost of Capital: Merck & Co.

The next ingredient in the production of Merck's 2003 EVA is the *dollar* cost of invested capital. In order to assess Merck's *one-step ahead* capital cost, one needs to know something about (1) the company's after-tax cost of debt financing, (2) the required return on common equity, and (3) the firm's "target debt weight" (if any) in the corporate capital structure.

Merck's pretax cost of debt financing can be estimated by using the information provided in the "Capital Structure Box" on the Value Line report. At 6.78%, the firm's pretax debt rate is obtained by dividing long-term interest expense, at $325.4 million, by the long-term debt figure, at $4,798.6 million. This pretax rate of interest can then be "tax-adjusted" by 35% to produce an after-tax gauge of the firm's "ex ante" cost of debt for 2003. These calculations result in a posttax cost of debt financing for Merck & Co. of 4.41%.

The Cost of Equity Capital: Merck & Co.

Merck's cost of equity capital can then be estimated with the familiar capital asset pricing model (CAPM). In this context, the firm's required equity return is obtained with knowledge of the risk-free rate of interest, the anticipated market risk premium, and the "systematic risk," or beta sensitivity of the stock.[5] With a risk-free rate of 5% (at that time), a "market risk premium" of 6%, and the Value Line beta estimate of 0.95, Merck's cost of equity is calculated according to:

$$\text{CAPM} = R_f + MRP \times \text{Beta}$$
$$= 5\% + 6\% \times 0.95$$
$$= 10.7\%$$

Thus, in a CAPM context, the stockholders of Merck are looking for the firm's managers to generate a 10.7% return on their equity capital. This expected return figure is slightly below the 11% rate that would be required on the equity of the average company in the marketplace. This happens because Merck's stock beta, at 0.95, lies below the beta of the market, which by definition is unity.

A Look at Merck's Debt Policy

If corporate debt policy (due to capital market imperfections) matters in the real world, then one needs to know something meaningful about the firm's "target debt weight" in the capital structure. For Merck & Co.,

[5] Note that the risk free rate of interest and the market risk premium are *external* to the Value Line report.

the "just-right" amount of financial leverage is somewhat elusive as long-term debt makes up 23% of capital as of 12/31/01 (see the Capital Structure Box) down to 10% of capital (taken as long-term debt *plus* net worth) out to years 2005–2007. In this context, the Value Line report suggests that the level of corporate debt at this pharmaceutical company is expected to decline significantly in the forthcoming years.

Thus, the issue of a meaningful target debt level for Merck & Co. is somewhat problematic. Assuming that Merck has an "optimal capital structure" that it is striving to reach over time, then one way of estimating the firm's target debt ratio is to use the forward-looking (ex ante) long-term debt and net worth (equity) figures provided on the Value Line report. In this regard, the published report shows that long-term debt makes up approximately *ten percent* of the estimated "book capital" (again, long-term debt plus net worth) for the three years covering 2005 to 2007.[6] If correct, then Merck's *ex ante* percentage of long-term debt relative to the *futuristic* capital employed in the business can be used as a reasonable estimate of the "target debt weight" in the firm's cost of capital calculation.

Combining the Capital Cost Inputs: Merck & Co.

The overall percentage cost of capital for Merck is a weighted average of the posttax cost of debt and equity capital. At 10.07%, the firm's estimated 2003 cost of capital is calculated according to:

$$
\begin{aligned}
COC &= w_d \times r_d + w_e \times r_e \\
&= (1/10) \times 4.41\% + (9/10) \times 10.7\% \\
&= 10.07\%
\end{aligned}
$$

In this cost of capital expression, w_d is the presumed target debt weight, r_d is the after-tax cost of debt, and r_e is the expected return on the stock (measured according to CAPM). At 10%, this figure represents the corporate-wide "discount rate" for Merck & Co. It will be used shortly as the *overall* required return for Merck in the calculation of its market value added (MVA).

Next, by multiplying the estimated 2002 book capital (long-term debt plus net worth[7]) for Merck & Co. by the weighted average cost of capital, COC, one obtains the firm's estimated *dollar* capital cost for 2003:

---

[6] On the Value Line report, long-term debt for years 2005–2007 is projected to be $3,000 million. Thus the projected debt-to-capital ratio is 10% ($3,000/$30,000).
[7] In practice, the "Debt Due" in current liabilities (see Current Position box on the Value Line report) should be factored into EVA debt. As a practical limitation, short-term debt is omitted from the EVA capital calculations because this figure is not available on the representative Value Line report after 12/31/01.

$$\begin{aligned}
\text{\$ Cost of Capital}(2003) &= C(2002) \times [COC/100] \\
&= \$21{,}825 \times [10\%/100] \\
&= \$2{,}183 \text{ million}
\end{aligned}$$

As with NOPAT, the dollar cost of capital is needed to calculate Merck's economic value added for 2003, and beyond.

Merck's Near-Term Expected EVA Stream

With this foundation, the *one-step ahead* EVA forecast for Merck & Co. is obtained by subtracting the estimated dollar cost of capital from the estimated net operating profit after taxes (NOPAT). Combining the relevant financial inputs yields Merck's estimated EVA for 2003:

$$\begin{aligned}
EVA(2003) &= NOPAT(2003) - \$COC(2003) \\
&= \$7{,}139 - \$2{,}183 \\
&= \$4{,}956 \text{ million}
\end{aligned}$$

This development is important not only because it produces a forecast EVA for 2003, but also because the same procedure can be used to calculate Merck's *four-step ahead* EVA out to year 2006 (taken as mid point of years 2005–2007 shown on the Value Line report). With the two EVA estimates separated in time, it is possible to calculate the *implied* near-term EVA growth rate, g_{NT}, for the three-year period from (year-end) 2003 to 2006. The resulting near-term EVA growth rate can then be applied to find the implied EVA estimates for 2004 and 2005.

However, in order to estimate Merck's EVA for year-end 2006, one needs the firm's estimated capital at year-end 2005. This book capital figure is necessary because the dollar cost of capital for any given year is generally based on the *beginning* of year capital stock. For convenience, the book capital figure, at $30,000 million ($3,000 long term debt plus $27,000 million net worth) shown on the Value Line report will be interpreted as book capital for year-end 2005.

Summarizing, upon interpreting the Value Line report for Merck in the same way that was used to estimate the firm's estimated EVA for 2003, one obtains the following results: (1) The estimated dollar cost of capital at year-end 2006 is $3,000 million; (2) the estimated net operating profit after taxes (NOPAT) is $9,201 million; and (3) the anticipated EVA for the pharmaceutical company is $6,201 million. Also, at 7.76%, the *implied* near-term EVA growth rate for Merck & Co. over the three-year growth phase covering 2003 to 2006 can be used to assess the firm's economic value-added for the missing years—specifically, 2004 and 2005—where financial data to measure EVA is noticeably absent from the Value Line report.

ESTIMATING MVA: MERCK & CO.

It is now time to calculate the market value added (MVA) for Merck & Co. using the two-stage EVA growth model. This procedure requires the calculation of (1) the present value of the anticipated EVA stream during the near-term growth phase, and (2) the intrinsic worth of the firm's long-term ability to generate EVA for the future. This latter valuation term is the present value of Merck's anticipated market value added at year-end 2006. The two-step MVA-pricing procedure (or template) for Merck & Co. is illustrated in Exhibit 12.4.

Combining the Valuation Results: Merck & Co.

Merck's *total* market value added at time period zero is thus the sum of (1) the MVA generated from the near-term EVA growth stage, and (2) the MVA contribution from the firm's long-term or mature economic growth stage. Upon adding the two pricing terms for Merck, the two-stage EVA growth analysis yields the aggregate market value added (or NPV) at time period zero:

$$\begin{aligned} MVA(0) &= \textit{Step A plus Step B} \\ &= \$17,474 + \$88,940 \\ &= \$106,414 \text{ million} \end{aligned}$$

In turn, Merck's enterprise value consists of the sum of the total capital employed in the business and the aggregate market value-added, $MVA(0)$. Based on the Value Line inputs for Merck & Co., we obtain:

$$\begin{aligned} EV(0) &= C(0) + MVA(0) \\ &= \$21,825 + \$106,414 \\ &= \$128,239 \text{ million} \end{aligned}$$

It is now a simple matter to calculate the intrinsic worth of Merck's stock. Specifically, with 2,273 million shares, and the $4,525 million in long-term debt outstanding (at year-end 2002), the intrinsic value of Merck's stock at year-end 2002 is $54.43. This present value figure results from dividing the pharmaceutical company's (estimated) equity capitalization, at $123,714 ($128,239 − $4,525) million, by the number of shares of common stock outstanding (again, taken as 2,273 million shares from the Capital Structure Box on the Value Line report).

EXHIBIT 12.4   Pricing Template to Estimate MVA: Merck & Co.

Step A: Calculate the MVA contribution at year-end 2002 from the estimated EVA stream during the abnormal growth phase: The following results show the estimated EVA figures for years 2003 through 2006, along with their current values when discounted at the Merck's 10% cost of capital. The *implied* near-term EVA growth rate, g_{NT}, used in these calculations is 7.76%.

Market Value Added: Merck's Near-Term Growth Opportunity ($ Millions)

Year	2002	2003	2004*	2005*	2006
Model Period (t)	0	1	2	3	4
EVA(t)	—	4,956	5,341	5,755	6,201
PVIF$_{10, t}$		0.909	0.826	0.751	0.683
PVIF$_{10, t}$ EVA(t)		4,505	4,412	4,322	4,235

*Implied EVA(t) estimates: EVA(t−1)(1 + g_{NT}) = EVA(t−1)(1 + 0.0776).
MVA(0) from Near-Term Growth Opportunity: $17,474 million = Σ^4 EVA(t)/(1.1)^t.

Step B: Calculate Merck's MVA contribution at year-end 2002 from the estimated EVA stream generated during the long term or mature growth phase. For convenience, we'll use a long-term EVA growth rate, g_{LT}, of 5% for this pharmaceutical company. This long-term EVA growth rate is approximately one-half of the EVA growth rate observed from Value Line information for years 1993 to 2003.* The resulting MVA contribution from this step represents the present (or current) value of the firm's anticipated Market Value Added at year-end 2006.

Market Value Added: Merck's Long-Term Growth Opportunities ($ Millions)

$$EVA(5) = EVA(4)[1 + g_{LT}]$$
$$= \$6,201(1.05)$$
$$= \$6,511 \text{ million}$$

$$MVA(4) = EVA(5)/(COC - g_{LT})$$
$$= \$6,511/(0.10 - 0.05)$$
$$= \$130,220 \text{ million}$$

$$MVA(0) \text{ from Long-Term Growth Opportunities} = PVIF_{10, 4} \times MVA(4)$$
$$= 0.683 \times \$130,220$$
$$= \$88,940 \text{ million}$$

* Merck's EVA using Value Line data for 1993 is $1,996 million. EVA for 2003 was previously estimated at $4,956 million. Hence the estimated 10-year EVA growth rate over the 1993–2003 period is about 10% (actually, 9.52%). Given that Merck cannot forever grow its EVA at a rate that is equal to the cost of capital, the estimated long-term EVA growth rate, g_{LT} is taken as *one-half* the observed 10-year EVA growth rate. With these figures, all of the information on the Value Line report—going back and going forward—is now being utilized to estimate MVA in the two-stage EVA growth model.

Interestingly, the two-stage EVA growth model reveals that Merck stock is "priced" just about right. This is based on the recognition that the EVA model produced an estimate of about $54 per share in the presence of the $55 stock price shown on the Value Line report (qualified of course by the time value of money difference between the April 26, 2002 report date and the year-end 2002 evaluation date).[8] In this context, the Value Line "timeliness" rating of "4" (on a scale of 1 to 5) seems *too* conservative for this wealth-creating (and low-volatility) pharmaceutical company. Moreover, from a traditional perspective, the return on equity (ROE) estimates for Merck & Co.—at 40.5% and 36.5% for years 2003 and 2006—are supportive of this relative performance assessment.

REAL-WORLD LINKAGE WITH THE CLASSIC NPV MODEL: MERCK & CO.

The wealth implications for Merck & Co. can be illustrated graphically in the context of the *two-period* NPV model. This two-period NPV (or MVA) representation is shown in Exhibit 12.5.[9] In this exhibit, it is important to recognize that Merck's *residual cash flow* (RCF) in the forthcoming year (year 2003 in our example) is a reflection of (1) the intrinsic value at period 1 of Merck's near-term EVA stream, and (2) the present value of the pharmaceutical company's long-term EVA growth opportunities when discounted back to that time.

For ease of calculation, it is helpful to recall that the expected residual cash flow, RCF(1), can be represented in terms of the firm's market value added at time period zero, MVA(0), *times* one plus the weighted average cost of capital; namely, [MVA(0)](1 + COC). Thus, at $117,055 million, Merck's residual cash flow (RCF) for period 1 (actually, 2003) can be expressed as:

---

[8] Note too that Value Line reports an equity capitalization for Merck & Co. of $125,000 (or $125 billion)—see the Capital Structure Box. Interestingly, this figure is close to the estimated equity capitalization of Merck stock, at $123,714, produced by the two-stage EVA growth model.

[9] Strictly speaking, the production possibilities curve, PPC, for Merck & Co. could be shifted to the left by the amount of its outstanding debt. However, in a well-functioning capital market the packaging of a company's debt versus equity has no material impact on shareholder wealth (NPV or MVA). Hence, this graphical complication is not included in the two-period illustration of Merck's current and future investment opportunities.

EXHIBIT 12.5   Wealth Creation at Merck & Co. ($ Millions)

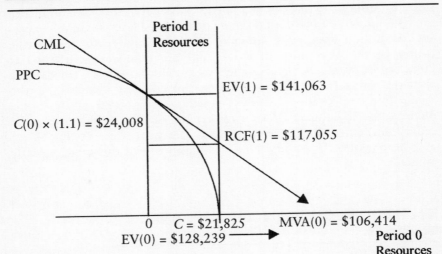

$$RCF(1) = \sum_{t=1}^{4} EVA(t)/(1 + COC)^{t-1} + PVIF_{COC,\,T-1}[MVA(T)]$$

$$= [MVA(0)](1 + COC)$$
$$= [\$106,414](1.1)$$
$$= \$117,055$$

The first term on the right hand side of the residual cash flow equation for Merck & Co. is the intrinsic value at period 1 of its expected EVA during the near-term growth phase. This component of RCF(1) is equal to $19,221 million. During the near term, Merck's EVA is presumably growing at an unusually high (or, possibly low) rate of growth—g_{NT} taken as 7.76% in the Value Line application. However, because of competition and/or technological advances within the pharmaceutical industry, the growth rate in Merck's economic value added settles down to g_{LT} for the long term—taken as 5% in the Merck application. Thus, the residual cash flow at period 1 generated by Merck's long-term EVA growth opportunities is equal to $97,834. Equivalently, this contribution to RCF(1) can be represented by Merck's MVA(0) from long-term growth opportunities *times* one plus the opportunity cost of capital, or $88,940 × (1.1).

Moreover, at $141,063 million, the two-period NPV illustration (again, see Exhibit 12.5) shows Merck's estimated enterprise value at time period 1. In this context, the pharmaceutical company's intrinsic worth at period 1 is obtained by growing its currently estimated market value, at $128,239 million, by the 10% cost of invested capital for one year. Most importantly, the two-period representation of Merck's variable growth opportunities suggests that EVA is a theoretically robust valuation metric for *any* company in *any* multiperiod framework.

A CLOSER LOOK AT INVESTMENT OPPORTUNITIES

Before completing our EVA valuation journey, let's take a closer look at the classic Investment Opportunities Approach to Valuation.[10] In this context, Fama and Miller show that the firm's enterprise value can be expressed in terms of (1) the intrinsic value of the expected net operating earnings, $X(1)$, that is generated by the firm's existing assets, and (2) the market value of the firm's anticipated future growth opportunities, G_f. In formal terms, Fama and Miller show that the firm's enterprise value can be expressed as:

$$EV(0) = X(1)/COC + \sum_{t=1}^{\infty} I(t)[RROC(t)/COC]/(1 + COC)^t$$
$$= X(1)/COC + G[I(t), RROC(t)]$$

In this expression, $EV(0)$ is the firm's enterprise value and $X(1)$ is the expected perpetual net operating cash earnings generated by the firm's existing assets. Also, $I(t)$ is the firm's *future* investment in real assets at period t, and $RROC(t)$ is the firm's assessed "residual return" on the capital additions at period t. Unless otherwise noted, the "Σ" sign in the enterprise value expression runs from $t = 1$ to ∞.

The IOAV approach to enterprise valuation separates the intrinsic value of the firm into two components. In particular, the first term on the right-hand side of the above expression is the present value of the net operating cash earnings, $X(1)$, generated by the firm's existing assets. The second and more complex-looking term is the intrinsic value of the firm's expected future growth opportunities, G_f. As shown, this pricing term is related to the capital additions at (t), and the assessed

---

[10] The strategic role of investment opportunities in enterprise valuation was introduced in Chapter 7. For a detailed explanation of this corporate valuation model, see Eugene F. Fama and Merton H. Miller, *The Theory of Finance* (New York: Holt, Rinehart and Winston, 1972), Chapter 2.

residual rate of return, RROC(t), on the firm's future investment opportunities.

In the IOAV model, the firm's investment opportunities make a value-added contribution to enterprise value when the anticipated return on the capital additions exceed the weighted average cost of capital, COC. On the other hand, when the after tax capital return is less than the assessed cost of capital the enterprise value of the firm falls when, for instance, corporate managers expand the real asset base for the purpose of expansion *per se*. Hence, the present value of the firm's future growth opportunities, G_f, is *positive* when the assessed "residual return" on the future investments, RROC(t), is largely positive.

It is now possible to make a formal connection between the classic IOAV model and the modern EVA measure. Based on the conventional definition of this financial metric, it is possible to express the firm's expected EVA on the future capital investments as:

$$
\begin{aligned}
eva(t+1) &= I(t)ROC(t) - I(t)COC \\
&= I(t)[ROC(t) - COC] \\
&= I(t)[RROC(t)]
\end{aligned}
$$

The first term on the right hand side of the above EVA expression, $I(t)ROC(t)$, is the firm's expected after-tax net operating cash earnings at period $t + 1$ on the (BOY) capital additions, and the $I(t)COC$ term is the firm's expected dollar cost of capital (at $t + 1$) on these future investment opportunities.[11] By substituting $eva(t + 1)$ for the $I(t)[ROC(t) - COC]$ term in the IOAV model, one obtains:

$$
EV(0) = X(1)/COC + \sum_{t=1}^{\infty} [eva(t+1)/COC]/(1 + COC)^t
$$

This expression indicates that the firm's enterprise value is linked to the ability of its managers to invest in growth opportunities having a measure of "economic value added." In this context, the market value of the firm's future growth opportunities, G_f, is based on shareholders' perceptions of the firm's underlying ability to generate EVA for the future. As expected, these investment opportunities make a positive contribution to the firm's intrinsic value when the anticipated after-tax return on invested capital, ROC(t), exceeds on the average the firm's weighted average cost of capital, COC.

---

[11] For modeling convenience, the cost of capital, COC, is presumed constant for all future time periods.

Moreover, the discounted EVA perpetuity in the brackets, namely, $eva(t+1)/COC$, is the "market value added $[mva\ (t)]$" from the firm's investment opportunity at period t. This present value interpretation reveals that G_f is the "market value added" at time period *zero* from all of the firm's expected future growth opportunities. With this development, the enterprise value of the firm can be expressed as:[12]

$$EV(0) = X(1)/COC + \sum_{t=1}^{\infty} [mva(t)]/(1 + COC)^t$$

IOAV and EVA: A Closer Look at the Present Value Linkage

As noted in Chapter 7, a simple rearrangement of the classic IOAV model reveals that the firm's enterprise value can be expressed as the firm's initial capital investment *plus* the present value of the anticipated EVA stream generated by both existing assets and expected future assets not currently in place. To show this present value linkage, it is helpful to recognize that the firm's net operating cash earnings, $X(1)$, can be expressed as:

$$X(1) = COC \times C(0) + EVA(1)$$

---

[12] Note that in this pricing development, EV(0) represents the enterprise value of the *unlevered* firm with positive growth opportunities, wherein the assessed residual return on future capital investment is positive (for some periods). If corporate debt policy is irrelevant as Miller-Modigliani contend, then EV(0) also represents the aggregate value of the *levered* firm. Otherwise, the unlevered and levered firms differ in corporate pricing terms by the present value of the *effective* debt tax subsidy received on the levered shares.

Also, there are helpful *finite* representations of the generalized IOAV model. For instance, in *The Quest for Value*, Bennett Stewart describes the enterprise value of an unlevered firm with a "forward plan (or positive EVA growth opportunity)" as:

$$EV(0) = X(1)/COC + [I(RROC)T]/COC(1 + COC)$$

In this expression, $X(1)$ is the unlevered net operating profit after taxes, COC is the familiar cost of capital, I is the normalized yearly investment in real assets, and T is the finite duration over which the firm can expand with a *positive* residual return on capital (that is, [RROC = ROC − COC] > 0). Also, Al Jackson, Michael Mauboussin, and Charles Wolf use this finite version of the IOAV model in their EVA growth illustrations. See, Al Jackson, Michael J. Mauboussin, and Charles R. Wolf, "EVA™ Primer," *Equity Research-Americas* (CS First Boston: February 20, 1996).

In this expression, the product of the firm's cost of capital, COC, and the initial capital investment, C(0), equals the *dollar* cost of capital on the firm's existing assets. Additionally, the EVA(1) term is the firm's anticipated economic profit at period 1. Upon substituting this expression for X(1) into the first term on the right-hand side of the IOAV model yields:

$$EV(0) = X(1)/COC + G_f[I(t), RROC(t)]$$
$$= C(0) + [EVA(1)/COC + G_f(.)]$$
$$= C(0) + MVA(0)$$

In this context, the IOAV-EVA linkage gives a powerful representation of the firm's enterprise value. The linked model suggests that the firm derives its market value added (MVA) from the present value of the anticipated EVA stream from assets already in place and the EVA earned on the likely capital additions for the future. In turn, the firm's total net present value is obtained by summing the two MVA-based pricing elements shown within the brackets.

More specifically, the EVA(1)/COC term represents the expected MVA contribution generated by the firm's existing assets. Also, the $G_f(I(t), RROC(t))$ function represents the net present value of the firm's anticipated future growth opportunities. Taken together, the two sources of economic value added—EVA from both current and anticipated future real assets—represent the firm's aggregate market value added (MVA) at time period zero.

Finally, the IOAV-EVA linkage provides some meaningful insight for wealth creators and destroyers. The model demonstrates that the firm's market value added is positive if and only if the expected after-tax return on future investment opportunities exceeds the *cross-generational* cost of capital, COC. The opposite MVA prediction applies for wealth destroyers having a largely negative expected residual return (RROC) on capital for the future.

RECAP AND SUMMARY

In the last couple of chapters, we looked at how EVA can be applied to estimate the enterprise value of the firm. In a nutshell, the firm's market value added (MVA) is equal to the present value of the anticipated EVA stream for all future time periods. From this perspective, it is possible to develop a series of practitioner-oriented models that use the EVA measure to estimate the value of the firm and its outstanding shares. Some helpful pricing variations on the general EVA model include the constant growth EVA model and the two-stage EVA growth model. Additional stages of growth in the firm's economic profit can of course be added should the valuation need arise.

In the constant growth EVA model, the firm's market value added (MVA) is expressed in terms of the current EVA outlook, as measured by EVA(1), and the company's assessed long-term EVA growth rate, g_{LT}. The model suggests that companies with positive EVA growth expectations—at some assumed constant rate for *all* future time periods—should see noticeable improvements in the enterprise value of the firm and its outstanding securities relative to a company with no future EVA growth potential. In effect, positive EVA growth enhances the stockholders residual claim on the firm's expected profits. Positive growth in EVA may also lead to credit upgrades in the firm's outstanding bonds.

The two-stage EVA growth model is a more realistic way of seeing how the firm derives its true corporate profitability. In the two-stage version of the EVA model, the firm's total market value added (MVA) is separated into the sum of (1) the present value of the EVA stream generated during the firm's abnormal growth phase, and (2) the intrinsic worth of the expected EVA benefits generated during the long-term (or mature) growth period. The total of these MVA-related pricing elements is the firm's total net present value. Moreover, with estimates of four easily identifiable parameters—including EVA(1), g_{NT}, g_{LT}, and COC—the two stage EVA pricing template can be used in practice by managers and investors.

Also, the benefit of using EVA to estimate the firm's enterprise value does *not* lie in its ability to produce a theoretically better estimate of the market value of the firm and its outstanding shares. For the "franchise value" of any company is derived from the intrinsic worth of the economic benefits—whether they be measured in terms of dividends, free cash flow, or EVA—that are being generated by the firm's capital assets (physical *and* human). This, after all, is one of the central valuation themes in financial economics more generally. It is also one of the major reasons why the firm's "capital structure" decision is largely irrelevant for firms operating in a well-functioning capital market.

Rather, the real benefit of using EVA technology to value companies is based on three considerations: First, since EVA is the *annualized* equivalent of the firm's total net present value, it makes a tangible connection with the economist's view on how wealth is truly created in an efficient capital market. This enterprise valuation point is clearly emphasized in the classic "Investment Opportunities Approach to Valuation (IOAV)"—wherein, the firm derives its aggregate market value added (MVA) from the anticipated EVA stream on both existing assets and future capital additions not currently in place. As noted before, the firm's capital assets make a meaningful contribution to the is net present value when the assessed "residual return on capital," $RROC(t)$, exceeds the cross-generational cost of capital, COC.

Secondly, the EVA pricing model is versatile because it can be used to value companies in a variety of real world settings. Unlike traditional dividend discount models (DDMs), the variable-growth EVA model can be used to value companies that operate in growth-oriented sectors of the economy—where, in many real-world instances, corporate plow-back ratios are close to unity. Also, since EVA looks at how the firm generates its overall corporate profitability, the derived pricing models have *joint* investment implications for the firm's outstanding debt (via credit upgrades or downgrades) and equity securities.

CHAPTER 13

Company Analysis Using EVA

Financial analysis is generally required to find the best companies in the marketplace. In the traditional "growth style" of investing, analysts look for companies having abnormally high product development and earnings growth prospects. By focusing research primarily on the "E," for earnings per share, it is anticipated that the "P," for stock price, will eventually catch up—if, in fact, it hasn't already done so. In practice, the revealed growth portfolio mostly consists of companies with a relatively high price-to-earnings ratio, a high price-to-book value ratio, and a low dividend yield. Moreover, this "P&E" view of the traditional growth style of investing is the essence of the "bottom up" approach to portfolio management that was used so successfully by the legendary Peter Lynch of Fidelity Investments.[1]

In the popular "value style" of investing, the research focus is primarily on the firm's stock price, rather than the recent growth rate in per share earnings. The investment presumption here is that the company's stock price has fallen too far and too fast in view of the firm's *future* earnings prospects and the quality of the assets employed in the business. In practice, the revealed value portfolio consists of companies having a comparatively low price-to-earnings ratio, a low price-to-book value ratio, and a relatively high dividend yield. Over time, it is anticipated that the debt and equity securities of these so-called "value" companies will appreciate to a level that is consistent with the firm's true wealth-creating potential.

Indeed, the real world importance of finding "good companies" in the market that are selling at attractive prices is no secret to that consum-

---

[1] Peter Lynch's view on the fundamental linkage between stock price and earnings per share can be found in, "Mind Your P's and E's," *Worth* (February 1996). From a modern perspective, the traditional "P and E" relationship can now be interpreted as, "Mind Your MVA's and EVA's!"

mate value-investor, Warren Buffet of Berkshire Hathaway, Inc. Also, a growing body of empirical research suggests that a value-focused investment strategy produces abnormally high risk-adjusted returns. In this context, studies by Eugene Fama and Kenneth French as well as Rex Sinquefield of Dimensional Fund Advisors suggest that abnormal return performance from a value style of investing applies to both the domestic U.S. and the international securities markets.[2]

Although the conventional growth and value strategies emphasize—to varying degrees—the importance of the "P" and the "E," there is a commonality among these active approaches to investing. In each case, the overall goal is to maximize the likelihood of financial success while minimizing the risk of paying *too much* for the shares of presumably mispriced companies. In the growth style, the investor tries to avoid paying excessive multiples for companies having unrealistic product development and earnings-growth expectations. In the popular value strategy, the active investor shuns the debt and equity securities of companies that may look "cheap" in the market, when, in fact, their low prices are an efficient market reflection of the firm's poor future growth opportunities.

This chapter looks at the question of value versus growth from an EVA perspective. We'll first build a foundation on an EVA-based growth approach to investing. In this context, we can distinguish between EVA growth "at a reasonable price" and fallen EVA growth at an overvalued price. Next, we'll build a foundation on an EVA-based value approach to investing. Here, we can distinguish between a real-value company with positive EVA momentum and a troubled EVA company that may be a "value trap." In this regard, we'll look at the profitability index ratio (defined as the return on capital over the cost of capital[3]) *versus* the value-to-capital ratio for a sample of companies that were selected in the first edition of *Foundations of Economic Value Added*.[4] We'll then "roll up" the EVA company analysis for U.S. wealth creators and destroyers into an EVA investment portfolio. Following that, we'll compare the stock market performance of the *ex ante* EVA portfolio with

---

[2] That "value wins" from a domestic U.S. perspective is described in Eugene F. Fama and Kenneth R. French, "The Cross Section of Expected Stock Returns," *Journal of Finance* (June 1992). That value "wins" from an international perspective can be seen in, Rex A. Sinquefield, "Where Are the Gains From International Diversification?" *Financial Analysts Journal* (January/February 1996).

[3] Note that when the profitability index ratio, ROC/COC, is greater than one, then a company has positive EVA. Conversely, when PI is less than unity, a company has negative EVA. This is just another variation—sometimes seen in practice—of the residual return on capital or the EVA spread.

[4] A benefit of repeating the initial EVA sample is that we can come back to assess the investment performance of the *ex ante* EVA portfolio in a forward time period.

the overall market (as measured by the S&P 500). We'll conclude the chapter with a look at the "top ten" EVA stocks among U.S. wealth creators and wealth destroyers for year 2000—based on the updated MVA and EVA data set used primarily in this book.

TOWARDS AN EVA GROWTH STRATEGY

A modern perspective on a "growth style" of investing should emphasize the positive EVA happenings at the firm. By focusing research efforts on those companies with abnormally high economic profit prospects, it is possible that one can discover the right kind of companies that will experience unusual growth in their market value added (MVA). In this context, it is no surprise to see (recall Chapter 5) that powerful wealth creators like General Electric, Microsoft, and Merck have relatively high enterprise valuations because, in principle, *they should have*. This happens because the net present value of these high growth firms tracks the explosive growth in economic value added. Of course, the security selection "trick" is to aying for the growth opportunities of wealth-enhancing firms.

3.1 provides some empirical insight on an EVA "growth . The exhibit plots the profitability index ratio (ROC/ 1ue-to-capital ratio for the 50 largest U.S. wealth 4.[5] As noted before, we'll begin with the EVA e first edition of *Foundations of Economic Value* .ators (and destroyers) so that we can (1) develop d value) approach to investing, (2) form an ex ante ,ortfolio and, (3) examine performance in a future .g that, we'll use EVA company analysis to develop a set of su at year-end 2000.

Sinc value-to-capital ratios in Exhibit 13.1 are noticeably above unity, it is clear that wealth-enhancing companies have substantially *positive* market value added. At year-end 1994, high-growth companies like Coca-Cola and Cisco Systems were selling for multiples of 8.19 and 10.47 times the capital employed in the respective businesses. In turn, the relatively high enterprise values for these growth companies are supported by profitability index ratios—at 3.55 and 4.25, respectively—that are considerably higher than one. Not surprisingly, the favorable "residual return on capital" for growth companies like Coca-Cola and Cisco Systems is the underlying source of their relatively high market valuations.

---

[5] The MVA and EVA data reported in the first edition of *Foundations of Economic Value Added* was obtained from the 1995 Performance Universe collected by Stern Stewart & Co.

EXHIBIT 13.1 Profitability Index Ratio versus Value/Capital Ratio for 50 Largest U.S. Wealth Creators at Year End 1994

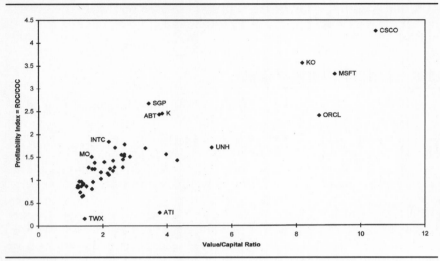

Oracle's positioning in Exhibit 13.1 makes for an interesting focal point to develop and EVA growth "style" of investing. In this context, Oracle is dominated by wealth creators from both above, and to the left of its position in real profitability (ROC/COC) and relative-value space. With a value-to-capital ratio near eight times, Coca-Cola's 3.55 profitability index ratio is considerably higher than the 2.40 figure observed on Oracle Corporation. Likewise, a look leftward in Exhibit 13.1 reveals that Abbot Laboratories also dominates this high technology company from a stock selection perspective. For about the same level of real corporate profitability (ROC/COC, near 2.4), Abbot's 3.75 value-to-capital ratio is dramatically lower than the 8.71 figure observed on Oracle. Hence, for differing active reasons, Coca-Cola and Abbot Laboratories were the preferred investment choices.

From a *strict* security selection perspective, it is interesting to see that Coca-Cola dominates Microsoft Corporation. Coke's profitability index ratio is higher than the corresponding 3.31 figure observed on Microsoft, while the beverage firm's value-to-capital ratio is lower than the 9.2 figure for the high-growth software services company. Also, in Exhibit 13.1, Kellogg Company is clearly the preferred active choice over AirTouch Communications, Inc. For a similar relative valuation (near 3.85), the cereal maker's 2.45 profitability index ratio is substantially higher than the dismal-looking 0.29 figure for AirTouch Communications.

Based on the 1994 valuations, the exhibit also reveals that Philip Morris Companies and Intel were the preferred investment choices over Time Warner, Inc. Generalizing these security selection concepts reveals that the best investment opportunities include those companies with the highest EVA prospects (measured here by the profitability index ratio) for a given level of the value-to-capital ratio. Indeed, firms that plot on the *leftmost* portion of the "company cluster" shown in Exhibit 13.1— such as Philip Morris, Intel, and Schering-Plough Corporation, as well as the high EVA-growth companies like Coca-Cola, Cisco Systems and Microsoft (just to be safe!)—seem to be "actively efficient." Investing in positive EVA companies like these appears to maximize the likelihood of financial success, while minimizing the active risk of paying *too much* for the (debt and equity) securities of wealth-creating firms. This is the EVA equivalent of buying growth at a "reasonable" price.

A Closer Look at the EVA Growth Strategy

It is also possible to use quantitative methods to identify the best growth opportunities in the marketplace. For instance, Exhibit 13.2 shows the actual versus *least-squares* fitted relationship between the profitability index ratio and the value-to-capital ratio for the 50 largest U.S. wealth creators at year-end 1994.[6] The predicted PI ratios for these large capitalization firms were estimated according to:

$$PI = 0.56 + 0.31 \text{ [Value/Capital]}$$
$$(5.73) \quad (11.09)$$

In this model, PI (dependent variable) is the ratio of the firm's after-tax return on capital to the cost of capital. The firm's economic value added is positive when the profitability index ratio is greater than unity, while its EVA is negative when the PI ratio is less than one. As expected, the "*t*-statistic" (shown in the parenthesis) on the enterprise value-to-capital factor (explanatory variable) for the 50 U.S. growth companies is highly significant.

In Exhibit 13.2, two points of reference are plotted for each company: (1) the actual profitability index ratio for a given level of the "value/cap" ratio, and (2) the predicted value of the PI ratio from the value-to-capital attributes of the linear regression model. In the exhibit, firms having profitability index ratios that are higher than those predicted by the regression model could be viewed as attractive *buy* oppor-

---

[6] At the end of this chapter, we'll look at the updated PI versus value-to-capital ratio in a nonlinear framework. This is more consistent with the present value dynamics of the PI and value-to-capital relationship.

tunities. Given the current relative value, their actual EVA is higher than that which was predicted for similarly valued growth companies. Conversely, growth firms with PI ratios that plot below the corresponding fitted values could then be placed on a *sell* or watch list, as their underlying EVA is too low in light of the relative valuation of their outstanding debt and equity securities.

In this context, Exhibit 13.2 shows why high growth firms like Intel, Schering-Plough, Coca-Cola, and Cisco Systems were attractive buy opportunities at year-end 1994. In each case, the actual profitability index ratio is not only greater than unity (consistent with highly positive EVA for growth companies), but also considerably above the fitted ratio that might normally apply for equally valued growth companies in the marketplace. At 3.55 and 4.25, the profitability index ratios for Coca-Cola (the top U.S. wealth creator at that time) and Cisco Systems were noticeably higher than the fitted values, at 3.11 and 3.82. Likewise, Intel was an attractive buy opportunity at year-end 1994 because its 1.84 profitability index ratio was some 48% higher than the 1.24 PI figure observed in the linear model.

EXHIBIT 13.2   EVA Growth Strategy: Profitability Index Ratio: Actual versus Least-Squares Fitted for 1994

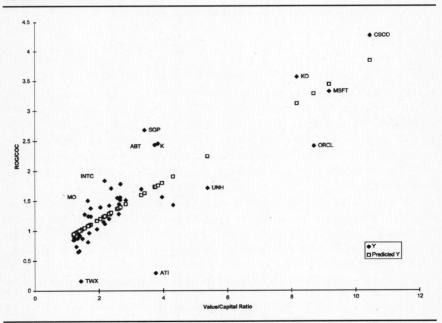

The least squares model can also be used to identify the growth companies that were priced too high in light of their (current) EVA characteristics. Given their relative valuations, Exhibit 13.2 shows that firms like Time Warner, Air Touch Communications, United Health Care, and Oracle Corporation had profitability index ratios that were substantially below the corresponding fitted PI ratios. For instance, Time Warner's actual profitability index ratio for 1994 was a paltry 0.16, while its fitted PI ratio was near unity, at 1.01. With a value-to-capital ratio of 1.44, the regression model suggests that the communication's giant should have had a capital return that at least paralleled the cost of capital. However, the firm's revealed PI indicates that its after-tax capital return was 84% *below* the weighted average cost of capital. Thus, Time Warner Inc. was an unattractive investment opportunity at that time.

For similar pricing reasons, it is easy to see why the securities of Air Touch Communications, United Health Care, and Oracle Corporation (no less) were also relatively overvalued at year-end 1994. The revealed profitability index ratios for these growth-oriented companies were 0.29, 1.71, and 2.40, respectively. In sharp contrast, the fitted PI ratios for Air Touch Communications, United Health Care and Oracle were significantly higher, at 1.73, 2.24, and 3.27. On balance, the quantitative analysis reveals that by focusing efforts on growth companies having profitability index ratios that lie above *and* below a fitted line (*or curve*), the active investor may see pricing trends that might otherwise go unnoticed in the marketplace. Moreover, because of possible credit rating changes, these EVA-to-valuation considerations have *joint* pricing implications for the firm's risky debt and equity securities.

TOWARDS AN EVA VALUE STRATEGY

Since EVA emphasizes shareholder value, there is a natural tendency to associate this metric with a so-called "value style" of investing. After all, the traditional value model—*à la Benjamin Graham in days gone by, or Warren Buffet in more recent times*—seeks to discover companies with favorable earnings prospects that have *unjustifiably* fallen out of favor with the consensus investor. Having said that, it is also important to recognize that the wealth-maximizing principles of corporation finance are applicable to all firms in the marketplace, regardless of whether their investment fundamentals (growth rates, price-relatives, or dividend yield) would lead investors to categorize them as either value or growth companies.

EXHIBIT 13.3   Profitability Index Ratio versus Value/Capital Ratio for 50 Largest
U.S. Wealth Destroyers at Year End 1994

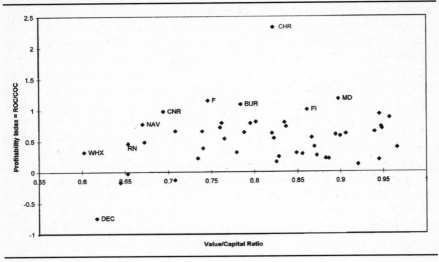

By analogy, a modern perspective on an EVA "value style" of investing would emphasize the importance of the "*M*," for market value
added, in view of the "adjusted-*E*," for economic value-added. In this
context, some firms with value-to-capital ratios that lie below unity may
have seen their security prices fall too far and too fast in view of the
company's fundamental ability to generate economic profit for the
future. By investing in the debt and equity securities of these presumably
mispriced companies, the active investor seeks to achieve windfall gains
on some, and possibly all, of the firm's outstanding securities. If correct,
then the securities (stocks and bonds) of these EVA value companies
should rise in the market as the future reveals the better than market-
assessed earnings prospects.

In light of the positive EVA announcements, the firm's risky debt
securities should rise in value due to unanticipated (from the bond
investor's viewpoint) "credit upgrades" on the junior and senior bonds.
Of course, the opposite pricing implications would apply for the firm's
risky debt (and equity) securities in the event that deterioration should
occur in the firm's future ability to generate economic value added.
Moreover, that fundamental changes in EVA may have information content for all of a company's security holders is one of the major pricing
features of the EVA approach to enterprise valuation.

Exhibit 13.3 sheds some interesting light on the "value-oriented
characteristics" of the 50 largest U.S. wealth destroyers listed in the

1995 Performance 1000 Universe. Not surprisingly, the exhibit reveals that all 50 companies had a value-to-capital ratio that fell below unity. At year-end 1994, the market capitalization (including the market value of risky bonds and stocks) of the so-called "wealth destroyers" were at a substantial discount from their aggregate invested capital. Knowledge of this overwhelmingly negative NPV finding for the bottom-50 U.S. companies in the Performance Universe is helpful, especially when attempting to develop a modern perspective on a real value approach to active investing.

Exhibit 13.3 suggests that large wealth destroyers have relatively low corporate valuations because, in principle, *they should have*. These U.S. large capitalization firms have negative MVA because their revealed profitability index ratios (ROC/COC) were mostly less than unity. In this context, 45 of the 50 (or, 90%) profitability index ratios for the companies shown in the exhibit are less than one. Hence, the economic source of the negative "net present value" finding for the 50 U.S. firms must in some sense be due to the low-returning (and therefore, negative EVA) capital investments that were being made by corporate managers. On balance, these adverse investment decisions are the kind, which ultimately lead to after-tax capital returns that fall short of the weighted average cost of capital.

As with the traditional value approach to investing, the challenge in the EVA approach involves finding those companies having low corporate valuations in the presence of positive earnings momentum. After all, buying securities of firms having favorable economic profit prospects at reasonable prices is what a real-value style of investing is really all about. In other words, an EVA value strategy is one that avoids persistently negative EVA companies that may be a "value trap." From an EVA perspective, the real-earnings factor can be measured either directly in terms of EVA, or possibly indirectly by looking at companies having a profitability index ratio (ROC/COC) that exceeds unity. In empirical terms, Exhibit 13.3 shows that only *five* firms pass the positive EVA (PI *greater than one*) and low relative valuation *(value-to-capital ratio less than unity)* screen. For 1994, these U.S. large capitalization firms were Ford Motor Company, Burlington Industries Equity, FINA, McDonnell Douglas, and Chrysler Corporation (noted as "CHR").

While companies like Navistar International, RJR Nabisco Holdings, and WHX Corporation had positive profitability index ratios, and notably low corporate valuations, their after-tax capital returns ranged from only 32% (WHX) to 77% (NAV) of the respective weighted average cost of capital. Hence, other things the same, their negative EVA excludes them from the active opportunity set. Among the five remaining candidates, Exhibit 13.3 shows that Chrysler Corporation was the best "value opportunity" at year-end 1994. That is, the automaker had the beneficial combination of a high profitability index ratio, ROC/COC at 2.33, in the presence of an aggregate corporate valuation (value-to-capital ratio at 0.82) that was 18% percent below the invested capital employed in the business. Assuming EVA consistency, Chrysler was a real value opportunity at that time because it had a comparatively low enterprise valuation and an after-tax capital return that was some 2.33 times the weighted average cost of debt and equity capital.[7]

Exhibit 13.3 also shows that Ford Motor Company was a better "value opportunity" than Burlington Industries Equity, McDonnell Douglas and FINA, Inc. With a profitability index ratio at 1.16, and a value-to-capital ratio at only 0.75, Ford Motor seemed to "minimize" the active risk of paying too much for the shares of companies having similarly positive EVA—when measured relative to the invested capital employed in the respective businesses. On the other hand, the exhibit reveals that Digital Equipment Corporation—with a 1994 after-tax capital return of –9.56%, and a cost of capital of 12.87%—was also a value-oriented investment of sorts, but from a *shortselling* perspective![8]

DIVERSIFICATION AND EFFICIENT MARKET CONSIDERATIONS

One of the limitations of an active strategy (value or growth) that deviates from the passive "market portfolio" is that the resulting combination of securities may contain an excessive amount of active risk. This residual risk consideration is problematic for the value-oriented investor because—in an efficient capital market—there can only exist a small number of firms having consistently positive EVA momentum and low relative valuations that haven't already been discovered in the capital market. Unfortunately, this portfolio risk dilemma for the active-minded investor doesn't go away by using quantitative techniques to identify the investable opportunity set of value-oriented companies.

---

[7] It is interesting to note that Daimler-Benz subsequently acquired Chrysler (in 1999). Thus, the stock or the company can be acquired when investors see a potential real value opportunity.

[8] In practice, an investor must consider a range of possible outcomes for a negative MVA and EVA company. Absent cyclical recovery, a negative EVA company will eventually (1) "go bust," (2) restructure for positive change, or (3) be acquired by a presumably more efficient company with a long-term focus on EVA improvement. In DEC's case, the firm was subsequently acquired by Compaq Computer, which, in turn, was acquired by Hewlett Packard!

EXHIBIT 13.4   EVA Value Strategy: Profitability Index Ratio: Actual versus Least-Squares Fitted for 1994

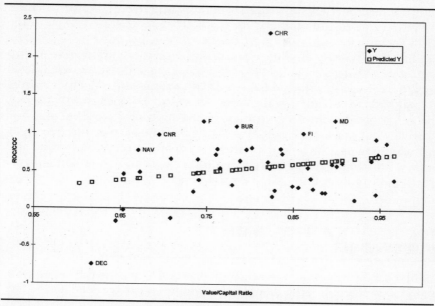

For instance, Exhibit 13.4 shows the actual versus *least-squares* fitted relationship between the profitability index ratio and the value-to-capital ratio for the 50 largest U.S. wealth destroyers at year-end 1994. Like Exhibit 13.2, two points are displayed for each company: (1) the actual profitability index ratio and, (2) the predicted PI ratio for a given value-to-capital ratio. In Exhibit 13.4, the fitted PI ratios for the bottom-50 companies in the 1995 Performance Universe were estimated according to:

$$PI = -0.33 + 1.09 \text{ [Value/Capital]}$$
$$(-0.63) \quad (1.70)$$

The profitability index ratio is again obtained by dividing the firm's after-tax return on capital by the weighted average cost of capital. Unlike the *t*-statistic reported on the value-to-capital factor for the top-50 companies, the *t*-statistic for the value-oriented companies is statistically insignificant.

In order to understand the findings in Exhibit 13.4, it is helpful to recall that when the firm's profitability index ratio is equal to unity, its after-tax return on capital is just equal to the cost of capital. When this happens, the company's economic value added is zero. This financial consideration is important because the two parameter estimates (intercept and slope) in the least squares model implies that the "value/cap" factor would have to equal 1.22 for the PI ratio to equal unity (therefore, showing positive EVA for investors in these negative MVA firms). However, the value-to-capital ratios for the bottom-50 U.S. companies in the 1995 Performance Universe were consistently below one.

In other words, the linear regression model predicted that the 50 largest wealth-destroyers in the 1995 Performance Universe would have negative economic value-added for 1994. As a result, the model offers *no* real basis for identifying the active set of value opportunities. Indeed, the empirical dearth of companies having both positive EVA and low relative valuations is a quantitative way of showing that there really is no such thing as a "free lunch." Real resources, in the form of time and money, must ultimately be expended to discover the "best of the best" stock opportunities in the capital market.

A COMBINED LOOK AT THE EVA GROWTH AND VALUE CANDIDATES

Exhibit 13.5 shows the "top-ten" companies that emerged from an EVA analysis of potential growth and value companies at year-end 1994. The eight growth-oriented firms—including Intel, Schering-Plough, Coca-Cola, and Cisco Systems—were culled from Exhibit 13.2, while the two EVA value companies—Chrysler and Ford Motor Company—were selected from Exhibit 13.4 because of their attractive PI/valuation characteristics. Among the 100 firms (top 50 and bottom 50 companies in the Performance Universe for 1994) included in the analyses, the ten large capitalization firms were chosen because of their positive EVA momentum and relatively low valuations. This enterprise value assessment was based on statistical analyses of the profitability index ratios (ROC/COC) and the value-to-capital factor.

Assuming EVA consistency, Chrysler Corporation stood out as one of the best investment opportunities at year-end 1994. With a value-to-capital ratio that was well below unity, the U.S. automaker had a profitability index ratio that paralleled the relatively higher-valued choices like Abbot Laboratories and Kellogg. Aside from Chrysler, Exhibit 13.5 shows a *positive* tradeoff between the profitability index ratio and the value-to-capital ratio for these U.S. large capitalization firms. Accordingly, this finding suggests that buying into companies with abnormally positive EVA characteristics—like Intel, Schering-Plough, Coca-Cola, and Cisco Systems—comes at a higher price, as the more growth-oriented firms have noticeably higher relative valuations.

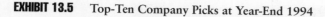

EXHIBIT 13.5   Top-Ten Company Picks at Year-End 1994

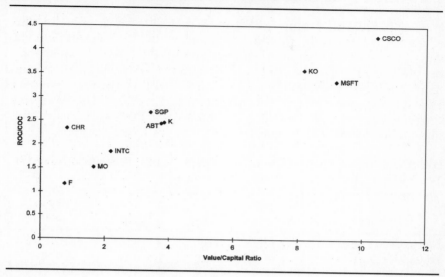

However, it is important to note that the ten best companies in Exhibit 13.5 were culled from two samples consisting of the top-50 and bottom-50 companies listed in the Performance Universe at year-end 1994. For each company selected—ranging from Ford Motor with a relatively low valuation, to Philip Morris and Intel with mid-level valuations, on up to the high end of the valuation spectrum with firms like Coca-Cola, and Cisco Systems—the revealed profitability index ratio was considerably higher than the predicted PI ratio that would normally be associated with similarly-valued firms in the marketplace.

In general, the active opportunity set can be expanded by screening firms from a larger universe. Such portfolio expansion would be beneficial for both performance *and* diversification reasons. Rather than looking at just the top-50 and the bottom-50 companies, the EVA analysis could be broadened to *discover* the best companies among all firms listed in the Performance Universe. On a larger scale, it seems that substantial performance benefits could be derived from an EVA-based approach to company analysis on both U.S. medium and small capitalization firms. Moreover, an international extension of the model might include an examination of the EVA-to-relative value characteristics of companies that operate in the developed foreign (MSCI-EAFE countries) and (IFC-based) emerging market regions of the world.

PERFORMANCE OF THE EX ANTE EVA PORTFOLIO

Having selected the "top-ten" EVA stocks for 1994—a point in time which turned out to be the starting point of the "bull market" of the mid- to- late 1990s—we can shed some empirical light on the stock market performance of the *ex ante* EVA investment portfolio.[9] In this context, Exhibit 13.6 shows the cumulative one-year, three-year, five-year, and six-year price return performance of the companies (*excepting Chrysler*) that were illustrated in Exhibit 13.5.[10] The stock market findings for the 1995–2000 period are interesting in several respects.

EXHIBIT 13.6 Stock Market Performance of the Ex Ante EVA Portfolio Formed at Year-End 1994

Company*	1-Year Return	3-Year Return	5-Year Return	1994 to 2000
Cisco Systems Inc.	112.82%	376.41%	2,646.67%	1,861.54%
Microsoft Corp.	43.59	322.91	1,428.14	467.80
Intel Corp.	77.69	340.10	931.58	653.38
Coca.Cola Co.	44.19	158.99	126.21	136.66
Schering-Plough	48.00	235.78	358.16	513.51
Philip Morris Cos. Inc.	56.91	136.05	19.98	129.53
Abbott Laboratories	27.59	100.80	122.62	197.00
Ford Motor Co.	3.57	74.17	91.22	46.96
Kellogg Co.	32.93	70.78	6.02	−9.67
Average-stocks	49.70	201.78	636.73	444.08
Market (S&P 500)	34.11	111.30	219.91	187.47
Cumulative Alpha	15.59	90.48	416.82	256.60

*Excludes merged Daimler-Chrysler

---

[9] Recall that these stocks were selected in the first edition of *Foundations of Economic Value Added*.

[10] Chrysler was omitted from the performance results due to a merger with Daimler-Benz in 1999. This is interesting because Chrysler had jointly negative MVA and positive EVA at year-end 1994 and, in turn, was one of the "top-ten" company picks at that time. Again, this brings to mind that either the stock *or* the company can be purchased when an investor (group) sees potential value going forward. Whether or not Chrysler was a "good fit" for Daimler-Benz is an issue for another day!

Regarding Chrysler, the one-year price return (1995) for the automaker was 12.5%, while the cumulative three-year return on the stock was −32.65%. With these figures, the average returns on the ten-stock EVA portfolio (with Chrysler) for one- and three-year periods was 45.98% and 178.33%—still much higher than the corresponding cumulative market returns.

First, it is interesting to see that the cumulative returns to the EVA portfolio were not only positive but also attractive for each of the forward time periods shown in Exhibit 13.6. In this regard, the EVA portfolio had positive returns over one-, three-, and five-year time intervals, including 49.7% for the one-year period, 201.78% for the three-year interval, and 636.73% for the five-year period. Also, the six-year cumulative return to the EVA portfolio during the 1995–2000 period was 444.08%, down considerably from the five-year results. These five- and six-year return differentials can be attributed to the general decline in the stock market that began in 2000 and the malaise in technology and telecom stocks in particular.

Second, Exhibit 13.6 shows that the EVA portfolio outdistanced the general stock market (as measured by the price return to the S&P 500) over short and intermediate time periods.[11] The one-year performance (1995) on the EVA portfolio was 49.7% compared with albeit lower, yet breathtaking stock market performance of 34.11%. Likewise, the cumulative three- and five-year performance on the EVA portfolio was 201.78% and 636.73% in the presence of what otherwise would be viewed as attractive cumulative market returns of 111.30% and 219.91%, respectively. Moreover, the *ex ante* EVA portfolio bested the market portfolio (cumulative "alpha") by 257% over the six-year period covering 1995 to 2000. This latter period includes the "bull market" run up in stock prices from 1995 to 1999 and the recent downturn in the market commencing in 2000.

There are also some interesting cross sectional differences in the short- to intermediate-term performance results shown in Exhibit 13.6. In this context, the exhibit shows that abnormal returns (alpha) to the EVA portfolio over one- and three-year intervals were prevalent *across* the actively selected stocks, including tech stocks such as Cisco Systems, Microsoft, and Intel, to beverage and soft-drink maker Coca-Cola, to health care company, Schering-Plough Corporation. In each case, these stocks outperformed the one- and three-year cumulative market returns of 34% and 111%. However, Exhibit 13.6 shows that the abnormally high five- and six-year cumulative returns (out to 2000) on the EVA portfolio were concentrated in the technology sector, with the notable exception of consistent stock market performer Schering-Plough in the health care sector.

---

[11] The author is aware that investment performance *should* be measured on a "risk-adjusted" returns basis. In this regard, the performance results are suggestive of what an EVA-based approach to company analysis might produce, but in *no* way are they conclusive. Moreover, the sample size is small and past performance is *no* guarantee of future investment results.

Moreover, while EVA stock picks Coca-Cola and Philip Morris performed well over one- and three-year periods, they *underperformed* the stock market over the five- and six-year time intervals. Also, EVA picks Ford Motor Company and Kellogg underperformed the general stock market over the short and intermediate time periods shown in Exhibit 13.6. On balance though, it seems that consistently high returns to the *ex ante* EVA portfolio were concentrated in wealth-creating technology stocks like Microsoft, Cisco Systems, and Intel Corporation and—as noted before—consistent stock market producer, Schering-Plough.

A LOOK AT THE TOP-TEN COMPANIES FOR YEAR 2000

Before moving on, it is instructive—*if not downright fun*—to form an *ex ante* EVA investment portfolio for year 2000—based on the updated MVA and EVA data used primarily in this book. In this context, Exhibit 13.7 presents a display of U.S. companies that were culled from the top-50 and bottom-50 companies in the Performance 1000 Universe at year-end 2000. The initial screening criteria used in the selection of these stocks consists of (1) a profitability index ratio greater than one (namely, positive EVA), and (2) an enterprise value-to-capital ratio less than 15. The relative value restriction is employed to achieve some conformity in the enterprise value-to-capital range reported in the first edition of this book and, practically speaking, to avoid paying excessive multiples in a negative year for the stock market—namely, 2000.

Given the initial screen, a nonlinear regression was performed to find the "best of the best" stocks among the EVA value and growth candidates shown in Exhibit 13.7.[12] Stocks that plot above the curve are considered the best (buy) opportunities, while stocks that plot below the curve are relatively unattractive based on valuation considerations. From this, we can easily identify ten stocks for the ex ante EVA investment portfolio at year-end 2000. As before, the active EVA strategy is to fix the enterprise value-to-capital ratio at any given level, then select those stocks with the highest profitability index ratio—presuming that the currently announced EVA has information content for future EVA generation). Based on the above considerations, Exhibit 13.8 presents a potential list of the "top-ten" company choices at year-end 2000.

---

[12] For further discussion on the EVA approach to company analysis in a nonlinear context—including the development of "theoretical company analysis" using economic profit principles—see James L. Grant and James A. Abate, *Focus on Value: A Corporate and Investor Guide to Wealth Creation* (New York: John Wiley & Sons, 2001).

EXHIBIT 13.7   EVA Company Analysis (Year-End 2000)

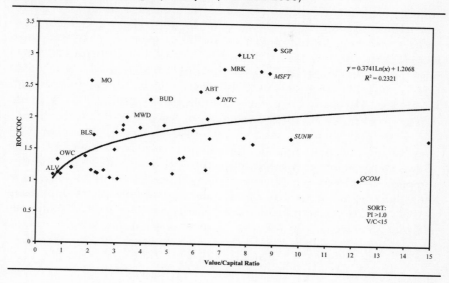

EXHIBIT 13.8   Top-Ten Companies for the *Ex Ante* EVA Portfolio at Year-End 2000

Ticker	Company	EVA Style
ALV	Autoliv Inc.	Value
OWC	Owens Corning	Value
BLS	Bell South	Growth
MO	Philip Morris	Growth
MWD	Morgan Stanley Dean Witter	Growth
BUD	Anheuser Busch	Growth
ABT	Abbott Labs	Growth
MRK	Merck	Growth
LLY	Lilly (Eli) & Co.	Growth
SGP	Schering-Plough	Growth

Possible Diversification Substitutes:

INTC	Intel Corporation	Growth
MSFT	Microsoft Corporation	Growth

Note however that the EVA stock picks for year 2000 are heavily concentrated in the health care sector. Without any industry or sector restriction, Exhibit 13.8 shows that 40% of the top-ten company choices are concentrated in this sector. These positive EVA companies include Abbott Labs, Merck, Lilly & Co., and, not surprisingly, Schering-Plough. Some attractive EVA-to-valuation candidates that might serve as possible substitutes (or additions) to the active portfolio include Intel[13] and Microsoft Corporation. Aside from these tech stock candidates, there are several other companies in Exhibit 13.8 that had attractive EVA and relative value characteristics. Again, assuming EVA consistency, any company that plotted *above* the curve shown in Exhibit 13.8 was a possible real value opportunity at year 2000. Note too that companies—such as Sun Microsystems and QualComm Inc.—that plotted *below* the curve were relatively unattractive investment opportunities at that time. Moreover, this EVA-based approach to company analysis cuts *across* both value and growth styles of investing.

SUMMARY

This chapter looks at how EVA principles can be used to identify the best companies in the marketplace. In the EVA growth strategy, the active investor seeks companies—due in large part to their exceptional research, product development, and marketing capabilities—having an uncanny ability to generate economic value added for the future. By way of contrast, the EVA value strategy emphasizes the security selection importance of firms with attractive EVA prospects that may have mistakenly fallen out of favor with the consensus investor.

While value and growth are often viewed as two distinct "styles" of investing, it is important to emphasize that there exists a commonality between these active approaches to investment management. In each case, the active goal is to *maximize* the likelihood of financial success while *minimizing* the active risk of paying too much for the shares of mispriced firms. In the EVA growth style, the investor tries to avoid paying excessive multiples for companies having unrealistic product development and earnings-growth expectations. In the EVA value strategy, the investor tries to avoid investing in the debt *and* equity securities of companies that may look "cheap" when, in fact, their seemingly low

---

[13] Since the Performance Universe was used to calculate the profitability index ratios in Exhibit 13.7, there may be cost of capital issues that impact the final stock selection choices. Recall the cost of equity comparison—CAPM versus EVA factor model—for Intel Corporation in Chapter 11.

prices are an efficient market response to the firm's poor future growth opportunities. Indeed, troubled companies with jointly negative MVA and (persistently) negative EVA are a "value trap."

It should also be emphasized that a correct assessment of whether a company is truly overvalued or undervalued needs to be based on an assessment of the firm's *future* ability to generate economic value added—in view of its current valuation in the marketplace. Owens Corning, for example, was considered a buy opportunity at year-end 2000 based on the presumption that its abnormally high EVA was a positive signal about the firm's long-term ability to generate economic profit for the shareholders. Given the negative MVA, if this composite materials producer were efficiently priced at year 2000, then investors may have been exceedingly pessimistic about the firm's future EVA capabilities in light of the currently favorable EVA announcement. This misestimation possibility is an unfortunate (from the active investor's perspective) yet integral component of active risk.

Finally, *real security analysis* involves a look beyond the numbers. In this context, it is helpful to remember that companies are manned by real people who produce real goods and services. This means that for any given earnings estimate (EVA-based or otherwise) to be realized, the firm needs to receive—within normal variation—the estimated number of orders that are consistent with the projected revenue growth rate, the product needs to be produced in a cost-efficient manner, and it then needs to be packaged and delivered in a timely fashion to the customer. Meaningful bottlenecks along the way will impact the firm's realized performance. Moreover, the firm's market value added (and therefore, its enterprise value) is also shaped by forces that are *beyond* the control of its managers. These general forces include unanticipated shifts in consumer demand, technological change within an industry, legal and regulatory rulings, and economy-wide and geopolitical changes.

CHAPTER 14

Industry Analysis Using EVA

While significant empirical advances have been made since the first publication of *Foundations of Economic Value Added*, there still exists a dearth of research that focuses on the relationship between industry EVA and net present value. This empirical void is unfortunate because one of the basic tenets of a free market economy is that wealth is created when resources flow to their highest valued use. Fortunately, by using EVA (and related value-based metrics) in an industry context, it is possible to see those economic sectors that have created wealth and those sectors that have not measured up to their true wealth-enhancing potential.

In this regard, EVA can be used to find industries or sectors that offer promising investment rewards.[1] By focusing research efforts on economic sectors having favorable EVA prospects *and* reasonable valuations, it may be possible to form actively managed investment portfolios that outperform similar risk-indexed passive strategies. Moreover, since EVA emphasizes total firm valuation, the methodology has industry-wide pricing and rating implications for equities *and* bonds. In an attempt to shed some empirical light on these financial possibilities, we'll first look at the wealth-creating and wealth-destroying features of U.S. industries that were reported in the first edition of this book. Then, we'll look at several quantitative-based EVA models in an industry context. Following that, we'll look at the MVA and EVA experiences (at year-end 2000) of U.S industries based on the MVA and EVA data used primarily in this new edition.

---

[1] For convenience, the words, "industry" and "sector" will be used interchangeably in this chapter.

MVA AND EVA FOR U.S. INDUSTRIES: THE INITIAL RESULTS

To begin, Exhibit 14.1 shows the MVA and EVA experiences of the top- and bottom-*five* U.S. industries that were listed in the 1995 Performance Universe—ranked by average market value added. The upper portion of the exhibit reveals that the top-three wealth-creating industries for 1994—Beverages, Personal Care, and Drugs and Research—had positive average EVA in the presence of their favorable net present values. The EVA values ranged from $114 million in the Personal Care and Drugs & Research industries, up to an average of $253 million for the high-growth Beverages sector. At that time, the average MVA for the top-three U.S. industries (measured in dollar terms) ranged from $4,569 million for the Drugs & Research group, up to $9,465 million for the Beverages' industry.

The positive MVA and EVA association observed on the top-three U.S. industries for 1994 is due to their relatively high average return on capital in comparison with the respective average cost of capital. With a profitability index ratio (ROC/COC) of 1.28, the after-tax return on

EXHIBIT 14.1   Top-Five and-Bottom-Five MVA-Ranked Industries in Performance Universe at Year-End 1994 (U.S. $ Average Millions)
Section 1: Top-Five MVA-Ranked Industries

#	Industry	$MVA	$EVA	%ROC	%COC	PI*
1.	Beverages	$9,465	$253	14.744	10.138	1.45
2.	Personal Care	4,645	114	14.742	11.234	1.31
3.	Drugs & Research	4,569	114	15.932	12.409	1.28
4.	Telephone Companies.	4,196	−351	7.408	9.304	0.80
5.	Conglomerates	3,605	−91	11.301	11.609	0.97

Section 2: Bottom-Five MVA-Ranked Industries

#	Industry	$MVA	$EVA	%ROC	%COC	PI*
52.	Aerospace	$253	−124	8.217	10.881	0.76
53.	Trucking & Shipping	249	−51	6.068	11.840	0.51
54.	Railroads	−30	−202	8.825	11.818	0.75
55.	Aluminum	−169	−452	3.440	11.510	0.30
56.	Cars & Trucks	−6,982	385	13.059	11.834	1.10

*PI = Profitability Index Ratio (ROC/COC).

capital for the Drugs & Research industry is 28% higher than the average capital cost for companies in this economic sector. Similarly, a look at the profitability index ratio for the typical beverage company reveals productive returns that exceed the weighted average cost of capital by some 45%. On the other hand, the upper portion of Exhibit 14.1 reports negative average EVA figures for the Telephone and Conglomerate industries at year-end 1994.

At –$351 and –$91 millions, the negative EVA averages for the Telephone and Conglomerates sectors are interesting in light of their *contemporaneously* positive net present values. This industry-pricing anomaly has at least two possible explanations: In particular, if the U.S. capital markets were largely efficient at that time, then investors must have been highly optimistic about the *future* earnings (EVA) prospects of companies operating within these economic sectors. On the other hand, if the capital markets were largely inefficient, then investors may have jointly mispriced (leading to overvaluation) the stocks and bonds of the average company within the Telephone and Conglomerates industries.

With respect to the five lowest MVA-ranked industries for 1994, the bottom portion of Exhibit 14.1 reports that these sectors had mostly negative average economic value added. Four industries in particular—ranging from Aerospace (#52) down to Aluminum (#55)—had consistently negative average EVA in the presence of low positive-to-negative net present values. Indeed, the average after-tax return on capital for the Aluminum industry was only 30% (profitability index ratio at 0.3) of its 1994 average cost of capital, while the Aerospace and Railroad industries had average capital returns of about 75% of the underlying cost of capital.

In sharp contrast, the Cars and Trucks industry (#56) stands out as a noticeable exception to the empirical finding that low positive-to-negative average MVA industries have negative average EVA values. At –$6,982 million, the large negative average net present value figure for the automobile sector seems way out of line with its positive average EVA, at $385 million. With a profitability index ratio of 1.1, the average return on invested capital for the Cars and Trucks industry during 1994 was 10% higher than the average cost of debt and equity capital. As with the financial interpretations for the Telephone and Conglomerates industries, this anomalous pricing association between MVA and EVA for the automobile industry has (at least) two meaningful explanations.

One interpretation of the negative average MVA finding for Cars and Trucks is that investors may have grossly underestimated the long-term ability of this sector to generate economic value added. If correct, then the vehicle manufacturers that operate in this industry—spearheaded in particular by Chrysler Corporation—would have been an attractive "buy opportunity" for investors at year-end 1994. However, if the U.S.

capital markets were generally efficient at that time, then the large negative average MVA figure for Cars and Trucks (at –$6,982 million) would
indicate that investors were correctly pessimistic about the *future* EVA
growth opportunities of the representative automobile company.

TOWARDS A MODERN APPROACH TO INDUSTRY ANALYSIS

On a broader scale, Exhibit 14.2 shows the MVA-to-Capital and EVA-
to-Capital ratios for the 56 U.S. industries listed in the 1995 Performance Universe. From an investment perspective, these size-adjusted
ratios can be used to identify those sectors that offered attractive EVA
prospects for any given level of market value added. For instance, the
exhibit shows that on average firms operating within the Glass, Metal,
and Plastic Container industry were the better "buy opportunity" in
comparison with companies that were operating in both the Aluminum
and Steel industries. While the three industries have (somewhat) comparable MVA-to-Capital ratios, the Glass, Metal, and Plastic Containers
industry had positive EVA at a time when the EVA-to-Capital ratios for
the Aluminum and Steel industries were below –6%.

EXHIBIT 14.2   MVA/Capital versus EVA/Capital Ratios: 56 U.S. Industries at Year
End 1994

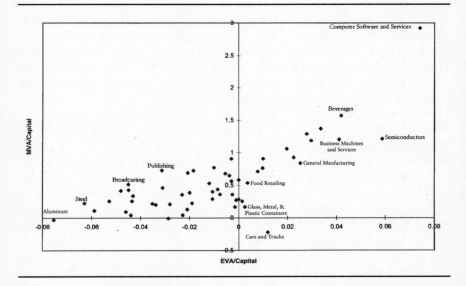

Exhibit 14.2 also shows that Food Retailing companies offered better investment prospects in relation to Broadcasting companies at year-end 1994. For about the same MVA-to-Capital ratio (near 0.5), Food Retailing had positive EVA, while this earnings metric for the Broadcasting industry was negative. At that time, the average firm within the General Manufacturing sector offered better EVA prospects than companies operating within the Publishing industry. By extension, it appears that a modern-based approach to industry analysis boils down to finding those sectors of the economy having *maximum* EVA prospects for any given level of industry valuation. This industry selection theme is of course consistent with the approach used before to identify the best companies in the marketplace.

A closer look at Exhibit 14.2 reveals some attractive industry candidates at year-end 1994. In this context, the low yet positive EVA (and mostly "unfashionable") industries like Cars and Trucks, Glass, Metal, and Plastic Containers, Food Retailing, and General Manufacturing offered attractive earnings prospects for their relative sector valuations. In a similar manner, the high EVA-generating industries like Business Machines and Services, Semiconductors, Beverages, and Computer Software and Services had attractive EVA prospects for their noticeably higher industry valuations.

Taken together, these wealth-creating industries describe an "efficient set" of active investment opportunities for 1994. For instance, Exhibit 14.2 shows that four economic sectors in particular—including Cars and Trucks, General Manufacturing, Semiconductors, and Computer Software and Services—occupy the *rightmost* position on the investable set of industry opportunities. At that time, these economic sectors had the beneficial performance/risk characteristics of (a) *maximum* EVA prospects for any given MVA-to-Capital ratio, and (b) *minimum* industry valuations for their given levels of economic profitability. Moreover, it is interesting to see (Exhibit 14.2) that the empirical relationship between the MVA and EVA-to-Capital ratios for U.S. industries seems nonlinear.[2]

A CONVENTIONAL LOOK AT INDUSTRY ANALYSIS USING EVA

The benefit of using EVA in an industry analysis context can also be shown in a more conventional profitability *versus* relative valuation framework. In particular, Exhibit 14.3 shows a comparison of the profitability index (ROC/COC) ratio versus the value-to-capital ratio for the 56 U.S. industries listed in the Performance Universe at year-end 1994. The sector-wide pricing happenings in this exhibit are interesting in many financial respects.

---

[2] We'll look at various quantitative approaches to EVA-based industry analysis at a later point in the chapter.

EXHIBIT 14.3   Profitability Index versus Value/Capital Ratio: 56 U.S. Industries at Year End 1994

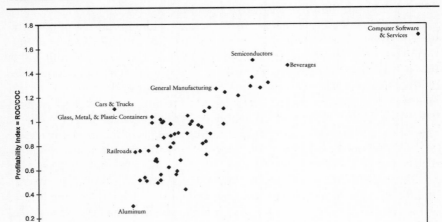

Exhibit 14.3 indicates that the "cluster" of U.S. industries looks like the typical display of asset classes in a more conventional "asset allocation" approach to investment management. From an EVA perspective, the active goal is to invest in the equity *and* debt securities of those economic sectors having the highest profitability index ratio for any given level of industry valuation—measured in the exhibit by the value-to-capital ratio. Alternatively, the sector allocation goal is determined by minimizing the value-to-capital ratio for a specified level of corporate financial success. In this way, the active investor avoids paying *too much* for any given level of industry earnings—as determined by the spread between the sector's average return on capital and its overall average cost of capital.

The location of the "best industries" for active investing is clearly evident in Exhibit 14.3. Looking at industries having a profitability index ratio that exceeds one (for positive average EVA), one sees a variety of U.S. sectors that were attractively priced at year-end 1994. Given the EVA results shown in Exhibit 14.2, it is no surprise to see that EVA-generating industries like Cars and Trucks, General Manufacturing, Semiconductors, Beverages, and Computer Software and Services were among the most attractive set of industry opportunities. Indeed, it seems that a portfolio of these mostly wealth-creating industries would trace out an "efficient frontier" of real industry opportunities at year-end

1994. Assuming EVA consistency, the performance findings revealed in Exhibit 14.3 suggest that the Cars and Trucks industry was the best "active bet" among the investable set of U.S. industries.

The exhibit also reveals that the Railroad and Aluminum industries have a relatively low valuation because their profitability index ratio is less than unity (for negative EVA). As a result, it seems that the active investor could construct a "two asset" portfolio consisting of securities in the Glass, Metal, and Plastic Containers and the Cars and Trucks' industries that would offer a preferred combination of economic profit opportunities for about the same relative valuation (near one). Better yet, Exhibit 14.3 suggests that it would have been possible to construct a "four industry" portfolio (at year-end 1994) consisting of Cars and Trucks, General Manufacturing, Semiconductors, and Beverages that would have dominated the problematic multitude of U.S. industries having profitability index (ROC/COC) ratios that fell below unity.

QUANTITATIVE INSIGHTS ON INDUSTRY ANALYSIS USING EVA

In light of the industry opportunities shown in Exhibit 14.3, let's look at the information content of this graph from a more quantitative perspective. In this context, we'll look at three models to describe the formal relationship between the profitability index ratio (ROC/COC) and the value-to-capital factor. These performance models include (1) a simple linear model, (2) a log-linear model, and (3) a "Markowitz-based" approach to modeling the relationship between the profitability index and value-to-capital ratios.

EVA Implications from a Simple Linear Model

The industry selection findings that were visually apparent in Exhibit 14.3 are reinforced by the *linear* regression results shown in Exhibit 14.4. In particular, the exhibit displays the actual profitability index ratio versus the fitted *PI* ratio for the 56 U.S. industries at their relative industry valuations. The intercept and slope estimates on the sector-wide profitability index ratios at year-end 1994 were 0.223 and 0.438, respectively. The percentage of industry economic profit explained (adjusted R^2) by the value-to-capital factor is 57%, while the t-statistic, at 8.55, on the reported slope estimate is highly significant.

$$PI = 0.223 + 0.438 \times \text{Value}/\text{Capital}$$
$$(t\text{-value}) \quad (2.66) \quad (8.55)$$

EXHIBIT 14.4   Actual *PI* Ratio versus Linear Fitted Ratios: 56 U.S. Industries at Year End 1994

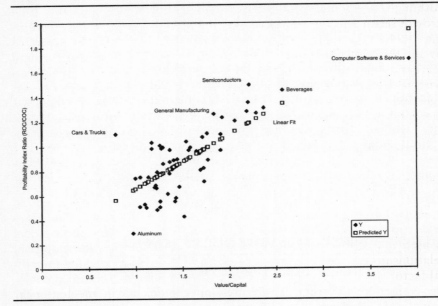

Exhibit 14.4 shows that the actual profitability index ratio for Cars and Trucks, General Manufacturing, Semiconductors, and Beverages industries were substantially higher than the corresponding "fitted values" from the linear model. For 1994, the expected profitability index ratio for the Cars and Trucks industry was only 0.57, while the revealed *PI* ratio for the average automaker was 1.1 (for positive EVA). Likewise, the estimated (fitted) profitability index ratio for the Semiconductor and Beverages industries were 1.19 and 1.35, while the actual *PI* ratios for these high growth sectors of the economy were 1.5 and 1.45 respectively.

At the lower end of the valuation spectrum, Exhibit 14.4 shows that the 1994 profitability index ratio for the Aluminum industry (at only 0.3) fell well below the 0.65 ratio that was predicted for its sector valuation. In effect, the actual EVA for the Aluminum industry was below the negative EVA measure that was expected for this traditional manufacturing sector. Additionally, if linearity is *supposed to* prevail in "real world" capital markets, then the simple regression model indicates that the Computer Software and Services industry—at the high end of the relative valuation spectrum—was relatively overvalued in the marketplace in view of its revealed (current) ability to generate economic value added.

With a value-to-capital ratio at 3.92, the anticipated profitability index ratio for the Computer Software and Services industry was 1.94. Although the actual profitability index ratio (at 1.7) for this high growth sector was the highest among the 56 U.S. industries covered during 1994, it fell short of the corresponding *PI* ratio that was predicted by the least squares model. That is, with linearity *and* efficient capital markets, this sector's valuation should have been more closely aligned with the relative valuations observed in the Semiconductor and Beverages industries. On the other hand, if real world capital markets are more aptly described by nonlinear relationships in key financial variables—like the *PI* and "value-cap" ratios—then this technology sector may have been priced "just right" at that time.

EVA Implications from a Log-Linear Model

Exhibit 14.5 expands the scope of the regression analysis by graphing the actual 1994 profitability index ratio versus the fitted *PI* values from (a) a simple linear model, and (b) a log-linear model. This latter model is used to capture some of the apparent "curvature" in the empirical relationship between the profitability index ratio and the value-to-capital factor shown in Exhibit 14.3—especially, at the high end of the relative valuation spectrum. The regression coefficients in the log-linear model were estimated according to:

EXHIBIT 14.5 Actual *PI* Ratio versus Log-Linear Fitted Ratios: 56 U.S. Industries at Year End 1994

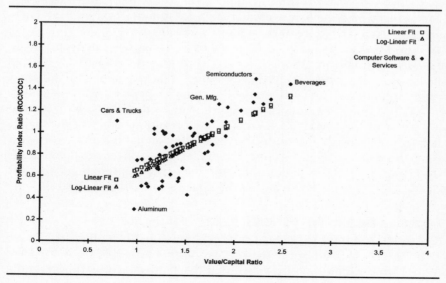

$$PI = a(\text{Value}/\text{Capital})^B$$
$$= 0.617(V/C)^{0.817}$$

In this model, the coefficient a, in log form, is the regression intercept, and B is the estimated sensitivity of the PI ratio to the (logged) value-to-capital factor. The reported t-statistics on the estimated parameters were -8.03 and 6.62, respectively, while the adjusted R^2 value in the power (or log-linear) model for 1994 was 43.79%.

On the forecasting side, the log-linear model produces a better estimate of the actual profitability index ratio for the Computer Software and Services industry in comparison with the simple linear model. At year-end 1994, the actual PI ratio for the Computer Software and Services sector was 1.7, while the fitted value from the power model was 1.88. This compares favorably with the forecasted profitability index ratio—at 1.94—for the Computer Software and Services industry using the simple linear model. In effect, the log-linear model captures some of the visible "curvature" between the revealed PI ratios and the value-to-capital factor at the high end of the enterprise valuation spectrum.

Exhibit 14.5 also reveals that at the lower end of the pricing spectrum, the curvature generated by the log-linear model produces a better estimate of the actual profitability index ratio for the Aluminum industry when compared to the forecast PI ratio from the simple linear model. The actual 1994 PI ratio for this raw material sector of the economy was only 0.3, while the log-linear model produced a somewhat more optimistic PI ratio assessment of 0.6 (the linear fit for industry #55 was 0.65). Taken together though, the predicted EVA estimates for the Aluminum industry from the two regression models were negative.

On the other hand, the percentage of PI variation explained for the 56 U.S. industries by the log-linear model was somewhat lower than that observed in the simple linear model. The R^2 values in the two regression models for 1994 were 44% and 57%, respectively. As shown in Exhibit 14.5, the induced curvature in the fitted PI ratios from the log-linear model effectively decreases the forecast accuracy of the model for the high-growth EVA industries like Semiconductors and Beverages. From a comparative perspective, the model also reduces the predictability in the profitability index ratio for the attractive-looking Cars and Trucks sector, at the lower end of the relative valuation spectrum.

EVA Implications from the "Markowitz Model"

Some interesting EVA insights can also be obtained by describing the set of industry opportunities in the context of a two-asset Markowitz portfolio. If, for instance, one assumed that the "age of information technology" were here to stay, then investors might consider forming a "two-asset" portfolio consisting of a representative "market portfolio," combined with an active "tilt" on the (presumed) high-growth technology sector. At that time, the expected performance/risk features of the Computer Software and Services industry would characterize the investment opportunities in the information technology sector. With these passive/active choices, the investor then chooses the "asset mix" that *maximizes* expected portfolio return for any perceived level of investment risk. In this scenario, passive investors would emphasize the "market portfolio," while proactive growth investors would place a high percentage of portfolio funds in, say, the information technology sector (*or* other fortuitous industry deemed to have abnormally attractive EVA prospects).

If one makes the simplifying assumption that the *revealed* profitability index ratio is a fundamental measure of an asset's expected return, then the two-asset class portfolio return can be described by:

$$E(R) = w_M E(R_M) + w_T E(R_T)$$
$$= w_M [PI_M] + w_T [PI_T]$$

The first expression shows that the expected portfolio return, $E(R)$, is equal to a weighted average of the expected returns available on component assets in the portfolio. In this expression, w_M represents the proportion of portfolio funds invested in the so-called "market portfolio," while w_T (or, $1 - w_M$) represents the portfolio weight assigned to the presumably high EVA growth technology sector. The second $E(R)$ expression is written in terms of the profitability index ratios (PI) for the jointly *passive-active* investment opportunities.[3]

Upon substituting the observed profitability index ratios (for 1994) on the Performance Universe (passive EVA opportunity) and the Computer Software & Services industry (active EVA opportunity) into the expected portfolio return equation, one obtains:[4]

$$E(R) = w_M [PI_M] + (1 - w_M)[PI_T]$$
$$= w_M [0.876] + (1 - w_M)[1.702]$$

---

[3] Fabozzi and Grant develop the concept of passive-active investing—as opposed to passive *versus* active investing—in *Equity Portfolio Management*. See Chapter 4, "Blueprint for Passive-Active Investing," Frank J. Fabozzi and James L. Grant, *Equity Portfolio Management* (New Hope, PA: Frank J. Fabozzi Associates, 1999).

[4] The *PI* ratio for the "market portfolio" is based on the capital-weighted profitability index ratio for 1994 that was available in the 1995 Performance Universe. Since Stern Stewart revamped their weighing scheme in favor of market-value weights in their 1996 Performance Universe, this capital-based return series is no longer available.

In this expression, the expected return on the two-asset portfolio is described by the respective profitability index ratios and the proportion of portfolio funds invested in the representative market portfolio, w_M.

With a two-asset portfolio, the expected risk can be captured with knowledge of (1) the investment portfolio weights, (2) the "own" volatility estimates—measured by return standard deviations—and, (3) the correlation among the asset class returns. In formal terms, the Markowitz portfolio risk equation for a combination of two assets can be expressed as:

$$SD(R) = \{w_M^2 SD(R_M)^2 + w_T^2 SD(R_T)^2 \\ + 2w_M w_T SD(R_M) SD(R_T) p(R_M, R_T)\}^{0.5}$$

In this portfolio risk expression, the SD terms represent return standard deviations, the w refers to asset weights, and the $p(R_M, R_T)$ term measures the correlation between the market and technology sector returns.

If one now makes the simplifying assumption that the *actual* value-to-capital ratio is a measure of the "active risk" of paying too much for the shares of wealth-enhancing companies or industries, then the expected risk for the "two-asset" portfolio can be modeled in terms of (1) the known "value-cap" ratios for the market portfolio and technology sectors, and (2) the estimated correlation between EVA measures for these asset classes. Upon substituting the "own volatility" estimates, at 1.451 and 3.923, respectively, along with the (ten-year) EVA correlation of 0.1806 into the portfolio risk equation, one obtains:

$$SD(R) = \{w_M^2 [1.451]^2 + w_T^2 [3.923]^2 \\ + 2w_M w_T [1.451][3.923]0.1806\}^{0.5}$$

With this information, it is possible to calculate the "plot points" for the two-asset Markowitz frontier, simply by varying the proportion of funds invested in the market portfolio, w_M (since, $w_T = 1 - w_M$).

The resulting two-asset Markowitz curve is shown in Exhibit 14.6, in conjunction with the plot points for the 56 industries that were available for 1994. At the lower end of the curve, the "P1000" (for Performance 1000) point represents the own return/risk combination for the passive "market portfolio"—as measured empirically by the profitability index ratio on the Performance Universe at the revealed value-to-capital ratio of 1.451. In a similar manner, the highest expected return/risk combination on the Markowitz curve consists of a 100% active investment in the information technology sector—as represented by the plot point in the exhibit for the Computer Software and Services industry.

EXHIBIT 14.6 Industry Selection using the Markowitz Model: 56 U.S. Industries at Year End 1994

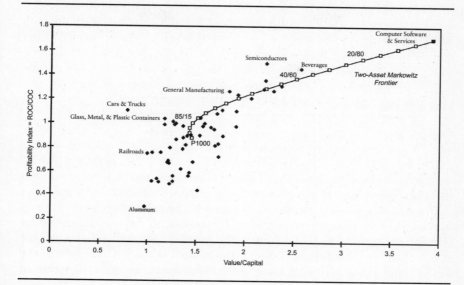

Among the findings in Exhibit 14.6, the two-asset curve reveals that the 85/15 combination lies at the lower end of the *positively* sloping portion of the Markowitz curve. This passive-active mix of the market portfolio and the information technology sector at year-end 1994 is interesting because a 100% allocation to the market portfolio alone results in a passive portfolio with negative EVA. This, in turn, suggests that a judicious mix of the market index (P1000) along with an active tilt toward technology produces a higher expected return for the same amount of risk. At the 85/15 mix, the portfolio has a profitability index ratio of precisely one (for zero EVA), while the market index at that risk level has negative EVA. That is, with a profitability index ratio at 0.876, the projected after-tax return on capital for the average firm in the 100% passive portfolio falls short of its average cost of capital. Again, it is important to emphasize that these industry-based portfolio results were based on EVA versus relative value findings for 1994.

Additionally, the Markowitz curve can be used to identify those industries that provided the best active opportunities (in retrospect) at year-end 1994. Cyclical industries like Cars and Trucks, Glass, Metal, and Plastic Containers, and General Manufacturing—that plotted above the two-asset "efficient frontier"—had better risk-adjusted performance than that available from the passive-active mix of the market index and the Computer Software and Services sector. Likewise, at the higher end of the Markowitz curve, the Semiconductor and Beverages industries stood out (once again) as clear expected performance winners for 1994. At that time, Semiconductors had a profitability index ratio of 1.5, while the profitability index for the 50/50 mix of the market portfolio and high technology was 1.29.

MVA AND EVA FOR U.S. INDUSTRIES: FAST FORWARD TO 2000

Given the earlier findings, Exhibit 14.7 now shows the updated MVA and EVA experiences of the top- and bottom-*five* U.S. industries in the 2001 Performance Universe—this time ranked by capitalization—weighted average market value added.[5] The upper portion of the exhibit (Section I) reveals that the top five wealth-producing industries for 2000—Capital Goods, Pharmaceuticals and Biotechnology, Software & Services, Technology Hardware and Equipment, and Retailing—had jointly positive average EVA in the presence of their favorable net present values. The average EVA values ranged from $263 million in the Technology Hardware and Equipment industry, to about 1,700 million in the Pharmaceuticals/Biotechnology and Software & Services industries, up to $2,741 million in the Capital Goods industry. At that time, the weighted average MVA for the top five U.S. industries (measured in dollar terms) ranged from $84,898 million for the Retailing group, up to $200,429 million for the Capital Goods industry.

Not surprisingly, the positive MVA and EVA experience of the top five U.S. industries at year-end 2000 is due to their relatively high *residual* return on invested capital. For example, with a profitability index ratio (ROC/COC) of 1.81, the after-tax return on capital for the Pharmaceutical and Biotechnology industry is 81% higher than the average cost of capital for companies in this high-growth sector. Similarly, a look at the profitability index ratio for the typical Computer Software and Services and Capital Goods company, respectively, reveals productive returns that exceed the weighted average cost of capital by some 45%. Moreover, at year-end 2000, the average return on invested capital in the Retailing industry was 11% higher than the average cost of capital for companies in this industry.

---

[5] Over the years, there have been a few important structural changes to the Performance Universe, including weighing schemes and industry coverage (ranging from 56 U.S. industries in the 1995 Performance Universe down to 23 industry-sectors in the 2001 Performance Universe).

EXHIBIT 14.7 Top-Five and Bottom-Five MVA-Ranked Industries in Performance Universe at Year-End 2000 (in U.S. $ Average Millions)

Section 1: Top-Five MVA-Ranked Industries*

Rank	Industry	$MVA	$EVA	% ROC	% COC	PI
1	Capital goods	200,429.01	2,740.73	14.95	10.27	1.46
2	Pharmaceuticals and Biotechnology	111,416.27	1,657.44	16.11	8.92	1.81
3	Software & Services	108,440.69	1,758.60	19.02	13.14	1.45
4	Technology Hardware & Equipment	92,230.32	262.89	15.53	12.75	1.22
5	Retailing	84,897.72	631.59	10.96	9.87	1.11

Section 2: Bottom-Five MVA-Ranked Industries*

Rank	Industry	$MVA	$EVA	% ROC	% COC	PI
19	Materials	7,482.90	−61.43	8.22	8.59	0.96
20	Consumer Durables & Apparel	1,590.08	−55.36	8.52	9.01	0.95
21	Transportation	1,537.95	−116.97	6.86	7.43	0.92
22	Real Estate	485.67	−21.86	8.12	8.62	0.94
23	Automobiles & Components	−4,398.14	175.74	8.22	7.58	1.08

*Note: ROC in the Performance Universe is NOPAT/Beginning Capital. This produced an exceptionally high ROC of 238% for FBN, which we think is an outlier. To normalize the industry average, we set FBN's ROC equal to COC. Also, the industry rankings are based on average MVA rather than total MVA generated by the industry.

In turn, the lower portion of Exhibit 14.7 reports the weighted average MVA and EVA experiences of the bottom-five companies in the 2001 Performance Universe. With respect to the lowest average MVA-ranked industries, Section 2 reveals that these industries had *mostly* negative average economic value added. Four industries in particular—including Materials, Consumer Durables and Apparel, Transportation, and Real Estate—had consistently negative average EVA in the presence of relatively low positive net present values. Along this line, the average after-tax return on capital for the typical firm in the Materials industry was 96% (profitability index ratio at 0.96) of the average cost of capital, while the average capital return for the representative firm in the Transportation and Real Estate industries had invested capital returns ranging from 92% to 94% of the respective average cost of capital.

Interestingly, the Automobiles and Components industry stands out as a noticeable exception to the empirical finding that low positive to negative-average MVA industries have negative average EVA values. At –$4,398 million, the large negative average net present value figure for the automobile and components sector seems out of line with its positive average EVA of $176 million. With a profitability index ratio of 1.08, the average return on invested capital for the typical firm in this sector during 2000 was 8% higher than the weighted average cost of debt and equity capital. This seemingly anomalous pricing association between MVA and EVA for the automobile and components industry has (at least) two meaningful explanations.[6]

One interpretation of the negative average MVA for the Automobiles and Components industry is that investors may have grossly underestimated the long-term viability of this sector to generate economic value added. Other things the same, then the representative automaker and components' company would have been an attractive "buy opportunity" at year-end 2000. However, if the capital market were largely efficient at that time, then the large negative average MVA for the Automobiles and Components industry (at –$4,398 million) would suggest that investors were correctly pessimistic about the *future* EVA generating abilities of the representative automobile and components company.

ANOTHER LOOK AT THE MODERN APPROACH TO INDUSTRY ANALYSIS

With updating, Exhibit 14.8 shows the MVA-to-Capital versus the EVA-to-Capital ratios for the 23 U.S. industries that were listed in the 2001 Perfor-

---

[6] Note also that there are two meaningful interpretations of the jointly positive and negative-average MVA and EVA experiences of the first four bottom-ranked industries at year-end 2000—an inefficient markets explanation and an efficient markets explanation.

mance Universe.[7] Again, from an investment perspective, these size-adjusted ratios can be used to identify sectors that offered attractive EVA prospects for a given level of market value added. At year-end 2000, the exhibit shows that on average firms operating within the Energy industry were the better "buy opportunity" when compared with companies operating in the Media industry. While the two industries had comparable MVA-to-Capital ratios (about 0.8), the Energy industry had positive EVA at a time when the EVA-to-Capital ratio for the Media industry was –4.8%.

Likewise, Exhibit 14.8 shows that the average capital goods company offered better investment prospects than the average utility company at year-end 2000. For about the same MVA-to-Capital ratio (near 1.5), the average company in the Capital Goods industry had positive EVA, while economic profit for the representative firm in the Utilities industry was negative. The exhibit also shows Pharmaceutical and Biotechnology companies were the better investment opportunity than Software & Services companies. With updating, we again see that a modern approach to industry analysis boils down to finding those sectors of the economy having *maximum* EVA prospects for any given level of industry valuation. This industry selection theme is of course consistent with the economic profit approach to company analysis explained in Chapter 13.

EXHIBIT 14.8 MVA/Capital Versus EVA/Capital Ratios: 23 U.S. Industries at Year End 2000

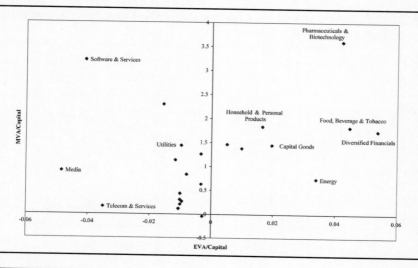

---

[7] Recall that there are 23 industry codes reported in the 2001 Performance Universe *versus* 56 industry designators in the 1995 Performance Universe (among other structural changes, including weighing schemes).

Most importantly, Exhibit 14.8 (like Exhibit 14.2) can be used to describe an "efficient set" of active investment opportunities. In this context, the exhibit shows that five sectors in particular—including the Energy, Capital Goods, Diversified Financials, Food, Beverage, and Tobacco, and Pharmaceuticals and Biotechnology industries—occupy the *rightmost* position on the set of investable industry opportunities at year-end 2000. Notably, these economic sectors had the beneficial performance/risk (to value) characteristics of (1) *maximum* EVA prospects for any given MVA-to-Capital ratio, and (2) *minimum* industry valuations for a given level of economic profitability (measured in Exhibit 14.8 by the EVA-to-Capital ratio).

ANOTHER LOOK AT THE CONVENTIONAL APPROACH TO INDUSTRY ANALYSIS USING EVA

As shown in Exhibit 14.3, the EVA approach to industry analysis can be recast in a conventional profitability *versus* relative valuation framework. In this regard, Exhibit 14.9 shows an updated version of the profitability index (ROC/COC) ratio versus the value-to-capital ratio for the 23 U.S. industries that were listed in the 2001 Performance Universe. The updated EVA and industry pricing happenings in this exhibit are interesting in several respects.

EXHIBIT 14.9   Profitability Index versus Value-to-Capital Ratio: 23 U.S. Industries at Year End 2000

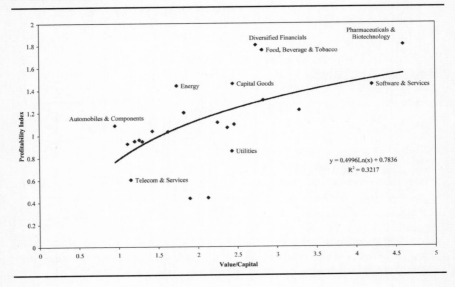

In visual terms, Exhibit 14.9 reveals that the "cluster" of U.S. industries looks like the typical display of asset classes in a more conventional asset allocation approach to investment management. As explained before, the active goal is to invest in the equity *and* debt securities of those sectors having the highest profitability index ratio for any given level of industry valuation—measured in the exhibit by the enterprise value-to-capital ratio. Alternatively, the sector allocation goal is determined by minimizing the value-to-capital ratio for a specified level of the profitability index ratio. In this way, the active investor avoids paying *too much* for any given level of industry earnings—as determined by the spread between the sector's average return on capital and the average cost of capital.

Along this line, the location of the "best industries" for active investing at year-end 2000 is clearly evident in Exhibit 14.9. Looking at industries with a profitability index ratio that exceeds one (for positive average EVA), one sees a variety of U.S. sectors that were attractively priced at that time. Given the EVA results shown in Exhibit 14.8, it is no surprise to see that wealth-creating industries like Energy, Capital Goods, Diversified Financials, Food, Beverage, and Tobacco, and Pharmaceuticals and Biotechnology were among the most attractive set of industry opportunities. Also, it is interesting to see that Automobiles and Components companies—with an average *PI* ratio above one *and* a value-to capital ratio below unity (for market-assessed negative NPV) looked like an attractive real value opportunity at year-end 2000. On balance, it appears that a portfolio of industries like those identified above would trace out an active frontier of investable industry opportunities. In quantitative terms, those industries plotted above the fitted curve to the *PI*/valuation points in Exhibit 14.9.[8]

RETURN ON CAPITAL *VERSUS* THE COST OF CAPITAL: 23 U.S. INDUSTRIES AT YEAR-END 2000

Before proceeding to explore the macroeconomic aspects of EVA in the next chapter, it is helpful to have a basic understanding of the return on capital and the cost of capital in the cross section of U.S. industries. In this context, Exhibit 14.10 shows the after-tax return on capital versus the cost of capital for the 23 U.S. industries that were listed in the 2001 Performance Universe—from top-ranked (capitalization weighed) average MVA to bottom-ranked average MVA. As noted before (Exhibit 14.7), the top-ranked indus-

---

[8] While it is easy with modern computing power to fit a curve to a scatter of data points (such as that shown in Exhibit 14.9), this does *not* mean that a nonlinear fit is necessarily better than a linear fit. Indeed, the R^2 from a linear fit to the data shown in Exhibit 14.9 is slightly higher than the R^2 value reported in the exhibit.

tries—such as Capital Goods and Pharmaceuticals and Biotechnology—had average capital return figures that were noticeably higher than the respective average cost of capital, while bottom-ranked industries—with the notable exception of the Automobiles and Components industry—had an average return on capital that fell short of the average cost of capital.

While top- and bottom-ranked clusters of U.S. industries at year-end 2000 had consistently positive or consistently negative residual capital returns, respectively, Exhibit 14.10 shows that for the most part the average return on invested capital *across* U.S. industries fluctuates both above *and* below the industry-wide cost of capital. This fluctuating, yet relatively neutral value-added positioning (representing *zero*-overall average EVA in the cross section of U.S. industries listed in the 2001 Performance Universe) of the after-tax return on capital versus the cost of capital is an important prelude to the next (and final) chapter—where we'll examine economic profit happenings at the macroeconomic level.

EXHIBIT 14.10   Return on Capital versus Cost of Capital: 23 U.S. Industries at Year End 2000

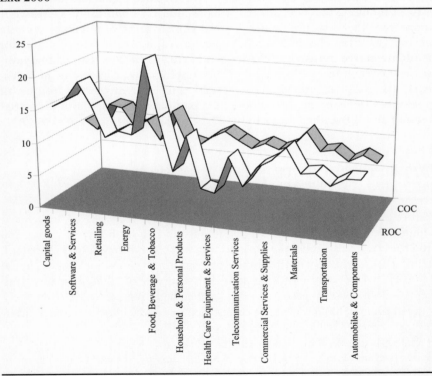

SUMMARY

The benefits of using EVA analysis in an industry context are twofold: First, the MVA and EVA metrics provide a *direct* way of measuring the wealth impact of resource allocation in a free market economy. This empirical recognition is perhaps most transparent when one looks at the positive net present values that are being generated in today's wealth-enhancing industries such as Capital Goods, Diversified Financials, Pharmaceuticals and Biotechnology, and Computer Software and Services, among others. These wealth findings contrast sharply with the relatively unattractive recent MVA profiles of industrial sectors like Materials, Consumer Durables and Apparel, and Transportation, based on the empirical findings reported in Exhibit 14.7. Indeed, EVA analysis can be used to capture the sector-wide NPV happenings as economies evolve from the agrarian, to manufacturing powerhouses, on up the financial ladder to the present-day age of information technology.

EVA analysis can also be used as a screening tool to find those industries that offer attractive investment rewards. By focusing research efforts on those sectors having attractive EVA forecasts *and* reasonable industry valuations, it may be possible to form active strategies that outperform similar risk-indexed passive portfolio strategies. At year-end 2000 attractive industries that were reported at the low end of the valuation spectrum (recall Exhibit 14.9) include sectors such as the Automobiles and Components industry and the Energy industry. Moreover, positive EVA-generating sectors (at year-end 2000) like Diversified Financials, Food, Beverage, and Tobacco industries, on up to the Pharmaceutical and Biotechnology industry offered attractive return possibilities even though their enterprise value-to-capital ratios were at the mid-to-high end of the industry-pricing spectrum.

Finally, it is important to emphasize that industry-based EVA analysis is still at its infancy. The preliminary findings reported in this chapter are encouraging in that many sectors of the U.S. economy—like Capital Goods, Diversified Financials, and Pharmaceuticals and Biotechnology—generate substantial value-added for their shareholders. However, the research analysis also indicates that several industries fail to live up to their true wealth-enhancing potential. This finding is supported by the fact that 35% of the 23 U.S. industries examined for 2000 had after-tax capital returns that fell short of the weighted average cost of capital. On the troublesome side, these negative average EVA happenings in the industry cross section may be symptomatic of lingering structural problems in the U.S. economy. On a more positive note though, the fluctuating industry EVA spread—both above *and* below zero—may be a sign of the normal ebbs and flows in a well-functioning, free market economy.

CHAPTER 15

Macroanalysis Using EVA

EVA offers some exciting insights on the source of wealth creation at the macroeconomic level. Specifically, when the economy-wide return on capital is higher than the cost of capital, then a nation's economic profit is positive. In principle, the favorable residual return on capital situation should lead to positive net present value (MVA) for the entire economy. In contrast, if the economy-wide return on capital falls short of the average cost of capital, then national EVA will be negative—even though the economy-wide return on invested capital (ROC) may be higher than the general level of interest rates.

If the adverse EVA situation persists, then the ensuing decline in national wealth will lower a country's overall standard of living. This macro-EVA prediction suggests that a nation's financial well being hinges on the balance between two macroeconomic drivers: the after-tax return on productive capital (ROC) and the economy-wide cost of capital (COC). Equivalently, the sign of the residual (or surplus) return on capital can serve as a test of whether a nation is increasing or decreasing wealth. On balance, a positive RROC is wealth increasing, while a persistently negative residual capital return at the economy level will ultimately destroy a nation's wealth.

While at the microlevel the primary responsibility for creating shareholder value rests on the firm's managers, the general economic climate can impact a company's ease or difficulty in meeting its fiduciary duties to the shareholders. For example, fiscal policy steps that are designed to *permanently* lower taxes, decrease business regulation, and spur capital formation (via, say, investment tax credits for physical and human capital) make it easier for firms to collectively increase the level of national wealth. On the other hand, adverse fiscal policy decisions that lead to higher personal and corporate taxes, nonproductive governmental spending, more business red-tape, and other investment disincentives ultimately impede the wealth-creating opportunities of firms operating in the real economy.

Additionally, monetary policy actions can either support or hinder the wealth-enhancing efforts of companies at the microlevel. On the positive side, central banks can support the EVA-generating efforts of firms by taking monetary steps that keep inflation in check, and therefore interest rates at favorable levels for productive business expansion. As the general level of interest rates decline in the economy, the collective NPV of companies rises, as the EVA streams of otherwise unacceptable projects now look acceptable. Also, central bank actions that seek to enhance investor confidence about the economic stability of a nation can have a *doubly* beneficial effect on the economy-wide cost of capital. This happens when a wealth-enhancing decline in the "risk-free" rate of interest is reinforced by a fall in investors required premium for bearing economy-wide business risk.

MACRO-EVA: THE EMPIRICAL EVIDENCE

Knowledge of macro-EVA drivers can be used to make some interesting inferences about the strength of an economy as well as the implied direction of security prices. In this context, Exhibit 15.1 presents a listing of the U.S. return on capital (ROC), the economy-wide cost of capital (COC), and the U.S. "residual return on capital" (RROC) for the 19-year period spanning 1982 to 2000.[1] Broadly speaking, the exhibit is important in a key EVA respect: Specifically, Exhibit 15.1 shows that the average return on U.S. capital over the 19-year reporting period is just about *equal* to the average U.S. cost of capital. That is, the average return on U.S. capital during the 1982–2000 period was 11.28% while the average economy-wide cost of capital was 11.84%. This macro-EVA finding is important because it is consistent with the classical economists' notion of *zero* economic profit generation (that is, zero economic "rents") on the average in an open and perfectly competitive economy.[2]

---

[1] The macro-EVA findings reported in this chapter are based on data listed in the 2001 Stern Stewart Performance 1000 Universe.

[2] Note that if a market economy—such as the U.S. economy—generates zero-average EVA, then a nonmarket economy must, in principle, generate negative-average EVA. This macroeconomic profit prediction is consistent with an insightful recent comment by Peter Bernstein—"After all, most of us subscribe to the notion that free markets organize production and allocate resources more efficiently than other systems, and especially in contrast to planned economies. See, Peter L. Bernstein, "Revisiting the Little Planned Society," *Journal of Portfolio Management* (Summer 2002).

EXHIBIT 15.1   U.S. Capital Returns and Capital Costs during the 1982–2000 Period

	Return on Capital (ROC%)	Cost of Capital (COC%)	Residual Return on Capital (RROC%)
1982	10.22	15.56	−5.34
1983	10.36	14.21	−3.84
1984	12.80	14.98	−2.18
1985	11.77	13.84	−2.07
1986	11.91	11.42	0.48
1987	11.70	11.92	−0.22
1988	13.20	12.42	0.78
1989	13.02	12.18	0.84
1990	11.89	12.40	−0.51
1991	10.12	12.10	−1.98
1992	10.83	11.54	−0.71
1993	11.33	10.71	0.62
1994	11.80	11.19	0.61
1995	12.15	10.73	1.41
1996	9.89	10.32	−0.42
1997	10.84	10.15	0.69
1998	9.28	9.59	−0.31
1999	11.98	9.89	2.09
2000	9.27	9.77	−0.50
Average	11.28	11.84	−0.56
Standard Deviation	1.19	1.76	1.84

   While the average return on U.S. capital over the 1982–2000 period is close to the average U.S. cost of capital, it is somewhat troubling to see that only eight of the 19 reporting years had average returns that were higher than the economy-wide cost of capital. Equivalently, the sign of the U.S. residual return on capital can be used to assess positive or negative EVA generation in the underlying economy. For example, during the 1980s, the U.S. residual return on capital (RROC) was positive in 1986 (0.48%), 1988 (0.78%), and 1989 (0.84%). During the 1990s, the U.S. residual capital return was positive during 1993 to 1995 (ranging from 0.61% to 1.41%), 1997 (0.69), and *especially* 1999 (at 2.09%).

On the other hand, the U.S. residual return on capital was negative for 11 of the 19 reporting years shown in Exhibit 15.1. For example, the U.S. residual capital return was sharply negative (although rising) during the 1982–1985 period—ranging from −5.34% in 1982 to −2.07% in 1985. At −0.22% and −1.98%, respectively, the economy-wide RROC was also negative in 1987 and 1991. In recent years, the macro-EVA spread was negative in 1996, 1998, and 2000. Moreover, Exhibit 15.1 shows that volatility is present in both the U.S. return on capital *and* the U.S cost of capital. The standard deviation estimates on these macro-EVA drivers over the 19-year reporting period were 1.19% and 1.76%, respectively. These macro-EVA findings are consistent with an overriding message of this book—namely, the return on capital must be *joined* with the cost of capital when making inferences about economic profit (EVA) generation and the process of wealth creation.

A CLOSER LOOK AT EVA GENERATION IN THE U.S. ECONOMY

Let's take a closer look at economic profit generation in the U.S. economy. In this context, Exhibit 15.2 provides a graphical display of the U.S. return on capital, the economy-wide cost of capital, and the U.S. residual return on capital for the 1982–2000 period. For discussion purposes, the exhibit will be framed in terms of four- to five-year subperiods that represent phases of economic profit acceleration and economic profit volatility

EXHIBIT 15.2   Macro-EVA Drivers: 1982–2000

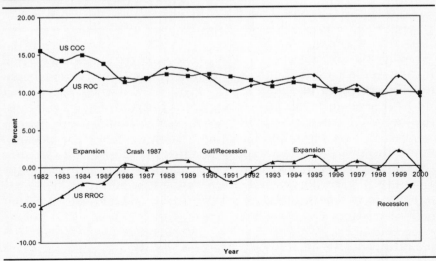

and deceleration in the U.S. economy. The representative subperiods can be used to demonstrate the qualitative nature of a two-factor EVA model—with a joint emphasis on the economy-wide spread between the return on productive capital and the cost of capital—*versus* a single-factor return on capital (ROC) or single-factor cost of capital (COC) model.

EVA ACCELERATION: 1982–1986 *(RAISE THE EVA FLAG!)*

We'll begin the macro-EVA journey with the 1982–1986 period. As shown in Exhibit 15.2, this subperiod is characterized by economic profit acceleration in the U.S. economy. Specifically, a phase of economic profit generation in the U.S. economy can be identified in the exhibit by either (1) the narrowing of the gap between the U.S. return on capital and the U.S. cost of capital, or (2) the rising U.S. residual return on capital (lower series) observed over the five-year reporting period. Moreover, the 1982–1986 period can be used to identify two distinct periods of economic profit improvement at the economy level—namely, EVA improvement during the 1982–1984 period and EVA improvement during the 1984–1986 period. These finer subperiods of economic profit acceleration can be attributed to varying patterns in the behavior of the U.S. return on capital versus the U.S. cost of capital.

Consider first the three-years 1982 to 1984: This period is interesting from an EVA perspective because the after-tax return on U.S. capital was rising in the presence of a declining U.S. cost of capital. At that time, the U.S. ROC rose substantially due to productivity gains in the underlying economy, while the U.S. cost of capital began to fall in tandem with a more general decline in the U.S. rate of inflation. At year-end 1982, the U.S. return on capital was 10.22% in the presence of an exceptionally high U.S. cost of capital, at 15.56%. By year-end 1984, the U.S return on invested capital stood at 12.8% in the presence of a U.S. capital cost of 14.98%

These favorable EVA events during the 1982–1984 period are also captured by a rise in the U.S residual return on capital series. At year-end 1982, the U.S residual return on capital (*equivalently*, the macro-EVA spread) was sharply negative, at –5.34%(!). By year-end 1984, the U.S residual capital return was –2.18%, which represents a 316-basis-point rise in the U.S. RROC from its former low point (see Exhibit 15.2) in 1982. With sustainability, this kind of EVA improvement at the economy-wide level is a precursor to a time of significant wealth creation. As evidenced by the macro-EVA drivers during the 1982–1984 period, a foundation for wealth creation at the economy-wide level can be identified by a rising return on capital in the presence of a falling cost of capital—which ultimately, leads to a fundamental change of sign in the macro-EVA spread from negative to positive.

Next, consider the 1984–1986 period: As shown in Exhibit 15.2, we see a different—yet equally important—pattern of economic profit improvement over this time period. This three-year period is interesting from an EVA perspective because the U.S. after-tax return on capital was actually *falling* in the presence of a continued rise in the U.S. residual return on capital (RROC). Of course, the driving force behind this period of economic profit improvement lies solely in the behavior of the U.S. cost of capital. During 1984 to 1986, the economy-wide cost of capital was decelerating—due to a sharp decline in U.S. Treasury bond yields—at a *faster* rate than the decline in the U.S. after-tax return on capital.[3] Indeed, at year-end 1984, the U.S. cost of capital was still at a high rate of 14.98%. By year-end 1986, the economy-wide cost of capital had declined some 356 basis points, down to 11.42%

In contrast, Exhibit 15.2 shows that the U.S. return on capital fell from 12.8% at year-end 1984 to 11.91% at year-end 1986. This represents an 89-basis-point decline in the return on U.S. capital over the two-year reporting interval. Taken together, the exhibit shows that the *spread* between the U.S. return on capital and the U.S. cost of capital increased from –2.18% in 1984, up to 0.48% by year-end 1986. This fundamental improvement in macroeconomic profit is captured in Exhibit 15.2 by the upward-sloping behavior of the U.S. residual return on capital (RROC) series covering 1984 to 1986.

Thus, we see that economic profit was increasing at the economy-wide level during the 1982–1986 period. As explained before, the source of the macro-EVA improvement over the five-year reporting period is different. During the 1982–1984 period, EVA was increasing in the presence of a rising return on capital and a falling cost of capital (alas, a made in EVA heaven combination). In turn, during the 1984–1986 period, EVA was increasing because of a precipitous decline in the U.S. cost of capital. Again, these macro-EVA findings reinforce a consistent message of this book. That is, the discovery of economic profit and wealth creation is fundamentally linked to two EVA factors—namely, the magnitude and behavior of the return on invested capital and the cost of capital.[4]

---

[3] We'll look at the time series behavior of U.S. Treasury yields over the 1982–2000 period in an upcoming section.

[4] Actually, there are three macro-EVA drivers if one considers that growth in invested capital at the economy-wide level can be either positive *or* negative. The comments in this chapter regarding the sign of the EVA spread and wealth creation presume that invested capital growth is on the average positive for the overall economy.

Indeed, the two-factor EVA model discussed above—as reflected in the changing sign of the U.S. residual return on capital (RROC) series from negative to positive—suggests that the wealth-enhancing potential of the U.S. economy was improving during the 1982–1986 period, even though at times a single-factor return on capital (ROC) focus would suggest otherwise. Also, the cutting of the U.S. COC function from *below* by the U.S. ROC series captures the crossing over from negative to positive EVA for the U.S. economy in 1986. More generally, knowledge of this economy-wide crossing point—as captured by the changing sign of the residual return on capital—provides a foundation for understanding the ultimate source of economic profit generation and "the wealth of nations."[5]

EVA DECELERATION: 1987–1991 *(LOWER THE EVA FLAG!)*

The next focal period of interest consists of the EVA happenings during the five years spanning 1987 to 1991. This subperiod is interesting from an economic profit perspective because it represents a phase of EVA volatility and decline. Exhibit 15.2 shows that in 1987 the U.S. cost of capital (COC) was rising in the presence of a declining return on U.S. capital. At year-end 1987, the U.S. return on capital was 22 basis points below the economy-wide cost of capital. This macro-EVA turning point is evident in Exhibit 15.2 by the sign change from positive to negative in the U.S. residual return on capital series that occurred between 1986 and 1987.

Following that, Exhibit 15.2 shows that the U.S. return on capital (ROC) actually "peaked" (at 13.2%) in 1988, just one year after the U.S. stock market experienced Black Monday, October 19, 1987. Coincidentally, the exhibit shows that the U.S. residual return on capital (RROC) returned to a positive mark in 1988. Moreover, at year-ends 1988 and 1989, the U.S. RROC series was at a turning point of what ultimately became a period of significant economic profit decline for the U.S. economy. In numerical terms, the U.S. residual return on capital was 0.78% in 1988, and at year-end 1989 the U.S. surplus return on capital was 0.84%.

Economic profit in the U.S. economy then began a substantial period of decay when the U.S. residual return on capital series (again, see Exhibit 15.2) was moving from positive to negative. Unfortunately, the economy-wide EVA turned negative in 1990 and 1991, at −0.51%

---

[5] Note that growth in invested capital (including physical *and* human capital) is also a key macroeconomic profit consideration.

and −1.98% respectively, when the U.S. cost of capital (COC) was cut from *above* by the downward spiraling return on capital (ROC) series. Indeed, the cutting of the COC series from above by the ROC series— equivalently, a sign change from positive to negative in the RROC series—should be viewed as a warning sign of forthcoming economic profit malaise.

The 1987–1991 period of EVA volatility and decline is also interesting in light of the efficient *versus* irrational markets' interpretations of the October Crash of 1987.[6] For obvious reasons, it has been difficult for efficient markets' proponents to argue that the U.S. stock market was indeed efficient in the sense of reflecting "full information" at the time of the 1987 Crash. For in the absence of any surprise negative information that might have sparked such a collapse, what was the point of the 20% decline in U.S. security prices on Black Monday, October 19, 1987? As a result, behavioral economists with their simplifying claims of market "bubbles" seized the explanatory moment of the day.

Despite the plethora of irrational-based characterizations of the October 1987 market break, the EVA evidence is somewhat consistent with a more "*positivist*" view of this adverse financial event. In this context, Exhibit 15.2 reveals that it is plausible that the October Crash of 1987 occurred because investors perceived that a powerful negative change was about to impede the U.S. economy's ability to generate economic value added for the future. If correct, then security prices should have fallen dramatically when investors perceived that the forward-looking negative EVA happenings at the economy-wide level would ultimately destroy wealth.

Conjecture aside, the benefits of looking at the economy from an EVA perspective should now be transparent: During the 1984–1986 period, a single-factor focus—by say, market strategists or equity analysts—on a traditional profitability measure like ROC would have led to an incorrect assessment of macroeconomic profit developments—as *favorable* interest rate and cost of capital happenings ruled the EVA day. Likewise, a single-factor focus—by "Fed watchers" or bond analysts, for example—on interest rate happenings in the U.S. Treasury bond market (an integral component of COC) from 1987 through 1991 (see Exhibit 15.2) would

---

[6] The finance literature abounds with interesting research on the events surrounding Black Monday, October 19, 1987. For this author's interpretation—concerning an unanticipated change in equity risk—see James L. Grant, "Stock Return Volatility During the Crash of 1987," *Journal of Portfolio Management* (Winter 1990).

For a speculative "bubble" view of the October 1987 market break, see Robert J. Shiller, "Who's Minding the Store?," *The Report of the Twentieth Century Fund Task Force on Market Speculation and Corporate Governance* (New York: The Twentieth Century Fund Press, 1992)

have led to a faulty assessment of the financial strength of the real economy—as *unfavorable* capital return developments ruled the EVA day.

Indeed, the disparate EVA phases containing (1) a sharply rising spread between the U.S. return on capital and the U.S. cost of capital from 1982 to 1986, and (2) the subsequently volatile and sharply falling EVA spread over the 1987–1991 period is a *powerful* justification for utilizing the information content of a two-factor (ROC and COC) economic profit model.

A Closer Look at the 1989 to 1991 Malaise

Before moving on, let's look at the macro-EVA experience during the 1989–1991 period in the context of the changing balance between the U.S. return on capital and the U.S. cost of capital. As noted before, this three-year period is characterized by economic profit malaise due to the sharp decline in the U.S. after-tax return on capital in the presence of a relatively stable cost of capital. At year-end 1989, the U.S. after-tax return on capital was 13.02%. By 1991, the economy-wide capital return had declined some 290 basis points, down to 10.12% Meanwhile, the marginal decline in the U.S. cost of capital, at only eight basis points, during these troubling years offered *no* assistance in helping to prevent the "free-fall" in the national EVA—and therefore, the general well being of the U.S. economy.

These ROC and COC patterns (Exhibit 15.2) eventually led to the "bottoming out" in the U.S. residual return on capital (RROC) series in 1991. For that problematic year, the U.S. residual return on capital was −1.98%—although fortunately, it was nowhere near the negative macro-EVA spread of −5.34% that occurred in 1982. In a nutshell, the macro-EVA model indicates that a powerful recession was underway during the 1990 and 1991 years. Moreover, the two-factor (ROC and COC) economic profit model shows that the source of the recession in the years 1990 and 1991 is mostly due to the sharp decline in the U.S. return on capital in the presence of an interest rate environment that was largely unsupportive.

EVA ACCELERATION: 1992 TO 1995 *(RAISE THAT EVA FLAG!)*

As a breath of fresh air, consider the 1992–1995 period. That a powerful EVA acceleration phase was underway is clearly evident in Exhibit 15.2 by the rising U.S. residual return on capital series, crossing over from negative to positive in 1993. Notably, at year-end 1992, the U.S. RROC was −0.71% (up from −1.98% a year earlier). By year-end 1995, the U.S. "surplus return on capital" had risen to 1.41%—a watershed mark for the U.S. RROC over the 1982 to 1995 reporting period. Moreover, the recovery in the U.S. economy—with its inception traced back to 1992—is revealed in the exhibit by the rising U.S. return on capital series in the presence of a falling U.S. cost of capital (*again*, a made in heaven EVA situation).

Particularly, at year-end 1992, the U.S. return on capital stood at 10.83% (up slightly from 10.12% at year-end 1991). In contrast, by year-end 1995 this measure of economy-wide profitability had risen to 12.15% (actually, a "peak" rate for the U.S. ROC during the 1990s). In turn, the rise in U.S. return on invested capital was reinforced by a decline in the U.S. cost of capital. At year-end 1992, the U.S. cost of capital stood at 11.54% (down slightly from 12.1% at year-end 1991). By year-end 1995, the U.S. COC had declined to 10.73%. Taken together, the 340-basis-point change in the U.S. return on capital and the U.S. cost of capital (viewing a decrease in COC as a positive EVA factor) lead to a period of significant macroeconomic profit acceleration in the post-1991 years through 1995

EVA VOLATILITY AND DECLINE: 1996 TO 2000 (OOPS, LOWER THAT EVA FLAG!)

In the aftermath of the peak in the U.S. residual return on capital in 1995, it is troubling to see that the U.S. RROC was quite volatile, moving from a positive to negative value some three times over the 1995 to 2000 reporting period. Exhibit 15.2 shows that the U.S. residual return on capital was negative in 1996, 1998, and 2000, ranging from about –0.3% to –0.5%. In contrast, the U.S. RROC was positive in 1997 and 1999, at 0.69% and 2.09% respectively. Indeed, the U.S. residual return on capital series fluctuated from –0.31% in 1998 to 2.09% in 1999, the highest value reached for the U.S. economy over the 1982–2000 reporting period.

Equivalently, the time series behavior of the U.S. residual return on capital can be explained in the context of what was happening to the U.S. return on capital and the U.S. cost of capital. In this context, it is interesting to see that volatility in the U.S. RROC during the 1996–2000 period is mostly attributed to volatility in the U.S. return on invested capital. Over this period, the U.S. return on capital fluctuated from a low of about 9.3% in 1998 and 2000 to a high of nearly 12% in 1999. Meanwhile, the U.S. cost of capital fluctuated in a range of about 10.3% to 9.6% during the 1996–2000 period. Thus, the time series behavior of the U.S residual return on capital (or the macro-EVA spread) during the five years covering 1996 to 2000 is largely attributed to volatile happenings in the U.S. return on capital in the presence of a relatively stable U.S. cost of capital.

ROLLING UP THE MACRO-EVA RESULTS

Stepping back, it is interesting to identify the subperiods of EVA acceleration and deceleration. Consider again the periods of EVA acceleration shown in Exhibit 15.2. In this context, the exhibit shows that EVA was accelerating during (1) the 1982 to 1986 years and, (2) the 1992 to 1995 years. These EVA acceleration periods in the U.S. economy can easily be seen in Exhibit 15.2 by the upward sloping behavior of the U.S. residual return on capital series—which ultimately crossed zero and turned positive in 1986 and 1993, respectively. While periods of EVA acceleration can be easily identified by the time series behavior of the U.S. RROC, it is important to emphasize (again) that the reasons for economic profit improvement were different.

Look again at the 1982–1986 period. During this subperiod the U.S. residual return on capital rose by some 580 basis points. In this period, the packaging of the rise in the EVA spread consisted of a 169-basis-point rise in the U.S. return on capital in the presence of a most accommodative decline in the U.S. cost of capital of 414 basis points. By contrast, the U.S. residual return on capital rose by some 340 basis points over the post 1991–1995 period. The packaging of this rise in the U.S. residual return on capital consisted of a 203-basis-point rise in the U.S. return on capital in the presence of decline in the U.S. cost of capital of 137 basis points.

Taken together, it is evident that EVA acceleration during the 1982–1986 period was largely driven by supportive interest rate and cost of capital developments, while EVA acceleration during the 1992–1995 period was mostly driven by economic profit considerations that drive the U.S. return on capital. Moreover, a similar dissection and analysis of the U.S. residual return on capital series can (and should) be made when evaluating periods of economic profit volatility and decline. Periods of economic profit volatility and malaise at the economy level look like those troubling subperiods shown in Exhibit 15.2 covering 1987 to 1991 and 1996 to 2000 (*actually*, through 2002 at the time of this writing).

INTEREST RATE DEVELOPMENTS AND THE TWO-FACTOR EVA MODEL

Let's now look at interest rate developments over the 1982–2000 period. Exhibit 15.3 presents a time series display of the U.S. return on capital, the 10-year U.S. Treasury bond yield,[7] and the U.S. residual

---

[7] Data for the 10-year U.S. Treasury bond series is obtained from the web site of the Board of Governors of the Federal Reserve System. See *www.federalreserve.gov*.

return on capital over the 19-year reporting period. Among other things, the exhibit can be used to reinforce the power of the two-factor EVA model over a single-factor interest rate model.

In particular, Exhibit 15.3 shows that while the U.S. after-tax return on capital was *everywhere* higher than the corresponding (pre-tax) Treasury bond yield during the 1982–2000 period, the U.S. residual return on capital ranged from positive to negative some five times over the 19-year reporting period. This finding implies that knowledge of inflation and, therefore, interest rate happenings in the U.S. Treasury bond market are a necessary but *insufficient* condition for understanding how wealth is truly created in a well-functioning capital market.

To illustrate this point, consider the post-1988 behavior of the U.S. cost of capital shown previously in Exhibit 15.2 in view of the interest rate happenings revealed in Exhibit 15.3. In the former exhibit, the U.S. cost of capital was largely falling because U.S. Treasury bond yields (Exhibit 15.3) were generally declining in the post-1988 years. However, the two-factor EVA model—with its *joint* focus on the relationship between after-tax capital returns and capital costs—shows that the economy-wide EVA was falling sharply out to 1991. In turn, the adverse RROC development that emerged in the post-1989–1991 period occurred because the economy-wide return on capital was falling at a *faster* rate than the general decline in interest rates (as reflected in a downward shift in the U.S. Treasury yield curve).

EXHIBIT 15.3   U.S. Return on Capital, 10-Year Treasury Yield, and U.S. Residual Return on Capital: 1982–2000

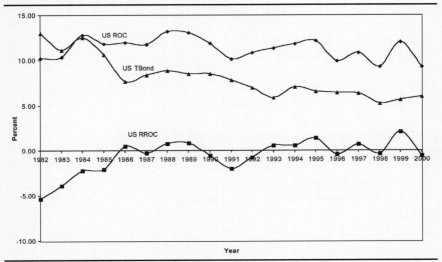

Other things being the same, a decline in interest rates should lead to an improvement in the economy-wide EVA and (therefore) the national wealth level. For better or worse, Exhibit 15.3 shows that interest rate changes rarely occur in a vacuum. For example, when interest rates "spiked up" in 1994 (due, perhaps, to harsh interest rate actions taken by the Fed), the economy-wide EVA spread remained unchanged from its former value in 1993. The exhibit also shows that when U.S. Treasury bond yields went up between 1998 and 1999, the economy-wide EVA spread actually reached an all-time high for the 19-year reporting period.

Surely, the economy-wide EVA did not remain unchanged in the former instance or go up in the latter instance because market participants thought that higher U.S. Treasury bond yields were somehow good for the overall economy. Rather, the economy-wide EVA remained flat in 1994 because the U.S. after-tax return on capital was rising at a rate that kept the rise in the U.S. cost of capital in check. Moreover, the "spike up" followed by the "spike down" in the U.S. ROC over the 1998–2000 period drove the sign of the EVA spread even though interest rates and the U.S. cost of capital were on the rise.

This EVA focus on the after-tax return on capital should *not* be taken to mean that a single-factor focus on the economy-wide ROC leads to more meaningful insights about the direction of a nation's economic profit or its national wealth in comparison with a single-factor emphasis on COC. In this regard, Exhibit 15.3 shows the U.S. residual return on capital (RROC) was rising over the 1984–1986 period when the U.S. after-tax return on invested capital was actually falling. This positive EVA development occurred for that three-year period because the U.S. cost of capital (led by sharply declining U.S. Treasury bond yields shown in Exhibit 15.3) was declining at a faster rate than the overall decline in the U.S. return on capital.

Taken together, Exhibits 15.2 and 15.3 suggest that the "real key to creating wealth" for a nation lies in a keen understanding of the economic prominence of the residual (or surplus) return on capital. Such knowledge is in turn derived from an appreciation of the economic relationship between the after-tax return on invested capital (ROC) and economy-wide cost of capital (COC).

EVA IMPLICATIONS BY PRESIDENTIAL YEARS

The macro-EVA survey can now be applied to assess the strength of the U.S. economy during recent Presidential periods. Although the positive or negative wealth consequences observed here do *not* necessarily mean that they were caused by the particular party in office—either Democratic or Republican—the historical possibilities are interesting to explore just the same. In this context, Exhibit 15.4 presents a time series plot of the U.S. after-tax return on capital, the economy-wide cost of capital, and the U.S. residual return on capital for seven of the eight Reagan Years including 1982 through 1988, the Bush I Years spanning 1989 to 1992, and the Clinton Years including 1993 through 2000. While not shown graphically, some EVA inferences will be made regarding the Bush II years to date.

The Reagan Years

The Reagan Years span the first and second EVA phases that were explained before in the context of Exhibit 15.2—namely, a period of EVA acceleration and then the makings for a period of EVA volatility and decline. During the first five years shown in Exhibit 15.4—spanning the first and second terms of the Reagan Presidency—the U.S. residual return on capital rose sharply from 1982 to 1986. During the last two years of the Reagan Presidency, the U.S. RROC was negative in 1987— the same year as the October Crash of 1987—and then it turned positive again in 1988. On balance, Exhibit 15.4 shows that the Reagan Years (especially for the *first* term of the Reagan Presidency) were largely EVA-increasing (although not necessarily associated with positive EVA) because the after-tax return on U.S capital was moving in a direction that eventually (in 1986) cut the U.S. cost of capital series from *below*.

EXHIBIT 15.4   Macro-EVA by Presidential Years: 1982–2000

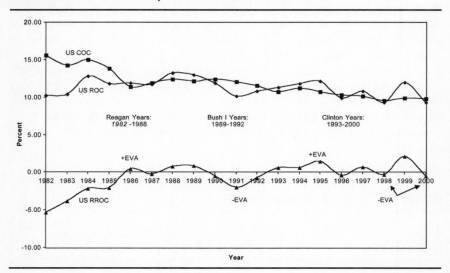

Moreover, the beneficial combination of a rising U.S. return on capital in the presence of a sharply falling cost of capital during the first term of the Reagan Presidency was the underlying source of the positive residual return on capital (and therefore, EVA) generated by the U.S. economy through 1986. Not surprisingly, the U.S. stock market boomed as a sustained acceleration in economic profit is directly related to wealth creation in the underlying economy.[8] However, in 1987, the cutting of the economy-wide cost of capital series from *above* by the U.S. return on capital was a possible warning sign for futuristic EVA volatility and decline. As a matter of conjecture, some of the anticipatory negative wealth effects were possibly "priced" on Black Monday, October 19, 1987 as part of the capital market's longer-term EVA outlook for the duration of the 1980s.

The Bush I Years

While EVA was largely accelerating during the Reagan years, Exhibit 15.4 shows that EVA was mostly decelerating during the Bush I years. Indeed, the Bush I Presidency is coincident with the post 1989 to 1991 malaise where the U.S. return on capital was declining in the presence of a relatively flat (thankfully!) cost of capital. Specifically, at –1.98% in 1991, the U.S. residual return on capital reached its lowest point since 1984 and 1985. During that problematic year, the U.S. cost of capital was 12.1%, while the after-tax return on U.S. capital was down at 10.12%.

However, after "bottoming-out" in 1991—the third year of the Bush I Presidency—it is interesting to see that the U.S. residual return on capital was on the rise in 1992. This view that EVA was increasing in the last year of the Bush I Presidency can be identified in Exhibit 15.4 by either (1) the upward turn in the RROC series from 1991 to 1992 or equivalently, (2) the rise in the U.S. after-tax return on capital (ROC) during 1992 in the presence of a falling U.S. cost of capital (COC). In effect, the free-fall in EVA that occurred over the post-1989–1991 period began a positive turnaround at the end of 1991. Contrary to what some revisionist historians might say, the EVA evidence indicates that the start of the recovery phase of the U.S. economy during the early 1990s began in the last year of the Bush I Presidency.

The Clinton Years

While some might quarrel about the exact turning point of the economy during the early 1990s, Exhibit 15.4 shows that the first term of the Clinton Presidency was associated with a period of rising EVA. Indeed, from 1992 to 1995, the U.S. after-tax return on capital was rising

---

[8] Indeed, the U.S. stock market (as measured by the S&P 500) rose by 147% over the 1982–1986 period.

sharply in the presence of a (mostly) falling cost of capital. When, in 1993, the U.S. ROC series passed the U.S. cost of capital series from *below*, this macro-EVA happening set the stage for the strongly positive residual return on capital that occurred in 1995. Equivalently, in 1993, Exhibit 15.3 shows that the U.S. residual return on capital (and therefore, the economy-wide EVA) passed through *zero* with an upward-sloping vengeance toward 1995.

As with the first term of the Reagan Presidency, the first term of the Clinton Presidency was associated with considerable EVA improvement in the underlying economy. Interestingly though, a comparative inspection of the two-factor EVA model shows that the U.S. residual return on capital (RROC) was largely rising during the Reagan Presidency because of a sharp decline in the U.S. cost of capital from 1982 to 1986. The U.S. capital cost declined during the Reagan years because of the favorable news conveyed by falling inflation (therefore Treasury bond yields) and presumably to a decline in the required market risk premium. In contrast, the first term of the Clinton Presidency was associated with a period of sharply rising capital returns in the presence of a comparatively smaller decline in the U.S. cost of capital.

Notably, while the economic and political circumstances may differ by presidential terms, the passing of the COC series from *below* by the economy-wide return on capital signaled the EVA recoveries that happened during both the Reagan and Clinton years. Moreover, when the ROC series is rising at a time when the cost of capital is falling, this, in principle, sets the stage for a powerful upward movement in *both* bond and stock prices. Indeed, the explosive growth in the U.S. stock and bonds markets that occurred during the Reagan and Clinton years seems consistent with a longer-term efficient market prediction of the two-factor EVA model.

However, Exhibit 15.4 shows that the second half of the Clinton Presidency is associated with a period of EVA volatility and decline. On the volatility side, the U.S. residual return on capital varied from positive to negative from 1995 to 1996, from 1997 to 1998, and then again from 1999 to 2000. During the last year of the Clinton Presidency, the U.S. residual return on capital was negative, as a recession was on the rise in the presence of a sharply downward turning ROC series between 1999 and 2000.

Interestingly, the U.S. stock market boomed in the 1995 to 1999 years even though the U.S. residual return on capital experienced considerable volatility (moving above and below zero) during the second term of the Clinton Presidency.[9] Indeed, the post-1995 EVA experience

---

[9] During the five years 1995 to 1999, the U.S. stock market rose by a breathtaking 250%.

for the U.S. economy suggests that the U.S. stock market was overvalued and therefore ripe for a significant decline at the century turn.

Bush II Years to Date

Next, some EVA inferences for the Bush II Presidency to date. Like the Bush I Presidency, Exhibit 15.4 suggests that Bush II was in the challenging position of inheriting a period of EVA volatility and decline that, *typically*, follows a period of rapid economic profit acceleration in the underlying economy. In this context, the EVA troubles for the first few quarters (Q1 to Q2, 2001) of the Bush II Presidency were caused by problematic happenings in the U.S. return on capital in the presence of a relatively stable cost of capital.

In turn, the tragic events of September 11, 2001 exacerbated the freefall in the U.S. return on productive capital. Also, this horrific event presumably led to a dramatic rise in the U.S. cost of capital—even though U.S. interest rates were then falling. The economic source of the presumed rise in the U.S. cost of capital—therefore the presumed source of the exacerbated decline in the U.S. residual return on capital in the aftermath of "9/11"—was due to a sharply rising market risk premium that, unfortunately, was likely *not* captured by conventional approaches to measuring the cost of capital via the capital asset pricing model (CAPM). Going forward, the "good news" (see Exhibit 15.2 or 15.4) is that periods of EVA volatility and decline are eventually followed by periods of significant economic profit improvement.

PERSISTENCE IN MACRO-EVA: 1982–2000

Finally, the macro-EVA evidence reported so far points to periods of structural persistence in macroeconomic profit. As highlighted in Exhibits 15.2 and 15.4, there is clear evidence of structural persistence shown by (1) the two phases of EVA acceleration, including the 1982–1986 period and the 1992–1995 periods, and (2) the two phases of EVA volatility and decline, including the 1989–1991 years and the 1996–2000 period (predictably, given the recession and "9/11" happenings, through 2002 at the time of this writing). More formally, the question of persistence in economic profit at the economy level can be addressed in the context of serial correlation among the yearly macro-EVA estimates over the 19-year reporting period.

Exhibit 15.5 shows a time series plot of the U.S. residual return on capital at year t, denoted as RROC(t) in the graph, *versus* the residual capital return at year $t - 1$, denoted as RROC($t - 1$). Without getting into all the details, there is clearly evidence of persistence in the lagged

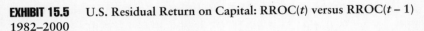

EXHIBIT 15.5   U.S. Residual Return on Capital: RROC(*t*) versus RROC(*t* – 1)
1982–2000

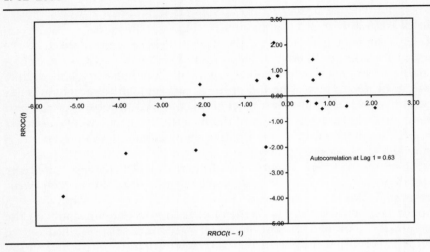

residual capital returns. For example, when the U.S. RROC was negative in 1983, it was preceded by a grossly negative residual capital
return in 1982. When the U.S. residual return on capital was sharply
positive in 1995, it was preceded by a positive residual capital return in
1994. This notion of persistence in macroeconomic profit is reinforced
by a serial correlation estimate at lag 1 (representing a one-year time
interval) of 0.63.[10] A further inspection of the correlative structure of
the U.S. residual return on capital reveals that the serial correlation at
lag 2 is 0.51, while the autocorrelation at lags 3 and 4 (3- and 4-year
time intervals) dampens down to about zero—actually, 0.095 and –
0.075, respectively.

SUMMARY

This chapter focuses on the benefits of using EVA in assessing the underlying strength of an economy. The macro-EVA model offers some major
economic and financial insights with its two-factor emphasis on the bal-
ancing between the after-tax return on capital and the cost of capital. In

---

[10] This implies that roughly 40% of the variation in the U.S. residual return on capital
at year *t* can be explained by happenings in the residual capital return at year *t* – 1.
On the other hand, 60% of the variation in the residual return on capital at *t* is explained by factors unrelated to the residual capital return at *t* – 1.

particular, when the after-tax return on capital exceeds the economy-wide cost of capital, then national EVA is positive. In principal, the positive residual (or surplus) return on capital situation is a powerful precursor to wealth creation in the underlying economy.

Additionally, the macro-EVA model suggests that the level of national wealth (or aggregate NPV) should be rising in the presence of a narrowing of the *spread* between the economy-wide return on capital and the cost of capital. This economic prediction makes sense if the positive EVA spread is joined with a *positive* growth rate in invested capital in the underlying economy. In contrast, the macro-EVA model predicts that the national wealth level (and presumably, a country's overall standard of living) decelerates when the residual return on capital (for varying ROC and COC reasons) is declining. These changing wealth conditions are both powerful and testable implications of the two-factor macro-EVA model.

The empirical results reported in this chapter are important in several respects. On the positive side, the macro-EVA spread was positive some eight times during the 1982–2000 reporting period. By definition, the U.S. residual return on capital was then negative 11 times over the 19-year reporting period. These positive and negative EVA happenings were not unique to any particular political party in office as the national EVA was improving substantially during the Reagan Years *and* the Clinton Years.[11] Indeed, the fact that the U.S. economy experienced economic profit acceleration during the 1982 to 1986 years and then during the 1992–1995 period suggests that wealth creation transcends the Presidential parties in office.

Moreover, on the research front, macro-EVA analysis offers a powerful synergy for those financial institutions that are traditionally separated along bond and equity market lines of research. By jointly focusing research efforts on the positioning of the return on capital relative to the cost of capital, both "Fed watchers" and equity market strategists alike can see powerful economic and financial trends that might otherwise go unnoticed in a more conventional realm of "top-down" macroeconomic analysis. In essence, EVA brings these seemingly unrelated bond and equity research groups back to a financial place called "home."

---

[11] Conversely, EVA for the U.S. economy was mostly decelerating during the Bush I and Bush II years (to date).